Losing Labour's Soul?

New Labour and the Blair Government
1997–2007

Eric Shaw

Routledge
Taylor & Francis Group

LONDON AND NEW YORK

First published 2007
by Routledge
2 Park Square, Milton Park, Abingdon, Oxon, OX14 4RN

Simultaneously published in the USA and Canada
by Routledge
270 Madison Avenue, New York, NY 10016

Routledge is an imprint of the Taylor & Francis Group, an informa business

Typeset in Times New Roman by
Taylor & Francis Books
Printed and bound in Great Britain by
MPG Books Ltd, Bodmin

British Library Cataloguing in Publication Data
A catalogue record for this book is available from the British Library

Library of Congress Cataloging in Publication Data
1. Labour Party (Great Britain) 2. Socialism–Great Britain. 3. Great
Britain–Social policy–1979- 4. Blair, Tony, 1953- 5. Great Britain–Politics
and government–21st century. I. Title.

JN1129.L32S458 2007
324.2410709'0511–dc22
2007025391

ISBN13: 978-0-415-35499-8 (hbk)
ISBN13: 978-0-415-35500-1 (pbk)
ISBN13: 978-0-203-00161-5 (ebk)

Dedicated to the memory of my grandparents:
Jeanette Weinstein (born 1895, died Auschwitz 1942)
Maurice (Meyer) Weinstein (born 1889, died Auschwitz 194?)

'The party I lead must have more than a set of policies – we must have a soul.'
(Gordon Brown's speech accepting the leadership of the Labour party, *The Independent*, 28 June 2007)

Contents

Acknowledgements

In June 2007 Tony Blair resigned from the leadership of the Labour party and the premiership. Whatever one's views of Tony Blair – and they range very widely – no-one can dispute that he has been one of the party's seminal figures. So now appears to be the right time to take stock and reflect upon the way in which Labour has been transformed – some would say out of existence – during the years when he stood at its helm.

I recall a conversation a while back with an MP – someone I've know since we were at university years ago, and a very shrewd and thoughtful politician. I was reflecting on the fact that, despite a record which easily bears comparison with Labour governments in the 1960s and 1970s, the Blair Government appeared to generate an extraordinary amount of anger among its erstwhile supporters. My MP friend suggested that it was a typical case of the 'betrayal' syndrome – left-wing Labour party members who were never happier than when bewailing the perfidies of their own government. I replied that the anger extended well beyond the usual suspects (and we were not even talking about Iraq!). He paused, reflected, and then commented, 'you know, Eric, my wife is very angry. She is threatening not to vote Labour again!' Trying to understand the reasons for that anger – *despite* what seem to be to be the considerable accomplishments of the Blair Government – helped shape the key themes of this book.

It has its origins in the earliest months of the Blair Government and it has proceeded at the pace of a tortoise on sedatives! Over the years I have accumulated many debts. I owe much to the patience and tolerance of my family who have had to put up with my distracted and ever more reclusive ways for far too long. My greatest debt, as ever, is to my wife Susan who endlessly encouraged and sustained me over the many years it took me to write this book. Without her it would never have been completed. The writing of books on the Labour party has been a strand running throughout our marriage and this, the fourth, is, I promise, the last.

I am immensely grateful to the following who read and made extremely useful comments on various chapters in the book:

- Chapter one: Prof. Jim Cronin and Prof. Stephen Ingle;

- Chapter three: Fiona Millar;
- Chapter five: Frank Dobson MP, Consultant Ophthalmic Surgeon Simon Kelly, Prof. Julian Le Grand, Consultant Physician Norman Peden, Prof. Martin Powell, Simon Stevens, Consultant Neurophysiologist Aline Russell;
- Chapter six: Dr Steve Ludlam; Employment Law specialist Brian Morron.

I would like to thank Jonas Hinnfors who read a number of chapters and John Callaghan and Luke Martell who very generously read and commented on the whole of the manuscript.

The following also provided invaluable assistance in lots of different ways: Charlotte Atkins MP, Liz Atkins, Tony Duckworth, Simon Kelly, John McTernan, Martin Powell and Perri 6.

Thanks too to Craig Fowlie of Routledge for his patience and understanding after, well, one or two broken deadlines.

I would like to acknowledge the help of the Carnegie Foundation for Scotland for providing help with travel and accommodation expenses.

Finally, I would like to acknowledge the contributions made by many people, both inside and outside the Labour party in many discussions over the years, which have helped me to come to such understanding as I have of the Labour party.

A note on sources

I have sought, as best I can, to ensure that ever major point, interpretation advanced and conclusion reached in this book is supported by evidence. I have inspected a host of documents over the years and have drawn heavily upon them. These include House of Commons Select Committee reports and minutes of evidence; the reports of the Audit Commission and the National Audit Office; Government White Papers and press releases and reports from a range of other government agencies and bodies. Studies produced by specialist research institutions, such as the King's Fund, the Institute for Fiscal Studies and the Rowntree Foundation, have been an indispensable source of data and interpretation. Press reports have also proved extremely useful – and the *Guardian* web site invaluable. I have ransacked journals from a wide range of disciplines including healthcare, education, social policy, industrial relations and contemporary history as well as, of course, politics.

In addition, I have interviewed over 40 politicians, political advisers and other office-holders in the course of writing this study, some on more than one occasion. Some of these interviews were conducted on an off-the-record basis: I list the names below. I was constantly impressed by the willingness of often extremely busy people to spend time discussing matters with an academic, so a great thanks to them all.

Interviews held

Andrew (Lord) Adonis; Graham Allen MP; Charlotte Atkins MP; Frances Beckett; Teresa Black; Charles Clarke MP; Paul Corrigan; Dan Corry; Dr Alan Curry; Jon Cruddas MP; John Denham MP; Frank Dobson MP; Dr Peter Fisher; Mike Gapes MP; Alan Glanzi; Brian Gould; Peter Hain MP; Chris Ham; Lord (Alan) Haworth; Keith Hill MP; David Hinchcliffe MP; Michael Jacobs; Dr Simon Kelly; Peter Kilfoyle MP; Julia Langdon; Neal Lawson; Julian Le Grand; Martin Linton MP; John McTernan; Michael Meacher MP; Alan Milburn MP; Ed Miliband MP; Fiona Millar; Geoff Mulgan; Doug Naysmith MP; Lord (Tom) Sawyer; Lord (Chris) Smith; Nigel Stanley; Simon Stevens; Graham Stringer MP; Lord (Stewart) Sutherland; Mathew Taylor; Paul Teasdale; Alan Whitehead MP; Jon Wood; Tony Wright MP; Phil Wyatt.

It goes without saying that none of the above bear any responsibility for the book's errors and blemishes, all of which are mine.

Introduction

For what and for whom does New Labour stand?

Doug Anderton, broadsheet journalist – 'The "Third Way". You're always banging on about it. What is it?'
Phil Trotter, Blairite Labour MP – 'What is it?'
DA – 'Yes.'
PT – 'How do you mean?' ...
DA – 'What is it. That's all I want to know.'
PT – 'Well, it's an alternative. An alternative to the sterile, worn-out dichotomy between left and right.'

(Jonathan Coe, *The Closed Circle*, Penguin 2004: 61–2)

'What', the little boy in a cartoon tugging at his father's hand and pointing to a figure in the distance enquired, 'is that man for?' What, we might well ask, is the Labour party (or, more precisely, 'New Labour') for? The object of this book is to take a stab at answering this question. Or, rather, two questions: *for what*, in terms of ideals, ambitions for social reorganisation and beliefs, does New Labour stand? Does it remain committed to the values with which Labour has been associated for its century-long history? Or has it broken with that tradition? Is it any longer a recognisably social democratic party? And *for whom*, in terms of social interests, does it stand? Having ceased to be a party of 'ordinary working people' has it developed into one which represents the community as a whole – or principally its more affluent sections? We shall expand a little on each of these questions.

For what does New Labour stand?

As Jane Lewis has observed, 'there has been a huge debate about what New Labour is, what it stands for' (Lewis, 2004: 208). Few observers query the proposition that under its new unofficial name of 'New Labour' the British Labour party has undergone a transformation – 'a fundamental re-ordering of the party's doctrine and ethos' (Chadwick and Heffernan, 2003: 1). Radical change is not, of course, confined to British Labour: social democracy in general 'is in the course of metamorphasising' (Moschanas, 2002:

327–8). As Gamble and Wright pointed out in 1999, there has 'never been such a widespread questioning of what social democracy stands for and whether it still offers distinctive policies and goals' (Gamble and Wright, 1999b: 1). This questioning in turn reflects the breathless pace of economic and social change which appears to undermine many of the established verities of social democracy.

Change is not itself a challenge social democracy has ever been able to evade. All political movements have had to adjust to new circumstances, shifting electoral configurations and fresh challenges to survive and, throughout their history, social democratic parties have grappled with 'the need to modernize and revise their policies and approach in the light of core principles and their understanding of the context in which they operate' (Gamble and Wright, 1999b: 3).

To this extent revision is implicit in the social democratic project. The key question in the debate about New Labour is whether, in adapting to new pressures, it has devised innovative and imaginative means to realise established ends – or engaged in a re-evaluation of those ends themselves. In what sense has it been 'renewed', for what purpose and with what effect? Does New Labour still embody a programmatic thrust that is recognisably social democratic? Does it, in its many innovatory efforts, prefigure a new, modernised social democracy – or the final exhaustion of that tradition?

There have been a multitude of responses to these questions. On the one hand there are those for whom New Labour is best understood as an ambitious project to modernise social democracy. For the leading progressive intellectual Tony Giddens, New Labour's 'new social democracy' preserves 'the basic values of the left – a belief in a solidarity and an inclusive society, a commitment to combating inequality and protecting the vulnerable' – by adapting to the new realities of globalisation, the new knowledge economy and more individualistic aspirations, a task that could only be accomplished by sloughing-off outdated ideas and policies (Giddens, 2002: 15). Green-Pedersen, van Kersbergen and Hemerijck concur: New Labour's 'third way' represents 'a fairly coherent set of social democratic ideas and policies ... that are clearly different from both old-style social democracy and neo-liberalism'. While it embraces a much more positive view of the market it retains an allegiance to 'the basic principles of social democracy' (Green-Pedersen, van Kersbergen and Hemerijck, 2000). Once account is taken of the fact that 'values are interpreted and expressed in a way appropriate to the particular social and economic context', Meredith contends, it is clear that 'the underlying values of democratic socialism elucidated by Crosland still endure' (Meredith, 2005: 252).

At the other end of the spectrum are those for whom:

> what is clearest about the third way is its rejection of social democracy. If the latter is taken to imply an unconditional right of access of all citizens to a comprehensive welfare state, a belief in democratic

economic governance ... and a commitment to egalitarian social outcomes. ... 'third way' political economy is post-social democratic.

(Hay, 2005: 3)

The Blair government's 'policy instinct', Chadwick and Heffernan similarly hold, is 'seemingly to prioritize the needs of the private wealth-creating sector over the public wealth-consuming sector when there is a conflict between the two'. It is no longer interested in 'constricting the market for a social purpose' (Chadwick and Heffernan, 2003: 8). Former cabinet minister and deputy leader, Roy Hattersley (from the party's 'Croslandite' right) concluded in 2005 that 'New Labour was created to reject much of what real Labour stands for'. New Labour was 'no longer recognisable as a political force on the democratic Centre-Left of British politics'. It ceased to believe that 'higher public spending is best paid for by a redistributive and progressive form of taxation' and 'the commodification of public space has now become an aggressive Blairite objective' (*The Guardian*, 7 November 2005).

These two broad approaches by no means exhaust the range of interpretations on offer. For Clarke, New Labour is the confluence of conflicting forces and pressures as it seeks to retain the loyalty of its traditional constituencies while developing a coherent programme for reforming public institutions and boosting economic competitiveness (Clark, 2004). Hall views the Blair Government as constituting a 'hybrid regime, composed of two strands, social democratic and neo-liberal'. While it retains a social democratic commitment to maintaining public services and alleviating poverty its 'dominant logic' is neo-liberal: to spread 'the gospel of market fundamentalism', promote business interests and values and further residualise the welfare system (Hall, S, 2003: 19, 13–14). Thus New Labour continues, on the one hand, 'to inhabit the terrain of the public and the social' but, on the other 're-articulates them towards neo-liberal meanings and practices' (Clarke, 2004: 43).

Driver and Martell also view New Labour as essentially a political composite. Pragmatic social democratic arguments for the mixed economy have been displaced by 'the celebration of competitive markets and private enterprise' with continued privatisation of public assets and services and the maintenance of a comparatively low tax regime. But equally a sustained effort has been made to mitigate social deprivation, refurbish (through a major boost in spending) the public services and extend opportunities for all – all policies that 'we might expect from a Labour administration' inspired by a 'social democratic and progressive ethos' (Driver and Martell, 2002: 21–22). Buckler and Dolowitz maintain that New Labour is offering a new synthesis which incorporates elements from both traditional social democracy and neo-liberalism, combining them in a way 'that transcends both' (Buckler and Dolowitz, 2004: 25). Thus it has abjured Labour's deep wariness towards the market and its traditional egalitarianism but remains fully committed to a 'politics of redistribution' defined in terms of 'the creation of opportunities for all, and particularly to the least well off groups, through the amelioration of background disadvantages' (Buckler and Dolowitz, 2000a: 107). It has arrived at a distinct programmatic profile which can best be encapsulated by the term 'social liberalism' (Buckler and Dolowitz, 2004: 25).

For Cronin, however, it is the repudiation of the party's past that is the defining feature of New Labour. This 'break with the past', a veritable *Kulturkampf* waged against 'labourism', is

> central to any understanding of New Labour. Its programme, for example, is at the very least a departure from the commitments of the party in the past and might even be regarded, at crucial points, as a direct repudiation; and it is consciously so. (Cronin, 2004: 2).

He argues that this rupture – in terms of ideology, policy, ethos, organisation and strategy – was vital because 'Old' Labour was locked into an impasse that it was wholly incapable of surmounting. The chrysalis of the past had to be shed if the party was to be renewed (Cronin, 2004: 3–4). It is precisely from this that its success, both in electoral and policy terms, derives: it has shaken off the detritus of the past.

For whom does New Labour stand?

There is an equal lack of consensus over the second key question this book addresses: for *whom* does New Labour stand? Parties are not simply organisations held together and informed by adherence to some body of principles – they are representative institutions. Contemporary analysis tends to focus on the role of parties as the representatives of blocs of voters but a crucial component of the modern political process has always been the representation of social interests. The representative function of parties thus also encompasses their role as repositories and aggregators of settled social interests, as these struggle to influence the disposition of societal resources. By exhibiting differential receptivity to the claims of competing interests, governing parties can have a profound effect upon the operation of the political system and the distribution of social goods.

Despite its importance the issue of the way in which social interests are represented within the existing political system has recently received very little sustained attention. Yet British party politics have always been structured by what Beer calls 'the theory of functional representation'. He defines this as 'any theory that finds the community divided into various strata, regards each of these strata as having a certain corporate unity, and holds that they ought to be represented in government' (Beer, 1969: 71). Thus in the nineteenth century the Tories were the party of the landed and mercantile interest, and the great traditional orders (the Church of England, the

Law etc.); the Liberals were the champions of the rising new Northern manufacturing interest and of religious (nonconformist) dissent. The Labour party was formed primarily because of a widespread sense that 'the labour interest' lacked adequate voice in the political system. Thus the party defined one of its main purposes as the promotion of 'the political, social and economic emancipation of the people and more particularly of those who depend directly upon their own exertions by hand or by brain for the means of life' (LP Constitution, Clause IV. 5, as published in Labour party, 1960). Labour's view of its representational function was best summed up by Cole's formulation: 'a broad human movement on behalf of the bottom dog' (quoted in Beech, 2006: 25). The new party sought, Crouch has argued, for the first time in modern British history 'to admit the voices of ordinary people into affairs of state' (Crouch, 2004: 4). The anchoring of social democracy in the political life of the early twentieth century can be seen as the institutionalisation of 'contentious politics'. 'Contentious politics' involves 'collective activity on the part of underrepresented claimants' and the posing of a challenge to 'existing power-holders in the name of a population which feels itself to be unjustly suffering harm or threatened with such harm' (McAdam, Tarrow and Tilly, 1995).

At the heart of the New Labour project has been a reformulation of the party's traditional representational role. Astonishingly, there has been no systematic analysis of the form this has taken – the manner in which the interests and claims of social and economic organisations have been intermediated by the Blair Government and incorporated into public policy. What equilibrium of interests does New Labour now seek to articulate? Given the shrinking size of the working class, its loss of cohesion, the waning of class identity, the blurring of traditional class lines and the emergence of issues only weakly if at all related to class, it was evident to most within the Labour party (that is both the right and the 'soft left') that the weight previously assigned to its function as custodian of working interests had lessened and that it must extend its angle of appeal to white collar workers. But the revision of the party's representational role by New Labour has been more dramatic. Old-style distributional conflicts have lost whatever relevance they once possessed. It was to be the party of both manual workers and 'Middle England', of both business and organised labour.

But could such divisions and tensions be transcended? In extending the hand of friendship to business and other elites has Labour – as one critic alleged – vacated its historical role as 'the political and ideological representative ... of the weak and oppressed, those disadvantaged by market forces'? (Rustin, 2000: 113). Has it relinquished the politics of contention in favour of competitive accommodation? It is at this point that it becomes evident that the two questions we have posed – for what and for whom does New Labour stand? – are, in reality, two aspects of the same problem: what role does the party now play in the wider political system?

The issue can be elucidated by using Jupp's distinction between 'adjustive' and 'programmatic' parties. The Liberals and Conservatives were 'adjustive' in that they saw their function as balancing and adjusting interests and preserving social harmony within the framework of the established institutional order. Social-democratic parties (such as Labour) were programmatic parties. By expressing a more critical view of the established order they sought 'to change basic institutions and social arrangements and cater for dissatisfied elements, labour, the poor and minorities' (Jupp, 1968: 30). Has Labour, under its present regime, been transformed from being a programmatic to an adjustive party?

The purpose and limits of this study

The starting point of this work is that questions about what and for whom New Labour stands can only be answered by analysing its conduct in government. Perhaps it may be useful to clarify what the book is *not* about. Its remit is confined. It does NOT seek to provide a general analysis of the record of the Blair Government. Given the restraints of time, space, resources and expertise such a task is well beyond the capacity of this author. Nor is it an attempt to identify the general dynamics of social democratic transformation which only a comparative approach would permit. It is definitely NOT a contribution to policy analysis – I claim no expertise in any of the areas of policy I cover. It is, simply, a study of the Labour party, the fourth of a series of books I have written on the subject. Its object is to identify the developmental path, 'the persistent tendencies ... the underlying framework of assumptions, the shaping philosophy' of New Labour (Hall, S, 1998: 14). This entails exploring the morphology of the New Labour creed, its 'casts of mind, habits of thinking and shades of sensibility' (Porter, 2000: 14). What practical meaning have the policies pursued by the Blair Government conferred on such core social democratic concepts as equity, social justice, community and equality and what dynamics have driven the process of policy selection?

The book is highly selective in its coverage of policy issues. I proceed largely through a series of case studies. These case studies contain detailed analyses of the issues at hand on the assumption that 'the more detailed the empirical account given, the more persuasive the argument based upon such evidence' (Wickham-Jones, 2002: 470). The criteria for their selection are as follows:

1. The policies examined have a direct bearing on the purposes of this work.
2. The policies are geared to addressing problems of real intrinsic significance.
3. The policies constitute central planks in the programme of the Blair Government.

4. The policies have ignited sustained disagreement within the party because they are seen by critics to signify a rebuttal of traditional Labour principles, aspirations and goals.

To qualify for inclusion in the work, policies have to meet all four criteria.[1] The result is some very notable exclusions, the most obvious being the huge controversy over the decision to send British troops to Iraq and to back the American-backed military assault and occupation. Equally ignored are major (and sometimes politically highly salient) domestic policy areas including law and order and the criminal justice system, housing, urban regeneration and the environment. I can only plead in exoneration for such gaps that my purposes are limited – to sift 'from the ebb and flow of everyday governance' (Porter, 2000: 14) the developmental tendencies which help us to disinter from its practice New Labour's underlying political logic, philosophy and strategic direction.

Theories of social democratic transformation

The discussion has so far assumed that we can infer something about the character and credal outlook of New Labour from the policy choices it has made. This implies that, to some substantial extent, it has control over its own destiny. In other words, a key assumption of this study is that what governments do is, at least in part, is the result of the operation of volition. By volition I mean the possession of 'the power of acting according to our will, or, in other words, the consciousness, when pursuing a certain course of action, that we might, if we had chosen, have pursued a different one' (Lecky, 1910 [1865]: x).

Of course this does not mean that key policy decisions can be seen simply or even primarily as outcomes of political will. Broadly speaking (and borrowing here from Clasen, 2005: 13), I see Labour's overall programmatic trajectory as a function of actor preferences operating within particular power configurations, evolving within institutional settings and responding to challenges arising from the external environment. Such an approach deviates from the two most influential theories of social democratic transformation – globalisation and 'varieties of capitalism' – both of which emphasise (though in different ways) the tight limits on human volition. Both identify as the key determinants of policy decisions environmental forces which establish very firm constraints upon the policy choices available to political actors. Globalisation theory holds that global economic forces are compelling all governments, irrespective of political stripe, to forsake traditional social democratic policies in favour of those that conform more or less closely to free market capitalism. Varieties of capitalism theory agrees that all countries confront the common challenge of globalisation but claim that the way they respond to that challenge is mediated by their historically configured and distinctive institutional complexes – their particular 'variant of capitalism'. However, given the United Kingdom's categorisation as a liberal, market-oriented form of capitalism, both reach broadly similar conclusions – that New Labour-style 'modernisation' represents the most rational, perhaps the only feasible, response to the pressures it confronts. These theories will now be briefly reviewed.

The globalisation thesis and 'the logic of accommodation'

The question of how far the pursuit of social democratic aims and values is compatible with the current levels of globalisation is a central issue of politics. The 'strong globalisation' thesis is perhaps the single most influential explanation of social democratic dilution. It holds that the 'social democratic era' with its commitment to an elaborate, ambitious and universalistic welfare state funded by high levels of taxation levied progressively is unsustainable in the new globalised world economy.

Globalisation is a complex concept but, for the purposes of this study, it can be seen as the conjunction of two inter-related forces, the globalisation of production and of finance. The globalisation of production has been defined as a process in which companies are becoming ever more globally integrated. It is manifested in the removal of barriers to the exchange of goods and services and in the paramount role played by multinational corporations in world production and investment. States have become increasingly dependent on attracting foreign capital to raise output and employment, secure access to new technology and boost competitiveness. In the competitive struggle to attract multinational capital and technological expertise and to avert corporate relocation (the globalisation thesis runs) governments are under pressure to weaken labour protection, cut non-wage social overheads, and reduce corporate and income tax rates. Further, the international scale of multinational corporations' operations gives them manifold opportunities to minimise tax liabilities via transfer pricing and corporate accounting systems, as well as to insist on subsidies and other fiscal concessions as conditions for fresh investment. 'Politically, internationalization of production has made the threat of exit more credible and thus has greatly strengthened the leverage of capital vis-a-vis both unions and governments' (Huber and Stephens, 2001: 224). As a result, the state is constantly being cajoled to cut marginal tax rates on capital, lower levies on the rich, acquiesce in the proliferation of tax havens, relax labour market regulation, slim-down social expenditure and gear policy to the needs of international corporate investors (Helleiner 1994: 173; Cerny, 1995: 610; Olsen, 1991: 120–1; Schmidt, 1995: 79; Garrett and Mitchell, 1999: 10).

For most globalisation theorists financial globalisation is an even more formidable barrier to the pursuit of social democratic policies. This has been defined as 'the reduction of direct controls and taxes on capital movements, liberalisation of long-standing regulatory restrictions within national financial markets, the expansion of lightly-regulated offshore markets, and the introduction of new technologies in the process of financial intermediation' (Pauly, 1995: 369). By the end of the 1980s controls on international capital movement had been removed in almost all advanced industrial countries. Huge volumes of currency are now regularly swapped on the foreign exchange markets as market players seek to capitalise on fluctuating currency ratios and shifting asset prices to maximise profits, and liquid capital floods from one capital market to another in the zealous search for the highest returns.

Financial globalisation inhibits social democratic politics in two main ways. First, the 'capital mobility hypothesis' holds that 'when capital is highly mobile across international borders, the sustainable macro-economic policy options available to states are systemically circumscribed' (Andrews, 1994: 193). Under deregulated capital markets, governments cannot control both the exchange rate and the interest rate, hence rendering the pursuit of Keynesian demand management policies virtually impossible. Countries can no longer use domestic capital controls to stimulate investment and employment by relaxing monetary policy without risk of precipitating currency depreciation, while the abolition of external capital controls severely impairs efforts to manage the economy through domestic capital market regulation (Huber and Stephens, 2001: 228, 230).

Second, the threat of currency crisis and capital flight weighing over governments means that they have to retain, by whatever modification of policy is deemed necessary, the confidence of international asset holders (Helleiner 1994: 173).

> Under conditions of complete and instant capital mobility, governments have come to realize that a reputation for 'unsound' fiscal policies will not only affect their credit rating and the interest rates they must pay, but will also make their currencies vulnerable to speculative attacks with potentially catastrophic economic consequences.
>
> (Scharpf, 2000: 7)

Judgements of credit worthiness depend in part upon the extent to which the policies governments pursue coincide with the free market creed, the touchstone (in the eyes of the financial markets) of economic soundness and responsibility. 'For many, the potential for massive capital flight has rendered the financial markets the ultimate arbiter of government policy. ... Governments are held to ransom by mobile capital, the price is high, and punishment for non-compliance is swift' (Garrett and Mitchell, 1999: 10).

To sum up: historically, the social democratic project has been pursued by the energetic utilisation of state power. Social democratic governments had sought to achieve full employment, a high level of output and investment, and the more equal distribution of income, wealth and life-chances through exercising a substantial level of control over the economy by means of demand-management, regulatory policies, interventionist industrial strategies and the welfare state. The liberalisation of the international financial and trade regimes, the rise of multinational capital, the ascendancy of financial markets and the widening disparity between the institutional capacity of the state and the structural characteristics of the global economy has progressively denuded governments of the capability to exercise any effective management of the economy in traditional Keynesian terms (Cerny, 1995: 598; Mishra, 1999: 97).

In short, the social democratic model of Keynesian demand management, progressive taxation, expanding welfare spending and redistribution is no longer a practicable proposition. Governments may not have been entirely disempowered but globalisation has narrowed the perimeter in which choices can be made and effectively given to financial asset-holders a veto on policy. The outer limits of effective state action consist now of supply-side policies designed to jack up competitiveness and promote a favourable environment for transnational capital by providing a circumscribed range of goods which the market is disinclined to supply, such as education, training programmes and infrastructure projects (Jessop, 1994: 264–5; Andrews, 1994: 201; Garrett and Lange, 1991: 546; Cerny, 1995: 611; Yeates, 1999: 374; Swank, 2001).

From this angle the jettisoning by New Labour of traditional social democratic policies represents a realistic appraisal of the possibilities and limits of political action. Governments in these circumstances have no alternative but to rein-in social spending, lower tax rates and ease tax regimes to attract foreign investment from internationally mobile firms, allay fears of inflationary pressures and placate international financial markets by pursuing orthodox fiscal and monetary policies (Swank, 2001). The reconfigured state thus has no real option but to acquiesce in 'the loss of key traditional social and economic state functions', focusing its energies instead on activities that promote national economic competitiveness (Cerny and Evans, 2004: 60). We can call this explanation of New Labour 'the logic of accommodation' since it stipulates that social democratic parties such as Labour have no option but to accommodate to the policy imperatives of globalisation (Hay, 1999: 29).

However, a growing body of literature has cast doubt on key propositions of the globalisation thesis. Some of the most compelling criticism emanates from Garrett's work which queries both the empirical evidence and the theoretical assumptions of the 'strong globalisation' thesis (see, especially, Garrett, 1998). Garrett and Mitchell find 'the notion that globalization has undermined the welfare state somewhat surprising' given that 'most systematic empirical studies on the subject' demonstrate 'neither clear nor consistent globalization constraints on government spending or taxation in the OECD' (Garrett and Mitchell, 1999: 6, 31). Indeed Weiss reported in 2005 that average social spending in the OECD over the past 20 years had actually increased as a share of national income. To finance this still heavy welfare effort the overall tax yields (including from corporate taxes) had also risen – not fallen – in this period (Weiss, 2005: 347–8). 'On most measures, most European welfare states are larger and more generous today than they have ever been before' (Rhodes, 2002: 38) In short, 'Globalization has not induced a pervasive race to the bottom in welfare state regimes' (Garrett and Mitchell, 1999: 33).

Why is this? 'Strong globalisation' sceptics have advanced two explanations. First, the 'compensation thesis'. The swelling size of the constituency of the vulnerable and economically insecure has strengthened political pressure for more generous social compensation while, at the same time, placing a premium on measures to sustain social order and cohesion whose loss would be deemed by investors to raise the risk attached to investment. Second, the assumption that high levels of public spending are necessarily economically damaging is questionable. Such a view overlooks the reliance of capital on the state to perform crucial functions such as 'the provision of infrastructure, education, training and the maintenance of social stability' (Yeates, 1999: 376). Business firms are influenced not only by low wage costs and low taxation when determining where to invest: they also want a sophisticated infrastructure, a skilled, well-trained workforce and a stable business environment, all of which entail an active state role. From this perspective 'government spending is an investment, enhancing productivity and securing collective goods that are under-supplied by the market' while even 'non-productive' social spending plays a vital role (for business) in helping to underpin social cohesion (Pierson, C, 2001: 463. See also Rhodes, 2002: 42). This leads Garrett to the conclusion that far from debilitating the capacity of social democratic governments to further develop their welfare systems, globalisation has enhanced the economic functionality of progressive social policy (Garrett, 1998, 10–11).

'Varieties of capitalism' and institutionalist theories

However it does NOT follow from this account that extensive welfare states and systems of labour protection are functional to all economies. Much depends upon which 'variety of capitalism' prevails. The core 'variety of capitalism' proposition is that policy responses to exogenous forces (such as globalisation) are filtered by institutional configurations – variously defined in terms of the organisation of decision-making within the polity, patterns of welfare provision and economic and industrial systems – which act as intervening variables. 'Actors do not inherit a blank slate that they can remake at will'. Rather they find that 'the dead weight of previous institutional choices seriously limit[s] their room for manoeuvre' (Pierson 2000a: 810; Pierson 2000b: 493). Major decisions taken at 'critical junctures' establish institutional patterns that channel future action. 'Critical junctures' are 'moments when substantial institutional change takes place thereby creating a "branching point" from which historical development moves onto a new path' (Hall and Taylor, 1998: 10). Once constructed 'institutions typically endure for significant periods of time, influencing political dynamics and associated outcomes in subsequent periods' (Lieberman, 2001: 101–3). Through the process of what is called 'path dependence' institutions reduce the range of policy options given serious consideration by structuring the ways decisions are made and by helping shape the way societal actors define and promote their interests (Weiss, 2005: 349; Huber and Stephens, 2001: 32) External forces are fed into policy choice only as they are mediated by institutional arrangements which thereby 'exert a tremendous influence over the pace, scope, character and style of policy adjustment' (Hall, P, 1993: 9).

'Varieties of capitalism' theory arrives in two – in many ways largely complementary – forms: 'production regime' and 'welfare state regime' theory. 'Production regimes' are defined as 'economies with specific relations between enterprises, financial institutions, labour, and the government, and specific constellations of labour market and economic policies' (Huber and Stephens, 2001: 23). There are two main 'production regimes': the coordinated (or concerted) and the liberal market.[2] In the former highly organised and centralised peak associations of capital and labour play a key role in orchestrating economic life in partnership with the state via a pattern of concertation (or institutionalised cooperation). There is an elaborate fabric of labour protection, wages and conditions of work are regulated through extensive collective bargaining networks and competitive strength is sustained by a highly skilled labour force coupled with a high-trust system of industrial relations (Huber and Stephens, 2001: 23; Howell, 2004: 4). Powerful trade unions and other representative and consultative agencies (such as works councils) impose a consensual style of decision-making on firms that propel them to seek productivity gains via innovation in the organisation of work and product quality rather than by cutting wage costs, while concerted bargaining between strong trade unions and employers associations ensures that wage increases match productivity growth (Hall, P, 1998: 5, 8). Examples of such production regimes typically include the Scandinavian countries, Germany, Holland and Austria.

In liberal market production regimes relationships are structured to a much greater degree by market transactions. Financial markets play a key role in supplying finance for investment, with access to funds being heavily dependent on short-term profitability and rising dividend and stock values. There is a high degree of labour market flexibility, collective bargaining (in the private sector) is normally weak and patchy and operates primarily at the firm or plant level while for many the employment contract is individually negotiated. Corporate managerial authority is only feebly checked by countervailing forces and management retains substantial prerogatives over hiring and firing, with competitiveness sustained by relatively low wage costs (Howell, 2004: 4; Hall, P, 1998: 3). The main examples of the liberal market regime are in the English-speaking world, notably the United States and the United Kingdom.

There are clear parallels with the 'welfare regime' typology. In a highly influential work Esping-Andersen distinguishes between 'the three worlds of welfare capitalism' (Esping-Andersen, 1990): the so-called social democratic, liberal (or market-oriented) and conservative (or corporatist) welfare regimes. The use of the term 'regime' denotes 'the fact that in the relation between state and economy a complex of legal and organizational features are systematically interwoven' (Esping-Andersen, 1990: 2). The regimes are differentiated in terms of their scope and spending levels and, more fundamentally, their institutional logic in assigning welfare functions to the state, the market and the family. Only the first two need (for the purposes of this study) detain us here. The social democratic welfare state (found mainly in Scandinavia) is characterised by generous social entitlements universally distributed, with high levels of income security and considerable redistributionary impact. The liberal welfare regime (exemplified in the United States and the United Kingdom) is more limited in scope, less well-funded, with a more of a restrictive approach to eligibility for benefits that emphasises means testing and more encouragement for citizens to obtain risk protection through the market (Myles and Quadagno, 2002: 39–40; Hall, P, 2002: 41; Huber and Stephens, 2001: 111).

There is a definite correspondence between the two typologies. Ebbinghaus and Manow note certain 'institutional complementarities between different production regimes, industrial relations practices and social protection systems' (Ebbinghaus and Manow, 2001: 3–4), while Huber and Stephens see 'social democratic welfare states [as] embedded in a mutually supportive relationship with co-ordinated production regimes' (Huber and Stephens, 2002: 48). Thus if we combine the two typologies we can then distinguish between the concerted market economy associated with a social democratic welfare state on the one hand, and the liberal market economy associated with the liberal welfare state on the other. The logics of both path dependence and institutional (functional) complementarities predict self-reinforcing processes of development (Pierson, 2000a: 812). Thus though the impulses transmitted by globalisation are powerful their impact is 'refracted through both very different political institutions and very different models for organizing relationships among economic actors' (Myles and Quadagno, 2002: 44). The theory predicts that the social democratic welfare regime buttressed by a concerted market economy is well placed to protect the welfare state and resist neo-liberal reforms whereas in liberal regimes the pressure will be towards further liberalisation, deregulation and welfare retrenchment. 'The clear implication' is that despite certain commonalities in the pressures they face, 'the paths taken by social democratic parties in Europe should diverge' according to the variety of capitalism that defines their basic structures (Hall, P, 2002: 32).

There *is*, in short, an alternative to neo-liberalism's logic, but *only* for those countries with the requisite institutional architecture (Hay, 2002b: 13). This excludes the United Kingdom since virtually all analysts agree in classifying it as a liberal production/welfare regime. As a result both glo-balisation and varieties of capitalism theory predict that for an incoming Labour government the only feasible set of policies is, effectively, market-oriented ones (Hall, P, 2002: 42–3). From the perspective of the former, Mishra contends that, under globalised conditions, 'left-of-centre approa-ches to social policy are virtually excluded', including any sustained expan-sion of the public sector, a return to more progressive and redistributive taxation, the narrowing of the income and wealth divide differentials and greater universality in social programmes (Mishra, 1999: 102. See also Cerny and Evans, 2004: 55). Varieties of capitalism theorist Peter Hall equally agrees that the incoming Blair Government was more or less constrained to pursue policies such as fluid labour markets, limited labour protection and a retrenched welfare system which are congruent with the dynamics of its liberal economic and social model (Hall, P, 2002: 42. See also Huber and Stephens, 2001: 32).

In short, both theories converge in their expectations for a British Labour government. As Clasen points out, 'much of the current literature on wel-fare state restructuring assumes that the colour of the governments is largely irrelevant in the light of economic globalisation, Europeanisation or other forms of external and internal socio-economic pressures' (Clasen, 2002: 71). If true, then a phenomenon (such as the emergence of New Labour) can best be accounted for by exploring the objective conditions, forces and inherited institutional forms to which it would be a necessary response. Such an approach presumes that political outcomes and events are always the product of objective and determinate forces over which human volition has little, if any, control. It takes for granted, as Sassoon puts it, that 'whatever happened had to happen' and thereby discounts the possibility that 'within determinate circumstances (this is not a minor proviso), things could have proceeded differently' (Sassoon, 2000: 18–19).

This book suggests an alternative way of explaining New Labour.[3] It rests on two assumptions. First, that political parties *matter*. However much their role may have been challenged by new patterns of power and constrained both domestically and globally they continue to provide an essential link between society and the sphere of executive action, articulating and aggre-gating interests, mobilising voters and legitimising state decisions (Becker and Cuperus, 2004: 7; Yanai, 1999: 10). It remains the case that (in the United Kingdom at least) 'once in government, political parties are the central actors in determining government policy outputs', a function 'per-formed by the transformation of the parties' manifesto and campaign pro-mises into law' (Dalton and Wattenberg, 2002: 9). The second assumption is that political action is intentional and strategic, that is to say political players – whether individual or collective – are not simply conduits for broader social forces, hemmed in by structural exigencies and compulsions. Politicians 'act for reasons to achieve consciously established goals. They are able to monitor their actions and to evaluate them' (Lloyd, 1986: 63).

This study follows Wickham-Jones in viewing the direction of New Labour policy as 'largely determined by actors occupying dominant positions within the institutional configuration that defines the Party'. These actors make rational and considered choices in seeking to attain their preferences within the limits set by (their understanding of) external pressures (Wickham-Jones, 2002: 470). They also act strategically in that they 'judge the contours of the terrain', seek to 'project the likely consequences of different courses of action' and, on this basis, 'select the particular course of action to be pursued' (Hay, 2001). The premise that underpins the approach taken by this study is that, in Douglass North's words, 'ideas and ideologies matter because they shape the mental constructs that individuals use to interpret the world around them and make choices' and hence it is necessary to get 'to grips with the subjective mental constructs by which individuals process information and arrive at conclusions that shape their choice' (quoted in Yee, 1997: 1002). Thus a primary purpose of this work will be to try and identify the New Labour belief system, that is the prism that shaped its perception of political and social reality, its conception of the desirable ends of political conduct, its definitions of the nature of the problems it sought to tackle and its criteria for policy choice.

The first chapter seeks to place this study of New Labour in a historical context by identifying Labour's established creed, or what is called the British social democratic tradition. It postulates a two-dimensional tradition, comprising 'redistributive social democratic' and 'ethical socialist' strands. Chapter two charts the Blair Government's efforts to promote social justice through measures to redress problems of poverty and social exclusion. Chapter three extends the discussion to another core New Labour principle, equality of opportunity, and considers how it has been applied in the crucial area of secondary education. An oft-repeated axiom of the Government has been 'what matters is what works' – irrespective of ideological provenance. A principal application of this axiom has been the Private Finance Initiative (a policy devised by the Conservatives), a method for financing public sector investment projects in which the private sector is charged with the design, construction and supply of public facilities (such as schools and hospitals) which are then rented out to public authorities. Chapter four examines the extent to which the PFI 'is what works' and considers why it was adopted. Chapter five investigates the Government's programme for 'modernising' the NHS – a programme which ignited more sustained and vehement opposition from within the party than any other aspect of domestic policy. Chapter six turns to what has always been a pivotal policy area for the party: employment relations. Why, in a break with tradition, has the Blair Government espoused a light-touch regulation of the labour market? What does the conduct of policy in this area tell us about New Labour's stance on what has traditionally been a major concern of the party – the protection of the interests of 'ordinary working people'? The previous chapters having sought to identify the broad thrust of the

Blair Government's domestic programme in key areas of policy, chapter seven seeks to uncover its dynamics. To what extent is the trajectory of policy explicable in terms of globalisation or varieties of capitalism theory? If there are other forces at work what are they? The next two chapters seek to pull the various threads of the argument together and answer the inter-linked questions: for what (chapter eight) and for whom (chapter nine) does New Labour stand? The concluding chapter reflects on the question posed by the title of the book: under the 10-year long premiership of Tony Blair did Labour lose its soul?

1 The British social democratic tradition

Introduction: the two dimensions of British social democracy

A key assumption upon which this study rests is that ideas and ideals matter. Parties are not simply competing teams of politicians producing policies to maximise electoral support but are bound together by some common principles, however loosely held. Parties 'have encompassing beliefs and cultures within which specific policies and strategic emphases took shape and which provided the overall framework for policy and strategy' (Cronin, 2004: 7). All political action must, to some significant degree, be grounded in a creed of some sort for, as Jack Straw explained, all politicians need a 'framework of belief' to provide a 'template for the scores of individual decisions which they have to make every day' (Straw, 1998). For this reason vote-seeking – however crucial this may be – cannot alone explain the political trajectory of the Labour party.

A central question that this work addresses is whether New Labour's 'framework of belief' is social democratic. How much credence is there to Tony Blair's claim that, under his leadership, 'we have re-discovered the ideals of community, equality and solidarity that are the foundations of our party, applying them in new ways to the massively changed world in which we live'? (Blair, Foreword to Diamond, 2004). Or is there more truth to Cronin's contention that New Labour 'had not forgotten its traditions: rather it had consciously and explicitly rejected those traditions and the policies to which they were attached'? (Cronin, 2004: 394).

Plainly such questions can only be answered on the basis of some understanding of Labour's established creed and values – what, in this chapter, is also called the British social democratic tradition. The concept of a party tradition implies the existence of what Durkheim termed a 'collective consciousness', the shared beliefs and aspirations which constitute an organisation's 'manners of acting, thinking and feeling' (Durkheim, 1982 [1895]). It is *collective* in that its elements come to constitute (in Durkheim's words) 'partially autonomous realities which live their own life' (quoted in Lukes, 1972: 8). It acquires the status of a *tradition* when 'a relatively coherent body of knowledge or thought' is transmitted from one political generation to another. A *party political* tradition (or creed or ideology)[1] refers to a body of thought diffused within a political party that 'is concerned with defining the good life for society, and serves as the principle basis for argument and action' (Hazareesingh, 1994: 5). A party then becomes 'the bearer of its own tradition' and this tradition is 'embedded in its identity, its conception of itself' (Moschanas, 2002: 243). The British social democratic tradition, in short, refers to the body of ideals, beliefs and goals which, in totality, constituted Labour's mental and moral outlook.

The way in which the terms tradition and creed are used here conform closely to Freeden's conception of ideologies as 'systems of political thinking, loose or rigid, deliberate or unintended, through which individuals and groups construct an understanding of the political world they inhabit' (Freeden, 1999a: 45). Creeds have both their analytical and normative aspects, that is notions both of how the world is and how it ought to be, and the two often blend into each other. The bias in this chapter is towards exploring the latter. It is with charting Labour's 'particular ethical view of the world' insofar *as this was translated into 'action in the domain of practical politics'* (Sassoon, 2000: 18. Emphasis added). In seeking to establish the principles and goals that distinguished Labour from its political rivals and imparted to it its most enduring characteristics a distinction is made between abstract 'ideals' and 'operative values'. An *ideal* refers to 'a conception of something in its highest perfection, especially as a thing to be aimed at' (*Shorter Oxford Dictionary*). *Operative values*, by contrast, refer to the conceptions of desirable future states of affairs which form themselves in the actor's mind as worthwhile goals and which they seek to further by legislative means. While ideals may embody pure aspirations, operative values are ideals accommodated to political realities: the need to build coalitions of electoral support wide enough to propel a party into office and keep it there; to respond to the preferences of powerful affected interests; and to take account of the problems of economic management and public administration. Thus, unlike ideals, operative values are primarily action-oriented, that is they represent desirable goals which (in the minds of their adherents) can be furthered by tangible acts in the foreseeable future.

Defining the British social democratic tradition is a complicated and elusive task. There is no authorised version, no formal, codified party programme as can be found, for example, with the German and Swedish sister parties. As Crosland noted, the Labour party was 'not founded on any body of doctrine at all, and has always preserved a marked anti-doctrinal and anti-theoretical bias' (Crosland, 1964: 80). From its origins it was steeped in the highly empirical, practical, down-to-earth culture of British trade unionism. Further, the party has always been proud to boast that it is a 'broad church' embracing a medley of different ideas, aspirations and ethical codes. There has never been, as Crosland added, 'a single constant and consistent body of socialist doctrine' (Crosland, 1964: 44).

So how, then, can the British social democratic tradition be identified? Three types of source material have been used: (1) official party documents which carry some authority and programmatic significance (such as manifestos, speeches by top political leaders, records of discussions and agreements); (2) the individual contributions of political thinkers who are widely acknowledged (by historians and other commentators) as exercising some formative influence on shaping Labour's collective mentality; and (3) evidence of values and intentions that can be derived from the actual behaviour of Labour governments. Inference here entails judgement. The form legislation takes reflects multiple influences and I have sought to distinguish, as best I can (and drawing heavily on secondary sources) *intended* from *constrained* action – while acknowledging the one often blurs into the other.

The object in this chapter is not to offer a systematic analysis of Labour's thinking over the years but to delineate the British social democratic tradition as a politically constituted space 'defined in terms both of values and of receptivity to certain kinds of policy instruments' (White, 2001: 3). It is to uncover the ideas, values and goals that operated as 'the orientations or premises of action' (Beer, 1969: 403) that guided and underpinned policy choices by successive Labour governments. My central organising hypothesis is that the British social democratic tradition has always been *two-dimensional*. This bipolarity is a recurring theme in the literature. The philosopher Gerry Cohen identified two values which he nominated as central to the Labour party: equality and community (or fellowship), 'the only values which the Left affirmed as a matter of principle and which the Centre and Right rejected as a matter of principle' (Cohen, 1994: 6). The political theorist (and now Labour peer) Raymond Plant pointed out that the party has traditionally stood for both social justice and equality on the one hand and solidarity and fraternity on the other (Plant, 1989: 2). Similarly Michael Young, drafter of the 1945 Manifesto and subsequently a highly influential thinker, saw British socialists as 'broadly of two kinds – the Fabians with their emphasis on efficiency and social justice, and their devotion to facts, and the idealistic socialists ... with their emphasis on the dignity of man and of labour' (Briggs, 2001: 93). Ingle, in his study of British political parties, also draws a distinction between ethical socialism, with its accent on fraternity, and scientific socialism, with its accent on efficiency and equity (Ingle, 2000: 104). To Greenleaf, on the one hand equity, 'organisation and efficiency', and on the other 'liberty, fulfilment and moral regeneration' represented two distinct motives or 'poles of endeavour within socialism' (Greenleaf, 1983b: 350. See also Ellison, 1994).

Miller offers the fullest exposition of this bipolarity. He identifies two distinct (though interlinked) critiques of capitalism (Miller, 1989). The first focused on the persistence within capitalism of pervasive deprivation and distress amid gross opulence, its inability, left to its own devices, to distribute resources equitably. This dimension of the social democratic tradition will be called the *redistributivist*. For the redistributive social democrat socialism was a matter of equality and social justice, and Labour's task the construction of social arrangements which engendered a much fairer allocation of resources and life-chances – though precisely what constituted a fair allocation, how much should be redistributed, to whom and on what basis were always matters of contention. The second critique emphasised the dehumanising effects of capitalism. It alienated people from each other by fostering relations of rivalry and suspicion rather than co-operation and trust. It nourished greed and the acquisitive instinct and it subordinated production for need to production for profit. It was an *ethical socialist* critique in the sense that it was about 'other people and how well or ill you behave towards them and they to you and to each other' (Young, 2000).

These strands were in many ways complementary. 'They could be pursued in tandem and in many respects reinforced each other' (Cohen, 1994: 6). To some degree they cut across the left–right division. This was particularly the case with redistributive social democracy where the degree of equality envisaged could differ quite starkly. Ethical socialism, in contrast, tended by its very nature to gravitate to the left since it entailed a major curtailment in the role of capital and the market in shaping the organisation of social relationships. The following two sections of the chapter investigate respectively the redistributive and ethical socialist strands of the British social democratic tradition. Both, it will be suggested, can be defined in terms of two central tenets: equality and collectivism for the former, fellowship and the public service ethos for the latter. The final section seeks to distil from the tradition a sense of how the party, as a collectivity, conceived its animating principles, its bedrock values, indeed its very reason for being. We call this distillation the party's 'soul'.

The first dimension: redistributive social democracy

Equality

For Labour's most eminent post-war thinker, Tony Crosland, the party's prime purpose was to promote 'wider social equality embracing also the distribution of property, the educational system, social class relationships, power and privilege in industry' (Crosland, 1974: 16). But what was meant by equality? It has now become customary (in New Labour circles) to counterpoise (New Labour) equality of opportunity with ('Old Labour') equality of outcome, with the latter assumed to mean a levelling of all incomes (Blair, 1998a: 3). However, as Plant has pointed out, the views on equality held within the Labour party over the years 'are far more complex and nuanced than can be caught in [this] very simple-minded contrast' (Plant, 2004: 117. See also Crick, 1984: 158). Indeed heated differences about the precise meaning of equality, how it should be applied and how far it should extend – in light of economic and electoral considerations – have been a fixed feature of the party since its birth. But all groups within the party were agreed on two points. First, absolute equality – or what Dworkin called 'the flat, indiscriminate, version of equality' (Dworkin, 1984: 173) – was neither feasible nor, indeed, desirable. It was generally accepted that ability should have its rent and that incentives were required to ensure that socially needed skills, energy and talent received a level of reward sufficient to ensure an ample supply. Indeed the most formidable figure on Labour's left, Nye Bevan, saw no reason 'to resent higher rewards where they manifestly flow from personal exertion and superior qualities' (Bevan, 1978 [1952]: 85).

The second agreed point was that the actual scale of inequality routinely generated within capitalism went beyond anything that could be justified on grounds of merit or efficiency. Rather than reflecting functional needs or differential deserts, the system of stratification in Britain was grounded in *class inequality*. A system of class-inequality existed (Crosland contended) to the extent that stratification patterns took the form of 'a few broad and deep incisions into the social body, as opposed to innumerable shallow cuts', and that 'these deep incisions coincide[d] to form a single set of national divisions'. The United Kingdom exhibited such a pattern since it was clearly evident that the various 'hierarchies of education, occupational prestige, and style of life all show pronounced and visible breaks; and these breaks broadly coincide[d]' (Crosland, 1964: 118, 119). This class-based system was unfair, party leader Hugh Gaitskell maintained, because a person's life-chances, his 'income, way of living, education, status and opportunities in life depend[ed] upon the class into which he is born' (Gaitskell, 1956: 3). Amplifying the point, Crosland saw inequality as offending social justice on three grounds:

1. Access to education was marred by gross inequalities which denied the right of all to equal opportunities in life.
2. 'An equitable distribution of wealth required that wealth should be the reward for the performance of a definite service and that all should have an equal chance of performing that function and so earning the reward.' This was plainly and emphatically not the case.
3. Class inequality caused a major concentration of power whose effect was to confer upon the rich and powerful a high measure of control over the lives of the less fortunate and enabled them to perpetuate their privileges.
(Crosland, 1964: 140–4)

What principles – operative values – should actuate the party's egalitarian drive? Two such values can be identified. First, equality of opportunity. This stipulated that all people, whatever their background, should be given an equal opportunity to fulfill their potential. Second, a more equitable distribution of income, wealth and power in which only such inequalities existed that clearly conduced to the common welfare. We discuss each in turn.

Equality of opportunity

The principle of equality of opportunity asserts that 'if there is to be inequality in the rewards and remuneration and status dispensed by social arrangements, all members of society should have equal opportunity suitably defined to gain the superior positions' (Arneson, 2002b). It is frequently asserted within New Labour circles that traditional party thinking – distracted by its obsession with 'levelling' – failed to grasp the importance of ensuring for all the ability to rise in the world. This claim is quite incorrect. Tawney encapsulated party thinking on the matter when he explained that

> a community must draw on a stream of fresh talent, in order to avoid stagnation. . . . The existence of opportunities to move from point to point on an economic scale, and to mount from humble origins to success and affluence, is a condition, therefore, both of social well-being and of individual happiness, and impediments which deny them to some, while lavishing them on others, are injurious to both.
>
> (Tawney, 1964a [1931]: 106)

Equally it was a proposition universally accepted within the party that the principal means by which a socially mobile society could be secure was the availability to all of a good standard of education. Educational opportunity was seen as the single most important determinant of future occupation, career and prosperity and there was a consensus within Labour's ranks that a prime cause of persisting class inequalities was a highly segregated educational system.

In this area the most radical of Labour administrations was, however, extraordinarily cautious. The Attlee government was content to respect the 1944 Butler Act which established the Eleven-Plus examination which effectively segregated the minority of the more 'academic' from the humdrum majority confined to inferior education and, hence, less well-paid and prestigious jobs. In the years in opposition after 1951 much more thought was given to how the right to a decent education could be extended to the population at large. By 1964, when Labour returned to power, there was a virtually unanimous recognition of the arbitrary character and highly divisive effects of the Eleven-Plus and the binary system it created. The institution of a comprehensive system of education was seen as vital to equalising educational opportunities (Chitty, 2004: 11–12). A shift away from the binary system was already underway prior to the election of the Wilson Government but a powerful impetus to reform was provided when Tony Crosland, an eager proponent of the comprehensive system, was appointed Education Secretary in 1965. He rapidly issued a circular urging all education authorities to abolish the Eleven Plus and progress towards a comprehensive system accelerated. By the time, after six years in office, the Labour Government had been relieved of power comprehensives had supplanted the binary system as the main form of secondary education.[2]

At the same time the Government was committed to extend the (at the time) highly restricted access to higher education. With the creation of a wave of new universities and the newly established Polytechnics the size of the higher education sector doubled. The Open University was established to provide another means by which a university education could be acquired by those beyond the school leaving age. There was, furthermore, a general recognition that educational standards could only be raised if more money became available and during the 1964–70 Labour Government spending rose substantially from 4.8 per cent to 6.1 per cent of national wealth (Ponting, 1989: 292).

There was, for the most part, a broad continuity between the policies pursued by the 1974–79 Government and its predecessor. The 1974 election manifestos committed the party to speed-up the phasing out of selection, give more priority to pre-school education and provide better education and training facilities for those who left full-time education at the age of 16. Straightened financial circumstances – the slicing-back of public budgets after 1975 in response to the economic crisis – meant that the pace of progress slowed, but by the time Labour left office in 1979 in most parts of the country comprehensives dominated secondary education.

New Labour has subsequently queried the effectiveness of the comprehensive system in improving both access to and the overall quality of secondary education. However the evidence suggests that the shift towards comprehensive education did, on balance, expand the educational opportunities for those who would otherwise have been consigned to secondary modern schools. A leading expert concluded that 'the averagely able and below average children definitely gained from comprehensive education' while the performance of the most able did not appear to be adversely affected (Glennerster, 2007: 142). Notwithstanding, it soon became evident that although the worst form of educational discrimination had been removed (in most of the country) with the abolition of the Eleven Plus a wide gap in educational attainment between the suburban and the inner-city comprehensive persisted.

Indeed, in retrospect, it is not the enthusiasm for educational levelling that seems so notable an aspect of Labour's educational policies in the 1960s and 1970s as their modesty of ambition. There were major accomplishments, notably the increase in spending and the abolition in most of the United Kingdom of the Eleven Plus. Notwithstanding, for many schools, the introduction of comprehensive education – in part because of lack of finance – made only slight inroads into educational inequality. The main beneficiaries of the expansion of higher education were middle-class youngsters – by 1979 there had been no improvement in the relative prospect of working-class children obtaining higher education (Blackstone, 1980: 226–7). The plainest evidence of the easily tempered ardour of Labour governments for educational equality lies in the treatment by successive Labour governments of the public schools. Although Crosland is best known for his opposition to grammar schools, he nominated the existence of a large private sector in education as 'the greatest single cause of stratification and class-consciousness in Britain' (quoted in Reisman, 1997: 78). Indeed, he very aptly queried 'why socialists could be so obsessed with the question of the grammar schools, and so indifferent to the much more glaring injustice of the independent schools' (quoted in Kogan, 2006: 76). Such schools, he argued, furnished not only a superior education but 'further crucial advantages of right accent, manners and dependability of character' which acted as 'a major determinant of occupation, and hence of income, power and prestige' (Crosland, 1964: 140). Indeed, as Glennerster points out, 'the public schools had long been an obsession with those on the left in British politics and for good reason' (Glennerster, 2007: 140).

Proposals to integrate the public schools into the state system were aired during the Second World War but they evoked no response from the postwar Labour Government (Attlee actually took a keen interest in aspiring Labour MPs who were educated at the same public school as himself). The party's 1964 Manifesto pledged – though only after 'hours of debate' – the setting up of an educational trust 'to advise on the best way of integrating the public schools into the state system of education' (Glennerster, 2007: 140–1). An enquiry was commissioned by Crosland as Minister of Education but no substantive action was taken, probably for two main reasons. First, many (especially on the right of the party) held that for the state to deny the right of those who so wished to spend money on purchasing a good education for their children could be construed as an abridgement of civil liberties. Second, so high a proportion of Britain's establishment (particularly the senior civil service, the media and finance) were educated independently that any major challenge to private education would incur heavy political risks. The abolition of public schools was thus never on Labour's agenda. What *is* surprising – given the status of the public schools as the real 'commanding height' of privilege – was that none of the various schemes mooted within the party to close the gap between the private and state sectors were ever implemented. Despite Manifesto pledges (e.g. Labour Party, 1974; Craig, 1990: 248) even the relatively modest promises to 'withdraw tax relief and charitable status from public schools, as a first step towards our long-term aim of phasing out fee paying in schools' were never fully implemented.

Indeed during the 1970s Labour Government faith in the efficacy of education as a mechanism for redistribution began to wane (Blackstone, 1980: 232). Concluding his discussion of the educational record of the 1974–79 Government, Lowe comments: 'out of the window went ... the drive towards a fairer society and an open democracy through education and in, an accent on economy, efficiency and employability' (Lowe, 2004: 137). For a party which claimed that the main lever for equality of opportunity was a more equal start in education, the outcome after 11 years of Labour government was only modest with access to positions of social advantage, in 1979, still highly correlated with social class.

This is puzzling given the repeated emphasis by the party on education as *the* crucial solvent of a rigid class structure. It seems reasonable to infer from this that, whatever the public declarations, the commitment to equality of educational access *in practice* never quite occupied the status of a *key* operative value. Thus apart from the phasing out of the Eleven-Plus, the 1964–70 Government 'took no major initiative of its own and showed little sign of tackling the roots of inequality in the system' (Ponting, 1989: 131). Labour's failure to commit more substantial resources to the educational needs of the less privileged sections of the community, Tessa Blackstone concluded in her review of the record of the 1974–79 Government, largely reflected the fact that a serious assault on educational disadvantage was never a top priority (Blackstone, 1980: 229–30, 232). Though the means chosen were (as we shall see) very different the circumspect and cautious approach towards evening-out educational inequalities adopted by the Blair Government has more in common with its predecessors in the 1960s and 1970s than critics allow, while the resources it committed were more generous. Contrasting the aspirations and discourse of earlier Labour governments with the actual record of their successor can produce misleading conclusions.

More equitable distribution

Opportunities to rise, Tawney declared, 'are not a substitute for a large measure of practical equality. … On the contrary, it is only the presence of a high degree of practical equality which can diffuse and generalize opportunities to rise.' He defined 'practical equality' in terms of 'the resolute elimination of all forms of special privilege, which favour some groups and depress others, whether their source be differences of environment, of education, or of pecuniary income' (Tawney, 1964a [1931]: 106, 30). How was greater 'practical equality' to be attained?

Until the 1940s (and, for the left, for many years later) the transfer of productive assets from the private to the public sector was seen as a major way in which gross disparities in resource-distribution could be rectified. This option had not been pursued with a great deal of enthusiasm by the post-war Labour Government (most of the industries nationalised were ailing and at best spasmodically profitable and their owners were handsomely compensated) and effectively abandoned afterwards.[3] By the time of Labour's return to power in 1964 it was widely accepted (in practice by the left too, as the Crossman, Castle and Benn diaries attest) that the most effective lever for countering and compensating for the regressive dynamics of the free-market economic system and securing a fairer distribution of life-chances was through what Titmuss called the 'institutional redistributive welfare state'. This envisaged redressing inequality at a secondary level by recycling, through additions to collective consumption, the proceeds of market-generated rewards. Extending public services and increasing welfare benefits (e.g. pension and family allowances) funded from progressive taxation was regarded both as a means to resolve specific problems (family impoverishment, poverty in old-age) and as part of the drive to spread resources more evenly by providing sources of income not contingent on position in the labour market. For example, in 1976 legislation was enacted tying increases in pensions with rises in wages rather than prices – the effect being a significant and sustained improvement in the material conditions of pensioners, who figured disproportionately among the poor.

The obverse to spending was taxing.

> Egalitarian policy involves altering the incidence of tax across the population, by increasing reliance on tariffs that relate to ability to pay, like income tax, and reducing that on those that ignore financial circumstance. It also involves setting the schedules of individual taxes (rates, bands, and the tax base) so more of the burden falls on the better-off.
>
> (Clark, 2001: 9)

Much has recently been made of the 'punitive' levels of taxation in the 1970s – 'taxation for taxation's sake' in Gordon Brown's quixotic formulation. The effects, allegedly, were to demotivate 'entrepreneurs', erode profits, discourage investment and sacrifice economic efficiency to a misplaced and lop-sided concern with economic equality. There is no doubt that the fiscal policies of successive Labour governments were designed to and did in practice have a discernable redistributive effect (Stewart, 1972: 88, 105). Extended public programmes financed by progressive taxation played an important part in sustaining the trend towards narrower material inequalities which was a pronounced feature of British society in the first three-quarters of the twentieth century. Whether the incidence and rates of taxation were ever such as to warrant the appellation 'punitive' or even steeply redistributive is another matter. Two economists concluded from an empirical analysis of the 1974–79 Government that 'the much-touted higher marginal rates of income tax were paid only by an extraordinarily small proportion of taxpayers' (Artis and Cobham, 1991: 275). While 'on paper marginal rates of income tax would seem to be high', another economist commented, 'in practice they are abated by tax allowances' (Bosanquet, 1980: 40).

Furthermore, as Crosland pointed out, 'the largest inequalities stem not from the distribution of earned incomes, but from the ownership of inherited capital' with unequal ownership 'still the major cause of inequalities in spending power'. Indeed inherited privilege was the main source of inter-generational transmission of inequality (Crosland, 1964: 171, 225). In 1957 Gaitskell pledged that under a future Labour government a higher proportion of the total tax yield would be drawn from those who profited from capital gains and inherited wealth (Ellison, 1994: 88). The 1959 Manifesto proposed taxation of 'the huge capital gains made on the Stock Exchange and elsewhere' and the blocking of loopholes and share purchases by public investment agencies to ensure that the community 'enjoys some of the profits and capital gains now going to private industry' (Craig, 1970: 227). Later manifestos committed Labour to siphon-off the gains accruing from inheritance and capital gains through wealth taxes.

All this would appear to signify a real determination to grapple with a major tap-root of inequality – one which contrasts starkly with the more benign regime for the affluent favoured by New Labour. The contrast is, indeed, real and genuine – but not as stark as might be supposed. In practice, action rarely matched rhetoric (Clark, 2001: 36–7). Labour did introduce a Capital Transfer Tax but there were so many exclusions that, by 1979, it was raising less revenue than Estate Duty, which, the then Chancellor later recalled, 'had become a laughing stock' since no-one who could afford an accountant paid it (Healey, 1989: 404). A Capital Gains Tax was enacted in 1965 but with so many exemptions that its effect was negligible (Ponting, 1989: 391). Equally, throughout the 1974–79 Government 'the corporate sector remained very lightly taxed' (Bosanquet, 1980: 37). Labour might have *aspired* to a more substantial redistribution of wealth but in practice was cautious and hesitant, wary of any measures that might jeopardise the process of capital accumulation – and increasingly so as profits were progressively squeezed in the 1970s.

None of this is to deny that Labour in the past was much more committed to greater equality in the dispersion of income and wealth than is at present the case. But it is worth noting that, in the late 1970s, the egalitarian consensus in the party favouring greater equality through a combination of high public spending and progressive taxation began to fracture as a significant section of the right queried both their economic benefits and even their moral justification. 'Socialism and equality', Crosland still maintained in 1974, 'require a relative transfer of resources from private consumption to public expenditure' (Crosland, 1974: 26). Others on the party's right – notably Roy Jenkins and his allies (most of whom were to defect to the Social Democratic Party in the early 1980s) – argued that the proportion of the nation's wealth spent on social programmes was beginning to exceed the socially, politically and economically acceptable (Clark, 2001: 9). Many ministers accepted the Bacon and Eltis thesis that high public spending was 'crowding-out' private investment and that high marginal rates of taxation destroyed incentives and weakened the supply-side (Jackson, 1991: 74; Benn, 1989: 668–9, 671. Entry 2 December 1976). By the end of the Callaghan Government, the short-term imperative of expenditure restraint, one expert commented, was transmuting into a 'permanent philosophy for public expenditure. The government seemed to have no belief in public services' (Bosanquet, 1980: 39).[4] The influence of this group abated after 1979 as many of its adherents quit Labour and the party in general swung heavily to the left. But the seeds had been planted for a later revival of a more restrictive approach to public spending as an instrument for equalising society.

Collectivism

The second major motif in redistributive social democracy was *collectivism*. This can be said to have two main features. First, a strong notion of a public good as something that often transcended the aggregated interests of private economic actors. Webb spoke of 'an order of social life, in which the common good overrules individual caprice' (quoted in Greenleaf, 1983a: 21). There was – contrary to what economic liberals claim – emphatically no natural 'harmony of interests. The world', Keynes maintained, 'is not so governed that private and social interest always coincide. It is not a correct deduction from the Principles of Economics that enlightened self-interest always operates in the public interest. Nor is it true that self-interest generally is enlightened' (quoted in Robinson, J, 1962: 81). While economic liberals emphasised the role of the individual and the maximisation of his or her rights, the collectivist highlighted 'the interests of the community which are regarded as primary claims morally superior to any individual demand' (Greenleaf, 1983b: 20). The second feature of collectivism was the idea of positive government that is the faith reposed 'in the benefit to be derived by the mass of the people from the action or intervention of the state' (Dicey quoted in Greenleaf, 1983b: 22). The state was the custodian of the public interest and it was with the progressive expansion in its role and reach that the needs of the community as a whole could most effectively be fostered.

Collectivism takes both economic and social forms. Economic collectivism refers to the transfer to public ownership of major industrial and financial enterprises and hence to the appropriation by society as a whole of the rewards which would otherwise accrue to capital asset holders; and to the replacement of the market and the profit motive as the governing principles of economic activity by some form of centralised economic planning. Cronin has argued that economic collectivism so defined constituted the common intellectual framework for the party at large (until the rise of New Labour). All groups within the party, imbued by a 'historic antipathy to the market and private capital', shared 'the same fundamental preference for collective solutions over market mechanisms and the same belief in collective provision over privately organized welfare' (Cronin, 2004: 10, 73–4). 'Businessmen were, at best, an interest that had to be reckoned with, but they were never seen as partners in generating economic growth' (Cronin, 2004: 74). This too is how New Labour construes 'Old Labour'. According to Gordon Brown it 'equated the public interest with public ownership and public regulation, and therefore.... assumed that markets were not in the public interest' (Brown, 2003).

This interpretation reflects a misunderstanding of the record of past Labour governments. It was true, as Crosland pointed out in 1956, that 'one often hears socialism equated not only with the nationalisation of industry, but with government planning ... or state collectivism' (Crosland, 1964: 66). Enthusiasm for planning and widespread nationalisation reached its peak in the 1940s but soon faded during the course of the Attlee Labour

Government when the advocates of 'physical planning' were routed by the Keynesians (Morgan, 1984: 170; Cairncross, 1985: 328). The issue of public ownership became the main domestic dividing line between Labour's 'revisionists' and 'fundamentalists' in the 1950s, but the former decisively triumphed – at least until the revival of the left in the 1970s (the issue is discussed at length in Minkin, 1978). Labour's National Executive Committee fell under the control of the left in the early 1970s and the outcome was the incorporation into the manifestos of 1974 of commitments towards extended public ownership and an elaborate system of planning, but this had very little influence on the policies pursued by the 1974–79 Government. Even in their most radical phases Labour governments were 'prepared to leave large swathes of the economy subject to market forces and private control' with 'the bulk of economic activity in private hands' (Patmore and Coates, 2005: 125, 127). As the Labour minister, financial expert and close Wilson confidante Lord (Harold) Lever observed, 'Clause 4 or no Clause 4, Labour's leadership plainly believes in a mixed economy' for 'it knows as well as any businessman that an engine which runs on profit cannot run faster without extra fuel' (quoted in Panitch, 1986: 342). The aim of successive Labour governments, however much they intervened in the economy (then, anyway, generally in vogue) was emphatically not 'to suppress market forces but to regulate them via Keynesian demand-management with its primary social purpose being secured through a universal welfare state' (Crouch, 1997: 353. For an extended discussion, see Hinnfors, 2006: 42–51).

Of course Labour in office did favour extensive and detailed state regulation of the economy – but this took the form of Keynesianism demand management, 'the philosophy of the mixed economy'. This envisaged state intervention in the market but without disrupting it, a humanising of capitalism 'without sacrificing consumer choice or entrepreneurial initiative' (Marquand, 1988: 18, 19). Keynesianism, as both Crosland from the right and Crossman from the centre-left of the party recognised, had 'undermined the old-fashioned economic case for socialism' (Crossman, 1960: 5). By regulating the level of demand through monetary and especially fiscal policy the state could dampen the oscillations of the business cycle, avoid depressions, maintain full employment and improve living standards while retaining a level of profitability sufficient for sustained business investment and growth. For Keynesians the issue of ownership was of little moment since they were confident that 'they had all the indirect controls they needed without going to the unnecessary expense and bureaucratic trouble of state ownership' (Callaghan, 2000: 11). By these means the more equitable distribution of goods and life-chances could be realised, distributional conflicts attenuated and the aspiration to social justice fulfilled (Callaghan, 2000: 11; Moschanas, 2002: 65).

What this meant in effect was that the defining feature of Labour's collectivism was the socialisation not of production but of *consumption*. The market should be left to determine the original distribution of income and wealth but public authority would then intervene to reallocate resources generated by private economic effort to ensure that social needs were met through schemes of collective risk protection. The principal institutional manifestation of collectivism, then, was not planning or public ownership but the social democratic welfare state 'defined in terms of citizenship rights distributed outside market according to the principle of socially recognised need, whose fulfilment was a matter of justice' (Harris, 1987: 29). Socially recognised need referred to those needs upon whose fulfilment rested the capacity of people to 'realise the full extent of their potential' and whose denial 'would cause injury or impairment' (Ignatieff, 1984: 15). Such needs (collectivist reasoning ran) created entitlements, in effect collective obligations, the undertaking of which required the commitment of public funds via higher taxation (Plant, 1991: 187). This notion of entitlement was given definitive expression in Marshall's famous theory of social citizenship. Earlier generations had established the right of British citizens to full civic and political rights but it was the particular contribution of the post-war Labour Government to extend these rights of citizenship to the social sphere. All citizens should enjoy a corpus of social rights extending from the 'right to a modicum of economic welfare and security to the right to share to the full in the social heritage and to live the life of a civilised being according to standards prevailing in society'. A key point was that these entitlements were 'not proportionate to the market value of the claimant' (Marshall, 1950: 11). As rights there were corresponding duties, but these were quite narrowly conceived.

In short, the concept of the citizen's social rights implied the responsibility of the state to provide for them. This was often conceptualised in terms of *social or mutual responsibility* which stipulated that the community had a duty to protect the social well-being of all its members. It can be contrasted with the laissez-faire doctrine of *individual* responsibility which emphasised people's responsibility for their own well-being and that of their families. The collectivist case was rooted in three propositions. First, that most of the risks to which people were exposed were either social (poverty, unemployment, bad health) or biological (disability, infirmity in old age, again poor health) and not individual in character. Second, that by spreading the burden of risk through the creation of a common fund upon which all could draw upon in time of misfortune, collective action was the most effective way of affording protection (Miller, 2003: 96). Third, that professionally staffed public organisations, motivated by considerations of public service and the common good, were best qualified to determine both the precise nature of social needs and the means by which they could be most fully met. These propositions were so firmly – indeed unquestioningly – a part of the Labour mentality that 'the collective provision of education, health, housing and social services by public-sector institutions' funded through general taxation became 'central to the theory and practice of post-war social democracy'. Indeed association with the public services came to lie 'at the heart of the Labour Party's political identity in post-war Britain' (Driver and Martell, 2002: 41). Social democratic policy was largely social policy. This was the essence of Labour collectivism.

In theory this took the form of commitment to the universal solidaristic welfare state – widely seen as a defining characteristic of social democracy (Esping-Andersen, 1990: 27–8). In practical terms, the issue was more blurred. Universalism was commonly contrasted to selectivity or means-testing and embodied the principle that all should contribute towards the financing of a service and all should benefit on the principle of need. This principle was eagerly espoused by social policy advisers, such as Titmuss and Townshend, and by left-of-centre politicians, such as Bevan, Crossman and Castle, but never really (in contrast to Scandinavian social democratic parties) became part of the party consensus. The point can be illustrated by the long battle during the 1960s and 1970s Labour governments over how best to combat child poverty. In 1967 the Pensions minister, Peggy Herbison, proposed to increase family allowances (a universal benefit) while clawing back part of the additional cost by raising tax for the better-off. A large slice of the cabinet, including the Chancellor, Jim Callaghan and Crosland preferred a means-tested approach. The dispute that erupted (Crossman recorded in his diary) was 'bitter and unpleasant' because it reflected a clash of social conceptions – in his words 'a fundamental difference in philosophy' over the desirability of universality (Crossman, 1976: 425. Entry 13 July 1967; 252–3. Entry 23 February 1967).

The battle eventually culminated, after further acrimonious dispute, in the enactment of the universalist Child Benefit scheme in 1976.[5] But its enactment was against the general drift in both the 1964–70 and 1974–79 governments which witnessed the rapid expansion of means-testing (Rhodes, 2000: 167). One reason for this was the economic failures of the two governments which led to constant public spending crises and pressures on the tax system. But the overall tilt of policy did, one expert concludes, raise questions about the strength of Labour's practical commitment to universalism and, indeed, 'to Marshall's concept of citizenship and unconditional entitlements' (Rhodes, 2000: 165). In short universalism may have been 'a central part of the Labour Party's own mythology' but its practical effect – its status as an *operative value* – was significantly weaker (Rhodes, 2000: 165). Labour was, assuredly, the party of social welfare and extended social rights but the depth of its practical commitment to the 'social democratic welfare state' should not be exaggerated. For this reason, the sharp contrast often drawn between past Labour's espousal of universalism and New Labour selectivity or targeting strategy is misleading..

The second dimension: ethical socialism

Fellowship and equality of social consideration

The redistributive dimension within British social democracy was always coupled with a second one, the ethical socialist. Crosland defined it as 'a

desire to replace competitive social relations by fellowship and social solidarity and the motive of personal profit by a more altruistic and other-
regarding motive' (Crosland, 1964: 54). As Marquand comments, it is not
difficult to trace a line of descent from Carlyle, Cobbett and Ruskin to
ethical socialists such as Tawney and Orwell, all united by repudiating the
image of '*homo economicus*, the rational, egotistic pleasure-seeker' (Marquand, 1988: 222). Most contemporary debate on the Labour party has
ignored this strand of thinking, yet the extent to which ethical socialist
thinkers have been invoked by senior Labour politicians as a formative
influence is quite striking. For example Attlee, Gaitskell, Bevan, Callaghan
and Barbara Castle all professed a keen admiration for ethical socialists
such as Morris and Tawney (Brivati, 1997: 29; Francis, 1997; Morgan, 1997:
764, 763; Perkins, 2003: 115). While the socialist system of values 'included
a distinctive view of equality and liberty' one only 'gets at the heart of its
ethical message with the concept of fellowship' (Beer, 1969: 128). Thompson
reminds us that 'the concepts of "fraternity", "solidarity" or "fellowship"
have been at the heart of ethical socialist thought for longer than the
Labour Party has existed' (Thompson, 2002: 1). The words might vary –
fellowship, fraternity, solidarity – but all connoted a co-operative ethic
which could morally integrate the community by nurturing a sense of
belonging and shared fate (Ranson and Stewart, 1989: 14). In the words of
Nye Bevan, the architect of the NHS, 'the outstanding task for the individual man is to build a home for himself in society' (Bevan, 1978 [1952]: 56).
Forty years later (1992) Gordon Brown repeated the sentiment. 'Democratic
socialism', he declared, 'was founded on the belief in the value of community;
its main inspiration is the ethos of community, not a theory of economy'
(quoted in Cronin, 2004: 361).

For the ethical socialist 'the revolt against capitalism had its sources, not
merely in material miseries, but in resentment against an economic system
which dehumanises existence by treating the mass of mankind as instruments to be manipulated for the pecuniary advantage of a minority of
property-holders' (Tawney, 1964c [1949]: 145–6). Capitalism was not only
inequitable but it devalued social relationships, sowed divisions among
people and fostered a fixation with material accumulation. For the ethical
socialist society was to be judged not simply by 'quantity of possessions'
but by 'quality of life. ... not by the output of goods and services per head,
but by the use which is made of them' (Tawney, 1964c [1949]: 174). Ethical
socialism objected not simply to the distributional consequences of capitalism but to the ideas and conceptions that both underpinned and validated
it. The issue can be clarified by utilising the distinction between '*homo
economicus*' and what Bowles and Gintis call '*homo reciprocans*'.

Capitalism rested on the presumption of '*homo economicus*' in which man
was conceived 'as an essentially isolated actor, calculating economic means
to ends which are individually identified, autonomously chosen and
privately consumed' (Hampshire-Monk, 1996: 201). Social order can be

sustained by human co-operation, but only where such behaviour could be seen to clearly service individual interests. Thus '*homo economicus*', the self-interested utility-maximiser, lived in a world structured around *specific reciprocity* in which co-operation occurs only when all partners have something specific to gain. This concept derived from a view of society as essentially composed of atomistic individuals in which, as Hume put it, 'every man ought to be supposed a knave and to have no other end, in all his actions, than private interest' motivated by 'his insatiable avarice and ambition' (quoted in Le Grand, 1997: 149). Ethical socialism, in contrast, conceived people as social beings or '*homo reciprocans*' only able to realise themselves and live meaningful lives in co-operation with others. Society was not (in Bevan's words) 'a multiplication of a number of simple self-sufficient social groupings, each able to detach itself from the other' but 'multicellular . . . Each part is connected as though by an infinite variety of nerves with the others' (Bevan, 1978 [1952]: 68).[6] '*Homo reciprocans*' thus 'cares about the well-being of others'. He exhibits a willingness to engage in 'strong reciprocity', that is, 'to cooperate and share with others similarly disposed' a world shaped by '*diffuse and generalised reciprocity*' or co-operation, that is as 'the action of working together for the same purpose or in the same task' (Bowles and Gintis, 1998/99).

But if ethical socialism regarded people as 'programmed for sociability' it also acknowledged 'we can be more or less sociable' (Marquand, 1988: 218). Character, motivation and behaviour were all social artefacts, the predominant form they took shaped by the norms, rewards and sanctions embodied in social arrangements. By its very nature as a profit-oriented, market-driven system capitalism legitimated, rewarded and thereby fostered '*homo economicus*'. 'By fixing men's minds,' Tawney maintained, 'not upon the discharge of social obligations . . . but upon the exercise of the right to pursue their own self-interest' it thereby offered 'unlimited scope for the acquisition of riches, and therefore gives free play to one of the most powerful of human instincts' (Tawney, 1961 [1921]: 32). Thus the institutional arrangements of free-market capitalism, economic exchange, competition and profit-maximisation, far from promoting social cohesion, corroded it.

It followed that the task of socialists should be to re-order society in such a way as to allow for the more co-operative and other-regarding human drives to come to the fore. But how could this be accomplished? By the 1950s only radical left wingers – with minimal influence in the Labour party – still dreamed of a society which dispensed with markets, private ownership of productive resources and the pursuit of profit. The experience of successive Labour governments underlined the fact that the fate of practical social democracy was 'inextricably bound to the promise of the successful management of the capitalist economy' (Scharpf, 1991: 24–5). Competitive markets, it was acknowledged, played a vital role in releasing energy, providing choice and increasing economic welfare and hence the organisation and provision of most consumer and capital goods must remain in private hands.

This was the conclusion reached by Labour's ascendant revisionists in the 1950s. Indeed Beer concluded that in its acceptance of the market, self-interest and profit-seeking as the main motors of economic activity 'revisionism attacked socialist ideology at its heart – the doctrine of fellowship' (Beer, 1969: 238). Twenty years later Plant reached essentially the same conclusion. Labour had traditionally stood for such end values as 'greater social solidarity and community, and seeing an intrinsic value in collective organization and action, not merely as a means to other ends but as an important way in which solidarity and fraternity were to be expressed'. But as the 'acids of individualism have eaten away at the basis of collective values' such notions had lost their hold on the party. Thus collective provision was no longer seen as 'valuable in itself as a way in which community values are expressed, but as an instrument of policy alongside markets and voluntary action, through which individual interests are best realised, the decision about which means to use being based largely on empirical rather than theoretical or moral grounds' (Plant, 1989).

However this view overlooks the crucial way in which ethical socialism evolved from the 1950s onwards. It is true that its compass shrank but its vision persisted. If the values of fellowship, solidarity, co-operation and public service could no longer be realistically viewed as norms which could regulate society as a whole they could survive as the governing principles of the welfare state. Thus Titmuss, a leading social policy advisor to the Labour party and an influential ethical socialist, saw the focus of social policy as developing the welfare state as a set of 'integrative institutions ... which promote an individual's sense of identity, participation and community' (quoted in Harris, 1987: 52). The collective organisation of welfare would operate as both an essential counterweight and a complement to the market system. Where the market rules unrestrained and unchecked 'the competitive pursuit of self-interest' and 'indifference, selfishness and acquisitiveness' would permeate all social relationships, subverting all social and moral bonds (Harris, 1987: 62). By bolstering sentiments of altruism and social responsibility the public and universal provision of key services (such as health, education) – from which all commercial considerations would be excluded – would supply the institutional basis of community feelings (Harris, 1987: 53–4). In programmatic terms ethical socialism was embodied in two key operative values, both promoted by the expansion of the welfare state: fellowship (with its entailment, equality of consideration or respect) and 'public service ethos'. We discuss each in turn.

Equality, we have seen, was a central defining value within the redistributive strand of British social democracy. Increasingly it was defined as an end in itself, in terms of equality of opportunity, that is of 'empowering individuals', giving all – particularly those handicapped by inherited background social disadvantage – the means to advance themselves and realise their freely chosen life-plans. Greater equality in material conditions, from this perspective, retained its importance but primarily as a *means*, a way of enabling all to compete more equally in a socially mobile society. For ethical socialism, in contrast, a major compression in income and wealth was an *end* in itself. This was because of its inextricable connection with fellowship, an absolutely core ethical socialist principle. There could be no real fellowship, no genuine sense of community without 'equality of social consideration' (Tawney, 1964d [1952]: 187). What precisely did 'equality of social consideration' entail? Here it may be useful to distinguish between two ways of viewing equality, in *allocative* and in *relational* terms. In the former case equality was a matter of securing the fairer distribution in initial life-chances. In the latter case it referred to a mode of human interaction in which people related and behaved towards each other as equals in a spirit of mutual respect.

For the ethical socialist, relational equality was impossible in a society characterised by cumulative, persisting and entrenched inequalities in the distribution of income and wealth, for these always gave rise to matching psychological inequalities of regard and social esteem – a pyramidal status order. In such an order a person's social status reflects his or her position 'in a socially-determined hierarchy of honour or prestige, signifying social superiority and inferiority' (Baker, 1987: 60). Thus, for Crosland, from their psychological aspect social classes were

> portions of the community ... marked off from other portions by accepted or sanctioned standards of inferiority and superiority. These socially-recognised relationships express themselves in the way a man is collectively treated and regarded by other people, as well as in the way he treats and regards them.
>
> (Crosland, 1964: 104)

The social-psychological and economic aspects of class were inextricably intertwined. Class systems were, Tawney maintained, historically associated with differences not merely of economic but of social position so that different groups were also demarcated from each other in terms of status, consideration and respect (Tawney, 1964a [1931]: 61). More than a century ago, in *The Theory of the Leisure Class*, Veblen described how increasingly wealth was becoming 'the conventional basis of esteem. Its possession has become necessary to have any reputable standing in the community' (quoted in De Botton, 2004: 194). Position in the status order was increasingly both defined and expressed by differences in life-styles and consumption pattern in turn a function of command over material resources. In such an order, sentiments of superiority and disdain on the one hand, and inferiority or resentment on the other were inevitable.

It followed from this that fellowship – rooted in equality of regard – was impossible in a society characterised by steep graduations, however meritocratically secured. Meritocracy, by justifying inequality in terms of merit and effort, had the effect of actually bolstering – by legitimating – a status hierarchy. To the extent that social and economic differentials could be construed as reflecting disparities in merit and hence desert, those who occupied the upper echelons could reassure themselves that their success was 'a just reward for their own capacity, for their own efforts, and for their own undeniable achievement' and could thereby savour the 'assurance of the best of moral titles to their fortune' (Young, 1958: 115, 106, 130). By the same token those who had faltered in the race of life could no longer console themselves with the thought that they had been denied opportunities. They were simply inadequate to the task – they had failed because they *were* inferior (Young, 1958: 107–8). 'To know that you are fairly allocated to poverty is little comfort and may actually increase the stigma attached to it; it certainly does nothing to reduce the pain of exclusion' (Wilkinson, 2005: 284).

To the extent that socialism was, as Wilfred Beckerman, economic advisor to the 1964–70 Labour Government contended, primarily 'about the dignity and status of the human being and his sense of being accepted as an equal and valued member of society irrespective of his particular role in it' (*New Statesman*, 19 January 1973) it could not be realised in a meritocratic social order. Such an order would encourage, on the one hand, the arrogance and condescension of the 'socially superior' and, on the other, the resentment, anger and alienation experienced by their 'inferiors' (Tawney, 1964d [1952]: 187). For the ethical socialist, it followed, the proper object of Labour's policy must extend beyond widening opportunities to encompass a major reduction in social and economic equalities, for only in such circumstances could equality of mutual respect and sentiments of fraternity and fellow feeling take root. This, in turn, required a generous, solidaristic welfare state funded by a steeply progressive system of taxation.

The public service ethos

The earlier ethical socialist vision of a society governed by fellowship, cooperation and altruism was replaced, it has been seen, by the drive to carve out a welfare sphere *within society* that could be regulated according to these principles – a specifically *public* domain. In ethical socialist thinking there was a whole range of public goods such as healthcare, education, welfare benefits and cultural activities from which market exchange and the commercial ethos should be barred *as a matter of principle*. Such goods were not commodities to be exchanged in the market in the pursuit of profit since they possessed an intrinsic value which could not be priced or traded. The public domain was to afford 'a space for forms of human flourishing which cannot be bought in the market-place' (Marquand, 2004: 27). From this perspective the development of public services, to be delivered by public organisations, was not simply a means – the best way, for example, of meeting social needs – but an end in itself. The set of norms and values by which conduct in the public sector should be regulated came to be known as the 'public service ethos' – a cornerstone concept in British social democratic thinking.

The term 'ethos' can be defined in two ways: as an empirical and as a normative concept. Plant uses the term in the former sense when he defines it as 'a matter of the spirit of an organisation; it is to do with how it shares understanding, perhaps even with a shared tradition within an organization. ... a matter mainly of the habitual way people do things' (Plant, 2001). This is the empirical usage of the term – *ethos as culture.* Ethos as *ethic* in contrast refers to 'a set of moral principles' and, more specifically, to 'the moral principles by which any particular person is guided' and 'the rules of conduct recognised in any particular profession or area of human activity' (*Shorter Oxford Dictionary*). It is a normative or prescriptive concept. Thus the Public Administration Select Committee characterised '*an ethos as a principled framework for action*, something that ... should also motivate those who belong to it ... *We see the* [public service] *ethos essentially as a benchmark, against which public service workers and institutions should continuously strive to measure themselves*' (Public Administration Select Committee, 2002: para 4. Emphasis added). The concept of the public service ethos uses the term in its normative sense – the sense in which Health Secretary Alan Milburn deployed it when he pledged his determination to maintain the public service ethos 'at all costs because it represents our values. Losing that ethos would break the NHS' (Milburn, 2001a).

Defining the term is a difficult task since there is no 'authorised' version. I have sought to give it a meaning that reflects *the way it has been customarily used* within the British Labour tradition, bringing out the range of associations that it commonly evokes. I conclude that it was essentially composed of two elements which can be labelled co-operation and professionalism.

Co-operation

Co-operation can be defined as 'the action of working together for the same purpose' and has typically been counterposed to competition, that is 'the action of competing or contending with others' (*Shorter Oxford Dictionary*). Co-operation as a behavioural precept within the public sector that applies to both *intra-organisational relations* (i.e. inter-personnel interaction within a single body, a school, university or hospital) and *inter-organisational relations* such as within the NHS or the system of secondary education as a whole.

Co-operative – in contrast to competitive – relations are by their nature high-trust. Alan Fox defines high-trust relationships 'as ones in which the participants share (or have similar) ends and values; have a diffuse sense of long-term obligation; offer support without calculating the cost or expecting an immediate return; communicate freely and openly with one another; are prepared to trust the other and risk their own fortunes in the other party; give the benefit of the doubt in relation to motives and goodwill if there are problems' (cited in Hunter, 2002: 71–2). *Institutionalised* trust, as envisaged by the public service ethic, is akin to social capital where this refers to 'features of social organization, such as networks, norms, and trust that facilitate coordination and cooperation for mutual benefit' (Putnam, 1993). High-trust relations would – so it was anticipated – enhance the capacity of public sector organisations to pursue the common interest more effectively than would be possible in a competitive and therefore low-trust system. While 'the market motivates productive contribution ... but on the basis of impersonal cash reward' the public service ethos encourages 'a commitment to one's fellow human beings' (Cohen, 1994: 9).

Trust and co-operative relationships and orientations, to survive and embed themselves, must be sustained by institutional rules and shared tacit understandings of appropriate behaviour. But how can one be confident that trust would not be abused and that, in the absence of competition and consumer pressures, those who worked in public organisations would not give priority to their interests and comforts at the expense of those they were supposed to serve? Espousal of the professional ideal was the second defining feature of the public service ethic.

Professionalism

Professionals here are defined as people who have acquired appropriate specialist training and expert knowledge, certified by formal qualification. Professional behaviour is behaviour regulated by a professional code of conduct which specifies the proper ends of the profession and commits its members to deliver services according to needs in an impartial and equitable manner. The professional ideal was a constituent feature of the public service ethic reflecting the social democratic assumption that the public domain was 'quintessentially the domain' of professionals: its 'values were their values' (Marquand, 2004: 53, 54). It was assumed that qualified public servants were more likely than those in the commercial sector to be professionally motivated and thereby be trusted to work for the public good (Le Grand, 1997: 155). Of course not all activity in the public sector was regulated by professional codes, at least not to any great extent, and in those areas (e.g. Direct Works departments in local government) the public interest might indeed be vulnerable. Where professionalism was seen as most vital, and most entrenched, was in the delivery of complex public goods such as healthcare and education. These were not products which could be precisely defined, itemised, measured and priced – hence neither markets (because contracts will necessarily be incomplete) nor bureaucracies (because rules and norms could not be codified in sufficient detail)[7] were appropriate ways of organising their supply (Smith, P, 2003: 25. See also Plant, 2003a: 567).

As pointed out above, the public service ethos was a prescriptive and not an empirical concept. It made no claim that public sector employees actually lived up to these ideals – Bevan, Crossman and Castle[8] in particular knew from hard experience that this was far from the case when encountering problems of professional exclusivity and corporative self-advancement – but, rather, that they should aspire to do so. But the precepts of co-operation and professionalism were (in our terminology) *operative values* and not merely ideals, that is they acted as principles for policy choice and institutional design. As such the public service ethos had one profoundly important corollary for the delivery of those public services which met basic human need: they must be supplied by public organisation. It was taken for granted that there was 'something that links many of these [public] services indissolubly to public bodies and public decision-making. The public realm, of collectively provided services and functions' was 'an essential component of a good society' (Public Administration Select Committee, 2002: para 27).

Indeed the belief that the domain of the public should be insulated from market forces and the commercial ethos emerged as a cardinal maxim of social democratic thought. On the one hand, as Titmuss put it, there was an economic sphere 'grounded in money and market exchange' but, on the other, a social one 'that met social needs, based on social values and altruism' (quoted in Piachaud, 2005: 350). Such needs were contrasted with commodities in that they were defined by their intrinsic value: they were peculiarly 'human' in that they were essential to human well-being and fulfilment (Keat, 2000: 26–7). For this reason it was regarded as axiomatic that the provision of services such as healthcare and education 'would be tainted by the association with financial exchange and profit' (Walsh, 1995: 4–5). Monopoly public supply of such public goods was a guarantee that social need was being given first priority and that they would be distributed in an efficient and equitable manner (Le Grand, 1998a: 415).

The maintenance of a large and expanding public sphere, governed by an ethic of public service, came therefore to be seen as the principal institutional expression of ethical socialist values. Its hold on Labour's mind-set was so tenacious that, alone of the policy prescriptions derived from ethical socialism, it was a constitutive principle, indeed a defining property of post-war British social democratic thought. 'Public sector institutions embody an ideal of public service, defined by the need of the service user, not his or her market power ... a space ... in which non-market values rule' (Michael Jacobs, *New Statesman*, 2 July 2001). As Gordon Brown was later to note, 'a well established ethos of public service rightly runs deep in our history, determines the character of our country, defines Britain's uniqueness to the world' (Brown, 2002a).

Labour's soul?

This chapter has sought to delineate the principles, beliefs and goals which actuated Labour's actions when in power and which could be said to compose its mental and moral outlook – its 'collective consciousness'. But can one distil from them a core of bedrock values defining what the party was, in the mind of its adherents, ultimately all about: perhaps something that we can call its 'soul'?

This concept is a curious one. It constantly recurs in Labour discourse. To give a few examples. A recent study of Labour's values was entitled 'The Struggle for Labour's Soul' (Plant *et al.*, 2004) – though the term 'soul' was never defined. Gordon Brown insisted that 'at every point in our history, Labour needs not just a programme but a soul' (BBC, 29 September 2003). The battle over New Labour NHS reforms had, the *Guardian* opined, 'escalated into an ideological battle for the soul of the party' (*The Guardian*, 1 May 2003), while the BBC, equally, interpreted the rift over the Blair Government's public sector reform programme as 'a contest for the party's soul' (Panorama, 2006a). The Blair/Brown clash has been described as a struggle for that very same soul (Peston, 2005: 13). Even former Conservative PM, Sir John Major lamented that New Labour had 'lost Labour's soul. It had a soul and a heart. I grew up in Brixton, with "old" Labour in Lambeth. I disagreed with them, but I admired what they stood for' (quoted by William Keegan, the *Observer*, 18 March 2007).

But what, precisely, is a party's 'soul'? And, if the concept is meaningful, what are the contents of Labour's soul? The *Shorter Oxford Dictionary* defines a soul as an 'essential or animating element or quality in something', a 'characteristic spirit as manifested in attitudes and aspirations', indeed a 'seat of emotion and sentiment'. A soul, in this sense, is what endows a party with its sense of being or, in Manheim's sense of the term, its utopia. Utopias 'transcend the social situation' since they 'orient conduct towards elements which the situation, in so far as it is realised at the time, does not contain' (Manheim, 1960 [1936]: 176). The 'utopia' may never be fully attainable but the striving towards it gives meaning to sacrifices. The concept of a 'soul' implies something that (unlike policies or programmes) is not contingent on circumstance but endures (though it might also evolve) over time.

But what is it, then, that forms *Labour's* 'soul'? Inevitably one has to be tentative and impressionistic for the concept is such an elusive one. According to Greenleaf the British socialist tradition in its essential elements encompassed 'a belief in mankind's inherent sociality, a feeling of human brotherhood, that abilities and powers are a social trust; the view that what is fundamental is not self-help or self-interest but a sense of social responsibility for general well-being; the idea that co-operation must replace competition in all areas of life especially the economic' (Greenleaf, 1983a: 13). Such ideas bore the imprint of one man whose work represented 'the pinnacle of ethical socialism' and which, more than that of any other, was 'profoundly influential within the ranks of the Labour party' (Carter, 2003: 164, 189). Tawney's thought 'has exercised such a profound and diverse influence upon socialist opinion in Britain,' Tony Wright judged, 'that it may be regarded as the central tradition of British socialism' (Wright, 1984: 81). His works – notably *The Acquisitive Society* and *Equality* – afforded 'probably the most widely influential modern statement of democratic socialism' (Dennis and Halsey, 1988: 149). For one party leader, Hugh Gaitskell, Tawney was 'the democratic socialist par excellence'; another, Jim Callaghan, professed himself deeply in his debt (Brivati, 1997: 291; Morgan, 1997: 764); while a third, Michael Foot, averred that his 'writings were read and *loved* – it is not too much to say – by one generation of socialists after another' (quoted in Wright, 1987: ix). One leading centre-left intellectual, Richard Crossman, called *The Acquisitive Society* his bible (Dennis and Halsey, 1988: 243), while from the party's radical left Tony Benn saw him as the greatest of socialist thinkers (*Tribune*, 1 May 1981). As Tomlinson notes, Tawney heavily influenced Labour's intellectual development with 'all shades of Labour opinion ... willing to pay obeisance to his writings' (Tomlinson, 2002: 14).

For Tawney 'the impulse behind the [Labour] movement has been obstinately and unashamedly ethical' (Tawney, 1964d [1952]: 176). The themes which recur most frequently in his writings are equality and fellowship. By equality he understood 'equality of environment, of access to education and the means of civilisation, of security and independence, and of the social consideration which equality in these matters usually carries with it'. It was 'the mark of a civilised society to aim at eliminating such inequalities as have their source not in individual differences, but in its own organisation' (Tawney, 1964a: 43, 57). To Tawney the recognition of the equal worth and value of all human beings was integrally related to fellowship for both were expressions of the essential human quality of sociability. William Morris' axiom that 'fellowship is heaven and lack of fellowship is hell' represented to Tawney 'the noblest aspect of the popular movement' (Dennis and Halsey, 1988: 213). Fellowship was not a matter, Crick explained, of 'radiating an abstract love of humanity: it arises from people actually working together towards common ends' (Crick, 1984: 22). It entailed a preference, wherever possible, for social arrangements which promoted co-operative rather than competitive behaviour actuated by the principle of common purpose rather than individual acquisitiveness.

In 1960 party leader Hugh Gaitskell sought to revise Clause IV of Labour's constitution in an attempt to update and render more relevant the party's expression of its own purposes. Knowing the bid would be highly controversial his aim was a pronouncement of fundamental party purposes which would have as broad an appeal as possible by encapsulating those ideas and principles – from both dimensions of the social democratic tradition – which resonated most strongly within all sections of the party.[9] The statement constituted – I suggest – a succinct and accurate description of Labour's 'soul'. It had the party stand for 'social justice, for a society in which the claims of those in hardship or distress come first; where the wealth produced by all is fairly shared among all; where differences in rewards depend not upon birth or inheritance but on the effort, skill and creative energy contributed to the common good; and where equal opportunities exist for all to live a full and varied life'. Equally, Gaitskell had the party disparage 'the pursuit of material wealth by and for itself as empty and barren,' repudiate 'the selfish, acquisitive doctrines of capitalism' with their belief that 'our relations with one another should be based ... on ruthless self-regarding rivalry' and strive 'to create instead a socialist community based on fellowship, co-operation and service in which all can share fully in our cultural heritage' (Labour Party, 1959: 12–13; Brivati, 1997, 340–1).

To this can be added a more recent statement of the party's fundamental purposes. Peter Hain commented of the late Robin Cook that 'when he was in the cabinet, people knew they had someone right at the top that could speak and act for Labour's soul' (*New Statesman*, 12 August 2005). A few months before his death he sought to 'identify what should be the core values' of a party committed to modern European social democracy. The echoes of both Tawney and Gaitskell's aborted Clause IV are strong:

> Top of anyone's list must come solidarity – the principle that the strength of a society is measured by the extent that its rich members support their vulnerable fellow citizens. Next comes our commitment to humanitarian rather than commercial priorities, and the corollary that the market should be managed to meet people's needs rather than the people harnessed to serve the market. ... [We] believe a collectivist solution is always preferable to individualism. Not only are we stronger if we work together, but the very attempt to find a common approach enhances social cohesion. (Robin Cook, *The Guardian*, 4 February 2005)

This chapter has sought to outline the components of the British social democratic tradition by selecting 'certain recurrent themes ... which have exercised a predominant influence' (Crosland, 1964: 51–2). It has focused on the action-orientations – values and habits of thought – that have informed more ephemeral responses and guided actual political action. Although it constituted a recognisable whole this chapter found that this tradition was an amalgam of ideas drawn from a range of sources, constantly evolving and with varying priorities and inevitable internal tensions. It has always been 'fluid and unstable, the synthesis of a variety of different traditions' (Francis, 1997: 15). These traditions, it has been suggested, can be subsumed into two dimensions: the redistributive social democratic and the ethical socialist. Recognising its bipolar character has (hopefully) provided a more accurate description of British Labour's thought which, in turn, will facilitate the task of assessing the extent to which the New Labour project lies within the British social democratic tradition – and whether it has preserved or abandoned Labour's soul.

2 New Labour and social justice

Introduction

'Equality,' Bernard Crick has contended, 'is the value basic to any imaginable or feasible kind of socialism' (Crick, 1984: 158). During 18 years of Conservative government inequalities in the share-out of wealth and income reached levels unprecedented since the end of the nineteenth century (Glennerster, 2001: 384). In 1979, the number of people living below half average income – the unofficial poverty line – was 5 million; by 1992/93 it had almost trebled to 14.1 million. During this period, average real income rose 37 per cent, that of the bottom tenth slid by 18 per cent, while that of the richest tenth leapt by 61 per cent. According to Eurostat, the European Union statistics agency, Britain had more children living in poverty than any other European country. New Zealand apart, Britain witnessed the most rapid growth of inequality of any industrialised country (*Guardian*, 28 July 1997; *Guardian*, 28 April 1997). 'Labour's biggest challenge', the *Guardian* declared shortly after its triumphant return to power, 'is the obscene inequality which has been generated since 1979' (*Guardian*, 12 May 1997). How did it respond to this challenge?

Giddens contends that 'the issue of inequality ... highlights the antagonism between the more traditional left and the modernising social democrats who advocate Third Way politics' (Giddens, 1999b). At the heart of any theory of distributive justice is the identification of the relevant criteria – the normative principles – to be applied to ascertain whether the existing allocation of resources is fair and, to the extent that it is not, to be invoked to formulate policies which can achieve greater equity. From its inception what set Labour apart from its mainstream political rivals was its insistence that the existing distributional order – that is 'the way in which the major social institutions distribute fundamental rights and duties and determine the division of advantages from social cooperation' (Rawls, 1971: 7) – was fundamentally unjust. Disparities in reward were acceptable to the extent that they could be 'justified by some notion of social utility or public welfare – some clear public benefit had to follow which could not otherwise exist' (Crick, 1984: 159), but in reality society was disfigured by class-based inequalities much deeper than was socially or economically warranted. Of course for successive Labour governments there were a host of considerations (economic, political, social etc.) which impeded efforts to promote equality and (as we noted in Chapter One) Labour's egalitarian drive in office was often tamer than both supporters and critics of New Labour have supposed. Notwithstanding, the compression of material inequalities was a key aspiration and it did, however loosely, set the line of march.

The New Labour theory of distributive justice, we shall suggest, can best be understood as a combination of traditional social democratic thinking, adjusted to meet shifting circumstances, and ideas more commonly associated with liberalism. Buckler and Dolowitz have designated this as 'social liberalism' (Buckler and Dolowitz, 2000b). It can be summarised in terms of four normative principles: social inclusion, fairness for all (or 'priority'), common advantage and equal worth/equality of opportunity. Social inclusion refers to the right of all to participate fully in society, fairness to all to the priority to be assigned to ending acute social deprivation and common advantage to the limits to redistribution imposed by the imperatives of wealth creation. The concept of 'equal worth' is in effect equated with equality of opportunity, defined in terms of ensuring that all people have the ability to realise their own potential. This chapter is devoted to defining the first three principles and exploring the way in which they were embodied in policies pursued by the Blair Government. The next chapter examines in more detail the application of the fourth principle, equality of opportunity, specifically in the field of secondary education.

Social inclusion

Social inclusion – or combating social exclusion – has emerged as a central New Labour organising principle. The socially excluded were those cut off from society's mainstream, outside the formal economy, dependent on benefits and the black economy, lacking skills, jobs and opportunities and often trapped in decaying, crime-ridden and drug-filled council estates (Blair, 1997b). The prime cause of social exclusion (for those of workable age and their dependents) was seen as lack of income deriving from paid work and, hence, the most effective remedy (for those so capable) was engagement in the labour market. How was this to be accomplished?

Traditionally, social democratic thinking in Britain has located the source of unemployment in structural factors, notably deficiency in demand for labour – the absence of a sufficient number of jobs at rates of pay and in conditions which it is reasonable to expect people to accept – or technological changes. For New Labour, this approach took insufficient account of supply-side factors causing a weak attachment to the labour market, whether through lack of skills or appropriate qualifications or (for groups such as single mothers) lack of adequate child care facilities. Equally it neglected the impact of the organisation of the welfare system – in terms of opportunities, incentives and penalties – on the operations of the labour market (HM Treasury, 1997). In consequence, New Labour's approach to tackling the problem was dual-pronged: enhancing 'employability', that is equipping people with relevant skills which facilitated their passage to work, and gearing the organisation of the welfare system more tightly to the needs of the labour market primarily via a strategy of 'welfare to work'.

Employability was a matter of developing the 'skills, knowledge, technology and adaptability' needed by employers which would then enable those who possessed them 'to enter and remain in employment throughout their working lives' (HM Treasury, 1997). In the high-tech, computerised and ceaselessly changing modern economy the most valuable resource has become human capital: the skill, knowledge, adaptability and creativity of the labour force. Human capital emerged as a key New Labour concept since, it held, competitive strength in the 'new economy' depended upon a well-educated, highly qualified, motivated and flexible workforce producing high value goods. It followed that the route to a secure and well-remunerated place in the labour market was not through outdated systems of labour protection but via possession of the relevant skills.

The second crucial feature of New Labour thinking has been 'welfare to work'. The welfare state, as the concept evolved after 1945, was grounded in the concept of social need. Because it was the obligation of society to guarantee the meeting of these needs to all its members they could be construed as social rights or entitlements – to healthcare, education, compensation for unemployment, infirmity and so forth – which enabled full participation in the life of the community (Harris, D, 1987: 49–50). 'As common needs, their moral force should be recognised by society and the means of their satisfaction financed out of general taxation' (Plant, 2003b: 155). This entitlement welfare philosophy, New Labour held, was flawed by its passivity. It failed to grasp that once large numbers of people grow used to relying on state benefits a culture of dependency emerges into which people are reared, severing them from the structure and rhythms of work which alone can promote self-discipline, diligence and self-reliance. The state 'can all too easily institutionalise poverty rather than solve it, lock people into dependency rather than give them the means to be independent' (Department of Social Security, 1998; *Guardian*, 2 June 1997, quoting a government source). In place of the 'passive' entitlement welfare state – with its invitation to free-riding – New Labour favoured the 'social investment state' (Giddens, 1998: 117–8). Lister has defined this in terms of 'RIO', that is responsibility, inclusion and opportunity. 'The exercise of responsibility, in return for the opportunities provided by government lies at the heart of New Labour's third way citizenship and social inclusion philosophy' (Lister, 2004: 169). This entailed replacing the older social democratic concept of social citizenship with a more contractual approach based on reciprocity. Influenced by the communitarian critique of the socially and culturally debilitating effects of weakening moral codes and severing rights from duties New Labour repudiated 'longstanding taboos on judgementalism' about personal behaviour (Deacon, 2003: 125). Government has a responsibility to ensure that all have the opportunity to better themselves by securing access to paid employment, through provision of education and training, subsidised employment and expert advice. The upshot would be that people would be equipped with the resources and incentives to manage their own lives (Jayasuriya, 2000: 285–6). In return, those helped had a duty to take advantage of the opportunities so furnished. People should not be free to choose a life on benefit but 'have a clear responsibility to help themselves' (Darling, 1999).

Plant calls this more contractual approach an 'achievement- or obligation-based conception of citizenship' which lays a stress on 'obligation, virtue and contribution' (Plant, 2003b: 155–6). Those who benefited from the fruits of social co-operation had an obligation to act in a more 'virtuous' manner by acquiring greater habits of social reliance and taking more personal responsibility for their own and their family's welfare needs. Equally they had a duty to society at large, by making a contribution to the social product (Jordan, 1998: 42). The aim was a 'something for something society' in which 'rights are matched by responsibilities' and all worked for the common good. The social investment state was a 'welfare to work' state.

The concept of welfare to work reflected (in New Labour's view) the functional imperative of integrating the welfare and labour market systems. Past Labour policy – it was claimed – had been characterised by the lack of any firm institutional articulation between the two systems. As a result the unchecked growth of spending on unproductive social programmes could be – and was – portrayed by the right as a burden on the economy (Clegg, 2005: 242). By demonstrating how – via welfare to work approach – active social and labour market programmes were vital to economic success, social spending could be relegitmated. There were two main themes in this approach: 'job facilitation' and 'labour activation'.

Job facilitation. Many people in the past, it was argued, had been effectively barred from the labour market and trapped in poverty by ill-designed policies and lack of resources. For example, as result of tax and benefit traps and the absence of adequate child care facilities, many people faced a situation where the lion's share of every extra pound earned went in tax. The Government sought to 'make work pay' – or widen the gap between paid work and benefit levels – by a range of in-work tax incentives such as the Working Families Tax Credit (which provides in-work subsidies), the minimum wage, which raised the floor of incomes, and child care tax credits to enable mothers (especially the large number of young single mothers) to afford childcare (Glennerster, 2001: 395; Taylor-Gooby et al., 2004: 581–2).

Labour activation and the New Deal. Under the Blair Government labour activation has principally taken the form of the various 'New Deal' schemes of assistance for the jobless, including education and training, work experience and personalised assistance to job-seekers by specially trained personal advisors. The best known example is the New Deal for Young

People designed to give work, education and other opportunities to those aged 18 to 24 who have been unemployed for over six months. Under its terms young people are guaranteed one of the following: a job linked to training; work helping the elderly, sick or handicapped; a post with an environmental task force or up to a year's full-time education or training. Subsidies are available for employers willing to take recruits. A key aspect of the New Deal for Young People (and, to a lesser degree, of other New Deals) is the principle of conditionality: the receipt of benefit is conditional on willingness to accept offers of work or training. Failure to do so is penalised by loss of benefit.

Subsequent 'New Deals' for single parents, the long-term unemployed and those on incapacity benefits have been introduced. The New Deal for lone parents, which is voluntary, offers personal assistance with job search, plus training and childcare facilities. The New Deal for the long-term unemployed (i.e. those out of work for more than 2 years) consists of a period of preparation followed by either subsidised employment or full-time education and training. All participants must attend a series of advisory interviews or risk loss of benefit. The New Deal for the disabled provides a personal adviser service and help with return to work (Daguerre, 2004: 49).

What has been the impact of New Labour's social inclusion measures? Taylor-Gooby and his colleagues report that 'New Labour has increased very substantially the resources available for training and advice, developed much more sophisticated and precise policies for particular groups of unemployed people and, perhaps most importantly, pursued policies to increase incomes for the low-waged' (Taylor-Gooby *et al.*, 2004: 579). Hirsch and Millar, summarising Rowntree research into the various New Deal programmes and fiscal measures, found that they had

- considerably improved financial incentives to work;
- made progress in tackling some key barriers to work, such as scarcity of child care facilities;
- provided help (through the personal adviser system) with job search or training for vulnerable groups who had previously received little or none;
- improved employment participation rates for targeted groups.

They conclude that the New Deal programmes offered 'a more wide-ranging and sustained approach to helping people enter the labour market' than previous ones and that the various tax credit schemes (such as the Working Tax Credit) together with the minimum wage had transformed support for working people on low incomes (Hirsch with Millar, 2004).

What have been the effects on unemployment? Labour force participation rates among the population of working age rose from 72.9 per cent in 1997 to 74.9 per cent in 2004, higher than the EU average, while the percentage of working-age people living in jobless households dropped from 13.1 to 11.6 over the same period (Levitas, 2005: 18–19). By 2005 unemployment was at its lowest level for 25 years, the numbers in work reached an all-time high and long-term unemployment among the under-25s had been very sharply reduced. This has been coupled with a remarkable degree of price stability and sustained and steady economic growth – a combination which has eluded all previous Labour governments (Clegg, 2005: 245).

The most effective measures in relieving poverty and 'making work pay' have probably been the minimum wage (first introduced in 1999) and the Working Families Tax Credit (WFTC). In 2006 the minimum wage stood at £5.35 for adults. By 2004, it has been calculated, 1.7 million were benefiting from it (Vigor, 2005: 160). A study by the Fabian Society published in 2006 reported that the wages of the lowest paid have increased faster than average earnings for the working population as whole and benefited two million people (*The Guardian*, 16 October 2006). The WFTC has also helped lever up the income of the low paid and, by increasing the gap between wages and benefits, helped 'make work pay'. However research by the New Policy Institute suggests that tax credits have also acted as a way of subsiding low-paying employers with public money. Workers have no incentive to seek wage increases since they would simply suffer a corresponding loss of benefit (or 'tax credit') so public funds are, to this degree, diverted into employers pockets (cited in the *Guardian*, 29 October 2004). To this extent the poverty trap persists.

Furthermore, while acknowledging the Government's accomplishments in reducing grinding poverty some have queried the Government's equation of social inclusion with paid employment. While, as we see below, it has concentrated its efforts on reducing poverty among families with children and pensioners, figures suggest that poverty among childless working age adults (who make up 39 per cent of the population) has shown no appreciable fall (Brewer *et al.*, 2006: 42). Government policy has contributed directly to the problem because benefit rates for the less favoured groups (i.e. the working-age out of work) have been tied to prices not incomes and hence dwindled in comparative value (Paxton and Dixon, 2004: 11, 13–14, 22). The Rowntree Foundation's *Monitoring Poverty and Social Exclusion* survey for 2006 found that 'at 6.2 million, the number of working-age adults in poverty now exceeds the pensioner poverty and child poverty combined'. Despite the gains arising from the minimum wage and WFTC 'the number of adults in in-work poverty has risen and now accounts for nearly half the total'. Given that half of the 3.4 million children living in poverty have a parent already in paid work, the same proportion as in the late 1990s, the report concluded by querying the central premise of the government's anti-poverty strategy – that work was the best route to social inclusion (Palmer *et al.*, 2006).

Fairness for all ('priority')

But what of those among the socially excluded – the young, the elderly, the disabled and infirm – not available for work? Here the second distributive principle of fairness for all, or priority, applies. To elucidate this concept it is useful to make a double distinction with egalitarian and 'safety-net' approaches. The principle of equality is a comparative one in that it measures the material position of one group compared to that of another and favours – as a principle – narrowing the gap that separates them. The principle of 'priority' is primarily concerned with combating social deprivation. Actuated by a 'benevolent and sympathetic concern' it imposes on society an obligation to alleviate the impoverished material conditions of the poor and to the meeting of their basic needs (Norman, 1999: 183–4, 188). Redistribution is only desirable to the extent that it contributes to this end.

But if the principle of priority can be distinguished from that of equality so, too, can it be from 'safety-net welfare' which is solely concerned with succouring people from the threat of absolute poverty. 'Priority' if not a 'comparative' concept is a 'relative' one in that it is defined in terms of providing the means to participate fully in the life of society according to the standards and expectations prevailing at the time. In other words, if living standards in general rise so too should expectations of what constitutes a sufficient standard of living. The Blair Government's commitment to this principle is illustrated by its decision to define poverty in *relative* terms, as living in a household with an income of less than 60 per cent of the median. So while, on the one hand, the Government was not concerned with lessening the *overall* hierarchy in the distribution of income and wealth, an important object of policy *was* the reduction of income inequalities between the poorest and those on median incomes (Brewer *et al.*, 2002).

Particular priority has been given to eliminating poverty among the young and the old. Brown has described child poverty as 'a scar on Britain's soul' (Brown, 1999: 8). In 1998 Tony Blair proclaimed that the elimination of child poverty (defined as children dwelling in a household with an income of less than 60 per cent of the median) was an 'historic aim' of his Government and – in an announcement that surprised observers – he pledged to reduce it by 25 per cent by 2004/5 and by 50 per cent by 2010/11. This is one of the most ambitious targets selected by the Government and attests to the seriousness of its commitment to this aspect of redistributive social democracy. 'In setting clear and measurable targets to reduce child poverty, the government is holding itself to account in a way that few governments have done before' (Robinson and Stanley, 2005: 276).

The decision to adopt these targets was strongly influenced by research which demonstrated that child poverty was closely associated with weak cognitive development, inferior educational attainment, psychological problems (e.g. low self-esteem), anti-social behaviour, low pay and poor employment prospects. Child poverty (Downing Street's Social Exclusion Unit reported) had 'an independent effect upon an individual's life chances and prospects for upward social mobility' (Social Exclusion Unit, 2004: 16). Given, too, that 'people's life chances are determined by who their parents were rather than their own talents and efforts' (HM Treasury, 1999b: 31) the principle of equality of opportunity enjoined that the breaking the cycle of disadvantage be one of New Labour's central policy aims (Deacon, 2003).

The Child Tax Credit emerged as the main tool for cutting child poverty. This was designed to replace various means-tested benefits, with low-income families allocated the maximum rate, though all families earning less than £58,000 pa were eligible (Hirsch with Millar, 2004). The aim was 'a single, seamless system of income-related support for families with children' paid direct to the caring parent (HM Treasury, 2002). In addition both the Working Family Tax Credits and universal Child Benefits have been increased and new child-care allowances introduced. Writing in 2005 Peston calculated that 90 per cent of families received some form of Working Tax Credit and Child Tax Credit, an estimated 20 million (Peston, 2005: 276).

To these cash benefits have been added preventative policies devised to snap the intergenerational cycle of disadvantage, notably the national childcare strategy. A key element of this was the development of high-quality childcare for all in the early years of life from which, research indicated, children from poorer homes would benefit most. In addition, the unusually low rate of lone parent participation in the labour force in the United Kingdom was seen as, in part, the consequence of the lack of decent and affordable childcare (Robinson and Stanley, 2005: 277). A pivotal role was assigned to the Sure Start programme whose aim was 'to improve the nurture and parenting of disadvantaged children through the provision of advice, support and nursery places' (Levitas, 2005: 52). The Blair Government's national childcare strategy amounts, social policy expert Ruth Lister wrote, to 'a breakthrough in British social policy ... the first time that government has accepted that childcare is a public as well as a private responsibility' (Lister, 2004: 169).

Between 1998/99 and 2004/5 child poverty fell by 700,000, from 4.1 million to 3.4 million children, reaching a 15-year low, (Palmer *et al.*, 2006) and the incomes of the poorest 20 per cent of households with children had risen since 1997 by around 15 per cent (Brewer *et al.*, 2005: 29). Financial support for children in total had grown in real terms by £10 billion, just over 70 per cent, since 1997 (Peston, 2005: 276). By 2002 the United Kingdom had moved from bottom to eleventh place in the EU league of child poverty, and by 2003/4 there were about one million fewer children in poverty (Paxton and Dixon, 2004: 10–11). According to Institute for Fiscal Studies research the steady reduction in child poverty after 1998/99 was 'the longest period of sustained fall' since data became available in 1961. For this, it concluded, Government actions –notably the decisions to raise substantially the scale of cash transfers and welfare-to-work measures and other steps to help parents find work – deserved much of the credit (Brewer *et al.*, 2006: 43–4). All this was achieved despite the fact that median income (and thus the poverty line) had grown significantly and that the proportion of children living in lone-parent families (which doubles the risk of poverty) had continued its upward curve (Brewer *et al.*, 2006: 61) 'It would appear,' Lister concluded, 'that we are witnessing a genuine, unprecedented, attempt to shift the social priorities of the state and nation to investing in children (Lister, 2004: 170).

A second example of the principle of priority was the emphasis on redressing poverty in old age. The poverty rate for pensioners (i.e. those below the 60 per cent median income line), the Rowntree Foundation calculated, fell from 27 per cent in the late 1990s to 17 per cent in 2004/5. Among single pensioners, the rate fell by half over the period, from 33 per cent to 17 per cent. Pensioners now account for just one-sixth of all the people in poverty (Palmer *et al.*, 2006) According to IFS figures, while there were 2.8 million pensioners who were poor (using an after-housing-costs measure) in 1996/97, this number had dropped by over a third to 1.8 million by 2004/5. Though a major factor was the rising prosperity of pensioners (in part because they benefited from higher-paying pension schemes than preceding cohorts) about 25 per cent of the improvement was due to Government policy initiatives (Brewer *et al.*, 2006: 61. See also Brewer *et al.*, 2007: 39). The Rowntree Foundation concluded that 'the big fall in poverty among pensioners, especially single pensioners, has been a major success of the anti-poverty strategy' (Palmer *et al.*, 2006).

However, if the objective of the principle of priority was widely applauded within the Labour party the means used – the decision to target help on those deemed the most exigent – has been more controversial. A new State Second Pension was introduced in 2002 which gave added entitlements to carers, the disabled and the low-paid who had not been able to accrue pension rights – potentially over 20 million people. A special fuel payment for pensioners was also legislated and progressively raised (Toynbee and Walker, 2005: 63). But the key Government initiative was the introduction of the means-tested Minimum Income Guarantee for Pensioners, later replaced and raised by the Pension Credit.

'Historically,' a leading authority has noted, 'a crucial political divide across the British political spectrum has been over the fundamental aims of the welfare state, with those on the Right ... seeing its role as predominantly that of poverty relief, while the Left has pushed towards provision of welfare services on a universal basis, not just to the poor' (Hills, 1998). Here it may be useful to distinguish between 'needs-testing' and 'means-testing'. Needs-testing was defined by Titmuss as 'positively discriminating on a territorial, group or "rights" basis in favour of the poor, the handicapped, the deprived, the coloured, the homeless, and the social casualties of our society' (Titmuss, 2000 [1968]: 48). Means-testing refers to determining eligibility to benefit according to income level. In practice (see Chapter One) the stance adopted by successive Labour governments oscillated between means- and needs-testing. That ambivalence has been removed by the Blair Government with a deliberate expansion of means-testing becoming 'one of the hallmarks of new Labour's social security policy' (Brewer *et al.*, 2002). Two controversial instances have been the decision not to reverse the Tories' decoupling of pensions from earnings growth, tying it instead to prices (which has led to a progressive diminution in its value) and the rejection of the recommendation of the Sutherland Royal Commission on Long Term Care that personal care should be freely available to the elderly infirm in favour of means-testing.[1]

Critics within the party have objected to this 'targeting' approach on a number of grounds. Applicants who are required to provide details of their financial position commonly experience this as intrusive if not demeaning. Means-tested benefits are expensive to administer. They usually entail time-consuming, complex and often baffling form-filling which deters many of those eligible from applying. As a result, take-up is substantially lower than for universal benefits (the Minimum Income Guarantee accounted for almost a half an estimated £1.4 billion of unclaimed benefits to which pensioners were entitled in 2000/1, Paxton and Dixon, 2004: 21). They discourage thrift and self-reliance. If the thrifty are forced to use up their savings while those who never saved receive help this provides a disincentive to save.[2]

In addition means-testing tends to create poverty traps, imposing what are in effect very high marginal tax rates: recipients normally forfeit a substantial proportion of any increase in income by withdrawal of benefits (according to a Treasury estimate about 1.7 million people on low incomes are subject to withdrawal rates of 60 per cent or more – as compared with a maximum tax rate of only 40 per cent on the rich. John Grieve Smith in *The Guardian*, 11 August 2004). Finally, critics claim, means-testing is unfair and ignores society's responsibility to care for the most vulnerable. Institutions acting on behalf of society, the Sutherland Report on long-term care for the elderly contended, had an overriding obligation to sustain the welfare of those of its members who 'unpredictably and through no fault of their own' fell victim to the vicissitudes of life. Since neither the 'incidence nor the scale of care needed' were predictable it was 'equitable and proper for the state to meet at least one element of these "catastrophic" costs for everyone' (Sutherland, 1999: 6.32–6.34, 10.13).

Means-testing (or targeting), the Government riposted, is the most cost-effective means of helping those in greatest need: it is no longer realistic, for financial and electoral reasons, to appreciably raise universal benefits. Universal benefits would mean either that existing resources would be spread too thinly, penalising those most in need, or a substantial hike in taxation, which was not acceptable to the voters. For example, the Government contended that universal free personal care for the elderly would 'consume most of the additional resources we plan to make available for older people through the NHS' (Alan Milburn, Health Secretary, *The Guardian*, 1 September 2000). Targeting ensures that resources go to those least capable of fending for themselves and hence is the most redistributive of policy options.

However means-testing remained controversial within the party with the Government twice defeated by Labour's conference for its refusal to restore the earnings link. Opposition extended well beyond the party and by 2006 the Government's confidence in its approach to pensions began to wilt. On the recommendations of the Turner Report it began to ponder seriously a return to a more universal system. However, despite mounting concern (in

England and Wales) that the Government's insistence on a means-tested approach to care for the elderly infirm was both ineffective and unjust (free NHS care was available for the elderly stricken, for example, by cancer but not for those suffering from dementia) on this issue the Government has shown no disposition to rethink its policy. This reliance on means-testing represented a significant shift in outlook compared to the past (Glennerster, 2001: 383).

Whatever its shortcomings, it is difficult to conclude other than that, in terms of practical achievement, the record of the Blair Government easily stands comparison with those of its predecessors in the 1960s and 1970s. We have already referred to findings on child poverty. A leading authority on social policy has concluded that the Blair administration

> has a commendable and effective policy of redistribution to the lower income working poor and their children. ... The attack on inequality may still look small in comparison to the powerful economic forces at work but it does move in the opposite direction to nearly two decades of budget policy.
>
> (Glennerster, 2001: 402)

If the population is divided into quintiles (groups of 20 per cent) Institute of Fiscal studies figures show that the income of the poorest two quintiles has risen faster than the rest since 1997 (Peston, 2005: 287). If the performance of the Blair Government is compared with the performance of previous Labour governments in the 1960s and 1970s – and not their rhetoric – then there is a strong argument to be made that it enjoyed greater success in implementing the key social democratic value of poverty relief. As Giddens observed, 'this may be the first Labour government actually to effect redistribution, rather than just talk about it' (Giddens, 2004b).

By the beginning of the Government's third term, however, the pace of progress began to slacken. It failed to reach its 'crucial milestone' of cutting child poverty by 25 per cent by 2004/5 (Harker, 2006: 43, 44) and from 2004/5 to 2005/6 the number of people in relative poverty (living in households with less than 60 per cent of the median income) actually rose (Brewer *et al.*, 2007: 2). The problem for the Government was that underlying trends within the labour market were continuing to depress the wages of the lowest paid (Harker, 2006: 44–5). The IFS observed that 'significant new spending measures' were required if the Government was to have any prospect of reaching its targets – but noted that social security expenditure was set to rise by a very modest 1.3 per cent per annum in real terms between 2004/5 and 2007/8, a third of the rate of increase between 1998/99 and 2004/5 (Brewer *et al.*, 2006: 57–8).

But here the Government confronted a political problem: survey evidence showed that for the majority of voters child (and, a fortiori, other forms of) poverty was not rated as a major object of concern. Public attitudes were in fact ambivalent and often contradictory. Seventy-three per cent of respondents in the 2005 British Social attitudes survey felt that the gap between rich and poor was too large and significant majorities (around 60 per cent) agreed that the government should redistribute income from the better-off to the less well-off and spend more on welfare benefits to the poor. However, only 43 per cent thought it was the government's responsibility to cut the gap between rich and poor (Sefton, 2005: 3–4, 24). Qualitative research commissioned by the Fabian Society indicated that there was no strong constituency favouring further redistributive measures with many attributing poverty (especially among the unemployed) to individual failings (Fabian Society, 2006: 33–4). The problem was that the New Labour policy of 'redistribution by stealth' meant that no real effort was made to alert a poorly informed public about the realities of widespread poverty in the United Kingdom and hence to mobilise support for pouring more resources into combating it. 'The result is that one of the government's most important priorities barely registers on the public's agenda' (Harker, 2006: 47). 'It must be a difficult task,' Robinson and Stanley commented, 'to win the electorate around to support a policy of tax and spend and redistribution (that is not too different from that of earlier Labour governments) when you have never openly acknowledged that this is at the heart of your social democratic reform project' (Robinson and Stanley, 2005: 281). Perhaps an even more fundamental drag on a sustained drive against social deprivation emanated from the Government's reluctance to return to a more steeply progressive tax system. In part this reflected considerations of electoral strategy (see Chapter Seven) but it was also a product of the New Labour belief that such a system would be economically damaging. It is to this that we now turn.

Common advantage

> "Well you deserve: they well deserve to have,
> That know the strong'st and surest way to get"
>
> (Shakespeare, *Richard II*)

> Money, it's a gas.
> Grab that cash with both hands and make a stash. ...
> Money, get back.
> I'm all right jack keep your hands off of my stack.
>
> (Pink Floyd, 'Money')

At the heart of the traditional social democratic critique of capitalism was the conviction that, left to itself, the market generated a grossly unfair distribution of resources, a relentless piling-up of riches that reflected both the dynamics of the market and the ability of the wealthy and powerful to perpetuate their privileges. The extent to which the state should seek to curtail inequalities and the most appropriate means of condensing them have long been debated within the Labour party but with the common presumption that they could and should be narrowed. To New Labour this mode of thinking was rooted in a reluctance or inability to grasp the benefits that a dynamic market economy supplied *to all*. For Giddens a defining feature of New Labour is the recognition that 'social justice must be tempered by the need to sustain a competitive economy' (Giddens, 2002: 22). The precept of common advantage focuses on the gains in efficiency, output and productivity accruing from high income disparities. It can be seen as an application of Rawls' 'difference principle' which holds that inequalities are justified where disproportionate benefits to some actually conduces to the welfare of all, especially the less well-off, by promoting the wealth-creating capacities of the market economy and thus expanding the amount of resources available for redistribution (Rawls, 1971). Heavy fiscal levies on high income earners and on business turnover are damaging in a globalised and integrated world economic order for they will discourage investment, stifle enterprise and penalise effort (Giddens, 2000). Blair and Schroeder, in their 'Third Way' manifesto, put the matter succinctly: 'modern social democrats recognise' that tax cuts for business and the wealthy 'raise profitability and strengthen the incentives to invest. Higher investment expands economic activity and increases productive potential. It helps create a virtuous circle of growth' (Blair and Schroeder, 1999).

The precept of common advantage has underpinned policy during the 10 years of the Blair Government. Income tax for the wealthy remains at a post-1945 low, at a 40 per cent maximum, while rates of taxation on corporations are less than in most comparable EU countries. Figures based on Inland Revenue statistics show that receipts from corporation tax fell from £34.3 billion for 1999/2000 to £28.8 billion in 2002/3, a period of increasing corporate profits. During the same years the yield from income tax levied on individuals rose from £93.05 billion to £105.1 billion (Sikka, 2003). Corporate tax payments now account for just 2.5 per cent of national income, the smallest share ever (Sikka, 2005).

The Government has been very wary about taking any steps that might jeopardise the United Kingdom's status as a favoured destination for inward investment and, in particular, might adversely affect financial institutions. A Downing Street spokesman emphasised that 'we are not prepared to sign up to anything that harms the City of London' (*The Guardian*, 1 December 1999). One interesting example is the Chancellor's success in blocking the proposed EU 'withholding tax'. This was to be a tax on holders of international bonds – issued by large companies, governments and international institutions – who (since tax was not deducted at source) could avoid taxation by transferring assets to lower tax countries. Brown condemned the measure on the grounds that it would undermine the wholesale Eurobond market in the City.[3] This prompted a bitter dispute within the European Union with the bulk of members backing the proposal (*The Guardian*, 22 November 1999, 30 November 1999). Critics (such as Will Hutton) contended that the Blair Government, by preserving 'the tax-haven status of the City was helping the rich minimise their tax liabilities (the *Observer*, 12 December 1999). The Government countered that the strength of the City was a major source of national economic wealth. Because of the EU requirement for unanimity the 'withholding tax' proposal eventually fell by the wayside (*The Guardian*, 21 June 2000).

Equally under New Labour the scale of individual and corporate tax avoidance, always impressive, has ballooned with no effective legislative restraint. No one knows precisely the scale of tax revenues lost. As a result of organised tax avoidance, it has been calculated that Britain is losing between £97 billion and £150 billion of tax revenues every year – representing at least 74 per cent of all income tax receipts (Sikka, 2007; BBC 2 *The Money Programme*, 2 March 2006; Lansley, 2006: 187). According to Prem Sikka, professor of accounting at the University of Essex, some of the country's most profitable firms, including Rupert Murdoch's NewsCorp, Richard Branson's Virgin empire and Philip Green's Arcadia Group, by making astute use of tax havens and other loopholes, pay little or no corporation tax – yet 'the Government has shown little interest in plugging the leakage of tax revenues to tax havens' (Sikka, 2007). 'A Labour chancellor', Brown had assured Labour's conference shortly before taking office, 'will not permit tax relief to millionaires in offshore tax havens' (quoted in Bower, 2004: 253). In fact, he did little and tax avoidance opportunities have continued to multiply. These range from registering profits made in the United Kingdom in offshore tax havens such as Jersey, the Cayman Islands and Guernsey, to generous interpretations of the concepts of residence, domicile, corporate personality and jurisdiction, to the use of trusts and 'transfer pricing' (i.e. ensuring that profits are highest in low-tax countries and vice versa) and to a host of other arcane and subtle tax management devices (Sikka, 2003). The same leniency has been extended to individual wealth. In 2006 Britain's 54 billionaires had an estimated income of £126 billion. Income tax liabilities should have been about £50 billion. But in fact they were estimated to have paid only £14.7 million – an effective tax rate of only 0.14 per cent (Sikka, 2007).

The Government's professed concern to curb tax evasion and avoidance has been modulated by its conviction that a business-friendly tax-collecting regime is vital to both efficient wealth creation and retaining the United Kingdom's allure for foreign investors.[4] Two years after pruning staff in divisions dealing with corporate tax avoidance (*The Guardian*, 28 September 2004) and in response to pressure from big business, the Treasury announced a 'culture change' at the Inland Revenue designed (according to the *Guardian*) to 'force tax officials to be less aggressive and obstructive to potential investors in Britain'. The Chancellor declared that he wanted a system 'more responsive to the needs of business' and which exhibited 'greater trust in companies' (*The Guardian*, 17 November 2006). Fortunes, one commentator concluded, 'have been swollen still further by a burgeoning, lucrative and largely unchecked tax avoidance industry'. Not only has Britain jurisdiction over numerous tax havens but the country 'itself is widely seen as a semi-tax haven, a country where large corporations and rich individuals can legally treat tax as a largely optional obligation' (Lansley, 2006: xiv, 185).

Traditional social democratic thinking, Blair and Schroeder averred in their 'Third Way' statement, had neglected 'the importance of individual and business enterprise to the creation of wealth' and failed to acknowledge the economically enervating effect of 'penal rates' of taxation (Blair and Schroeder, 1999). This mistake has not been repeated by the Blair Government. According to the Institute of Fiscal Studies the incomes of the richest 1 per cent have risen 25 per cent faster than any other percentile group under New Labour. While the 'extremely indigent' have registered little advance 'the very rich have actually benefited from Brown's conviction that economic growth requires entrepreneurialism and enterprise' (Peston, 2005: 285–6). Thus while over the past decade the average earnings growth for British employees as a whole had been 45 per cent, for top executives of FTSE 100 companies the figure was more than six times as fast at 288 per cent (Paxton and Dixon, 2004: 23). Research by consultants Independent Remuneration Solutions revealed that total remuneration for top executives in the United Kingdom's largest companies climbed 22 per cent per year between 1998 and 2003 – a total pay rise of 168 per cent over the 5-year period (Croner Webcentre, 24 May 2004).

The accent on common advantage reflects New Labour's adherence to the 'harmony of interests' thesis. Since society as a whole benefited from a dynamic and competitive market economy it follows that there was a broad correspondence between the needs of investors and entrepreneurs in the market and society at large – a natural harmony of interest. Since the welfare of society is contingent on business prosperity, there could be no opposition between the private interest of business and the public: whatever benefits business (and businessmen) would also benefit the population as a whole through a 'trickle-down' effect. The only way success could be guaranteed in an intensely competitive world economy was by oiling the engines of wealth creation through encouraging profitability, higher levels of investment and an entrepreneurial culture: wealth, it was vital to recognise, must be generated before it could be distributed.

New Labour and the pattern of the distributional order

It may be useful here to summarise the impact of 10 years of Labour Government on the shape of the United Kingdom's distributional order. Under the Conservatives, income inequality rapidly widened, though from the early 1990s (for various reasons) this levelled off. In the first couple of years of the new government the trend resumed. 'Between 1996/7 and 2000/01 income inequality rose to its highest level since comparable records began in 1961' but since then income inequality has returned to roughly the level that Labour inherited (Harker, 2006: 45).

The detailed picture is quite complex. The IFS found that 'between about the 15th percentile point and the 90th percentile point, it is generally the lower parts of the distribution that have gained most over the period 1996/97 to 2006/06'. Below the fifteenth percentile point, 'income growth is progressively lower the lower the income percentile, with real income falls in the very lowest part of the income distribution' (Brewer *et al.*, 2007: 17). As we have seen, those who have fared least well are working-age adults without children, with the proportion in poverty actually tending to rise. The richest 10 per cent, in contrast, had experienced a steady growth of income which curves steeply upward for the top 1 per cent (Brewer *et al.*, 2006: 21–2). Between 1995 and 2005 the number of those with incomes over £1 million increased eightfold (Lansley, 2006: ix). 'In the space of two decades or less, Britain has experienced an explosion of personal wealth, one of the fastest rates of personal enrichment on record' (Lansley, 2006: 20).

The data also indicates that, in line with New Labour intentions, the tax system does not operate as a major instrument of redistribution. The poorest 20 per cent of households pay 42 per cent of their incomes in tax and for the poorest 10 per cent this rises to 53 per cent. In contrast the richest 20 per cent pay 34 per cent and the richest 10 per cent a very affordable 33 per cent (Jackson and Segal: 2004: 49). Professor John Grieve-Smith 'estimated that in 2003/4, households in the lowest fifth of the income scale paid as much as 28 per cent of their incomes in indirect taxes, whereas the top one fifth only paid 11 per cent … the poorer you are, the higher the proportion of any extra income the state takes back in either reduced benefits or higher tax payments' (Grieve-Smith, 2006: 10). The IFS concluded that the net effect of two terms of the Labour Government 'was to leave income inequality effectively unchanged and at historically high levels'. There has been a slight rise in income inequality since 1996–97 as measured by the Gini coefficient (which measures inequalities in income distribution)[5] due largely to the difference between income growth at the very bottom and very top of the distribution (Brewer *et al.*, 2007: 21, 1). The distribution of wealth, which includes financial assets such as savings or shares and fixed wealth such as housing, has traditionally been much more uneven than that of income. The Gini coefficient for wealth distribution in 2001 was, at 0.7, double that for disposable income in the same year (Paxton and Dixon, 2004: 25). In 2002 the top 1 per cent of the population held 23 per cent of personal wealth, up from 18 per cent in 1990, while, over the same period, the share held by the top 10 per cent rose from 47 per cent to 56 per cent (Vigor, 2005: 163).

However, as noted above, the narrowing of inequality per se is not an important policy objective for New Labour. Its three central normative principles (as discussed in this chapter) – social inclusion, fairness to all and common advantage – have been geared to securing employment opportunities for all as the best way out of poverty, protecting the poorest and most vulnerable in society slipping below minimum standards (with a particular emphasis on eradicating child poverty) while ensuring that the prevailing apportionment of rewards and resources ensures optimal efficiency in the wealth-generating market economy. Inequality is seen as a functional requisite in complex market economies operating in a highly competitive globalised world economy (Merkel, 2001: 50).

3 Equality of opportunity

The case of secondary education

Introduction

We noted in Chapter Two that the four principles defining the New Labour concept of social justice were combating social exclusion, fairness to all, common advantage and equality of opportunity. Here we consider the fourth of these, utilising policy on secondary education as a case study. 'Our goal,' the Prime Minister proclaimed in 2002, 'is a Britain in which nobody is left behind; in which people can go as far as they have the talent to go; in which we achieve true equality – equal status and equal opportunity rather than equality of outcome' (Blair, 2002c). A just society was not one which levelled income and wealth but one in which all people could compete equally in the labour market for the positions which conferred the greatest prestige and the highest rewards: in short a meritocratic social order where advancement was based on effort, qualification and ability, not inherited wealth or family background. Improving the standard of education for all – ensuring 'that every pupil – gifted and talented, struggling or just average – reaches the limits of their capability' (Department of Education and Skills, 2005: 20) – was the indispensable means to realising this vision of a meritocratic Britain. The object of policy should be to snap the 'cycles of underachievement, low aspiration and educational underperformance' (Department of Education and Skills, 2005: 19) by active and sustained public intervention in the structures and processes generating educational opportunities. It was for this reason that Tony Blair declared that 'I don't just want education to be the number one priority of the government. I want it to be our passion as a party' (quoted in Smithers, 2001b: 422).[1] New Labour's education policy goals can be briefly enumerated as follows:

1. Tackling social exclusion by setting minimum standards so that all were able reach a basic level of literacy and numeracy. The central weakness of the British (more specifically English) educational system was (it was held) that it effectively failed a large slice of the younger population who left schools barely literate and numerate and entered the labour market with rudimentary skills (Department of Education and Skills, 2005: 19).

Since 'low educational attainment is one of the main mechanisms by which disadvantage is transmitted from one generation to the next' the availability of a decent education was vital in enabling those 'from a relatively deprived background to enjoy upward social mobility' (Social Exclusion Unit, 2004: 16).

2. 'Excellence for all'. Also called the 'standards agenda' this stipulated continuous and sustained improvement of the education system 'so that all learners receive high quality provision which enables them to achieve as highly as possible' (Ainscow and Dyson, 2006: 5) by reducing the gaps between the outcomes achieved by the educationally most and least advantaged. As the then Education Secretary, Ruth Kelly, put it: 'I see my department as the department for life chances. . . . Our task is to make sure that for everyone involved in learning, excellence and equity become and remain reality' (quoted in Dyson, Kerr and Ainscow, 2006: 51).

3. Developing human capital. A crucial purpose of raising levels of educational achievement was to add to the stock of skill, knowledge and adaptability – or 'human capital' – which was seen as a precondition for maximising the competitive capacity of the UK economy in global markets.

Blair summarised the aims of his policy thus: to improve the overall quality of education, to 'tackle the pockets of deep educational disadvantage' and ensure the state sector would provide 'as good an education ... as anyone can buy in the private school system' (Blair, 2005). These were ambitious aims and the major and sustained expansion of educational spending which occurred after 1999 demonstrated the Government's commitment to them. After 1999, the education budget rose rapidly with a planned overall increase of 60 per cent between 1998/99 and 2007/8. 'The scale and continuity of these increases,' according to the Chief Economist at the Department for Education and Skills (and a leading academic authority), 'are unprecedented in recent history' (Johnson, 2004: 175). Total spending in cash terms was £30 billion in 1997 and was due to hit £64 billion by 2007/8, while capital investment leapt from £680 million in 1997 to an estimated £5 billion in 2005 (*The Guardian*, 9 July 2004). All this was associated with 'a deluge of policies on education' (Walford, 2005: 5) including nine separate Education Acts, and countless separate initiatives: a level of educational activism that no preceding government, Labour or otherwise, could match.

Yet – puzzlingly as it might seem – Government educational reforms encountered a degree of sustained opposition from within the party greater than in any area of domestic policy other than healthcare. The main reason for this was that key pillars of its educational strategy posed a very direct challenge to long-held tenets of belief. Nowhere was this more so than in the field of secondary education, where New Labour not only broke with the party's generation-long dedication to a uniform system of comprehensive education but pursued controversial policies extending performance management, choice, competition and the role of the private sector. This chapter will explore these policies, why they were selected and the extent to which they seemed likely to achieve the New Labour objective of 'an education system achieving excellence for the great majority' not simply a minority (Blair, 2004c).

For a generation between the 1960s and the 1990s Labour was a staunch advocate of the comprehensive principle – it had become 'one of the articles of the Labour faith' (Wilby, 2006b: 215). Pupils of all ability ranges and (as far as was feasible) social backgrounds should be taught in schools designed to serve the local community. The large-scale application of the comprehensive model from the 1960s 'formed a key moment in the constituting of the social democratic settlement that pursued social justice based on redistribution' (Harris and Ranson, 2005: 571). Of course, there was always a gap – often very wide – between principle and practice and the contrast between the high-achieving suburban comprehensive and the inner city 'sink school' was a familiar one. Notwithstanding, Labour retained a belief that with an appropriate level of funding the community-rooted comprehensive school represented the model of education which would bring the widest benefits to the largest number of children.

This belief came under sustained assault during the Thatcher and Major governments with the shift towards a 'quasi-market'. The Conservatives introduced open enrolment, school-managed delegated budgets, the right to opt-out of LEA control, a funding system based largely on the number of pupils on the school roll, greater diversity of school provision (e.g. the establishment of City Technology Colleges and Grant-Maintained schools), a national system of inspections (conducted by the newly created Office for Standards in Education or Ofsted) and a well-publicised system of performance tables based mainly on exam results. The role of LEAs was weakened, funding advantages were delivered to self-governing schools and the principle of selection was extended by giving some schools control over their own admissions policies (Driver and Martell, 2002: 49; Glatter, 2004: Ev 4; Taylor, Fitz and Gorard, 2005: 51).

Labour reacted with indignation. In 1994 party leader John Smith denounced Tory policy as 'driven by consumerist dogma, by oppressive dictation by a central state, and by a false and inadequate theory of choice' (quoted in Lawton, 2005: 118) and a report on education policy prepared before his death pledged the scrapping of league tables and reviving the power of the LEA. But Blair's accession to the leadership brought 'a dramatic turnaround in Labour education policy' (Smithers, 2001b: 406). The new Labour Government reversed the Tory neglect of deprived areas by establishing Education Action Zones which targeted extra resources onto educationally deprived areas (Coates, 2005: 134). But, to the distress of many within the party and the education profession, it enthusiastically embraced many of the innovations introduced by the Conservatives, including tests and league tables and financial delegation to schools (Smithers, 2001b: 405). Grant Maintained schools were retained as foundation schools and CTCs as City Academies. Rather provocatively Blair insisted on maintaining in post the Ofsted chief closely associated with Tory policies, the much-reviled (in traditional Labour and education circles) Chris Woodhead.

Two steps of considerable symbolic and practical significance are worth noting. First, the Blair Government resolved the traditional Labour ambivalence – the gulf between rhetoric and practice – towards public schools. Though the Government abolished the Assisted Places Scheme (in effect a subsidy to the public schools) the long-running commitment to ending their charitable status (hence tax advantages) was scrapped. A schooling system which had been denounced by Crosland as a principal cause of entrenched privilege and class inequality was now – for the first time in Labour's history – fully and formally accepted as an essential part of Britain's pattern of education. As the then schools minister (Estelle Morris) announced in 2000, there had been a 'huge cultural change' in the party's perception of public schools: it had come to 'like the independent sector in the same way that we like the other sectors' (quoted in Paterson, 2003: 172).

Second, the new government effectively terminated efforts to end selection by Eleven-Plus which still persisted in a number of areas of the country (including large authorities in Trafford, Greater Manchester and Kent. There were 164 grammar schools whose selective policies affected some 500 other schools, *in toto* almost 15 per cent of all children in the state education system). A system of parental ballots of such mind-boggling complexity was instituted that a positive vote for abolition was 'effectively unwinnable' (Education and Skills Select Committee, 2005: 28). While new grammar schools were not allowed to open existing ones could expand and, as a result, both the number of children attending and the numbers effected by the Eleven-Plus system was higher after a decade of Labour Government than when it came to power (Wilby, 2006a).

The New Labour programme for improving education took time before it acquired its definitive form. This was for two main reasons. First, anticipating strenuous opposition both from the teacher unions and from within the party, the Government initially elected to proceed with some circumspection (David Blunkettt, Education Secretary from 1997 to 2001 in 'Panorama', 2006a). Second, public sector reform was not the overriding priority in Labour's first term while in the second – and as the money really began to follow – it became (as one senior Downing Street advisor put it) the 'key domestic agenda' (interview, 2007). We can sum up the key prongs of the strategy as it eventually emerged in the second term as follows:

- *Stringent performance management* with a host of centrally set targets and rigorous monitoring and inspection regimes – all with the object of hoisting standards.
- *Competition and choice.* League tables and other sources of information about comparative school performance would enable parents to make

informed choices about where to place their children which would release competitive pressures for improvement.

- *Autonomy.* Choice and competition would only operate effectively if the producers were able to respond to shifting patterns of demand. This meant giving successful schools the right to expand, innovate and manage themselves, empowering parents to establish new schools and placing failing schools under tough remedial 'special measure' regimes or even closing them down.
- *Diversity.* Choice would be widened, innovation fostered and competition given a sharper edge by encouraging new types of providers (including private ones) to enter the market.
- *Collaboration.* This was designed to encourage schools in given localities to work more closely together. The object was to promote standards by pooling expertise, diffusing good practice and developing mutually supportive co-operative relationships. Since this component of the Blair Government strategy was not controversial it will only be mentioned in passing.[2]

The application of this strategy would, New Labour believed, impart the energy, motivation and drive that was required to boost the overall quality of educational provision, establish access of all to quality schooling and ensure that teaching was geared to individual pupil needs and talents (Blair, 2004a: 3). In combination these principles amounted, we shall suggest, to a sea-change in the party's educational philosophy. The next section charts the attempt to put these principles into practice by examining three key policy initiatives: performance management, specialist schools and City Academies. It concludes by discussing what can be seen as the culmination of the Government's reform agenda, the highly contentious 2006 Education Act. The penultimate section assesses the extent to which the Blair Government's educational reform programme appears on course to attain its objectives and the final one seeks to account for the shifting trajectory of Labour's (secondary) education policy.

Performance management

Labour had energetically opposed the performance regime instituted by the Conservatives but by 1997 had swung round to the view that it was an effective way to raise standards. The 1998 School Standard and Framework Act set out a framework for assessing and measuring standards of performance and from this flowed a relentless stream of initiatives ranging from numeracy and literacy targets to ever more complex and elaborate output measurement regimes. Teachers were to be 'performance managed' against individual objectives and a system of performance-related pay was launched.[3] The four key elements of performance management, as expounded by the PM's Strategy Unit, were as follows:

- Targets. These set specific ambitions for improvement in public services and provide publicly available performance information allowing comparisons of the performance of different providers.
- Regulation. This includes the setting of (national) minimum standards – which specifies the quantity, quality and/or type of service providers should offer users.
- Performance assessment, under which providers are monitored and inspected and their performance assessed as to whether they are providing an acceptable level and quality of service. Performance assessment provides triggers for intervention to tackle poor performance.
- Intervention mechanisms, which are used to tackle failing or underperforming providers.

(Strategy Unit, 2006: 34)

The testing, targeting and inspection regime was the core of performance management and had two principal aims. The first was to improve pupil performance by setting very clear targets (e.g. raising literacy and numeracy standards). Stringent recovery regimes ('special measures' was the preferred euphemism) were installed for schools which failed to reach requisite standards – a system that critics decried as 'blame and shame' and the cause of much demoralisation in beleagued schools. The second purpose merits (for the purposes of this study) more extended discussion: the institution (or consolidation) of a 'surrogate' market system. New Labour increasingly came to accept that as in the private sector so too in the public competitive impulses were an effective, indeed indispensable, mechanism for raising standards of service-delivery. Price plays a central role in markets since it operates as a summary indicator of quality, enabling consumers to compare a range of goods and services, thereby greatly facilitating informed consumer choice. The problem was the absence in state education of price signals – hence a substitute was needed. Here the Government accepted the system inherited from the Conservatives where league tables based on test results (though ostensibly to be 'value-added') coupled with other indicators of performance (e.g. Ofsted inspection reports) operated as surrogates for price (Smithers, 2001b: 419; Crouch, 2003: 27–8). Performance tables and inspections, Blair maintained, gave 'parents the information that has enabled them to make objective judgements about a school's performance and effectiveness' (Blair, 2004a: 3). The combination of the desire to enhance rank order in the league tables and the rewards attached to higher ranking would, it was assumed, 'incentivise' the drive to continuously lift standards (Smithers, 2001b: 410).

The Government's assumption that school performance, in terms of 'adding-value' to pupils' educational progress, could be effectively measured by target attainment and league tables was queried by academic experts (Harris and Ranson, 2005: 573). According to a team of researchers from London University 'the position of a school in published league tables, the criterion typically used by parents to select successful schools, depends more on the social profile of its pupils than the quality of the teachers.' This applied even if the tables were 'value-added'. The report estimated that more than 50 per cent of a school's performance is accounted for by the social make-up of its pupils (Taylor, M, 2006). Opposition swiftly mounted to other aspects of the performance management regime. Doubts were cast about the reliability of the data: progress in boosting standards was often exceeded (it was claimed) by ingenuity in statistical manipulation. There were mounting, insistent and widespread complaints that schools were increasingly 'teaching to test' to maximise exam results, which meant that broader educational purposes – such as critical reasoning and extending the capacity for experience – were being sacrificed to a blunt measure of attainment (Cribb and Ball, 2005: 123; Machin and Stevens, 2004: 163; Smithers, 2005: 278–9; Johnson, 2004: 176, 183, 185). The Blair Government's policy has been 'trapped in a language which militates against the broader moral dimension of education – the language of skills and targets, of performance indicators and audits ... of economic relevance and social usefulness' (Pring, 2005: 82–3). The state educational system was increasingly viewed as more or less exclusively a device for fitting people into the appropriate level of occupational hierarchy (Tomlinson, S 2005: 202–3). Furthermore the sheer drain of time and energy entailed in record keeping, and monitoring and route administration exasperated many (Crouch, 2003: 28). There was a general suspicion that performance indicators were chosen for ease of measurement and control rather than because they accurately measured the quality of performance, producing perverse incentives (O'Neill, 2002). Many teachers complained that what was intrinsically valuable but not easily measurable was neglected while those with special needs were often ignored (Gewirtz, Dickson and Power, 2004: 337; Russell, 2007).

The Government did acknowledge the force of at least some of this criticism and, in its second term, performance management was (particularly in terms of numbers of targets and scale of monitoring) relaxed somewhat. There was a significant shift towards 'earned autonomy' in which control over organisation, management and finance was devolved to 'good performers' (Strategy Unit, 2006: 43). However the Government (or, more accurately, Number 10) did not flinch in its commitment to league tables and other performance indicators for a simple reason: as price surrogates they were an essential part of the quasi-market system. It is to this that we now turn.

Choice and diversity: specialist schools

In Labour's second and third terms detailed, centrally powered performance management was increasingly coupled with institutional arrangements which emphasised choice, competition and diversity. Labour had inherited a system characterised by growing variety in secondary education provision. Aside from standard comprehensives and faith-based schools there were City Technology Colleges, specialist schools and Grant Maintained Schools.

Labour had opposed the Conservatives' legislation setting up these new structures but after Blair's accession to the leadership there was a growing convergence in outlook between the two parties (Tomlinson, S 2005: 90). Greater diversity became an increasingly insistent theme, especially after 2000. The object was to replace the dull uniformity allegedly imposed by the comprehensive system with a range of schools all able to differentiate themselves according to their individual ethos, special character and areas of specialist expertise (Taylor, Fitz and Gorard, 2005: 54). Diversity took a number of forms but in this account we concentrate on the two principal (and contentious) examples: specialist schools and City Academies.

Specialist schools – first established by the Conservatives in 1994 – were so designated because they specialised in one area of study, such as music, sport, information technology or languages. According to Education Secretary David Blunkett, they were vital for creating an education system which 'caters for the individual strengths of children rather than assuming a bland sameness for all' (quoted in Coates, 2005: 134). The aim was for all schools to become specialist ones and by 2005 around 2,000 schools had become so, about 60 per cent of those eligible (Smithers, 2005: 269). To be eligible for specialist status schools had to demonstrate high examination performance and a sustained record of school improvement. (In addition they had to raise £50,000 in unconditional sponsorship towards a capital project.) Specialist status provided extra state funding of £100,000 up front and over £100 per pupil per annum for 4 years (Taylor, Fitz and Gorard, 2005: 55; Johnson, 2004: 186). The Government's Five Year Strategy published in 2004 developed the concept further, anticipating the creation of 'independent specialist schools'. These were to be encouraged to specialise in up to two curriculum areas and would be authorised, by a vote of their governing body, to become 'foundation schools'. As such they would then own their own buildings and land, be able to work with private sponsors, employ their own staff, be given dedicated 3-year funding budgets and operate as their own admissions authority. They would be encouraged to forge long-term partnerships with external sponsors, including business, charitable and faith-based organisations who would, in return, obtain improved (in some cases, majority) representation on governing bodies (Education and Skills Select Committee, 2005: 39).

According to Education Secretary Charles Clarke 'specialist schools lie at the heart of our drive to raise standards and offer more choice in secondary schools' (quoted in Glatter, 2004: Ev 7). Such schools, Ofsted contended, benefited from 'working to declared targets, dynamic leadership by key players, a renewed sense of purpose, the willingness to be a pathfinder, targeted use of funding and being part of an optimistic network of likeminded schools' (quoted in Education and Skills Select Committee, 2005: 11). Tony Blair claimed that 'with external sponsors, strong leadership and a clear sense of mission' these schools 'driven by their acquisition and retention of specialist status improved faster than other comprehensives' (PM Foreword to Department of Education and Skills, 2005: 3). Given the short time period that has so far elapsed any assessment of this claim can only be tentative but informed opinion, overall, has not been convinced. The Education and Skills Select Committee wondered whether specialist status per se was the main driver of improvement. It might also reflect a 'privileged position within the education market' sustained by an ability to attract children from higher social backgrounds. Certified good management practices and extra funding – both conditions of specialist status – 'alone may account for better results' (Education and Skills Select Committee, 2005: 11). It was, one group of researchers concluded, 'unsurprising, therefore, that with additional resources and growing popularity, the specialist schools programme may appear successful to the government' (Taylor, Fitz and Gorard, 2005: 66). Equally relevant was the impact of specialist schools on the performances of other schools in their localities. Here there was 'some tentative evidence that specialist schools might be succeeding at the expense of neighbouring non-specialist schools' (Education and Skills Select Committee, 2005: 11; Glatter, 2004: Ev 6–7). There were also severe doubts about the concept of 'specialism'. Over half the schools surveyed in one piece of research reported that the specialism chosen for the bid was not the school's strongest teaching area: the main reason citied by schools for seeking specialist status was the additional money it would bring (Glatter, 2004: Ev 6). Further it was argued that locking pupils into a particular specialism at the early age of 11 was rather premature. The final objection was that, since only 10 per cent of the intake could be chosen on the basis of aptitude for the speciality, it was unclear how the scheme justified the claim that it catered for the individual strengths of *all* pupils (Smithers, 2001a).

City Academies

The decision to launch the City Academies programme was a major plank in the Government's drive to address the problem of low educational attainment in deprived – or 'educationally challenging' – areas. The objectives of the programme were to raise educational standards and achievements and to increase choice and diversity by creating a new type of local school. The initiative was an ambitious, even an audacious, one since the schools the Academies would replace generally were expected to have suffered from a history of low attainments, limited aspirations and poor behaviour among pupils (National Audit Office, 2007: 10–11). City Academies were publicly funded with the Department of Education paying most of the capital costs and all the running costs. The most controversial aspect of the programme was that each City Academy had to have one or more 'external sponsors'. The Prime Minister anticipated that sponsors from 'the business and voluntary sectors' would 'play a far greater role in the management of schools. ... If a successful school wants to engage with reputable external sponsors, this should not only be allowed – it should be strongly encouraged' (*The Guardian*, 12 February 2001). Such sponsors could include business, faith and voluntary organisations and wealthy individuals. External sponsors could pay up to 10 per cent of the capital costs, capped at a contribution of £2 million. In return for their donations sponsors (via their right to elect a majority on the governing body) had a considerable say over the curriculum, admissions and exclusions policies and the appointment (and dismissal) of the head. They could decide pay and conditions of staff independently of national pay scales and could shape an Academy's ethos – including whether it was faith-based (Francis Beckett in the *New Statesman*, 10 July 2000 and 17 January 2005; National Audit Office, 2007: 11). The Government initially planned to have 40 City Academies in place by September 2006 and 200 by 2010. However in November 2006 Tony Blair – as part of his effort to lay down his 'legacy' – announced plans to double the number of proposed City Academies to more than 400, which would mean that more than 10 per cent of secondary schools would become academies (*The Guardian*, 30 November 2006).

To the Government, the City Academies programme was a classic example of 'modern social democracy in action', in that it clung to traditional ends while being prepared to experiment with means, whatever the ideological provenance. Thus the ends (according to a senior Government advisor) were solidly social democratic: 'to narrow attainment gaps, widening opportunities and eradicate the inheritance of failure for generations of working class kids'. Choice of means, however, was grounded in a cool, dispassionate analysis of what worked. Thus research had demonstrated that City Technology Colleges (introduced by the Conservatives and the precursor of the City Academies) had worked 'astoundingly well' (interview, 2007) and for that reason the Government had opted to persist with them, in an amended form. City Academies, Tony Blair asserted confidently in 2005, were already improving 'at more than three times the national average in areas of the greatest challenge and disadvantage' (Foreword to Department of Education and Skills, 2005: 3).

It is much too early to reach any definitive conclusions about whether such claims are justified with research so far conducted producing conflicting results. On the one hand, an Edinburgh University study found that City Academies failed to raise standards (*The Guardian*, 22 May 2006) but National Audit Office research indicated that they added 'more value than schools in similar circumstances within two years of opening' while not damaging the performance of neighbouring schools (National Audit Office, 2007: 16, 19, 23). The Education and Skills Select Committee wondered whether better performance in some Academies was due to the higher rates of exclusion of disruptive children and to a fall in the proportion of children from deprived backgrounds (Education and Skills Select Committee, 2005: 15).[4] Equally there has been disagreement about *why* improvements have occurred. To the Government it was due to such innovations as the involvement of external sponsors with a solid track record of achievement in many fields (interview with senior Government advisor, 2007). It was certainly the case that a relatively modest investment gave sponsors a degree of discretion in how schools should be run greater than that conventionally enjoyed by LEAs – the Education Select Committee noted that the influence they acquired was being 'bought relatively cheaply' (Education and Skills Select Committee, 2005: 16). Others, however, attributed gains in educational attainment to the morale-boosting effects of new buildings, an influx of new staff and funding and the excitement of an experiment (Wilby, 2007; Roy Hattersley in *The Guardian*, 28 May 2007). Only the passage of time and the accumulation of research will enable a clearer judgement about the impact of the City Academy programme to be reached.

'A pivotal moment in the life of this government': the 2006 Education Act

After Labour's third and unprecedented election victory the tempo of educational reform accelerated with the publication (in October 2005) of an ambitious White Paper. Earlier measures had not fulfilled their promise because (Tony Blair felt) the Government had been insufficiently bold. 'Every time I've ever introduced a reform in Parliament', he told the party's conference in 2005, 'I wish in retrospect I had gone further' (quoted in Dyson, Kerr and Ainscow, 2006: 49). Hence – he declared – the radical new White Paper marked 'a pivotal moment in the life of this parliament and this government ... the crucial point where the reforms can be taken to their final stage' (Blair, 2005). Its core elements included the following:

1. All schools would be encouraged to become 'trust schools' with greater independence and freedoms to run their own affairs. Trusts, comprising representatives from businesses, charities, faith groups and voluntary associations, would lie 'at the heart of this new vision' (Department of Education and Skills, 2005: 24). They would be able to appoint the majority of a school's governing body, control its assets, vary the national curriculum and set admissions rules (within the advisory national code of practice).
2. The role of local education authorities would 'change fundamentally'. They would move from being a direct provider of services and from involvement in the day-to-day running of individual schools to a more strategic commissioning role. They would have a new role as 'commissioner' (rather than provider) of places and must offer advice and assistance to parents on their choice of school.
3. The education system would be 'opened up to real parent power'. Parent councils would give parents more control over the management and policies of schools and could even trigger the replacement of the school's leadership. Parents dissatisfied with existing comprehensive provision would have the right to set up new schools free from LEA control, even if there was already surplus capacity.

4. Choice would be facilitated by allowing good schools to expand and by the creation of a network of advisors to advise parents on what was available. Poor schools which failed to improve would be put out to tender.
5. There would be more diversity in admission procedures. All self-governing schools (foundation, voluntary aided and trust) would be free to 'use the approach to fair admissions that they think will best meet their local circumstances, as long as it is compatible with the Admissions Code'. They would retain the right to give priority for up to 10 per cent of their total places to pupils with particular aptitudes for the subjects in which they specialised (Department of Education and Skills, 2005: 46).

The proposals sparked off a massive wave of opposition within the Labour party. Comprehensive education, the left-wing weekly *Tribune* proclaimed,

> together with the NHS, lies at the heart of the Labour Party's core values of liberty and equality ... The reason why resistance among Labour MPs is building up so strongly against the proposals in the forthcoming education bill is because they threaten to overturn these founding principles.
>
> (*Tribune*, 20 January 2006)

An 'Alternative White Paper' written by a number of former ministers including John Denham, Angela Eagle, Alan Whitehead, Nick Raynsford and former Education Secretary Estelle Morris – none of them serial rebels – and signed by over half Labour backbenchers, was a full-frontal attack on the direction of Government policy. While the document commended important aspects of the White Paper (such as the accent on personalised learning, enhancing the role of parents, greater choice where appropriate, improved discipline and more effective leadership throughout the school system) they also advanced a battery of objections:

1. *A market in schools.* Empowering popular schools to expand with little or no regulation and making it easier for parents to establish new schools (including those catering for specific faith groups) would damage the collective interest by undermining the viability of other schools and by encouraging barriers between ethnic and religious communities, a growing and serious problem. Making a reality of choice – which necessarily entailed both closures and creating fresh (and surplus) capacity – would waste scarce resources which could be much more productively used.
2. *Local authority role.* Eroding the powers of LEAs would undermine their co-ordinating role and hinder the adoption of an integrated and cost-effective approach to the use of school resources within local communities. Equally, creating a more competitive environment would

discourage co-operation among schools which the Government professed to favour, while encouraging the setting up of schools outwith LEA control blocked the development of new community (LEA) schools irrespective of local need.

3. *Admissions.* A purely advisory Admissions Code, combined with the incentive imparted to schools to recruit pupils from more educationally oriented backgrounds, would further intensify trends to socially skewed intakes. It would also increase the numbers of pupils likely to be denied admission to their preferred school since competition for scarce places effectively meant that popular schools could choose pupils.

4. *More Bureaucracy.* The White Paper proposed the establishment of a new bureaucratic structure essentially duplicating functions previously performed by LEAs. A bewildering array of different schools and admissions procedures would create a cumbersome system complicating the task of parents seeking the best for their children.

5. *Privatisation.* The founding of independent trust schools represented an irreversible transfer of public assets into the hands of organisations subject to little public accountability (Denham *et al.*, 2005: 4–7).

6. *Recommendations.* The Alternative White Paper concluded with a series of recommendations including the strengthening of the strategic and regulatory role of LEAs, establishing the right of local authorities to set up new local community schools and creating a legally enforceable Revised Code of Practice on Admissions (Denham *et al.*, 2005: 9–10)

Added pressure was placed on the Government by unprecedented public criticism from former leader Neil Kinnock, who condemned the White Paper as 'at best a distraction and at worst dangerous'. It would 'lead to further fragmentation of our education system', with its array of specialist schools, trust schools and academies giving 'the appearance of choice [that] will not be available to many'. This fragmentation would 'have a damaging effect on schools, individuals and ultimately the level of educational performance' (*The Guardian*, 12 January 2006). The Government's embarrassment was then compounded by a highly critical report by the Audit Commission (the independent watchdog for public services in England) which expressed serious reservations about the White Paper and queried some of the fundamental tenets of the Government's strategy for widening educational opportunities. The White Paper (it commented) failed to grasp the contradiction between parental choice and cost-effectiveness since more choice meant creating surplus capacity (even more so if some new schools catered only to religiously defined sections of the population). Undermining the role of LEAs ignored the fact that schools were 'not self sufficient institutions' but required 'the strategic oversight and leadership' and clear lines of accountability provided by local authorities (Audit Commission, 2005a: 4, 6). Questioning the proposition that choice was an effective instrument for raising standards the Audit Commission noted that in much

of the country choice was 'neither realistic nor an issue of primary importance to parents'. There was an absence of 'the checks and balances necessary to secure equity of access and treatment of parents and children'.
Furthermore greater school freedom over admissions arrangements was
'more likely to work against the interests of the most disadvantaged, least
mobile and worst informed parents and children'. Rather than granting
schools more autonomy over admissions, it recommended that the Code of
Practice should be made binding and local councils should be made responsible for tracking admissions and appeals (Audit Commission, 2005: 4, 3).

Blair had little option but to compromise to mollify the massed ranks of
the critics. This was reflected in the final shape of the Act. On the one hand,
it enabled all schools to become trust schools by forming links with external
partners which (if the school agreed) could appoint the majority of the
Governing Body. Trust schools could own their own assets, employ their
own staff and set their admission arrangements (Department of Education
and Skills, 2006). They could also sift their intake by seeking reports from
primary schools on a child's conduct, motivation and attendance and even
on parental 'attitude' (Wilby, 2006a). On the other hand, under a strengthened Admissions Code selection of pupils by interview was prohibited and
schools were 'expected' to ensure their intake matched the social and class
mix of their catchment area; they would be barred from taking into account
a parent's marital, occupational or financial status, the pupil's behaviour or
attitude in other schools and their specialist interests. Local authorities
would be allowed to open new schools themselves, though subject to the
Education Secretary's veto, and retain considerable oversight over all
schools in the maintained sector while new trusts would get no extra funds
(*The Guardian*, 29 April 2006). The bill eventually passed in May 2006 –
though not before further extensive backbench protests including the largest
rebellion on a third reading since Labour first took office in 1924 (*The
Guardian*, 25 May 2006).

Education, social exclusion and meritocracy

Assessing the extent to which the Government is making progress in
achieving its objectives is no easy task and what follows is inevitably highly
tentative. It may be useful to distinguish between two such goals: the raising
of overall standards of educational attainment and promoting greater
equality of educational opportunity. These will be discussed in turn.

There is a broad measure of agreement that the rapid build-up of the
education budget, coupled with initiatives designed to raise standards in
educationally deprived areas (including substantial enhancement of pre-
school education) and the priority assigned to improving basic educational
skills have produced significant improvements in the overall quality of
education since 1999. Schools are better funded, better staffed, better
housed and given better facilities. The schools capital programme of

around £7 billion represents a ten-fold increase over 1997; revenue per pupil has increased by 50 per cent per pupil, teacher salaries have been substantially increased which, combined with new forms of recruitment, has brought an influx of top graduates into teaching.

By 2005 over three-quarters of children leaving primary schools had mastered the basics in English and Maths compared to a third in 1997, fewer secondary schools were failing, achievement for 14 year olds in core subjects had risen appreciably and school performance in deprived communities had progressed more quickly than the national average. For example 55 per cent of pupils in Birmingham left school in 2005 with five or more good GCSEs, compared with a third in 1997 (Department of Education and Skills, 2005: 7, 14–15). According to Ofsted the proportion of good or excellent teaching in primary schools jumped from 45 per cent in 1997 to 74 per cent in 2004 and from 59 per cent to 78 per cent in secondary schools. Not least there was an unprecedented programme of school refurbishment and rebuild under PFI schemes (Department of Education and Skills, 2005: 16). Some of Labour's most striking accomplishments (not reviewed here) have been in preschool education, including the provision of free nursery places for all 3 and 4 year olds; the Sure Start initiative targeting children under 3 and their families in disadvantaged areas; and its National Child Care strategy and its programme of Centres of Early Excellence (Lawton, 2005: 35). Other successes included higher standards, as measured by key stage tests, reductions in class sizes, literacy and numeracy hours and the introduction of citizenship education (the implementation of the Crick Report) (Johnson, 2004: 195–6). However the steady and sustained improvement evident most notably for the under-11s was not matched by older pupils with 'the story at age 16 and beyond', the IFS reported in 2006, being one 'of stagnation from around 2000 onwards' (Palmer, MacInnes and Kenway, 2006).

In terms of tackling the educational roots of social exclusion the record of the Blair Government has been impressive and certainly bears comparison with that of earlier Labour administrations. But, as we have seen, an equal priority has been to 'extend opportunities for all' in order to construct a truly meritocratic society. This requires that all children must 'have the same chance in life' and that 'every pupil – gifted and talented, struggling or just average – reaches the limits of their capability' (Department of Education and Skills, 2005: 20). To what extent does the evidence suggest that the New Labour education reform package is on course to deliver this goal? The Government contends that the impact of widening choice, more diversity, more competition and new providers would, by empowering all parents and not simply the more articulate and forceful middle class, contribute to the equalising of educational opportunities. Critics have countered that the logic of a quasi-market operating in a society in which income and wealth are apportioned in a highly unequal way would actually entrench rather than dilute middle class (or more accurately 'salariat')[5] advantage. Why is this?

Given the imbalance between the demand for and supply of places in high-achieving schools (ranked in terms of league tables), given, further, that in a rank ordering system such an imbalance is inherent and given, too, the ever-growing importance of educational credentials for career advancement, it follows that competition for scarce places is bound to intensify. Highly motivated middle class parents would naturally do their utmost to use the resources they command – in terms of know-how, communication skills, the social standing of their professions and so forth: 'cultural capital' for short – to secure a competitive edge. Furthermore not only would children from a 'salariat' social background have a competitive advantage in securing entry into the 'better' schools, but these schools themselves – benefiting from the imbalance between supply and demand – would be in a strong position to exert some choice over their pupil intake. As the Education Select Committee observed, 'the balance of power is slipping away from parents choosing schools for their children towards schools as admissions authorities choosing the children that they wish to admit' (Education and Skills Select Committee, 2005: 24). Given that research shows that 'selecting children whose homes are in high-status neighbourhoods is one of the most effective ways of retaining a high position in the league table' (Taylor, M, 2006) the more high-scoring schools would have a strong incentive to recruit pupils from a salariat background. Though pledged to block the extension of selection by ability the Government retained the policy, first introduced by the Tories, of selection by aptitude (in a specialist area of study) of up to 10 per cent of intake. In evidence to the Education Select Committee it claimed that selection by aptitude would increase choice by enabling 'young people with particular gifts and talents to have direct access to high quality specialist provision where over-subscription criteria might otherwise have ruled them out' (quoted in Education and Skills Select Committee, 2005: 26). However, the Education and Skills Select Committee doubted that aptitude (in the more academic subjects) could 'reliably be distinguished from ability at the age of 11' and reasoned that reserving places in an oversubscribed school for those with a particular aptitude meant denying choice and 'high quality provision' to pupils who might otherwise, on a catchment basis, have gained entry (Education and Skills Select Committee, 2005: 26, 29).[6]

Although judgement must inevitably be provisional, the evidence to date suggests the goal of greater equality of educational opportunity will, under present policies, prove elusive. Research reviewed by Professor Glatter indicated that 'competitive markets in schooling promoted social polarisation' with middle class families more likely to gain admission to significantly higher scoring schools (Glatter, 2004: Ev 6). Machin and Stevens similarly found that a 'quasi-market in education has actually reinforced existing inequalities in the education system. Children from lower income and social-class backgrounds ... are now even more concentrated in less-well-performing schools' (Machin and Stevens, 2004: 164; see also Harris and Ranson, 2005:

574). In an exhaustive review of the literature Taylor, Fitz and Gorard found that specialist schools with some autonomy over their admissions arrangements were less likely to admit pupils from working class backgrounds. For instance 43 per cent of specialist foundation schools and 57 per cent of specialist faith-based schools have become more middle class in intake over recent years (Taylor, Fitz and Gorard, 2005: 61–3). In general, 'LEAs with higher proportions of foundation, selective or specialist schools have higher levels of socioeconomic stratification between schools'. The real driver 'to a two-tier education system' appeared to be the combination of the '"specialist school" form of diversification with the "school autonomy" form of diversification, as represented by voluntary aided and foundation schools'. This was because specialist school status increased the popularity of a school which was then more likely to apply oversubscription criteria more favourable to the more able and (normally) more socially advantaged children (Taylor, Fitz and Gorard, 2005: 59, 61,66. See also Lawton, 2005: 146, 152; West, 2006). In Wales, where New Labour-style reforms had not been implemented, socioeconomic segregation between secondary schools was not only significantly lower than in England but continued to decline (Taylor, Fitz and Gorard, 2005: 66).

Evidence suggests that concentrating pupils from low income, disadvantaged backgrounds in the same school tends to create 'the kind of intake mix that has been shown to significantly influence a school's ability to improve its performance' (Harris and Ranson, 2005: 574). The Education Department's own review of performance data indicated no abatement in the link between social background and educational achievement (especially as measured by exam results) and no significant narrowing in the gap between schools with more or less disadvantaged intakes (Dyson, Kerr and Ainscow, 2006: 51). Given that 'the best educational achievement for the largest number of pupils will be achieved by having a broad social mix of pupils in as many schools as possible', academics from London University concluded, the outcome of the Government's choice and diversity strategy would be to diminish the *relative* educational prospects of poorer children (Taylor, M, 2006. See also Tomlinson, S, 2005: 175). The effect of extending parental choice in an educational market seems likely to 'reinforce the competitive advantage of middle-class parents, reinforcing … an emergent hierarchy and segmentation of schooling' (Harris and Ranson, 2005: 582). The result, in due course, would be a fall in social mobility (Taylor *et al.*, 2005: 59. See also Harris and Ranson, 2005: 572; Tomlinson, S, 2003b; Barry, 2005: 66).

Determinants of New Labour's education strategy

The Government – and the Prime Minister in particular – was prepared to invest considerable political capital, and run high political risks, in an ambitious programme of educational reform which broke sharply from party traditions and persisted with many of its predecessor's innovations. Why? Here we adumbrate a range of factors which played a part, though it is not as yet possible, given limits of documentary evidence, to assign any precise weights.

First, a decisive role was played in the shaping of education policy by the Prime Minister and his top aides. Blair exhibited a close and continuing interest in secondary education and most of the crucial initiatives in the choice and diversity agenda emanated from Number 10 rather than the Education Department. Two figures with a formative impact on policy were Andrew (now Lord) Adonis, Blair's education advisor who was later appointed an education minister, and Michael Barber, from 1997–2001 head of the Standards and Effectiveness Unit in the Department of Education and subsequently head of the Downing Street Delivery Unit (Seldon, 2004: 433; Smithers, 2005: 256–7). Adonis in particular was said to wield 'enormous power and influence in the formulation of New Labour education policy' (Chitty, 2004: 11). Blair, Barber and Adonis all shared a lack of confidence in the capacity of the comprehensive system – with its alleged 'one-size-fits-all' mentality and belief in 'uniform provision for all' – to raise standards and guarantee a good education for all, particularly the least advantaged and the most able. The misconceived effort to create equality through standardised education 'often produced deadening uniformity' (Blair, 2005).

Second, key policy-makers felt that there had been among earlier Labour governments too great a disposition to ignore the responsibility of schools for weak educational performance, especially among pupils from poorer backgrounds. They were unduly swayed by those in the teaching profession who held, one senior policy advisor observed, 'deeply pessimistic views as to the capacity of the educational system to improve standards with working class pupils'. Further, past Labour governments had shown insufficient determination to challenge those within the educational system who enjoyed 'massive vested interest in the status quo' (interview, 2007). New Labour, in contrast, was convinced that background disadvantage could be overcome by sheer effort within the schooling system. Well-resourced, properly monitored and effectively managed schools, with clear targets and appropriate incentives, and – not least – subject to tenacious parental pressures, could overcome social and economic disadvantage and very substantially bolster attainment (Tomlinson, S, 2005: 70). Here the very opposition reforms ignited from 'the forces of conservatism' within the education profession was seen as a positive bonus. Part of the problem of 'Old Labour' – so the reasoning ran – was that it was too closely associated with 'producer interests' in the public sector and too prone to defer to their wishes. 'Middle England' would be reassured that a Labour government was, at last, standing up to 'vested interests'. Such initiatives were guaranteed to elicit favourable mentions in 'Middle England's' favoured papers, the *Sun* and the *Mail*. As the Blair aide Peter Hyman observed, New Labour 'enjoyed the headlines that came from suggesting tough action on failure, pointing out that thousands of teachers were not up to it. ... It put us on the side of the anxious middle-class parent. It was part of our repositioning. It showed our reforming cutting edge' (Hyman, 2005: 270).

This brings us to a third point. The Government was convinced that a universal system of state education could only survive to the extent that it retained the confidence of the middle classes. Here the problem was growing middle class defection to the private sector. There was a fear that (as with the NHS) if the middle class deserted what they perceived as inferior state schools in large numbers their willingness to pay taxation to fund state education would also dwindle – and hence their propensity to vote Labour. The problem was especially acute in London. In July 2004 Education Secretary Charles Clarke expressed concern that while an average of 7 per cent of children were educated in private schools in England, the figure rose to 20 per cent or higher in parts of London. 'There is a significant chunk of people who go private because they feel despairing about the quality of education. They are the people we are after' (quoted in the *Guardian*, 9 July 2004). London was important for a range of reasons: because of its population size, because such a high percentage of people in the professional and managerial classes dwelt there, because developments and sentiment in the capital city were far more likely to be reported on television and in the press and hence set the political agenda, and because it held so many marginal seats. As the well-informed *Times* journalist Peter Riddell reported, 'Blair was particularly sensitive to the [educational] frustrations of middle-class people, notably in London' (Riddell, 2005: 103).

Conclusion

As Smithers points out 'it is difficult to reach a firm conclusion on the actual impact of [the Government's] educational changes because their effects will take a long time to really show through' (Smithers, 2005: 279). There can be no doubt about either the seriousness of the Government intent to tackle the often woeful weaknesses in schools provision (of which the more disadvantaged sections of the community were the main victims) and to develop a more equitable and higher-quality education system. Considerable resources have been ploughed into building new schools, improving facilities and recruiting new teachers by raising pay scales. Not least, a key aim had been has been to afford greater support for schools in poorer and more deprived communities.[7] Yet, at the same time, other policies appear to be having the effect of 'creating local hierarchies of schools' (Dyson *et al.*, 2005: 52). Taylor, Fitz and Gorard noted the apparent contradiction between 'fostering greater cooperation and networking between schools' as a strategy to raise overall standards on the one hand and the impact, on the other, of school choice and competition which discouraged collaborative efforts (Taylor *et al.*, 2005: 66. See also Pring, 2005: 84). For one critic 'the outcome was a structurally fragmented school system ... The public education system had become a franchised set of competing institutions democratically accountable to neither the public nor to their staff' (Tomlinson, S, 2005: 160). In part this reflected the multiple internal stresses and inconsistencies in the Government (interview, Fiona Miller, 2007). Thus the Education and Skills Select Committee, reporting in 2005, found it 'difficult to detect a coherent overarching strategy in the Government's proposals' and detected 'a number of policy tensions and contradictions' (Education and Skills Select Committee, 2005: 49). Not all ministers shared the single-minded zeal of the Prime Minister and his closest advisors for incessant and unflagging change, without pausing to consider what really worked. 'Despite the Government's proclaimed attachment to evidence-based policy,' the Select Committee added, 'expensive schemes seem to be rolled out before being adequately tested and evaluated compared to other less expensive alternatives' (Education and Skills Select Committee, 2005: 17).

Perhaps the heart of New Labour's predicament here lay in its bid to promote equality of opportunity while preserving the major differentials in rewards and wealth which – following the US model – it thought vital to ignite the spirit of enterprise and risk-taking essential to a dynamic and competitive economy. The Social Exclusion Unit noted that 'education plays a crucial role in explaining social outcomes and is especially important in accounting for long-range social mobility' (Social Exclusion Unit, 2004: 16, 84). But equally it pointed out that 'parental social class and educational attainment have a powerful influence over children's achievement at school'. Thus 'the social capital of the professional classes can provide their children with far greater opportunities than are available to children with a manual background' (Social Exclusion Unit, 2004: 84, 19). Writing in 2003 the Chief Inspector of Schools, David Bell, reiterated the conclusion of an earlier, 1993 report which stated that 'education by itself can only do so much to enable individuals to reach beyond the limiting contours of their personal and social circumstances and succeed' (quoted in Harris and Ranson, 2005: 575). Was the Blair Government, in seeking to combine equality of opportunity with conspicuous inequalities in outcome, trying to square the circle?

4 Is what matters what works?

The case of the Private Finance Initiative

Introduction

Perhaps the most oft-repeated of all New Labour formulations is the mantra 'what matters is what works'. New Labour believed in approaching issues 'without ideological preconceptions' and searching for practical solutions 'through honest well constructed and pragmatic policies' (Blair and Schroeder, 1999). To David Blunkett pragmatism meant an approach to policy-making 'guided not by dogma but by an open-minded approach to understanding what works and why' (quoted in Sanderson, 2003: 334). It makes decisions on the grounds of the merits of the case and the feasibility of all policy options grounded in a scrupulous investigation of their likely consequences (Temple, 2000: 320). It rests on a sharp distinction between means and ends. The Blair Government, the argument runs, has eschewed ideological formulae and displayed an agnosticism as to their ideological provenance.

This – it is argued – is best exemplified in its attitude to the provision of public services. The traditional Labour commitment to the state 'as the sole mechanism for provision and strategy in these areas has been rejected in favour of more pragmatic public–private partnerships' (Buckler and Dolowitz, 2000a: 311). Indeed 'the public–private model represents a focal point – a crucible almost – where the tenets of old and new Labour are exposed in their starkest form' (Reeve, S, 2006: 38). The most prominent policy innovation here is the Private Finance Initiative (PFI), described by the Government as the 'key element' in its 'strategy for delivering modern, high quality public services' (H M Treasury, 2000: 6). It emerged as 'a key attribute of the "New Labour" government's broad political strategy' (Greenaway, Salter and Hart, 2004: 519), the centrepiece of New Labour's pragmatic approach to 'the delivery of a higher sustainable level of public sector investment' (Robinson, G, 1998).

It was also one of the most contentious of New Labour's policy initiatives, arousing a storm of opposition within the labour movement. John Edmonds, general secretary of the GMB, warned that by his insistence upon the PFI strategy 'Tony Blair threatens to crack the foundations of the

Labour party. He has certainly tested the loyalty of Labour party members to destruction' (*The Guardian*, 10 September 2001). It was attacked both for 'creeping privatisation' and for imposing unacceptable costs on the public sector. 'Beyond the Iraq war' Kelvin Hopkins MP wrote, 'nothing has dismayed Labour supporters more than the government's relentless determination to privatise public services', notably its 'obsession with the private finance initiative' (*The Guardian*, 30 November 2006). A motion calling for an immediate moratorium was passed by the 2002 party conference, a rare defeat for the Government (*The Guardian*, 1 October 2002). According to Unison leader Dave Prentis 'the government is relentlessly pursuing a policy that wastes money, wastes time and fails any objective test of value for money'. Using PFI to pay for schools and hospitals was like 'paying for a mortgage through Barclaycard' (*The Guardian*, 19 September 2002). It was, former minister Michael Meacher averred, 'an exercise in down-sized semi-privatisation to dismantle the NHS' (*The Times*, 14 December 2004).

To a number of commentators, in contrast, the Blair Government's pursuit of the PFI reflected its determination to sweep aside outdated party shibboleths and take decisions on their merits. In the past (it is contended) Labour was stubbornly opposed to reliance on the private sector and market disciplines for supplying public services on grounds of dogma. It now exhibited a new willingness to set aside established ways of thinking and ground policy choice on a dispassionate analysis of the facts of the case. 'Old Labour' antipathy to the market has been replaced by a appreciation that, in some areas, 'the market works best'. It demonstrated a typically New Labour synthesis: 'practical judgement ... to be exercised within the context of a commitment to key values' (Buckler and Dolowitz, 2000a: 311). The PFI, in short, was the new politics of pragmatism in action. It reflected a 'pluralist approach to the delivery of public services' opening up 'established hierarchies without fetishizing market' (Bevir and O'Brien, 2001).

The prime purpose of this chapter is to explore, through the case study of the Private Finance Initiative, the nature of New Labour pragmatism. Was 'what mattered what works'? The next section examines the origins of the PFI, the principles underpinning it and the case the Government presented for its adoption. This is followed by a discussion of the case lodged by critics and an assessment of the relative merits of both sides of the argument. The final section seeks to establish the reasons for so vigorously embracing a policy that became 'ultimately a leitmotif of the Blair government' (Greenaway, Salter and Hart, 2004: 523).

The principles and goals of PFI

The Major Government launched the Private Finance Initiative in 1992. PFI contracts typically involve investment by a private consortium of construction companies, bankers and service providers contracting to finance, design, build, maintain and operate new public facilities (schools, hospitals, prisons etc.) which they then lease to the public sector, usually for periods of 25 to 35 years. The consortium provides finance and accepts some of the venture's risks in return for an operator's license to provide specified services to the relevant public body. Thus under the PFI the public sector 'does not own an asset, such as a hospital or school, but pays the PFI contractor a stream of committed revenue payments for the use of the facilities over the contract period' (House of Commons Library, 2003: 9). At the end of this period, the responsibility for the buildings will typically revert back to public control. It enabled public capital spending projects to be undertaken without adding to the Public Sector Borrowing Requirement (PSBR).

Labour initially denounced the PFI as 'totally unacceptable' and as 'the thin end of the wedge of privatisation' warning that (as applied to hospital building) it put the 'founding tenets of the NHS' at risk, and admonished the Tory Government for 'destroying by design or default the service people most value' (Margaret Beckett, shadow health secretary, cited in *Health Service Journal*, 1 June 1995; Labour Party, 1996: 280). In fact, when the Tories left office in 1997 the policy had languished with little progress made in signing PFI contracts. But by then Labour's initial hostility had been displaced by the zeal of the convert and its 1997 manifesto promised to 'overcome the problems that have plagued the PFI' (Labour Party, 1997).

It was as good as its word. The Blair Government set up and implemented the Bates Review (chaired by the businessman Malcolm Bates) which simplified the PFI process and swept away a range of legal and financial obstacles blocking its progress. Further, one of the first pieces of legislation passed by the new government was the National Health Service (Private Finance) Act which empowered NHS Trusts to enter into PFI agreements and (crucially) guaranteed financial payments over the life of the contract irrespective of public expenditure totals (Centre for Public Services, 2001). The effect 'was to provide a degree of momentum at the bureaucratic level that had hitherto been lacking' (Greenaway, Salter and Hart, 2004: 519). By 1999 the Government could present the 'revitalised PFI' as 'a key tool in helping provide effective and good value public services' (Milburn, 1999a).

A rapidly swelling proportion of public sector infrastructure projects were financed under PFI deals. In 1995 spending on PFI was a mere £670 million but by 2006 the Government had signed PFI projects worth around £40 billion and comprising 13 per cent of capital spending (Milburn, 2006: 13). By 2028 the huge sum of £110 billion, it was anticipated, would be absorbed by PFI payments. Alan Miburn pronounced the PFI 'a huge UK success story. We are blazing a trail that others will undoubtedly follow' (Milburn, 1999b). It was 'helping deliver the biggest hospital building programme the country has ever seen. ... hundreds of new and refurbished schools, alongside scores of fire and police stations, courts and prisons' (Milburn, 2006: 13). According to the Government the PFI was able to supply:

1. investment in the public infrastructure that would not otherwise have been possible;
2. higher quality projects; and
3. greater value for money (VFM). (Robinson, G, 1998)

There are in fact two arms to the case for PFI, the macro-economic and the micro-economic. The former holds that the PFI has made possible a scale of public sector investment – new hospitals, schools, prisons and many other facilities – that otherwise would not have been economically and financially feasible by providing a mechanism for a massive renewal of infrastructure without having to raise taxation or add to public sector borrowing. While borrowing to fund conventional public procurement was counted as adding to the public sector borrowing requirement, borrowing by the private sector of the same amount of money to finance the same investment, was not – even though the public body would be contractually bound to repay the private firm from its revenue budget. Because PFI spending does not count as capital spending it can be moved 'off balance sheet' (Sawyer, 2003). Thus it made possible high levels of public investment while conforming to Gordon Brown's strict fiscal rules, an essential pillar of the Government's economic strategy (Robinson and Dixon, 2002).

However, the crucial case for PFI was the micro-economic one. As the Chief Secretary to the Treasury explained, 'We use PFI where it offers best value for money – not to move public sector investment off balance sheet' (Smith, A, 2000). According to the Department of Education PFI schemes provided the public sector 'with better value for money in procuring modern, high-quality services from the private sector' (quoted in Audit Commission, 2003: 4). The crucial point levelled by critics is that PFI is actually more expensive because of the interest load burden it shoulders since public authorities can raise capital more cheaply in the financial markets than private concerns. The Government acknowledges that interest payments will be higher but counters that this will be more than wiped out by a host of compensating advantages: the efficiency gains deriving from commercially driven incentive to minimise costs, significant performance improvement through private sector innovation and management skills, synergies between design and operation and greater availability of private sector expertise and experience (Department of Health, 1999; Brown, 2003).

Better value for money is secured, the Government maintains, through a rigorous testing procedure. The Government insists that the PFI option was only selected over public procurement after a strict analysis of the relative costs. It is a comparative judgement: which promises better value for money, public procurement or PFI? All PFI schemes are compared with a notional publicly funded equivalent, the so-called 'public sector comparator', using an appraisal methodology 'under which the cash payments associated with each option are "discounted" and costs are adjusted to reflect "risk transfer"' (Gaffney, Pollock, Price and Shaoul, 1999b: 116). Initially the discount rate was pitched on the high side (at 6 per cent), lending the PFI option a favourable gloss, but this was later (after criticism) reduced to 2.5 per cent. However the crucial factor in determining whether PFI represents value for money is the amount of risk transferred. How much a private consortium receives under the terms of a contract is a function of the amount of risk transferred from the public sector, such as risks arising from construction cost overruns, design faults, higher than expected maintenance costs, unexpected variations in demand and so forth. The Department of Health stated emphatically that 'the majority of savings provided by PFI are due to risk transfer' (Boyle and Harrison, 2000: 22).

PFI: 'partnership that works'

PFI, Blairite outrider Alan Milburn confidently asserted, was 'partnership that works' (Milburn, 2006: 14). He cited National Audit Office figures indicating that whereas just 27 per cent of projects built under public procurement were delivered on budget, and 30 per cent on time, the comparative figures for PFI were 78 per cent and 76 per cent (Milburn, 2006: 14). But did PFI work? The case critics lodged against PFI can be analysed under four headings: competition, transaction costs, externalities and risk transfer. We review each in turn.

Competition

In conventional markets, the degree of competition is seen as a key determinant of efficiency, responsiveness and choice (Bartlett and Le Grand, 1993: 19). The PM's Strategy Unit pointed to the distinction between 'competition *in* the market' and 'competition *for* the market'. In the former case a range of providers continually compete with each other for the custom of individual users. In the latter case providers compete at one point in time when a contract to supply given services is up for tender, but not on an ongoing basis (Strategy Unit, 2006: 48). Competition for PFI contracts clearly takes this form. In such cases, the Strategy Unit stressed, 'competition will only succeed if there are enough alternative providers who are keen to provide services' (Strategy Unit, 2006: 54. See also Public Accounts Select Committee, 1999).

PFI contracts involve the public sector client specifying services which they wish to purchase and, through competition, selecting the most competitive bids. However, because of the sheer magnitude of the costs incurred by a potential contractor, the number of bidders involved in any one set of project discussions is usually very small. In four of the first fifteen PFI schemes to reach financial close there was only one final bid (Boyle and Harrison, 2000: 19). In the real world, the Treasury Select Committee pointed out, 'there is a trade-off between competition and the length and cost of [PFI] negotiations'. Few companies were large enough to cope with the large contracts and complex negotiating processes involved in PFI and the ongoing process of acquisitions and mergers was constantly reducing that number. Even where the procurement was competitive overall, the Treasury Select Committee added, the market 'may be too immature for competitive tension to provide value for money. ... In these circumstances, it may not be sufficient to rely only on competitive pressure to secure reasonable financing arrangements' (Treasury Select Committee, 2000). In its review, the Public Accounts Committee cited examples where there is only one bidder for the contract, or where the contractor raised the price after becoming the preferred bidder, and queried whether the taxpayer was 'always getting the best deal from PFI contracts' (Public Accounts Select Committee, 2003: 14).

Transaction costs

Transaction costs (in this context)[1] are the costs involved in arranging contracts. They include 'the costs encountered in drafting, negotiating and safeguarding an exchange agreement' and 'the costs of monitoring the outcomes of the exchange to check compliance with the exchange's terms after the transaction has taken place' (Bartlett and Le Grand, 1993: 27). Their magnitude has been recognised as a key issue in determining whether goods and services should be contracted out or handled in-house (Williamson, 1985). The more effectively contractual performance can be monitored and the more economically compliance can be enforced, the higher the chances of promised gains being made – a key point where contracts take the form of long-term binding agreements.

Thus transaction costs can vary very considerably according to the transparency and complexity of the services offered. If the delivery of a service or product can be easily prescribed and monitored, and the standard of the service provided measured with some precision, outside tendering may well make sense (Coulson, 1998: 30). The problem with PFI (critics reasoned) was that in a number of areas (e.g. the NHS) the negotiation and monitoring of contracts was almost invariably intricate, highly protracted and required a range of technical expertise that public bodies (such as NHS Trusts) lacked and had to purchase. But such expertise – in finance, law and accounting – is very expensive. Details obtained through Parliamentary Questions revealed that the advisors' costs of the first fifteen NHS PFI hospitals represented between 2.4 per cent and 8.7 per cent of the capital cost of the projects (Hansard, Written Answer, 28 February 2000, quoted in Centre for Public Services, 2001: 13). The Public Accounts Committee expressed 'alarm' in its report into the Dartford and Gravesham hospital contract that the Health Trust incurred costs from its advisors, KPMG and Nabarro Nathanson, which exceeded the initial estimates by almost 700 per cent (Public Accounts Select Committee, 2000). The NHS Confederation reported that NHS managers found negotiating PFI contracts to be slow, very costly, bureaucratic and immensely time-consuming (Health Select Committee, 1999).

Externalities

Externalities are costs (or benefits) external to the terms of a contract borne by (or accruing to) others who are not party to it. Thus PFI Value for Money analysis is conducted 'primarily in terms of benefits and costs to the purchasing public body, without regard to costs imposed on other public bodies' (Heald, 2003: 348–9). The argument advanced by critics here is that contractualisation, by its nature, ignores externalities and VFM analysis cannot catch the full costs of PFI. By focusing narrowly on costs and benefits within the terms of the contract it ignores wider needs whose formal responsibility lies with bodies or agencies not party to a contract, and thereby contributes to a fragmentation of overall service provision. An example would be adequate provision for the elderly, which requires close collaboration between suppliers of both primary and community care, responsibility for which is divided between the NHS and local government Social Service departments. As a result PFI obstructs the Government's professed objective of 'the planned delivery of health care across a full range of provision facilities' (Boyle and Harrison, 2000: 34).

Furthermore, by tying itself into 30-year contracts with specific PFI providers, the ability of the NHS to respond flexibly and efficiently both to changed patterns of healthcare needs and technologically different ways of meeting those needs has been curtailed. 'The fundamental flaw at the heart of the PFI scheme', a British Medical Journal editorial maintained, 'is its lack of flexibility' (Atun and McKee, 2005: 792). Changes in needs, technologies and treatments may, for instance, reduce demand for large acute PFI hospitals but the public sector will be contractually bound to a pre-set schedule of payments, reducing its ability to shift funds into other forms of health care (Dawson, 2001; Mayston, 2002). The Government itself began to question the value of the type of giant hospitals built by PFI. The 2006 Department of Health White Paper admitted that the days of the 'gleaming chrome and glass mega-hospital' were numbered and appeared to favour the revival of 'cottage hospitals' (*New Statesman*, 6 February 2006). The logic of the Government's policy of shifting care into the community could then render redundant many of the PFI super-hospitals well before the expiration of their contracts (Klein, 2006: 413).[2]

There are also broader and more long-term externalities. The Government insisted that, under PFI arrangements, 'while responsibility for many elements of service delivery may transfer to the private sector the public sector remains responsible for deciding, as the collective purchaser of public services, on the level of services that are required, and the public sector resources which are available to pay for them' (H M Treasury, 2000). But a growing share of the resources set aside for healthcare will be pre-committed, leaving less and less to the discretion of public authorities and democratic choice (Pollock, Shaoul, Rowland and Player, 2001). One of the first pieces of legislation passed by the new government was the National Health

Service (Private Finance) Act which guaranteed financial payments over the life of the contract irrespective of public expenditure totals. *The Financial Times* noted in July 1997 that 'future cash outflows under PFI/PPP contracts are analogous to future debt service requirements under the national debt, and, potentially, more onerous since they commit the public sector to procuring a specified service over a long period of time when it may well have changed its views on how or whether to provide certain core services of the welfare state' (*The Financial Times*, 17 July 1997). By the same token, if spending needs to be contained non-PFI expenditure would be disproportionately effected. Precisely this eventuality materialised with the NHS financial squeeze of 2006/7 when many of the hardest-hit trusts where those with PFI-built hospitals carrying heavy contractual commitments ('Health Funding' in *Private Eye*, 12 May 2006).

Risk transfer

Calculation of the amount of risk transferred to the private sector was normally crucial in determining whether a PFI deal was better value for money than standard public procurement. 'Transferring risks to the private sector,' Chief Secretary to the Treasury Andrew Smith explained, 'frees the taxpayer from unnecessary burden, creates a greater incentive for the private sector to deliver to budget and on time, and when they do, benefits the citizen – the consumer of public services' (Smith, A, 2001). But – critics queried – how accurate and objective were the costing estimations for risk transfer? To what extent did the financial terms of a contract correspond to the amount of risk actually borne by the contractor? And to what extent could the risks *in practice* (given statutory responsibilities and political realities) be off-loaded onto to private contractors? These issues – technical and political – are discussed in turn.

Prima facie evidence that payments for the actual amount of risk contractors were assuming were overly generous emerged with the development of new risk markets that allowed some PFI firms to capitalise on a 'risk premium'. As the Public Accounts Committee commented, refinancing in the form of changes to the debt or equity finance through the development of secondary markets during the life of the project was a normal feature of long-term projects. There was 'normally greater risk at the construction phase which, once completed, enables better financing terms to be obtained' (Public Accounts Select Committee, 2007: 3). The windfall gains made by some PFI consortiums in refinancing – deals under which they could borrow at lower interest rates and pocket the difference between the original and new financing costs – suggested that the original loan rates had substantially exaggerated risk exposure (*The Guardian*, 10 June 2005). The House of Commons Public Accounts Committee, investigating one complex refinancing scheme (involving increasing the level of borrowing and deferring repayment) discovered that the Octagon consortium responsible for the Norfolk and Norwich hospital contract made a windfall profit of £115 million, of which only £34 million was returned to the hospital trust. The refinancing scheme had 'lined the pockets of the investors', boosting their rate of return from 16 per cent to 60 per cent, and it was anticipated that the phenomenon would recur elsewhere (cited in *The Guardian*, 3 May 2006). Reporting in 2007 the Committee commented that some of these early refinancings 'had generated very high rates of return to the private sector investors and additional risks to the public sector in the form of higher termination liabilities and extended contract periods' (Public Accounts Select Committee, 2007: 3).

Some commentators have also queried the methodology by which risk exposure and transfer was calculated. 'Judgements about the relative importance of different kinds of risk,' David Heald, a leading expert in public finance observed, 'are likely to be crucial, for example the balance between construction risk, design risk, demand risk and residual value risk'. But those making the judgement were bound to be influenced by their appraisal of the alternatives. The Government clearly indicated that for many capital investment projects the option of public procurement was not really on offer. Public authorities in health, education and elsewhere were well aware of this and for this reason – in some cases at least – there was 'enormous pressure to make the numbers work out "right"' (Heald, 2003: 359, 347). In the oft-repeated phrase, 'PFI was the only game in town'.

Doubt also attached (according to critics) to the degree to which, in the real world, risk in large-sale public sector capital projects *could be* moved to the private sector. Former minister Michael Meacher contended that the transfer of risk to the private sector was 'a mirage. If a major PFI contractor went bankrupt, the Government would have little alternative but to bail it out.' On repeated occasions – the Channel Tunnel consortium, the Criminal Records Bureau, air traffic control, the Benefits Agency and the Passport Agency – the Government had had to pump in additional money (*The Times*, 14 December 2004). Blairite former minister Stephen Byers acknowledged that 'the private sector knows that whilst it might be able to walk away in many cases the government will need to step in' (Byers, 2003). 'It may be tempting for authorities to transfer as much risk as possible to the private sector,' the National Audit Office commented, 'but the ultimate business risk, that of delivering the public service, cannot be transferred' (Simons, 2006: 52. See also Lonsdale, 2005: 243; Shaoul, 2003: 193). In short, the final political responsibility and statutory duty remained with public authorities.

PFI: the balance sheet

The ultimate defence for PFI is that 'it worked', providing, the Chancellor claimed, 'the most cost-effective infrastructure for our public services' (Brown, 2003). Value for money, for the Government – which tended to take little account of considerations of transaction costs and externalities – was the overriding criterion for evaluating the success of PFI. Confining ourselves to this one yardstick, does the evidence suggest that PFI 'worked'?

Given the sheer range, diversity and scale of PFI projects, there is no easy answer to the question. The judgement of the National Audit Office – whose responsibility was to assess value for money – was that PFI had generally performed well in bringing projects into operation. In its investigation of PFI Construction Performance, the NAO found that projects had been completed 'with much greater time and cost certainty than had been the case under previous conventional procurement' (Simons, 2006: 48).[3] Its judgement of the *operational performance* was less enthusiastic. Here PFI's record was patchier – good on prisons – but less so elsewhere and especially poor on very expensive IT projects (Simons, 2006: 48, 50–1).[4] Early data suggested that significant efficiency gains in road and prison projects were not replicated for schools and hospitals (Allen, 2001: 32). An Audit Commission study comparing seventeen PFI schools with twelve built by traditional public finance found that 'the quality of the PFI sample of schools was, statistically speaking, significantly worse than that of the traditionally funded sample on four of the five matrices' (Audit Commission, 2003: 13). Equally, though it accepted that PFI did offer 'potential benefits' the study 'found no evidence that PFI schemes delivered schools more quickly than projects funded by more traditional ways' and 'did not as a matter of course guarantee better quality buildings and services, or lower unit costs' (Audit Commission, 2003: 21, 43).

The PFI appears to have performed least well in the NHS. The conclusions reached by Professor Mayston, a leading authority in NHS finance, in his memorandum to the Health Select Committee make sombre reading. The growth of PFI had pushed 'the NHS towards raising finance from the private sector via an inherently more costly route' which has encumbered public authorities with the 'substantial additional costs' incurred by 'contracting, negotiation, consultancy and potential litigation costs'. Furthermore, 'securing capital via the PFI route is itself likely to impose significant new risks upon the NHS' (Mayston, 2002). In June 2004 a report to the Government compiled by NHS chief executives stated that the PFI hospital building programme in England had produced poorly designed buildings, the wrong number of beds, often poor ventilation and insufficient flexibility to meet changing health needs (*The Guardian*, 22 June 2004).

In conclusion it may well be that it will prove more appropriate for some areas (roads, prisons) and less so for others (hospitals and perhaps schools). Equally there might well be a trade-off between short-term benefits in relying on the PFI (in terms of speed of construction, availability of use and cost savings) and longer-term policy constraints. The National Audit Office's overall conclusion, in 2006, was that while PFI was 'performing well in operation, there is no clear evidence of PFI's providing improved service delivery compared with conventional procurement' (Simons, 2006: 49).

According to senior Downing Street advisor Geoff Mulgan at least half of PFI projects did not in fact make a good deal of financial sense – though, he added, that was fairly typical of the outcome of exercises in policy experimentation (interview, 2006).

What is very plain is that the PFI was not self-evidently an instance of pragmatic, evidence-based policy-making: that it was chosen because 'it worked'. Indeed the well-connected economic journalist Bill Keegan reported in 2003 that he was 'struck by the way that even some of those officials who were most enthusiastic about the private sector partnerships at the beginning began to wonder whether ... the PFI had been worth the candle' (Keegan, 2003: 275). Why, then, did New Labour embark upon it with such enthusiasm? Why, indeed, did this verge (in Keegan's word) on an 'obsession' with PFI (Keegan, 2003: 269)?

Why PFI?

Economic factors

Greenaway, Salter and Hart attribute the emergence of the PFI to 'a rich mixture of forces: economic imperatives, ideological aspirations, party political calculations, complex bureaucracies ... and players from the private sector as well as "outside" parties' (Greenaway, Salter and Hart, 2004: 509). This section tries to unpick these forces.

As noted above, PFI spending was 'off balance sheet', meaning that debts incurred under PFI schemes did not add to the public sector borrowing requirement (PSBR). Though it would have been cheaper for public bodies to borrow directly from the capital markets (interest rates would have been lower) such charges would have had to be included in PSBR totals. PFI thus had the decided advantage of easing compliance with the Blair Government's fiscal rules, the so-called 'golden rule' that over the economic cycle current spending must be covered by revenue and not borrowing and the pledge that net debt should not exceed 40 per cent of the gross domestic product. According to the then Chief Secretary to the Treasury, Des Browne, (speaking in April 2006) if PFI projects had been brought on to the government books 'such movement on the balance sheet would put the country in a position in which it could not meet the sustainable investment rule and thus could not invest further in public services and our infrastructure' (quoted in *Private Eye*, 14 April 2006).

Whether this makes a difference in the long run is a moot point since PFI 'does not in the end provide a single penny of actual resource. ... Although the finance ... comes from the private sector all the funding comes from the public purse' (Health Select Committee, 2002: para 55). 'Off balance sheet' financing may have been (as Peter Robinson, senior economist at the Institute of Public Policy Research put it) 'little more than an accounting trick' (*The Guardian*, 3 October 2002), but as long as it did not add to government borrowing it fitted in well with Gordon Brown's insistence on sustaining a reputation for 'fiscal prudence' which, in turn, was vital in securing a crucial New Labour objective, winning the confidence of the financial markets. This goal was also facilitated by the fact that financial institutions were major benefactors of PFI projects. As McKibbin points out, under PFI 'higher spending has been accompanied by determined efforts to include the private sector in the rich pickings ... a goldmine not just for the contractors but for the lawyers and consultants who write the contracts' (McKibbin, 2007: 24). Indeed giving the money markets a vested interest in public spending programmes was an important part of PFI's appeal, as the Chancellor emphasised in 2000 when he reminded financiers that they would be investing in 'core services which the government is statutorily bound to provide and for which demand is virtually insatiable. Your revenue stream is ultimately backed by the government. Where else can you get a business opportunity like that?' (quoted in 'File on Four', 2004).

To this extent PFI had a symbolic as well as practical value. The claim that the criterion 'what works' drives the decision to opt for the PFT should not, perhaps, be taken too much at face value. As Brown's close associate Geoffrey Robinson (then Chief Secretary of the Treasury) told the BBC, 'it seems *quite axiomatic* to me that bringing together private capital, private building skills, together with public requirements and over all public oversight in these matters is a form of public partnership that *in principle* must commend itself' (BBC Radio 4 'World At One', 11 July 2002. Emphasis added). As a Treasury official closely involved with PFI told Keegan, 'it was a way of demonstrating they [New Labour] could do business with the City' (Keegan, 2003: 269).

Electoral factors

PFI, by the same token, fits neatly into New Labour political strategy. The concept of 'New Labour' hinged on a disassociation from 'Old Labour' with the entire penumbra of 'financial profligacy' this conjured up. Along with the decision to freeze public spending for 2 years the PFI can be attributed to 'fears that haunted New Labour' about past defeats and tabloid branding it as a tax and spend party. Brown's acceptance of PFI was thus 'a deliberate attempt to distance the Labour party from the past' (Keegan, 2003: 269). It allowed the Blair Government to uphold its muchcherished and hard-earned reputation for 'sound finance' while, at the same time, permitting a vote-winning unprecedented programme of hospital- and school-building. As Health Secretary Alan Milburn pointed out, 'in the end its [PFI's] compelling attraction as far as the National Health Service is concerned is that we can get more hospitals built more quickly' (Health Select Committee, 2002: para 94).

Whether this represents an optimal use of public funds is another matter. In effect future generations will incur long-term obligations for annual PFI payments – involving calls on tax revenues – for facilities which will primarily benefit the present generation. The exclusion of these obligations from the public sector balance sheet transferred the liabilities of the present generations of taxpayers to future ones (Mayston, 2002). 'Acquiring assets via the PFI is analogous to buying a house with a mortgage rather than paying cash for it up-front. You still have to pay for the house, one way or the other' (Sussex, 2001). However, there is a disjuncture between the repayment schedule and the electoral cycle for, long before the former has been completed, the politicians who claim credit for the massive public infrastructure building programme will have departed the political scene. It is notable that while there has been a rash of criticism from the trade unions, the medical profession and many experts – the country's leading health research institute, the King's Fund has pronounced the PFI-driven hospital construction programme as one of the Blair Government's 'few outright errors of policy' (*The Guardian*, 9 May 2002) – the PLP has been (in contrast to variable top-up fees and foundation hospitals) generally quiescent. As David Hinchliffe MP, the very independent-minded chair of the Health Select Committee from 1997 to 2005, candidly commented:

> I'm in a position where the hospital in my constituency is in a poor state of repair, we can't attract staff so if you know you'll have to wait much longer for a publicly-funded scheme then you'll go for PFI. I won't be around when the accountants tell us it cost us three times as much to have the PFI scheme and got us locked into a hospital structure which perhaps we won't want.
>
> (interview, 2004)

For Labour MPs the PFI is obviously 'the only game in town' and spanking new hospitals and schools in their constituencies is a sight that tended to quell all but the most restive spirits. The Government can claim (credibly) to be embarking on the largest hospital building programme in history without – it seems – placing unduly burdensome claims on the taxpayers purse.

Ideological factors

Yet it would be wrong to conclude that the policy is simply politically driven. Keegan noted New Labour's 'almost doctrinal obsession' with PFI (Keegan, 2003: 269). Equally Flinders concluded that 'the fact that Labour ministers are willing to proceed with these PPPs, often in the face of intense trade union opposition, demonstrates the centrality of this tool of governance within the New Labour project' (Flinders, 2005: 234), while Greenaway *et al.* see ideology as a 'driving force behind the new policy' (Greenaway, Salter and Hart, 2004: 517). Ideology, in this sense, refers to the New Labour operational code, or mind-set – its way of looking at and making sense of the world, its assumptions of what worked and why. A key factor here was New Labour's crisis of confidence in public service delivery. As a Treasury official who worked closely with Brown reflected:

> They had seen enough of the public sector at work to see that schools and hospitals went over budget, over time, and were not fit for that purpose. They had learnt from Mrs Thatcher that privatisation and contracting out produced better results.
>
> (Keegan, 2003: 269)

There is little doubt about Brown's key role in promoting PFI. Brown 'appeared passionate in his support for PFI' and threw his 'considerable political weight behind it' (Keegan, 2003: 286). It was taken more or less for granted that, by its very nature, the public sector was less efficient and effective in managing large projects because it has 'no incentive to make a profit or recoup the cost of capital'. As a result (the reasoning ran) there was an innate 'temptation to over specify, leading to gold-plated projects'. In contrast, under PFI private firms have 'every incentive for tight project management and the best use of capital' (HM Treasury, 1999a). Thus 'the "Jubilee Line overrun" became a mantra to be invoked when anyone questioned the supposed wonders of the PFI' (Keegan, 2003: 270). Former senior Downing Street advisor Geoff Mulgan recalled such thinking as a key factor driving policy on public sector procurement (interview, 2006). Keegan indeed wondered whether senior Labour figures like Blair and Brown have 'jump[ed] too far from an ideological belief in the powers of the state to a nai?ve belief in the wonders of the private sector' (Keegan, 2003: 275).

For the Government one of the virtues of PFI was the increasing inter-penetration between public authorities (central and local government, NHS Trusts and so forth) on the one hand and business concerns (private building contractors, financial institutions, accountancy and consulting firms) on the other. This would place at the disposal of the former the latter's managerial skills, expertise, entrepreneurial flair and drive. Thus in 1999 the Government readily accepted the recommendation by the Bates Review to set up Partnerships UK (PUK), a body 51 per cent of whose members were recruited from the private sector, charged with the task of engaging 'the private sector policy networks in the implementation of PFI on a systematic basis'. PUK became an increasingly influential conduit through which private firms could influence the determination of policy on issues of public procurement (Greenaway, Salter and Hart, 2004: 520). In short people who were 'not neutral referees but interested players' were located centrally within the decision-making system (Heald, 2003: 361).[5]

Not all have been enthusiastic about this trend. Not all are convinced of the benefits of delegating to 'private contractors too many decision-making powers affecting the interests and the welfare of citizens' (Vincent-Jones, 2000: 343. See also Broadbent and Laughlin, 2005: 93). Crouch warns that as leading companies become increasingly reliant on public sector contracts a premium will be placed on 'cultivating good relations with a few key decision-making individuals' with the result that 'the lobbying and temptations of mutual exchanges of favours become permanent' (Crouch, 2004: 96, 95). Indeed some officials have questioned 'the wisdom of the public sector becoming so reliant on [private sector] consultants' (Keegan, 2003: 275). Be that as it may, it seems that a new form of governance, characterised by the enmeshing of the public and the private, reflects an institutional logic embedded in the expansion of public–private partnerships. The growing entanglement between the two sectors, as exemplified most starkly by PFI, may be one of the Blair Government's most enduring legacies.

5 Modernisation in action
The case of NHS reform

Introduction

The future of the public services has been called 'the defining issue of our time' (*The Guardian*, 21 March 2002). Indeed Tony Blair described 'our second term mission' as 'the biggest reform programme in public services for half a century' (Blair, 2001a). Nowhere was this mission more energetically pressed or to prove more contentious than in the NHS. This chapter provides a case study in what was a crucial component in the New Labour strategy for public service 'modernisation': a radical overhaul of the National Health Service.

Healthcare is an explosive political issue.[1] It regularly tops polls measuring issue saliency. Neglect of the NHS was a principal cause of the Tories' downfall in 1997 and it was, undoubtedly, the issue upon which Labour most heavily relied to mobilise mass political support. The reason for this is that the NHS has been indissolubly linked in the public mind with the Labour party. Its creation was, Frank Dobson, Health Secretary from 1997 to 1999 proclaimed, 'Labour's greatest achievement. It is a working example of the best instincts of the people in this country. It is the most popular institution in Britain' (Dobson, 2003). It was, TGWU General Secretary Bill Morris declared, for Labour 'the jewel in the crown' (introduction to TGWU, 2002: 4). As Dobson's successor as Health Secretary, Alan Milburn, explained the NHS was 'in our blood. For many it is the touchstone of all that we stand for' (Milburn, 2003a).

Labour's 1997 manifesto warned that only the election of a Labour government could 'save the NHS'. The task the Government set itself was formidable for – even in less dilapidated systems – healthcare was under acute strain for economic, social and demographic reasons. In Britain, as in most Western countries, healthcare was the single most expensive item in the national budget and pressure on scarce resources was relentlessly intensifying. Rapid increases in longevity with its implications for widespread chronic illness (the average annual cost to the NHS of a person aged over 85 was, Gordon Brown calculated, approximately six times the cost for those aged between 16 and 44), the remorseless rise in the costs of medical technology and pharmaceuticals, the limited prospect for productivity gains in a highly labour intensive industry, all coupled with an insatiable demand for better healthcare meant that any government would be impelled to seek means to contain costs and utilise capacity more effectively (Brown, 2002b).

New Labour's objectives – reducing inequalities in access to healthcare, more rigorous systems of quality control and accountability, more patient involvement in healthcare in the delivery of services – were wholly in accord with party values. Many of the policies geared to putting these objectives in effect were greeted enthusiastically by its supporters. These included the creation of a Healthcare Commission to assess the performance of NHS institutions, a new regulatory structure to ensure that standards of care for conditions such as cancer and coronary heart disease were firmly evidence-based, the establishment of the National Institute of Clinical Excellence to assess the clinical and cost-effectiveness of treatment, and the creation of the National Patient Safety Agency (NPSA) to improve patient safety (King's Fund, 2005a: 10).

Despite the fact that in terms of both spending and outcomes the Blair Government's record easily bears comparison with its Labour predecessors since 1964, no domestic policy territory has been as bitterly contested within the party's ranks as its NHS modernisation strategy. As early as June 2001 David Hinchcliffe, Labour chairman of the Health Select Committee, warned that if pushed to its logical limits, its market-inspired reforms would amount to 'a complete betrayal of everything the Labour Party stood for' and 'would quite frankly cause outrage within mainstream Labour Party circles' (BBC Radio 4, 'On The Record', 24 June 2001). In 2005 more than two-thirds of *The Times* signatories to a 1997 statement backing Tony Blair's policies on health announced that they would not do so again. One signatory, Professor Vincent Marks, decried these policies as 'against the most fundamental principles of the NHS. Most of us feel that we have been badly let down. The dismantling of the NHS has continued apace' (EPolitix.com, 13 April 2005). Mounting disaffection within the party culminated in the passage of a resolution at the 2005 Labour party conference attacking the Government's move 'towards fragmenting the NHS and embedding a marketised system of providing public services with a substantial and growing role for the private sector'. Was 'an NHS driven not by patient need, but by profits and markets', Unison leader Dave Prentis demanded, 'really our vision?' (*Unison News*, 28 September 2005).

Why did reform of the NHS prove, as Driver and Martell observed, 'Labour's greatest domestic political challenge over two terms in power' (Driver and Martell, 2006: 120)? What were the key components of the NHS reform programme, what were its goals and for what reasons did it assume its specific shape? The first section of this chapter outlines the background to the formulation of what will be called New Labour's 'modernisation strategy'. The second, longer section analyses the key prongs of this strategy, namely choice, competition and private sector involvement – what they entailed, why they were introduced and why they proved so controversial. The final section assesses the debate over the impact of this programme. Did New Labour, as it pledged in 1997, 'save the NHS'?

Cost containment dominated the first two years of the Blair Government since the pledge to respect the Tories' spending plans denied the NHS any substantial replenishment. In terms of policy Health Secretary Frank Dobson, from the centre-left of the party, cautiously pursued a strategy of (in Powell's terminology) 'pluralism without competition' (Powell, 2003: 734). Labour had inherited a system which was moving – hesitantly and unevenly – towards 'managed competition' within the NHS, achieved by the creation of a purchaser/provider split in which health authorities were given responsibility for commissioning or purchasing services from a range of providers (Field and Peck, 2004: 256). However the so-called 'internal market' had proceeded tardily as an apprehensive Conservative Government was loath (for political reasons) to financially destabilise NHS Trusts.

Labour assumed power with a pledge to dismantle the internal market on the grounds that it had fragmented the health service, demoralised staff, widened inequalities, multiplied administration costs and reduced accountability – a view strongly held by Frank Dobson. The White Paper 'The New NHS: Modern, Dependable', issued in December 1997, espoused a 'third way' between the internal market and centralised control, based on partnership and collaborative working. The purchaser/provider split was maintained but long-term contracts were to substitute co-operation for competition. GP fund-holding was abolished, with their commissioning role assumed by Primary Care Groups (later Trusts) which were to compulsorily organise all GPs and community health providers. PCG/PCTs were to be responsible both for the provision of primary care and the purchase of secondary care services with the object of creating a primary-care-led NHS (Robinson and Bevan, 2002: 6; Powell, 2003: 734; Ham, 2004: 59). To this was added a determined effort to drive up performance by establishing national standards within 'a framework of clear accountability, designed to ensure that citizens have the right to high quality services wherever they live' (Office of Public Services Reform, 2002: 10). This entailed the development of a raft of targets and performance indicators and the establishment of quality-control and monitoring organisations (such as the Commission for Health Improvement – later incorporated into the Health Care Commission – and the National Institute for Clinical Excellence). The first phase of New Labour health policy thus signalled a retreat from the market and private sector involvement, more emphasis on co-operation and some decentralisation of decision-making, but within the context of the tightening of central regulatory mechanisms (Robinson and Bevan, 2002: 6).

However health policy-makers in this period were stymied by the self-imposed two-year moratorium on public spending. The decision to accept tight Tory spending plans – seen by New Labour strategists as an astute political move – reflected, Downing Street health policy advisor Simon

Steven recalled, a remarkable complacency about the effect of a strict diet-
ing regime on an anorexiç NHS already crippled by years of tight budgets
(interview, Simon Steven, 2006; see also Riddell, 2005: 51). The beds crisis
in the winter of 1999/2000 was a cruel awakening – 'absolutely dreadful' in
Milburn's words (interview, 2006) – with ministers swamped by an ava-
lanche of damaging publicity about clogged wards, elderly patients left for
hours on trolleys along hospital corridors and ever-swelling waiting times.
In Government circles there was 'the sense that the wheels were coming off'
(interview, Simon Stevens, 2006).

In January 2000, Tony Blair suddenly announced to bemused TV viewers
a major boost to the NHS budget designed, no less, to match average European Union levels of spending on health. In March 2001 Gordon Brown
set up a committee, headed by former senior banker Sir Derek Wanless, on
NHS funding. The 2002 Wanless Report concluded that a tax-funded
system was the most cost-effective way of financing a universal healthcare
system but that the NHS was seriously under-funded (Riddell, 2005: 105–6).
The Chancellor responded in his 2002 Budget by providing the largest ever
sustained increase in NHS funding. The result was an average annual
increase in real terms of 7.4 per cent between 2002/3 and 2007/8 taking total
net NHS expenditure from £55.8 billion in 2002/3 to £90.2 billion in 2007/8
(Department of Health, 2003: 4). Spending in real terms on health increased
between 1997–98 and 2002–3 by 6.3 per cent *per annum* and the Government
planned for gross NHS spending to rise to 8.2 per cent – the European Union
average – by 2007–8. This increase in investment in the NHS – used to improve
salaries and pay for more staff, equipment, buildings and medicines and in
part financed by a 1 per cent increase in both employer and employee national
insurance contributions – was unprecedented (King's Fund, 2005a: 19).

But the Government had become convinced that money was not the sole
answer. Ministers and key advisors feared that much of the new money
would be dissipated by weak management, stubborn resistance to more
efficient work practices and vested interests. Although really substantial
extra resources would not start flowing into the system until 2001 there was
a feeling that the additional funds which had entered the system in April
1999 had not been matched by a commensurate improvement in performance (communication from Simon Stevens, March 2007). Once the decision had been taken to pump more money in the Health Service, Simon
Stevens, Downing Street's senior health policy advisor at the time recalled:

> The terms of debate changed dramatically as the issue of getting value
> for money assumed decisive importance. The period between 2000 and
> 2002 was pivotal for it became increasingly clear that the additional
> resources made available were not being translated into more opera-
> tions and falling waiting times. The system was absorbing cash without
> producing results. Hence new incentives were needed.
>
> (interview, 2006)

What is significant is, as former Director of the Health Department's Strategy Unit, Chris Ham, later recalled, that this conclusion was reached despite the fact that sufficient time had not elapsed to determine whether policies in operation were not working. It was in part a result of the sheer impatience of ministers, quite inexperienced in managing change in large and complex organisations, who fretted if policies did not immediately deliver results – who always had an eye to the headline-grabbing potential of new initiatives (interview, 2007). But at the heart of the policy shift lay something more fundamental – a loss of faith in the capacity of the NHS to sustain long-term improvements in both cost-efficiency and the quality of care without drastic reform. Centrally defined targets and strict performance monitoring, Milburn reflected, were short-term measures designed to prod the lumbering NHS into action. 'We had to put in place,' he explained, 'a command and control system' – with central standards, inspection and so forth – to tackle the alarming problems (especially of massive waiting times and lists) inherited from the Tories. But this afforded no long-term solution. 'There was only so much you could achieve,' Milburn added, 'by finger-wagging and instructions. We had to move to a system that was sustainable in its own right' (interview, 2006).

Unravelling the internal market had been a mistake: indeed (it was now felt) the Tory failing was less that it had been introduced than that it had been introduced with insufficient verve and determination (interview, Milburn, 2006). 'There was a perception,' Stevens' successor as Number 10 health policy advisor Julian Le Grand recollected, 'that command and control had reached its limits' (interview, 2006). What was required was the embedding within the NHS's organisational fabric of incentives for relentless service improvement, and this could only take the form of reconstituting an internal market through a combination of patients' choice, competition and diversity. The result was a step-change in policy, first floated in the major policy document the NHS Plan (published in 2000) but taking firmer form in the 2001 consultative document entitled 'Extending Choice for Patients' (Greener, 2003: 57).

New Labour policy mark 2: 'modernisation' in action

Unlike its predecessor the Blair Government was wholly committed to the notion that the state had an obligation to provide healthcare to all on the basis of need – and, crucially, it was prepared to meet the price tag. The increase in investment in the NHS since 1999 has been greater than during any other period in the last 30 years. There was little disagreement between the Government and its critics over values and goals: fostering greater equality in access to treatment, improving efficiency and value for money within the NHS, raising the quality of care and promoting the capacity of the NHS to meet the general healthcare needs of the population. What was new and distinctive about New Labour were the methods used. The three key innovations, defining New Labour-style 'modernisation', were choice, competition and private sector involvement in the delivery of NHS services.

1. Choice was pivotal to the Blair Government's drive to transform the NHS from a 'provider-led' to a 'patient-led' service.
2. Competition was essential both to ensure choice and to prod providers into increasing efficiency and rendering them more responsive to their patients. Competition, in turn, required a system of financing in which money would follow the patient. The system was soon dubbed Payment by Results (PbR) though, strictly speaking, it was payment by activity.
3. Competition, in turn, if it was to act as a real spur to innovation and efficiency required new entrants to the market. The recruitment of new providers from the commercial sector would not only enlarge choice and raise capacity but intensify pressure on NHS producers to raise their game – or lose business.

In combination these reforms, experts have agreed, amounted to 'a dramatic break with the pre 1997 election stance' and 'the most radical departure from previous Labour policy' (Robinson and Bevan, 2002: 7; Glennerster, 2005: 287). Each of them will now be discussed in more detail.

Choice

By the beginning of the Blair Government's second term in office the concept of choice had emerged as a crucial organising principle of its public sector strategy. Traditionally Labour governments had reposed considerable faith in the benign effects of the enlightened state. The standard social democratic approach to public services favoured uniform provision in which professionals, on the basis of their expert determination of health needs, would decide on the most appropriate forms of treatment. 'Assumptions of professional expertise and standards reinforced by the orderly controls of rational bureaucracy were the defining conditions of the social democratic state' (Ranson and Stewart, 1994: 11). In *The Socialist Case*, published in 1937, the Labour thinker and politician Douglas Jay had written 'in the case of nutrition and health, just as in the case of education, the gentleman in Whitehall really does know better what is good for people than the people know themselves' (quoted in Nuttall, 2006: 58).

To New Labour this mode of thinking smacked of elitism. The 1945 settlement was (in Tony Blair's words) 'largely state-directed and managed, built on a paternalist relationship between state and individual, one of donor and recipient, [one in which] personal preferences were a low or non-existent priority' (Blair, 2002a). Centralised bureaucracies delivering uniform services rendered public organisations unresponsive to shifting public preferences, barnacled them to old habits and solidified structures in which producer interests too often took precedence over consumer needs. The public, Health Secretary Alan Milburn reflected, 'were supposed to be truly grateful for what they were about to receive. People expected little say and experienced precious little choice' (Milburn, 2003c). In Le

Grand's terminology service-recipients were treated as 'pawns' (Le Grand, 2003: 6).

New Labour envisaged a health service 'shaped around individuals' needs and preferences' and characterised by 'greater choice and shared decision-making between patient and clinical team over treatment and care choice' (Department of Health, 2004: 27). Choice, when coupled with voice, would, the PM's Strategy Unit opined, 'allow users to become more assertive customers and help to ensure that public services respond more promptly and precisely to their needs' (Strategy Unit, 2006: 65). The patient as 'pawn' would be replaced by the patient as 'queen' – as 'citizen-consumer' or 'active choice-maker' (Clarke, Smith and Vidler, 2005: 174). Only such an approach, it was argued, could realise traditional Labour aims – equity and high quality services responsive to patient needs delivered in a cost-effective manner – which the traditional approach had conspicuously failed to deliver.

What did choice actually mean? The Government sought to promote the following types of choice:

- over the quantity or quality of a service;
- over the specific form or content of the service, for example the type of treatment;
- through personalisation by tailoring services to fit the specific needs and preferences of individual users;
- between alternative providers, for example between an NHS or an independent sector hospital.

(Strategy Unit, 2006: 63)

A range of initiatives were taken after 2001 to give effect to this programme. For example heart surgery patients who had been waiting more than 6 months were given a choice of treatment in hospitals nationwide, in the private sector and even abroad. All patients were given the right to book a convenient time and place for their treatment after they had been referred to hospital by a GP (Appleby, Harrison and Devlin, 2003: 6). By 2005 patients requiring elective surgery were offered a choice of four to five providers – one of which had to be from the private sector – on referral, the menu of choices decided by the Primary Care Trust. By 2008 it was planned that all patients would be able to choose between any healthcare provider provided the price was reasonable and the quality met NHS standards (Department of Health, 2006: Ev 3). All these various measures were designed, as Health Secretary John Reid put it, to engineer 'no less than a change in the working culture of the NHS' so that patients were treated with the same promptness and respect that (it was assumed) they received as consumers of private goods and services (*The Guardian*, 29 August 2003).

Labour's market-oriented reforms signalled, the left-wing think-tank Catalyst maintained, a philosophical shift, 'a move away from the pursuit of equality to an agenda of consumer choice and preference; citizenship entitlements become defined in terms of the opportunities available to individuals in markets' (Mohan, 2003: 2). Yet, as Klein comments, 'it would be difficult to find a healthcare system in Western Europe where choice is not both seen as desirable and taken for granted' (Klein, 2005: 59). Indeed it is not at all clear that the advocacy of choice (in the wider sense of the term) per se represented the breach with social democratic values portrayed by some critics. 'The key issue concerning choice in the NHS,' the health policy research institute the King's Fund commented, 'is not whether choice is indisputably a bad thing or a good thing, but more an empirical question of where choice (and what type of choices) can bring benefits where the cost of doing so is judged acceptable' (King's Fund, 2005a: Ev 62).

In truth, much of the controversy aroused by Government reforms revolved less around the issue of choice per se than over its impact, especially on equality. The insertion of choice, its left-of-centre critics claimed, would inevitably widen health inequalities. 'The articulate and self-confident middle classes,' Hattersley contended, 'will insist on the receipt of the superior services. The further down the income scale a family comes, the less likely it is to receive anything other than the residue which is left after others have made a choice' (Hattersley, 2005: Ev 18).

The Government's response was that critics ignored the dismal failure of the NHS to tackle health inequalities. Since its inception, Health Secretary Patricia Hewitt declared, the NHS had been bedevilled by 'shocking inequalities in health and care' (Hewitt, 2005b, 2006b). These disparities – the reasoning ran – were a direct consequence of the absence of choice. The more articulate, knowledgeable and confident were more likely to be listened to and receive sympathetic consideration from medical staff (Le Grand, 2006a: 11). 'In the absence of choice,' Alan Millburn maintained,

> the ones who come out worst are the poorest because they haven't the option of paying, they don't know how to work the system, the least articulate. Why did they get worst treatment? Because they have very little power. Choice is a means to get the best service to those least well served under an ostensibly socialised system.
>
> (interview, 2006)

Inequality was, in short, in-built in the old-style NHS. Denying choice, Downing Street health policy advisor Julian Le Grand observed, 'meant that providers who offered a poor or a tardy service could continue to do so with impunity for those badly treated had nowhere else to go' (Le Grand, 2006a: 5). Or, rather, only the less well-healed did, for the ability of higher income groups to purchase medical services meant that they had access to choice denied to those who were solely reliant on the NHS. The same consultant not available for an appointment for months on the NHS could magically be made to materialise – by a private insurance premium – at a time that suited the patient. Government proposals extended to all choice which previously had been the prerogative of the rich. Ministers accepted that to make effective choices patients needed to be better informed. 'Knowledge,' Milburn commented, 'is power. To make choice work, the NHS will need to provide reliable and relevant information to patients in a way people can understand' (Milburn, 2003b). This the Government sought to do by disseminating information about the performance of providers (in the form of quality standards and outcomes, inspections, monitoring and evaluation) and by appointing choice advisors to guide patients.

Competition and payment by results

A degree of choice has always existed within the NHS, for example of GPs, maternity hospitals and (prior to Tory reforms) of specialists. But for choice (as the Government envisaged it) to work effectively producers must learn to compete for custom. 'The crucial point in generating sustained improvement in service quality,' a senior Number 10 policy aide emphasised, 'is having competition, some from private sector, most within public sector' (interview, 2007). The reason for this, Prime Ministerial health adviser Julian Le Grand explained, was that many of the serious weaknesses from which the NHS suffered – inefficiency, unresponsiveness, slowness to innovate, inequity – stemmed less from want of cash than from monopoly provision. He recalled:

> When I was working at No 10, I lost count of the number of times people came to me with often what seemed to be brilliant and innovative ideas, but incredibly frustrated by their inability to get the NHS even to try them out – let alone adopt them across the service. Simply demonstrating good ideas or good practice or even publicising them were not sufficient: the incentives for adoption were not there.
>
> (Le Grand, 2006a: 3)

In the private sector competitive pressures imparted relentless pressures to curb costs and deliver better value services, more flexibly and to a higher standard. If private firms failed to respond to 'the immediate needs of demanding consumers,' Blair pointed out, 'they go out of business. They know that poor service, lack of courtesy, massive delays, destroys their image and their success' (Blair, 2001a). Where the consumer was sovereign the producer must take heed. The public sector, in contrast, had no incentive to improve. It could not deliver 'even when its mouth was stuffed with gold' (Le Grand, 2006a: 4). Monopoly empowered producers at the expense of consumers. Without some form of external pressure clinicians lacked the motivation to adopt more efficient practices and even if they were proposed they were likely to encounter formidable resistance from vested interests or be bogged down in Byzantine bureaucratic negotiations. Without the spur of competition, public organisations tended to succumb to bureaucratic

inertia, a wasteful use of resources, rent-seeking behaviour, weak management and organisational arrangements designed to procure a more comfortable and rewarding life for public servants rather than those they served
(Le Grand, 2006a: 5).

The major policy instruments selected to help deliver a more competitive
system in which choice would flourish were:

1. Entrenching and extending the provider–purchaser split;
2. Giving greater autonomy to good providers;
3. Money following the patient (payment by results).

Entrenching the provider–purchaser split

The provider–purchaser split was introduced by the Conservatives and largely
retained by Labour in 1997. The purchaser was given the responsibility for
planning and commissioning services involving, inter alia, the determining
of local needs and priorities, the choice of the providers to use, the designing and negotiating of contracts and the assessment of clinical quality
(Lewis and Dixon, 2005a: 16). The provider supplied the services contractually negotiated with the commissioners. In 2002 303 Primary Care
Trusts (PCTs) were created, controlling around 80 per cent of the NHS
budget, with responsibility for providing primary health care and commissioning secondary care services. A further shift in policy occurred when the
Government decided to devolve commissioning powers to general practice
level with the development of Practice-based Commissioning (PbC). From
April 2005, all practices have had the right to commission care for their
registered patients using an 'indicative budget' in which, though commissioning resources remained formally under the control of the PCT, power to
allocate these resources was passed to practices (Lewis and Dixon, 2005a:
5). PbC's objectives were to give GPs more freedom to respond to patient
need, to entrust them with more responsibility for the public money they
spent and to give them an incentive to provide treatment at the primary
level – with the object of expanding community-based services – rather than
the more expensive secondary care sector (Hewitt, 2005b; Blair, 2006).

Giving greater autonomy to good providers

The value of a provider–purchaser split was broadly accepted within the
party. The next Government initiative was not. By 2001 the faith that the
Government had exhibited in its first few years in the capacity of a flood of
centrally driven targets to achieve its goals had begun to wane and it began
to espouse a new 'localism' to release local initiative and encourage more
responsiveness to local communities (Hunter, 2005: 210).

Decentralisation took a number of forms but, within the secondary care
sector, the most important was the setting up of Foundation Trust hospitals.

The powers and status of Foundation Trust hospitals can be summarised thus:

- They were given access to increased financial freedoms, including the freedom to borrow capital, sell off assets and retain surpluses.
- Department of Health controls were eased and the trusts awarded greater management freedoms, including increasing flexibilities to reward staff.
- A new, more decentralised, form of governance was instituted with a Board of Governors elected in part by local communities.
- Foundation status would take the form of 'earned autonomy'. All NHS trusts which had received a 'three star' rating – demonstrating high clinical standards, effective leadership and sound finances – were eligible to apply for Foundation Trust status.
- Foundation trusts remained part of the NHS. A legal lock on their NHS assets was installed ensuring their continued use for NHS patients and the proportion of the income they could earn from private patients was capped.

(Health Select Committee, 2003: 5; Milburn, 2003a)

The measure ignited in 2003 the biggest backbench rebellion to date. Foundation Trust status, critics claimed, would establish a two-tier system in which some hospital trusts would be better resourced than others, thus widening health inequalities, health services would become fragmented, care in the community downgraded and money squandered in yet another reorganisation.[2] The Labour-run Health Select Committee warned that Foundation Trusts, because of their stronger resource base, would be able to attract more custom, and with money following patients, 'poorer performing hospitals will see their revenue streams dry up ... locking them into a downward spiral of poor performance that may ultimately culminate in their closure' (Health Select Committee, 2003: 41). Opposition to the proposal steadily built up in the PLP, led by Frank Dobson and Labour chairman of the Health Select Committee, David Hinchliffe, with no less than 124 Labour backbenchers signing a critical motion.

To the Government these criticisms reflected a fundamental misunderstanding of the role and purposes of Foundation Trusts. Owned and controlled by and accountable to local communities, unequivocally not-for-profit organisations, 'wholly part of the NHS' and 'subject to NHS standards and inspections', they represented 'a new model of public ownership, firmly rooted in the cooperative and mutual tradition' (Milburn in *The Guardian*, 14 March 2003). Blair and Milburn, however, found themselves caught in a pincer attack as left-wing and trade union critics were joined by the Chancellor. Milburn was keen to maximise the financial autonomy of foundation hospitals by giving them complete freedom to borrow from the private sector, to buy and sell assets and to boost their income from commercial ventures. Brown's objection was three-fold. First, he was not prepared to grant foundation hospitals the right to accumulate liabilities for which the

Treasury would ultimately be responsible: this would jeopardise public spending discipline. Second, he was worried that foundation hospitals would have an incentive to maximise income from private patients, threatening the integrity of the NHS. Third, he feared that Foundation Trusts would financially destabilise PFI, since PFI-built hospitals would be contractually bound to service and rental payments to the private sector irrespective of income.[3]

The outcome of protracted negotiations was a compromise. It was agreed – as Blair and Milburn wanted – that foundation hospitals would be independent of Whitehall direction with ownership and control over their own assets and with powers to borrow from both public and private sources. But Brown ensured that borrowing would come off departmental expenditure limits, competing with other commitments (Peston, 2005: 296–7, 301–2). In addition restraints were placed on the freedom of foundation hospitals to treat private patients and vary pay rates (*The Guardian*, 14 March 2003; Dixon, 2003a: 1344).[4] However the various concessions were not sufficient to dispel widespread anxieties. A rebel amendment was defeated by only 286 votes to 251 and the bill scraped past the Commons with a majority of 17, the lowest since 1997. The bill only survived on the back of votes from Scottish Labour MPs, despite the fact that it would not apply to – and foundation hospitals had been rejected in – Scotland (*The Guardian*, 8 July 2003 and 26 November 2003). The wider party also signalled its opposition when Conference passed a motion condemning foundation hospitals – only the third conference defeat Blair had suffered since becoming party leader (*The Guardian*, 2 October 2003).

Despite the passions ignited, the furore over Foundation hospitals in due course abated: 'who now talks about them?' Alan Milburn reflected a little later (interview, 2006). Part of the reason why interest waned may be that the issue was overshadowed by yet more controversial ones: the introduction of payment by results and commercial provision of NHS services.

Money following the patient (payment by results)

The institution of an effective market, the Government recognised, depended on the introduction of a system in which money followed the patient. Traditionally hospitals had been financed by block grants unrelated to either the quantity or quality of their work. Under this system, the Prime Minister averred,

> There were no financial incentives to treat more patients, nor for hospitals to cut their costs. This meant that the inefficient hospitals would have little incentive to improve. If they overspent they would be baled out. Nor was there any incentive to be efficient since, if you were, the resource that you gained would be taken from you and given to a hospital that was overspending.
>
> (Blair, 2006)

Real competition for custom would only be embedded if funding for activity followed individual choice. Hence perhaps the single most far-ranging measure in health policy introduced by the Government – the reform 'which makes everything else possible' (Timmins, 2005a: 1141) – was a system of payment by results (PbR) first unveiled in the 2002 policy statement *Delivering The NHS Plan*. Under PbR existing block contracts were to be replaced by specific contracts based on agreed levels of activity with a national tariff of set prices for different procedures, whereby hospitals were paid a fixed amount for each medical intervention (e.g. a hip replacement).[5] These tariffs would be based on the national average cost for each activity, though account would be taken of variations in costs arising from, for example, higher salary costs in London (Appleby and Jobanputra, 2004: 196). The introduction of a set national tariff was designed to remove the need for time-consuming price negotiations and focus discussion on the quality of care (Department of Health, 2004: 70). Given that they controlled over 80 per cent of the NHS budget, PCTs would (it was envisaged) have an incentive to avoid inappropriate admissions to hospital, thereby releasing resources for other purposes such as improving the quality of care for those with chronic and long-term conditions (Department of Health, 2004: 70).

PbR was introduced in stages. Implemented for acute inpatients in some areas in April 2004, the following year it was extended to elective activity in all NHS trusts, then to non-elective and outpatient care and by 2006 to the 80 per cent of hospital admissions that were unplanned emergencies (Audit Commission, 2005b: 3).

PbR's prime purpose was to reward the successful and exert 'consumer' pressure on poorly performing hospitals. It did not amount (as sometimes alleged) to straight marketisation. In markets price signals guide consumers in making purchase decisions and the organisation of supply responds to purchaser preferences. In the internal or quasi-market patients did not directly pay for services. Rather these were purchased on their behalf by public authorities on their estimations of need and hence would not be driven by consumer demand (Powell, 2003: 726). Equally, the price mechanism did not direct the flow of services and resources since the national tariff for procedures meant that providers could not compete over the cost of treatment. But PbR did seek to capture the benefits of competitive markets. Competitive pressures would impart, the Health Secretary claimed, 'a very sharp incentive for hospitals to improve the quality of care they provide – and an equally sharp challenge to the medical profession to change old vested interests and protective practices if they are holding back patient care' (Hewitt, 2005a). Whatever the uncertainties about how the system would operate in practice there can be little doubt that PbR constituted a 'financial revolution' which would have profound effects on the operations of the NHS' (Appleby and Jobanputra, 2004: 195).

Involvement of the private sector

Of all New Labour's health policies 'the most contentious ... highly politicised and emotionally-charged' has been the institutionalisation within the NHS of private provision of public healthcare ('File on Four', 2006). Labour's 1997 manifesto made it clear that it was opposed to the use of the private sector in the supply of clinical services. Three years later its position had been reversed with the signing of the 'Concordat' with the Independent Healthcare Association which encouraged the active participation of the commercial health sector in the delivery of NHS care. The recruitment of commercial suppliers was initially presented as a hard-headed, practical solution to the problem of massive waiting times and lists – the precipitating factor being the 1999–2000 winter's heavily publicised bed crisis (*The Observer*, 19 November 2000; *The Guardian*, 25 October 2001; *New Statesman*, 13 August 2001). Milburn emphasised that healthcare would still predominantly be supplied by the NHS: 'our policy is about not creating a mixed economy in healthcare in this country' (*The Guardian*, 30 May 2001).

However it soon became evident that this was precisely what the Government had in mind. The key policy initiative was the commissioning in December 2002 of so-called 'Independent Sector Treatment Centres' (ISTCs). The Government had already agreed to the development of NHS diagnostic and treatment centres which, free of the responsibility for emergency surgery, would be able to concentrate on carrying out elective procedures. This was widely welcomed. The ISTC initiative was far more of a challenge to existing practices. Under ISTC agreements private providers were contracted to carry out relatively simple, high-volume surgical procedures, initially in the fields of ophthalmics and orthopaedics. The first ISTCs began operating in 2003 and a second procurement wave followed two years later with the intention that the private sector would provide up to 15 per cent of all affected procedures by 2008 (Health Select Committee, 2006a: 7; *The Guardian*, 26 January 2005).

In embarking on this initiative, the Government was throwing down the gauntlet to party traditionalists (and many within the NHS too). A willingness to accept that 'NHS healthcare no longer needs to always be delivered exclusively by line-managed NHS' organisations and to recognise commercial supply of NHS healthcare as 'a permanent feature of the new NHS landscape' amounted, as Health secretary Alan Millburn acknowledged, to nothing less than a 'fundamental change' in outlook (*The Guardian*, 25 May 2002). There appeared to be two interconnected reasons for this change. First, the Government was persuaded that only with the recruitment of fresh and eager entrants could a truly competitive market capable of pressurising NHS hospitals to adopt more productive and effective practices be created (Department of Health, 2006: Ev 2–3; Strategy Unit, 2006: 54).[6] The effect of the spread of ISTCs would be, Health Secretary Patricia Hewitt contended, to 'incentivise' the spread of best practice and innovation throughout the whole service by placing NHS providers under commercial pressure (quoted in Health Select Committee, 2006a: 23).

In its memorandum to the Public Administration Select Committee the Government spelt out the logic of its case:

> Looking at the case of choice of provider, those providers who are not chosen have a strong incentive to raise their game. They will have to improve the quality of their service (at least in the eyes of the users), to increase their responsiveness to the users' expressed needs and wants, and to use their resources more efficiently so as better to attain these ends.
>
> (Public Administration Select Committee, 2005a: 39)

This takes us to the second reason for the policy shift. Exposing NHS hospitals to the harsh and chastening blast of competition was designed to achieve two interlinked objectives: to weaken the entrenched power of consultants and their professional organisations over the organisation and practices of the NHS, and to impel consultants to commit more of their time to the Health Service. The problem of professional power in the NHS had dogged Labour governments ever since (to rally the support of the Royal Colleges) Bevan had felt impelled to concede the right of NHS consultants to engage in private practice and to accept a very large degree of clinical autonomy and control within the NHS. Earlier Labour governments had more or less acquiesced in the status quo created by the Bevan compromise but New Labour was determined to act, and to do so by ending the NHS consultants' clinical monopoly. This meant confronting the issue of 'perverse incentives'. Clinicians (the reasoning ran) had a vested interest in long waiting times since this guaranteed them (at least in some specialities and in some areas) a very lucrative additional source of income from those with the means to pay for swift treatment. Banning private practice was not politically realistic and the Government's attempt to compel newly qualified consultants to restrict private practice in their first years of NHS service in a first version of a long promised new consultant contract failed.

The ISTC programme, by ending the monopoly of NHS clinicians and NHS hospitals, would expose them to commercial pressures. They would be obliged (so the reasoning ran) to put more effort into cutting excessive waiting times through improving their work practices or risk the loss of valuable contracts to the commercial sector, their new rivals. Reducing professional discretion over clinicians' conditions of work would curb professional power. Shortening waiting times would, in turn, squeeze the private medical insurance and private secondary care market (which profited from the opportunities it offered for 'queue-jumping') and – as a senior Government policy advisor put it – permit the 'breaking of private practice cartels' (interview, Simon Stevens, 2006). The rationale was spelt out by

Klein: if the NHS could not 'get a grip on the spare time activities of its consultants' through a contract that would have given NHS managers first call on their spare time 'at least it can buy them from the same doctors working in the private sector' (Klein, 2005: 54).[7]

The benefits envisaged by augmenting the role of the private sector were, in short, multiple. More innovatory and efficient working practices would be introduced. To the extent that the private sector contracted and queue-jumping by the more affluent became less common, then ability to pay would cease to take precedence over clinical need in elective surgery. The grip of the consultants over the machinery of the NHS, which had thwarted reforming efforts by successive Labour governments, would be loosened. The more affluent sections of the middle class would be less likely to defect and their allegiance to a public healthcare system fortified.

The Government removed any doubts about its enthusiasm for a mixed economy of healthcare when a Health Department White Paper published in January 2006 announced a plan to open up primary care to commercial bidders (*The Guardian*, 31 January 2006). Private participation in public health-care delivery had emerged as a pillar of the New Labour strategy for 'promoting quality, efficiency and equity in public services' (Joint Government Memorandum, 2005: 1).

These interlinked components of the Government's reform programme – choice, competition and private involvement – all incited hostility within the party. For New Labour they were the only means by which a future for the NHS could be secured. But it was precisely this proposition that its critics within the party's ranks (and the medical professional too) challenged. The NHS, they insisted, was being subverted, its founding principles violated. Indeed, the temper of the debate rose to such a pitch that one commentator concluded that 'the NHS risks becoming Labour's Iraq on the home front' (Polly Toynbee, *The Guardian*, 22 September 2006). The next section seeks to explain why.

Safe in New Labour hands?

The NHS bequeathed by the Tories was in crisis, starved of funds, with overflowing hospitals, massive waiting lists and plunging morale. Since 1997 the NHS has enjoyed the largest sustained increase in funding in its history and by the end of 2008 it was estimated that NHS funding will have reached nearly 10 per cent of total national wealth – around the European average. The extra money allowed the NHS to recruit 193,000 extra staff, including 23,000 more doctors, 67,900 nurses, 26,500 therapists and technical staff, and 71,700 clinical support workers (*The Guardian*, 8 March 2006). In an audit of the Blair Government's record published in 2005 the King's Fund reported that significant improvements had occurred in the quality of care with 'huge progress' in the reduction of waiting times and 'more and better services'.

Long waits for treatment have been virtually eradicated ... the Government has reversed a previously inexorable upward trend in the numbers of people waiting for treatment – the first time this has been done since the NHS was founded. Therefore, the Government looks set to meet all of its targets in this key area of NHS performance.

(King's Fund, 2005a: 8, 79)

Whereas in 2002 a quarter of patients on waiting lists had been waiting for more than five months, by March 2006 no-one was (Klein, 2006: 412). By 2008, the Government pledged, no one would have to wait more than 18 weeks from GP referral to hospital treatment (Hewitt, 2005b). After a survey of over 80,000 patients the health watchdog the Healthcare Commission reported in 2007 that 90 per cent rated the overall care provided by NHS hospitals as 'excellent', 'very good' or 'good', with just 2 per cent describing it as poor (Healthcare Commission press release, 16 May 2007). The overall results of its audit, the King's Fund declared, were 'very positive' (King's Fund, 2005a: 6, 81).

Yet, puzzling as it might seem, within the Labour party Blair Government health policies have stirred up heated and impassioned debate. Many shared former Health Secretary Frank Dobson's apprehension that the outcome of New Labour-style modernisation could be 'the end of the NHS'. The internal market which it had created would fragment the NHS, erode its capacity to supply healthcare according to medical need and was 'alien to the spirit of the Labour party' (*The Guardian*, 14 March 2003). The 2006 party conference overwhelmingly carried a Unison motion urging the Government to 'rethink the headlong rush to a competitive system' and called for a moratorium on key planks of its NHS strategy including payment by results for hospitals and private sector involvement (*The Guardian*, 28 September 2006). After a stormy meeting, Labour's normally extremely compliant national executive only rejected a motion critical of the Government by the narrowest of margins – 16 votes to 15. How can we account for this response? Was the NHS, as critics alleged, no longer safe in New Labour's hands?

Answering these questions requires addressing three major issues of contention: first, the impact of choice on equality of access to healthcare treatment; second, the effects of commercial competition on the organisational and financial integrity of the NHS and its capacity to deliver healthcare according to need; and, third, the strain placed on the NHS by the sheer cost in terms of money, time and energy of the market-oriented reform programme. We explore each of these in turn.

The issue of equality

The Government has insisted that a more equitable distribution of services has been a principal aim of its installation of choice and competition mechanisms. Equality in healthcare can be defined in terms of equal access to treatment, with priority based on clinical need. Critics claimed that the main benefactors of consumer choice would be those from more comfortable and more highly educated backgrounds 'with the capability, time and resources to make informed and determined choices' (Rustin, 2004a: 93). The Government riposted with two points. First, the traditional system was a two-tier one. 'Our supposedly uniform public services were deeply unequal. ... The affluent and well educated ... had the choice to buy their way out of failing or inadequate provision ... It was a choice for the few, not for the many' (Blair, 2003c). Second, within the state sector, and in the absence of choice, 'voice' mechanisms prevailed and this tipped the balance of advantage decisively in favour of the 'more articulate, more confident, and more persistent' middle class (Le Grand, 2006b). The Government insisted that its reform programme would curb both forms of inequality.

First, inequality arising from the existence of a two-tier, public and private system. A prime purpose of the ISTC programme of introducing commercial competition was to end this system both by placing surgeons under pressure to devote more effort to their NHS responsibilities and by reducing demand (by cutting waiting times) for private treatment. As a result, Downing Street Health Policy advisor Simon Stevens maintained, it would help to 'deliver the old Labour dream of reducing the demand for privately funded care – thereby sustaining cross-class support for an equitable, tax-funded healthcare system' (Stevens, 2005). There is indeed some evidence that patients are being seen more rapidly and waiting times are falling because of a rise in the pace of NHS surgical activity and service redesign in the specialities (ophthalmology and orthopaedics) most affected by intensified competition from ISTCs. Whether this is the *consequence*, as the Government claims, of ISTCs has as yet to be conclusively established. On the one hand *Financial Times* journalist Nicholas Timmins reported that:

> NHS managers, usually off the record ... are not short of examples where they say the arrival of an independent treatment centre locally has suddenly made conversations with NHS consultants about how services are organised and how waiting times can be cut much easier.
>
> (Timmins, 2005b: 1194)[8]

The effect has been – Derek Machin, chairman of the BMA's private practice committee, commented – to reduce 'incentives for both corporate and individual subscribers to take out medical insurance' (*The Guardian*, 3 July 2004). After Bevan and Castle had, unavailingly, 'fought tooth and nail to stop private practice damaging the NHS', Polly Toynbee opined, 'they will have the last laugh as the NHS is now beginning to devour private practice' *The Guardian*, 23 June 2004).

On the other hand, critics of ISTCs pointed out that specialities such as ophthalmology were already modernising their working methods. Surgery waiting times for cataract operations, for example, had fallen year on year due to greater productivity (pump primed by modest injections of new capital via the NHS 'Action on Cataract Scheme') *before* the ISTC cataract scheme became operational (Kelly, 2005: 1691; Wood, 2007: 107) – a point accepted by Bob Ricketts, a senior official at the Department of Health, in oral evidence to the Health Select Committee.[9] In its report on the ISTC programme the Select Committee concluded that 'waiting lists have declined since the introduction of ISTCs, but it is unclear how far this has happened because the NHS has changed in response to the ISTCs or because of additional NHS spending and the intense focus placed on waiting list targets over this period' (Health Select Committee, 2006: 25).[10]

What of the second form of impact of inequality arising from 'middle class voice bias'? Proponents of the Government's reforms contend that choice benefited the less well-off precisely because it *curtailed* the middle class voice – Health Secretary Patricia Hewitt adduced evidence from pilot experiments that lower income groups were among the keenest supporters (and users) of choice (Le Grand, 2006b; Hewitt, 2006a). On the other hand, the Public Administration Select Committee reported widespread anxieties among its witnesses 'that greater choice would merely give the articulate and the prosperous an even better opportunity to take advantage of the best in public services' (Public Administration Select Committee, 2005a: 24). Unfortunately insufficient data has as yet accumulated to allow any firm conclusions to be reached on this issue (Lewis and Dixon, 2005a: 13).

The organisational and financial integrity of the NHS

The debate over equality strained relations between the Government and its critics but the real focal point of intra-party dissension was the effects of its policies on the financial and organisational integrity of the NHS as principal supplier of healthcare. Protagonists of the market-oriented reform programme contended that in response to competitive pressure from private firms 'some dramatic improvements in NHS efficiency and productivity' were occurring. Independent sector treatment centres were carrying out operations three or four times faster than NHS ones, forcing the latter to raise their game or lose business to their commercial rivals (Le Grand, 2006a: 25, 28). Its critics, in contrast, claimed that the headlong rush to a more marketised system was in fact jeopardising the future of the NHS. NHS producers were being exposed to unfair competition in two ways: first, because the new system allowed ISTCs to 'cream skim' and, second, because the market was rigged in their favour. These two claims will now be investigated.

Cream skimming. Profit-maximising firms (it was contended) were bound to optimise their income streams by engaging in 'cream skimming', or 'cherry-picking', that is seeking to lower costs and minimise work by dealing 'with the most straightforward (and therefore most profitable) cases' (Public

Administration Select Committee, 2005a: 43). Commercial companies, Frank Dobson contended, would 'cherry-pick the profitable end of the business, leaving the NHS with the rest' (*The Guardian*, 13 September 2003). Privately owned diagnostic and treatment centres would have no responsibility for complex operations, or accident and emergency cases, and would only carry out routine and simple procedures on the fittest patients for clinical safety reasons. ISTCs were contractually barred from accepting the more challenging – and thus expensive – cases. The PbR tariff structure did not properly discriminate between complex cases and the routine and straightforward medical procedures carried out by ISTCs. Hence the market would be skewed against NHS hospitals for such cases would 'significantly increase the NHS hospitals' average cost per patient thereby leading to worse performance-target records and a decline in competitiveness' (Lane, 2005; see also BMA, 2006: Ev 58). 'The "cherry picking" of simple cases ... leaves the local NHS Trust with the complex, higher risk and more expensive cases' (British Orthopaedic Association, 2006: Ev 63. See also Royal College of Anaesthetists, 2006: Ev 121).[11] The Royal College of Ophthalmologists pointed out that as resources were directed to those procedures stipulated by contracts (such as cataracts) patients with other eye ailments were ignored by the ISTC providers while the NHS Eye Unit was starved of funds that would facilitate general eye care for all patients – including those with much more serious or sinister eye problems (Royal College of Ophthalmologists, 2006: Ev 128). The effect of the ISTC programme, the BMA concluded, was that money and NHS resources were 'being redistributed to the independent sector often to the detriment of existing NHS services elsewhere' (BMA, 2006: Ev 56).

As yet insufficient data has been gathered to allow one to determine the extent to which these fears have proved justified. A survey of clinical directors conducted by a BMA research team in 2005 did find that independent treatment centres were ignoring the more difficult, complex and hence expensive cases which accordingly remained with NHS Trusts (BMA, 2005: 8–9). But more research and evaluation is required before firm conclusions can be reached.

Market-rigging? A second objection lodged by critics was that the NHS market was 'rigged to protect private entrants against fair competition'. Not only were privately run independent treatment centres 'paid substantially more than the rates laid down in the NHS national tariff for standard low-risk surgery', Labour MP Michael Meacher claimed, but the Government was putting NHS commissioning bodies under pressure to sign contracts with commercial providers (*The Guardian*, 12 January 2006).

The Government acknowledged that in order to ensure the viability of the programme ISTCs had been guaranteed payment for an agreed number of surgical procedures irrespective of whether these were actually performed (Health minister John Hutton, Public Administration Select Committee, 2005b: Ev 145, Ev 146). As the Chief Executive of a leading contractor,

Netcare UK, told the BBC this guarantee was necessary as a 'sweetener' for the private sector ('File on Four', 2004a). Further, 'for the purpose of seeding a new market', the Government agreed to pay ISTCs a premium (11.2 per cent above equivalent NHS cost for 2004/5) (Department of Health 2006: Ev 4).[12] Finally, under the choice programme, PCTs were obligated by Government to include at least one ISTC among the contracted providers: in effect, 'a proportion of the PCT budget was top-sliced by requiring them to purchase minimum volumes of services from an ISTC' (Palmer, K, 2006: 7).

ISTCs had originally been justified as a quick way to provide additional capacity to over-stretched NHS services. But what would happen if a PCT decided that existing capacity sufficed and it did not require an ISTC contract? This was the case for a number of commissioning authorities, including PCTs in Southampton, Rochdale, Oxfordshire and Cheshire, who concluded that contracts with ISTCs would not be a cost-effective use of funds. They immediately came under pressure from the Department of Health which insisted that such contracts must be signed and a number of Trust members who resisted were forced to resign (Jacky Davis, *The Guardian*, 27 June 2005; 'File on Four', 2004a).

But a more general complication soon arose. Under the Government's doctrine of Patient Choice, it was up to doctors and patients to decide together where to refer for treatment. However ISTCs had to be paid irrespective of how many procedures they actually carried out once a contract had been agreed. Hence there was 'a powerful incentive to PCTs to encourage patients to use ISTCs rather than NHS Treatment Centres' (Health Select Committee, 2006a: 34–5. See also Ruane, 2006). BBC Radio Four's 'File on Four' reported in 2006 instances in which a number of Primary Care Trusts had sought 'improper influence over patients' decisions about where to go for operations' including the use by the PCT of Referral Management Schemes to redirect patients to ISTCs ('File on Four', 2006). In Greater Manchester special payments were made to GPs who referred patients to the ISTC run by Netcare's Greater Manchester Surgical Centre in Trafford (*The Guardian*, 11 May 2006).

The whole point of the ISTC programme, as we have seen, was to expose NHS providers to the lash of competition. Whether or not this shift of capacity from NHS to commercial providers 'in practice proved good value for money', the Health Select Committee report on ISTCs concluded, was impossible to determine because the Government was unwilling to supply the appropriate evidence. However the Committee did express its own lack of conviction 'that ISTCs provide better value for money than other options such as more NHS Treatment Centres' (Health Select Committee, 2006a: 38, 47).[13] A note of uncertainty was sounded by the Government itself when it announced in December 2006 that a significant chunk of the second wave of the ISTC programme would be abandoned (*Health Service Journal*, 4 December 2006).

The impact of commercial competition raised the key question of the longer-term consequences for the NHS of private firms acquiring a larger share of the healthcare market (in elective procedures). The greater the volume of services that PCTs commissioned from ISTCs the less they could afford to purchase from NHS providers. The problem was that far from supplying additional capacity to over-stretched services the introduction of ISTCs has led to under-utilisation of NHS Diagnostic Centres and other NHS services,[14] leaving the latter with unused or 'stranded' capacity (Palmer, K, 2006: 7). Given that the NHS had to shoulder fixed costs the result was to push up the unit costs of the services they provided, rendering them less competitive than ISTCs. Hence it seemed likely, the Health Committee judged, that the ISTC programme would 'affect the viability of many existing NHS providers', leading to the closure of major NHS hospitals and the transfer of a proportion of elective services they currently provided to ISTCs (Health Select Committee, 2006a: 36).[15] There was already evidence that in one of the two main specialities where ISTCs were most active, ophthalmics, a previously planned expansion of NHS services was curtailed (Kelly, 2006: 7). The problem worsened from 2005 onwards when (for a variety of complex reasons) a substantial number of NHS Trusts were hit by deficits and having to slice back their services, including cutbacks in beds and medical staff. In the circumstances, as the leading health economist Professor Alan Maynard commented, it was 'very frustrating for people in the NHS to see private sector facilities getting this rather outrageous price premium and then not actually filling their beds' ('File on Four', 2006).

Transaction costs

Transaction costs are conventionally defined as the costs involved in establishing the governance structures required for markets to operate effectively (Williamson, 1985: 46; see also Deakin and Walsh, 1996: 39). The term is used here more broadly to embrace the costs – in money, time, energy and morale – entailed in embarking on and implementing organisational change. Thus a distinction is made between *specific* transaction costs, that is those arising directly from the specific form that reforms have taken; and *general* transaction costs, that is those incurred by the costs of re-organisation per se. These are discussed in turn.

Specific transaction costs. Former minister Michael Meacher defined these as the costs of 'providing information, operating the pricing system, and monitoring and enforcing contracts'. He claimed these would be 'very high', act as 'a serious barrier to value for money' and therefore damage the financial viability of the NHS (*The Guardian*, 12 January 2006). Ex-Health Secretary Frank Dobson similarly charged that massive amounts of money were being lavished 'on management consultants and franchising operations to the private sector and by the costs of introducing payment by results.

Paperwork used to cost 4% of the NHS budget, but now costs 15–16%' (*The Guardian*, 24 March 2006). Does the evidence substantiate these charges?

According to the Audit Commission the shift to PbR had been 'time-consuming and costly to implement'. Although it did envisage eventual benefits in greater efficiency, the additional burden on senior management, in regulating conflicts and implementing the new scheme would be significant, while it anticipated that the full implementation of practice-based commissioning and patient choice would further add to the administrative cost (Audit Commission, 2005a: 34). Figures released by the Information Centre for Health and Social Care in spring 2006 indicated that while overall the NHS workforce in England had grown by 30 per cent over the past decade the number of managers had doubled (BBC News Web, 24 April 2006). According to figures leaked to *The Sunday Times*, the cost of hospital administration rose from £3 billion in 1997 to £5 billion in 2004 (Tallis, 2004: 158). Many of the changes introduced entailed new specialist skills and types of expertise, which, it was felt, the NHS could not supply and, thus, required hiring them from outside sources. Between 2003 and 2004 alone NHS spending on management consultants leapt 340 per cent, from £25 million to £85 million. By 2005 this figure had (according to a Department of Health report) risen to £133 million – more than the £94 million projected net deficit for the NHS in 2006 (*Health Service Journal*, 30 November 2006). The cost of the 'Choose and Book' computer system that was intended to facilitate consumer choice for surgical treatment ballooned from an original £65 million to (in 2006) over £200 million (Craig with Brooks, 2006: 3, 191). A National Audit Office report estimated NHS spending overall on business consultants employed to advise on project management and IT systems had jumped more than fifteen-fold from £31 million to more than £500 million in two years (*The Guardian*, 15 December 2006). To this had to be added general transaction costs.

General transaction costs. Sir Andrew Foster, chairman of the Audit Commission, expressed his 'worry about the sheer mass of structural change there has been … and whether that will really bring the result that is needed' (quoted in Lang, Wainwright and Sehdev, 2005: 35). Although the Government was sometimes inclined to depict the NHS as a lumbering monster in an arrested state of evolutionary development, in fact it had experienced incessant and major changes under the Tories. Health policy expert Kieran Walshe lamented that the NHS had been 'in a state of almost continuous reform and restructuring for two decades or longer'. Insufficient account had been taken of the fact that 'organizational restructuring tends to divert time and effort from the challenges of improving healthcare delivery' even though the benefits were often 'negligible' (Walshe, 2003: 106. See also Tallis, 2004: 84, 146–8, 154–7; Edwards, 2005: 1464). Unending change in organisational roles and responsibilities, one commentator cautioned, 'destroys the inter-organizational communication channels, decision processes and shared understandings required for collaborative success … the ties that bind organizations ... and are the basis on which mutual trust emerges' (McMurray, 2007: 79). Although the Government regularly deployed the language of 'modernisation' and reform', implying a forward progression in structure and techniques, in fact many of these changes were cyclical in character. The revamped PCTs were not wholly unlike old district health authorities, practice-based commissioning bore more than a passing resemblance to the Tories' model of fund holding, and payment by results represented a return to John Major's internal market (McMurray, 2007: 80). Far from installing a self-renewal mechanism the effects of incessant organisational restructuring, critics claimed, was to strengthen change-aversion and encourage NHS managers to take a short-term view on the assumption that the next stage in musical chairs would not be long delayed (Walshe, 2003; Walshe *et al.*, 2004).[16]

The Government's response was that relentless centrally driven change was vital if the NHS (and other public sector organisations) were to be shaken up and revitalised. The Government was, according to former senior advisor Chris Ham, deliberately pursuing a policy of 'organisational destabilisation' or 'creative destruction' to ensure that the urge to improve and innovate was internalised and to prevent the forces of inertia from reasserting themselves: almost a 'permanent revolution' syndrome (interview, 2007). The assumption was that the costs of relentless change would be more than generously outweighed by the benefits of the new, more market-oriented regime. The Government, Ham concluded, was taking a big gamble: 'that the instability its policies are generating will eventually deliver change that is more far-reaching than targets and spending can deliver on their own. It is no exaggeration to suggest that the future of the NHS depends on the success of this gamble' (Ham, 2006).

Conclusion

Under New Labour 'the National Health Service in England has embarked on one of the most radical and far reaching set of reforms in its history'. The stakes could not be higher for their success or failure 'will determine the future of the NHS and perhaps even whether it has one' (Lewis and Dixon, 2005a: 1). For New Labour's most severe critics, if present policies were to continue, it would not have one (or at least in any recognisable shape). Private enterprise was 'penetrating and corroding the fabric of the NHS at every level'. The NHS has been 'dismantled and privatised ... and commodified. ... The institutions that made the NHS strong, economical and popular are being dissolved ... In their place are market mechanisms: invoicing, customers, segmented risk pools, legal contracts, and a myriad of competing suppliers' (Pollock, 2004: 1, 214, 215). Other commentators strongly dissent. For Klein, talk of privatisation was 'nonsense'. The reforms were 'in the means, not the aims: market dynamics are to be harnessed in the service of equity and social solidarity' (Klein, 2006: 411).

'Introducing choice and diversity,' Driver and Martell suggest, 'challenges social democratic political economy where choices remain attached to property rights. But where choices remain attached to public money, and those choices reflect need not private resources, they do not' (Driver and Martell, 2006: 136).

The root of the argument (at least within the Labour party) lay in differing conceptions of the NHS. For the traditionalists the founding principles of the NHS required that healthcare service had not only to be financed and commissioned but also provided by the NHS; and that services should be provided in an integrated way in which all organisations would co-operate to meet general health needs.[17] For the Government, in contrast, the two cornerstone principles of the NHS were 'equal access to treatment for all, based on clinical need and regardless of the patient's ability to pay'; and 'collective funding of the NHS, through national taxation' as the guarantor that 'quality care would be available to all' (Health Secretary John Reid's introduction to Department of Health, 2004). Under the mixed economy of healthcare, responsibility for supplying services would be apportioned to a plurality of providers, public, private and voluntary, who would compete with each other to maximise efficiency and quality. As long as care and treatment were freely provided via the NHS, Milburn explained, whether it took place in 'a private sector hospital or a NHS hospital is, frankly, a secondary consideration' (Health Select Committee, 2002).[18]

Whatever the truth of the matter New Labour has set in motion powerful forces about whose longer-term consequences nobody can be sure. Paradoxically for a government elected on the pledge to 'save the NHS', 'the only certainty is that at no other time in the NHS's history does its future appear so uncertain' (Hunter, 2005: 212).

6 New Labour's representational role
The case of employment relations

Introduction

Representation is a key function for political parties since they act as 'channels for articulating, communicating and implementing the demands of the governed' (Sartori, 1976: 27). Contemporary analysis tends to focus on the role of parties as the representatives of blocs of voters but the essence of politics has always been 'who gets what, when and how' and, since government decisions are so often about the allocation of scarce resources, parties in office necessarily must adjudicate between the claims of competing social interests. For the purposes of this book the function of party interest representation is defined as the promotion of the interests and concerns of groups differentially located within a social structure and their translation into acts of public policy.

This chapter sets out to analyse how New Labour has enacted its representational role by exploring one particular policy area: employment relations and conditions of work. This is for a number of reasons. First, because traditionally Labour has regarded as one of its prime purposes the advancement of the interests of 'ordinary working people'. Second, because employment status has a profound impact upon people's lives and the resources they can command. Third, because the recasting of the party's stance on industrial relations and the labour market and the reformulation of its relations with business and trade was absolutely central to the New Labour project.

Any analysis of interest representation inevitably begs the question of establishing what the interests of specified groups are – a most difficult task. As Lukes has pointed out, the concept of interest 'is an irreducibly evaluative' one, but proceeds by distinguishing between three approaches. The 'liberal' equates interests with subjective wants or policy preferences as articulated in the political arena, typically by parties and interest groups. For the reformist, interests may be latent, that is subjectively held but not articulated in the political sphere since the prevailing arrangements of power may cause them to be 'deflected, submerged or concealed'. The 'radical' takes this a step further by suggesting that interests may exist apart from people's apprehension of them. They can be defined as what people 'would want and prefer, were they able to make the choice' (Lukes, 2005: 37–8). Unlike in the first two cases the assumption is that interests can, at least to some degree, be regarded as 'objective' and need not be conflated with subjective preferences.

The approach taken here, for the purposes of this chapter, is a synthesis of the 'liberal' and the 'radical'. It follows the liberal model in assuming a large measure of correspondence between the interests of employers and employees and the policy preferences of the bodies which claimed to represent them. Hence it seeks to establish the degree to which New Labour policies (in the relevant areas) conformed more closely to the preferences of the one or the other. It follows the radical model in postulating the existence of objective interests which can be said to attach to groups with a particular location in the social order, irrespective of whether they are advanced on their behalf by some representative body. These interests are equated with needs which, in turn (and drawing upon Gough), are defined in terms of the maintenance of physical and mental well-being (Gough, 1994). The hypothesis advanced is that some light can be on shed New Labour's representational role by assessing the impact of its policies on the physical and mental health of employees.

The first section of the chapter sketches the historical background to the relationship between Labour and the unions; the second (using a 'liberal' conception of interest) discusses Blair Government policies on the regulation of employment, pay and conditions and the organisation of the work process. The third section (using a 'radical' conception of interest) draws upon available evidence to assess the impact of Government policies on employees' physical and mental well-being. The fourth section reaches some initial conclusions about the performance by New Labour of its representational role.

The advent of New Labour

A crucial aspect of the transformation of European Social Democratic parties has been a recasting of their relationship with trade unions and 'a reconceptualization of the appropriate role of organised labour in the political economy of the Left' (Howell, 1998: 3). Received wisdom (readily accepted and promulgated by New Labour) held that past Labour governments, especially in the 1960s and 1970s, had exhibited a deferential, reverential and often supine attitude towards the 'barons' of the union movement. Ludlam and Taylor dub this the *union-dominance* model, where unions 'are able to dominate the direction of party policy-making' (Ludlam and Taylor, 2003: 728). In reality, as Minkin (1991) demonstrated with an immense wealth of detail, the party–union connection corresponded much more closely to what Ludlam and Taylor called the *union-party bonding* model, where unions are integrated into the party, have guaranteed governmental positions in its organisational structure, but do not dominate policy-making (Ludlam and Taylor, 2003: 728). Though numerous changes altered the form organisational linkage took (culminating, during the Smith leadership, in the introduction of 'one member one vote' in the casting of trade union votes) in essentials the bonding model survived intact until 1994.

The party–union relationship, Minkin observes, 'was defined in terms of a common loyalty and a deeply felt commitment to a wider entity and purpose – the Labour Movement'. The protection and promotion of the industrial interests of the unions and their members became the 'anvil upon which "labour alliance" was forged' and formed the party's 'most basic and unifying purpose' (Minkin, 1991: 4, 11). But equally the alliance was (in Minkin's phrase) a contentious one, which came under immense strain during the Labour governments of the 1960s and 1970s. These governments grappled with the huge problems of, on the one hand, sustaining full employment and growing public expenditure to finance its welfare ambitions while, on the other, containing mounting inflationary pressures and seeking to tackle low productivity in industry. These problems were exacerbated by a rate of growth that lagged behind major competitors, vulnerability to currency crises and inflated pretensions as to the United Kingdom's proper role in the world. The classical social democratic model (most closely associated with Scandinavia) suggested that full employment, rising living standards and an expanding welfare state could best be reconciled with growth, industrial order and price stability through a system of political exchange. This stipulated that the unions would exercise wage moderation to contain inflationary impulses and improve competitiveness in return for social reforms and an institutionalised role in a 'corporatist' system of policy formation knitting together labour, capital and the state.

British social democracy's predicament was that the institutional conditions which could sustain such a system were at best only partially and spasmodically present and at worst wholly absent in the United Kingdom. The governments of both 1964–70 and 1974–79 made some effort to erect a quasi-corporatist institutional and policy-making apparatus to master inflationary pressures but, in both cases, they 'failed visibly and spectacularly' (Cronin, 2006: 54). There were many reasons for this (discussed in Shaw, 1996) but a principal cause was the absence of a centralised, cohesive trade union movement and a pattern of national co-ordinated industrial bargaining systems 'which, as a vast literature has shown, constitute the best possible institutional infrastructure for harmonizing wage-equalization, full employment, and growth' (Esping-Andersen, 1999: 17). In consequence Labour governments faltered as they wrestled with low growth, paltry levels of investment, industrial strife and (above all) intensifying inflation that eventually culminated in the twin shocks of the 1976 IMF crisis and the 1978/9 Winter of Discontent.

For Labour leaders in the past, while undoubtedly part of the problem the unions were also an essential part of the solution. For New Labour they were, more simply, the problem. Far from being (as party tradition would have it) a source of strength the union connection was the party's Achilles heel. What the party's principal political strategist, Philip Gould, called 'trade union domination' was seen as a major bar hindering Labour's 'modernisation' and a major cause of its bleak electoral performance since the 1970s (Gould, 1998: 19). As Howell has observed 'ending the association, in the minds of voters and business, between the Labour Party and organized labour ... is the defining core of the modernization project. It is seen as central to the ability to appeal to more affluent swing voters, and to win the confidence of employers and financial interests' (Howell, 2001: 28–9).

In the New Labour political economy, too, organised labour was assigned a modest role. Learning, it believed, from experience the Blair administration envisaged relations with the unions, and hence questions of employment relations policy, in a manner starkly different from its predecessors. Blair himself (and many of his closest advisors) had a somewhat jaundiced view of the unions and the role they had played both in the party and the country at large, and believed that the Conservative legislative assault on union power had benefited both the economy and the conduct of management–labour relations (Taylor, R, 2001a). New Labour's 'modernisation project' 'deliberately sought to develop a positive and intimate relationship with business and a more arms-length and unsentimental one with trade unions' (Taylor, R, 2001a: 246). Price stability was now to be secured not by incomes policies or social contracts but by a combination of transferring control over monetary policy to the Bank of England (which would operate as an anti-inflationary anchor)[1] and maintaining a deregulated labour market where (in the private sector at least) wage levels would be determined principally by market forces. The co-operation of a much weakened trade union movement was no longer needed.

What the incoming Blair Government promised the unions was 'fairness not favours'. 'Not favours' meant, on the one hand, that the industrial relations settlement that had emerged from the Conservative years was, in its essentials, to be respected. Thus the 1997 Labour election manifesto pledged emphatically that 'the key elements of the trade union legislation of the 1980s will stay – on ballots, picketing and industrial action'. There would be 'no return to flying pickets, secondary action, strikes with no ballots or the trade union law of the 1970s' (Labour Party, 1997). Indeed, for New Labour, marginalised unions and a lightly regulated labour market would ensure that Britain would continue to be an attractive location for inward investment. On the other hand, the Government promised 'fairness'. It was committed to redressing the harmful consequences of Conservative policies – a rapid growth in income inequality, the effective absence for many employees of protection against exploitation and, above all, mass unemployment. It pledged to introduce 'basic minimum rights for the individual at the workplace', a minimum wage, rights for workers to join a union and for a union to secure recognition by employers 'where a majority of the relevant workforce' balloted in favour. Finally, in contrast to the Major Government, it promised to sign the European Union's Social Chapter (Labour Party, 1997).

Three major statutes have been enacted: the Employment Relations Act (ERA) of 1999, the Employment Act of 2002 and the Employment Relations Act of 2004. These aimed, as far as was practicable, to balance and reconcile a number of objectives: to establish a network of legally enforceable rights for employees which would protect them against gross abuse and exploitation; relieve the trade unions from some of the legal impositions which unfairly impaired their ability to represent the interests of their members; foster a spirit of harmony and co-operation between management and labour; and promote higher productivity and greater competitiveness by sustaining a flexible labour market which had given the United Kingdom a competitive edge against some of its economic rivals. The next section explores how these aims were realised by examining policy in three aspects of labour relations: security of employment, pay and conditions and the organisation of the labour process. The Blair Government's measures are placed in the context of the system of labour relations bequeathed to it by the Conservatives. In each case we examine how it struck a balance between re-regulation on the one hand and the preservation of market determination (or 'flexibility') on the other.

Blair Government and labour law

Employment regulation

Flexibility in conditions of employment refers to the capacity of employers to hire and fire employees at will, and to use part-time, temporary and short-term contracts to match production to shifting market demands. Greater employment flexibility was pursued by the Conservatives by a variety of measures such as the dismantling of employment protection legislation, weakening employment rights over unfair dismissal, privatising industries and thereby removing workers from the umbrella of collective agreements, and enforcing competitive tendering in the public sector. In many sectors (and partly as a result) the proportion of the labour force on part-time and temporary contracts steadily rose in the Tory years, enabling employers to tailor the size and composition of the workforce to market demand. The most decisive step taken was to institute new industrial relations legislation impairing the capacity of unions to organise and bargain effectively (Michie and Wilkinson, 1994: 17).

The Employment Relations Act, the Blair Government's major contribution to revising the labour relations legal code, moved some way to satisfying trade union calls for a re-regulation of the labour market. It imposed restraints on the right to fire, most notably by strengthening unfair dismissal provisions and banning discrimination against union members (Glyn and

Wood, 2001a: 61). The qualifying period for protection against unfair dismissal was restored to 12 months (it should be noted that John Smith had promised to scrap the qualifying period entirely) bringing an additional 1–2 million workers into its fold. Further, the maximum compensation figure, initially set at a level highly unlikely to deter employers prepared to risk an unfair dismissal case to rid themselves of employees, was very substantially raised (Hamann and Kelly, 2003: 647). One result of this was the growth of compromise agreements in which employers and dismissed workers informally worked out compensation levels.

A number of other steps increased employee rights, driven primarily by European Union legislation. In July 2000, for example, the Government enacted the Part-time Workers Regulations as required by EU law which, for the first time in Britain, extended statutory employment protection to employees engaged in 'atypical work' such as part-time workers. However the effect of this was attenuated when the Government limited coverage to those classified as 'employees', a definition which excluded 'temporary' agency and nominally self-employed workers, and the legislation as eventually implemented left (according to the Government's own figures) more than 90 per cent still unprotected (McKay, 2001: 294). TUC pressure to extend protection to all workers mounted as it became evident that employers were increasingly using 'temporary' agency staff to cover positions previously held by permanent workers. The European Commission proposed a directive covering temporary and agency workers, which would have given them the same employment rights and pay as their permanent counterparts. However, this was blocked by the Blair Government. Equally, it was loath to take effective action to regulate the growth of 'gangmasters', effectively a system of providing cheap labour with minimal rights to low-paying employers. The gangmasters' licensing law, introduced in 2004, covered only agriculture and food processing, deliberately leaving out caring, cleaning, catering and hospitality. Aside from widening the pool of easily exploited employees, the growth of this source of labour supply tended to depress wages in sectors where low pay was rampant. Pressure by unions (and some Labour MPs, notably Jon Cruddas) on the Government to take action has been (at time of writing) quite unavailing.

Regulation of pay and conditions

Wages, free market theory runs, are the price paid for labour and in a properly functioning market should operate as signal for both workers and employers as to how labour resources can be most productively used. Employee cost rigidities, either through the use of trade union bargaining power or state-imposed regulations, have the effect of artificially inflating the cost of employees beyond market equilibrium. Inspired by free market theory, the Conservative Government implemented a variety of measures to render pay and conditions more responsive to market pressures. These included abolishing wage councils (which had set minimum pay in low-wage industries), contracting out public services where the existing staff was often re-employed at lower rates and with fewer fringe benefits, and trade union laws which hampered the ability of unions to resist changes in wages and conditions. The scaling down and tightening eligibility for social benefits was designed to lower the 'reservation cost' of labour by pressurising the unemployed to accept low-paid jobs rather than hold out for better-paid ones. The spread of temporary and part-time contracts and self-employment also reduced costs since their holders were not normally eligible for holiday pay, sickness entitlements or pension contributions. The Blair Government, as a result, inherited a wages system far more market-oriented than those found among most other West European countries. It sought to strike a balance between sustaining this system while taking steps to protect labour against grosser abuses. What emerged was a patchwork quilt of measures, a pattern which combined substantial advances in worker protection in some areas with rudimentary regulation in others.

A key commitment in Labour's 1997 manifesto was the introduction of a minimum wage. Although often seen as a defining feature of the Blair Government's approach to employment relations it was, in fact, an iron-clad pledge bequeathed by the John Smith leadership which enjoyed fervent support within most of the trade unions. However, its significance should not be under-estimated. By placing a floor beneath wages, it signalled a forthright rejection of the pure market approach to pay determination. To foster agreement between the unions and employers a Low Pay Commission was set up headed by the academic Professor George Bain and with repre-sentatives from both sides of industry. It was charged with making recom-mendations as to the appropriate level for the minimum wage. Initially set, when enacted in April 1999, at £3.60 an hour the National Minimum Wage now (spring 2007) stands at £5.35 for adults. It has been calculated that, by 2004, over 1.7 million poorly paid (and mainly part-time) workers had benefited (Vigor, 2005: 160). Its effect was to push up the reservation wage by ensuring that no employee (within the law at least) would receive less than the statutory minimum. Coupled with the various tax credit schemes to supplement low wages, the effect has been to significantly increase the earnings of the lowest income decile (Hamann and Kelly, 2003: 646). How-ever, unlike most comparable EU countries, the Government elected to establish a 'soft' inspection regime with only 100 compliance officers to cover the country to enforce the legislation. Prosecution of rogue employers has been very rare and with the maximum penalty set at £5,000, there is little effective deterrence (Polly Toynbee, *The Guardian*, 25 May 2007). Fur-thermore, a BBC investigation in April 2007 disclosed the existence of a large underworld of migrant labour employed at rates well below the minimum wage, but the Government has yet to take action (BBC News, 25 April 2007).

If the minimum wage was one major step taken by the Government to regulate the labour market, a second, no less significant, was the Government's decision to abolish the two-tier workforce in local government. A two-tier workforce refers to the differences in pay and conditions which arise when workers are transferred from the public sector to the private sector and when new workers are recruited to carry out jobs previously undertaken in the public sector but with different pay and conditions. A major prong of Conservative employment liberalisation was the enactment of compulsory competitive tendering of local authority services, which moved many workers (especially in local authorities and the NHS) from the public to the private sector and led to a notable deterioration of conditions in terms of wages, employment status (i.e. from regular to temporary contracts), holidays, pensions and sick pay.

The end to the two-tier workforce was a key union demand incessantly pressed upon the Government. Unions insisted that previously publicly employed workers transferred to the private sector and those who moved into jobs formerly in the public sector – as a result of contracting-out and PFI deals – should be guaranteed 'no less favourable' terms and conditions than those still employed by the state.[2] The Government initially resisted these pressures on the ground that private contractors could only improve efficiency and make savings if they had the freedom to vary wages and conditions, dismantle rigid public sector working practice and introduce more flexibility in staff deployments, though it was prepared to concede that pay and conditions should be 'broadly comparable'. By early 2003 increasingly impatient and disgruntled union leaders warned of serious industrial action if steps were not taken to end the two-tier workforce. It became evident that the whole relationship between the unions and the Government was coming under serious strain over an issue that was plainly a top priority for what had once been called the 'industrial wing of the movement'. Eventually the Government decided that this was a matter on which it could concede to the unions and a deal was reached effectively ending the two-tier workforce – which left the CBI 'fuming' (Ludlam, 2004: 81). A further step was taken with the so-called 'Retention of Employment' clause under which workers employed in cleaning, catering, portering and security services which under NHS PFI agreements became the responsibility of PFI consortiums (see Chapter Four) were allotted the status of NHS employees on secondment to private contractors (Maltby and Gosling, 2003: 15, 12–13).

However, if on issues of the minimum wage and the two-tier workforce the Government proved amenable to union representations, and agreed to a significant measure of re-regulation on other issues, it proved adamant in its insistence on maintaining a high degree of flexibility. 'One of the most essential ingredients in the organisation of work,' John Monks, then TUC General Secretary, maintained, 'is time – when we work, for how long and how we are able to balance working time with our time outside of work' (quoted in Taylor, R, 2001b: 9). The time-effort-wage bargain has always been an 'inherently contested aspect of the employment relationship' with employers seeking to maximise control over time-deployment which unions have sought to resist by, for example, establishing a standard working day (Rubery, Ward, Grimshaw and Beynon, 2005: 92). After falling steadily for generations after 1979 the number of hours worked began to creep up again. Research by Professor Green showed that the average British household with two adults was working seven hours a week more at the end of the 1990s than in the early 1980s, and that the rise in work intensity had been steeper than in any other country in Europe (cited in *The Guardian*, 21 June 2000). In 1999 the annual European Labour Force Survey reported that British employees worked some of the longest hours in the European Union (the *Guardian*, 22 August 1999). Recent research covering both the public and private sectors indicated that not only were workers being required to work longer hours but the right to additional pay for working unsocial hours was being progressively removed. 'We found that time was being used as a means of securing greater effort for the same reward whether extracted through an intensification of work or a prolongation of working hours. In effect the work-effort relationship' was being 'quite fundamentally restructured' (Rubery, Ward, Grimshaw and Beynon, 2005: 98, 103). Growing employer control over the length, tempo and shape of the working week meant that the concept of a standard working period was being eroded and the balance between work and family/private life upset, often at the cost of increasing stress at work (Rubery, Ward, Grimshaw and Beynon, 2005: 103–4).

In a major shift in strategy the TUC has sought to reverse the drift to longer hours not through collective bargaining but via full enforcement of restrictions to the working week agreed by the European Union. The EU's Working Time Regulations stipulated that workers must not be normally required to work over 48 hours per week. However, ignoring TUC representations, the Blair Government excluded millions of workers from coverage by allowing workers to 'waive' their rights under the regulations (seeking 'derogations') and by exempting a number of occupational categories (Smith and Morton, 2001: 123; Glyn and Wood, 2001a: 63). The effect of the opt-out clause has been that many of the lowest paid have been more or less obliged to sign the 'voluntary' declaration as a condition of obtaining work (Toynbee, 2003: 33).

As a result the effect of the Working Time Directive in the United Kingdom has been slight. Indeed between 2000 and 2002 the number of men working more than 60 hours a week has increased from one in eight, to one in six and the number of women working long hours has doubled from one in sixteen to one in eight (*The Guardian*, 6 January 2003). The TUC lobbied strenuously for the lifting of the exemptions and for tougher enforcement while in 2005 the European Parliament demanded that the opt-out from the working time directive be scrapped by 2010 at the latest. However the Blair Government blocked these proposals and the opt-out has been preserved (*The Guardian*, 3 June 2005).

The Government has also doggedly resisted the extension of protection to atypical (part-time and fixed-term) and agency workers who number among the most vulnerable and poorly paid groups in the British labour market (Smith and Morton, 2006: 413). Many of these jobs were filled by floods of migration workers, both legal and illegal, eager to take jobs at levels of pay uncongenial to the indigenous population. The United Kingdom was one of only three countries in Europe where employers could legally hire temporary workers on lower pay and poorer conditions than other staff. Many of the workers recruited to fill these jobs – mostly menial, poorly paid, insecure and unpleasant – especially in London were, as the BBC's business correspondent reported, newly arrived (Mason, 2007). As one senior Downing Street source acknowledged, this flow of migrant workers played a key role in holding down wages and may account for why income at the lowest deciles remained stubbornly low (interview, 2007). Not surprisingly the unions called for the Government to improve labour protection, with one of their priorities being the enactment of the EU Temporary Agency Workers Directive, which would afford agency workers equal treatment on pay and other employment conditions with permanent employees. The Government, however, orchestrated opposition to the measure which, despite widespread support from most other EU countries, remains in abeyance (TUC Press release, 21 November 2003; TUC workSMART newsletter, September 2005 issue 39; *The Guardian*, 25 May 2007). Equally it resisted trade union pressure to extend legally enforceable worker rights to those employed in firms with 20 or fewer workers 'mainly as a result of successful business lobbying from the Federation of Small Businesses' (Taylor, R, 2005a: 189).

Inevitably relations between the Government and the unions became strained over these issues. TUC General Secretary Brendan Barber expressed the 'despair' of trade unionists 'as our Government has appeared systematically to oppose every recent positive European initiative in the social field', denying proper protections to some of the most vulnerable members of the workforce (TUC Press release, 20 May 2004). Derek Simpson and Tony Woodley, general secretaries respectively of Amicus (the engineering union) and the Transport and General Workers' Union (now merged in the super-union 'Unite') complained that because of Government obstruction 'British employees work longer hours, with greater job uncertainty and a bleaker pensions future than those elsewhere in Europe' (*The Guardian*, 30 June 2004). The Government's riposte was that it was seeking to protect the competitive advantage that Britain's flexible labour market afforded, which in turn guaranteed a flow of new jobs and a rate of growth that consistently surpassed the EU average. Indeed Blair and Brown frequently contrasted the dynamism of the British economy with the sclerotic social market economies of Western Europe (especially France and Germany) urging that they emulate UK success by liberating their business sector from the employment-stifling rigidities of their labour markets (Taylor, R, 2005a: 186–7).

Regulation of the work process

According to free market theory, competitive efficiency requires effective managerial control over the work process to enable the entrepreneur to sweep aside restrictive practices and adapt to ever-fiercer economic competition. The Conservative Government after 1979 launched a determined and remorseless drive to restore managerial prerogatives by breaking union power. Secondary picketing was banned, mandatory strike ballots imposed and individuals given the right to refuse to abide by majority decisions. Unions could be sued if they went on strike without fulfilling complex and detailed statutory procedures and firms were empowered to replace collective agreements by individual contracts (Michie and Wilkinson, 1994: 17; Hutton, W, 1995: 92). The culmination of almost two decades of Conservative rule was a dramatic reassertion of employer authority: for the first time in generations the wages and conditions of the bulk of employees (especially in the private sector) were set by 'unilateral rule-making by management' rather than collective regulation (Undy, 1999: 322; Towers, 1999: 91).

Labour's 1997 manifesto stated boldly that 'the key elements of the trade union legislation of the 1980s will stay – on ballots, picketing and industrial action'. However the party believed that Tory legislation had been one-sided and promised to return to employees rights they should properly enjoy. It pledged that people 'should be free to join or not to join a union. Where they do decide to join, and where a majority of the relevant workforce vote in a ballot for the union to represent them, the union should be recognised' (Labour Party, 1997).

Intense controversy accompanied the framing of the Blair Government's provisions on union recognition and the outcome, as it eventually emerged in the Employment Relations Act, was very much a compromise – and one which satisfied key union demands. For the first time a legal right of employees to trade union representation was established. Two methods of statutory recognition of trade unions by employers for collective bargaining over pay and conditions were introduced. Under the first a union would be recognised if a majority of those voting *and* at least 40 per cent of those eligible to vote supported it. Under the second where the union could show a majority of the employees in the proposed bargaining unit were members of the Central Arbitration Committee (CAC) it could insist on trade union recognition (Gennard, 2002: 585; Smith and Morton, 2001: 124). The 40 per cent threshold was steep – it was a (much) higher proportion of those eligible to vote than any of the three Labour governments elected since 1997 were able to secure. Blair, a senior TUC official commented, was 'fixated on the 40 per cent. He seemed to regard it as a symbol of New Labour's determination to stand up to the unions' (interview, 1998). The second method eased the hurdle for the unions somewhat but it still proved difficult to surmount. The effectiveness of the recognition procedures was further reduced by two other clauses: firms with fewer than 21 employees were exempted (excluding over 5 million workers) and employers were under no obligation to bargain in good faith even when recognition had been conceded.

But the most 'notable absence' from the Employment Relations Act 'was any weakening of the constraints on industrial action that had been introduced by previous Conservative governments' (Brown, W, 2000: 302–2; Blair, 2001d). Though a new 8-week protection from unfair dismissal for workers taking official strike action was introduced the UK legal regime regulating industrial action persisted as the most restrictive in the European Union. Solidarity action is banned, legally permissible industrial action defined very narrowly and balloting procedures required for such action are extraordinarily complex and demanding.[3] Further, an employer still cannot be compelled to reinstate those who successfully claim unfair dismissal and the restrictions preventing employers dismissing those who are on strike are limited (McKay, 2001: 297; Glyn and Wood, 2001a: 61–62; Towers, 1999: 86–7; Brown, W, 2000: 302–3).

Notwithstanding, the Act was welcomed by the TUC and its affiliates as the first piece of favourable legislation for 20 years. It took much patient and assiduous lobbying not only of the Government but of backbench Labour MPs, with union negotiators convinced that the threat of a major PLP revolt was needed to push the Prime Minister into a more conciliatory frame of mind (interview, senior TUC official, 1998). Indeed, according to Jon Cruddas MP, Downing Street industrial relations advisor from 1997–2001 and closely involved in discussions with the unions over the framing of the 1999 Employment Relations Act, 'every single labour market initiative has to be fought line by line, almost street by street' (Cruddas, 2002).

Plainly, the Blair Government's approach to employment relations law is sharply different both from the stance traditionally taken by Labour and that followed by the Conservatives. Thus while new labour rights *have* been created these are primarily *individual* ones (enforceable through employment tribunals and other public agencies) rather than *collective* (trade union) ones (Howell, 2004: 12). The list is a substantial one, including: reducing the qualifying period before benefiting from claims for unfair dismissal; giving workers on fixed contracts the right to claim unfair dismissal; raising the cap for unfair dismissal compensation; providing the right of employees to be accompanied by a trade union official during a disciplinary or grievance hearing whether or not a trade union is recognised; extending maternity leave and introducing the right to paternal leave (Gennard, 2002: 584; Howell, 2004: 9). However the formal existence of such rights should be distinguished from their effective exercise since research has found that trade unions are frequently the main enforcers of such rights whose implementation in their absence (in the private sector) is patchy and sporadic (Brown, W, 2000: 304; McKay, 2001: 298). Hence the failure of the unions to make significant progress in re-establishing an effective presence in great swathes of the private sector suggests that many of the new individual rights acquired will be, for many of the most vulnerable workers, largely paper ones.[4] Employment rights remain narrow in scope, difficult to activate and with weak enforcement mechanisms. 'The resurgence of the managerial prerogative, which so characterized the 1990s', Smith and Morton concluded, 'has continued' (Smith and Morton, 2006: 414).

Employment relations: promoting whose interests?

So far (following Lukes' terminology) a 'liberal' concept of interest has been used in which the interests of a group are broadly equated with the demands made on its behalf by a representative institution. Of course the Blair Government disputed the trade union interpretation of employee interests claiming that its own policies catered for their 'real' interests. Defining the nature of these 'real' interests (as against those they profess or are professed on their behalf) is a task riddled with methodological and substantive difficulties. It has been suggested that 'real interests' can be equated with 'needs' but, as Gough comments, 'the absence of a theoretically grounded and operational concept of objective human need has inhibited the development of a common calculus for evaluating human welfare.' However he suggests that all persons have an objective interest in having the means to 'enable sustained participation in one's form of life' (and avoiding serious harm that inhibits this) and the prerequisites for this include the possession of sufficient material means (income) and physical and mental health (Gough, 1994: 25). Following this, in this chapter we operationalise these prerequisites by examining the impact of Government policies on, first, the availability of work, second, the level of remuneration and third, physical and mental well-being. It is, of course, difficult (given the limitations of this study) to pursue these issues in any detail, to establish with any precision the conditions required to meet the prerequisites and, indeed, to explore any trade-offs (e.g. between jobs and wage levels) that may exist. However some preliminary and inevitably tentative observations can be made.

The availability of work. This issue has been investigated in a little more detail in Chapter Two (see pp. 46–7) so comment here can be confined to a couple of summary points. Those who undoubtedly have benefited from Government policies include the very large numbers whose entry into the labour market has been facilitated by its legislative measures. The Government's record in reducing the jobless queue has been quite impressive in comparison to other EU countries (though overall levels of economic inactivity in the male 50–65 age-group remain astonishingly high). The percentage of the working-age population in paid employment rose from 70.8 per cent in 1997 to 74.7 per cent by the end of 2004, from 25.7 million to 27.4 million (Taylor, R, 2005a: 196). What had appeared to be the intractable problem of a large number of young jobless was at least partially resolved. In 2004 Brown told the CBI that the United Kingdom now had 'the highest levels of employment and the lowest levels of unemployment in our history' which, at 4.8 per cent, stood at about half the eurozone's 9 per cent (*The Guardian*, 2 July 2004). A host of initiatives, notably the various New Deals for the young, long-term unemployed, lone parents and the disabled, were implemented to promote full employment and although commentators differ in assessing their impact there can be no doubt on two points: that creating jobs was a Government priority and that the overall impact of its policies on the labour market has been quite positive.

Wages and conditions. The Minimum Wage has provided a platform below which wages cannot (legally) fall while the Working Families Tax Credit has subsidised low wages by publicly provided funds. More broadly the Government contends that higher rates of growth made possible by a more competitive economy benefit all, both directly by feeding into higher wages and indirectly by enabling the Government to extract additional resources from a thriving economy to fund more generous public services. Equally, the Government has disavowed any intention of competing through lowering wage costs – the so-called 'race to the bottom'. Its 'human capital' strategy is geared to boosting the performance of British firms by upgrading employee capabilities. Traditional social democratic approaches, with their accent on labour protection, social entitlements, high reservation wages and extensive collective regulation of the labour market, are seen as counterproductive in causing disequilibria in the matching of the supply and demand of labour and by imposing heavy social costs which discourage labour recruitment. Thus a top priority has been the avoidance of the toll on efficiency allegedly imposed by what are deemed 'institutional rigidities'.

'The successful economies of the future,' Blair declared, 'will excel at generating and disseminating knowledge, and commercially exploiting it. . . . The main source of value and competitive advantage . . . is human and intellectual capital' (quoted in Coates, 2005: 71). However, in practice spending on skills acquisition and retraining has (in comparative terms) remained low. Labour's strategy, one expert has concluded, seems to be 'not so much based on training and raising skill levels but more on relatively inexpensive job-search-focused programmes to move people into regular employment which might be low paid and thus publicly subsidised'. The scope of training elements within the various New Deal programmes which might lead to raising human capital have been 'modest' (Clasen, 2003: 26–7. See also Layard, 2005b: 191). The Treasury itself acknowledged that Britain continued to suffer from a 'poorer skills mix than many other countries' (quoted in Taylor, R, 2005a: 201). For some commentators, the Government is simply obeying the precepts of economic rationality: the Blair Government's labour market policies were 'congruent with the demands of a liberal market economy for highly fluid labour markets [and] readily available labour at low cost' (Hall, P, 2002: 42–3). However, despite much public preening on European stages by the Prime Minister and his Chancellor about the United Kingdom's remarkable economic accomplishments, labour productivity failed to improve and indeed was well below competitors such as France and Germany (Taylor, R, 2005a: 200–1). Nor is this surprising. Research conducted by Michie and Sheehan indicates that the characteristics associated with flexible labour markets – such 'low-road practices' as the use of short-term and temporary contracts, job insecurity and low levels of training – are negatively correlated with innovation (Michie and Sheehan, 2003: 138). Indeed economists have argued that the availability of a constant flow of low-cost and lightly protected labour actually 'encourages competition based on cost and price rather than on high quality, good design and product and process innovation' (Kitson, Martin and Wilkinson, 2000: 633). A paper by economists John Schmitt and Jonathan Wadsworth, exploring the 'flexibility is good for you' thesis, concluded that 'the international data for 1990–2000 gives little support to the view that greater flexibility in the US and the UK benefited less skilled or otherwise disadvantaged workers in those economies' (quoted by Larry Elliott, *The Guardian*, 22 March 2004).

The Government's own Trade and Industry website makes clear its view of the areas where it believes the British economy enjoys comparative advantage:

> Total wage costs in the UK are among the lowest in Europe … In the UK employees are used to working hard for their employers. In 2001 the average hours worked a week was 45.1 for males and 40.7 for females. The EU average was 40.9 hours … UK law does not oblige employers to provide a written employment contract … Recruitment costs in the UK are low … The law governing conduct of employment agencies is less restrictive in the UK. The UK has the lowest corporation tax rate of any major industrialised country.
>
> (quoted by Polly Toynbee in the *Guardian*, 11 February 2004)

Thus employment growth (outside the public sector) has largely been in hotels and catering, retailing and contract cleaning – where low pay and poor working conditions are endemic, managerial controls tight and trade union membership is extremely low – and not in the much-lauded high tech industries. Problems of low pay and employment insecurity, it should be added, affected only a minority of the workforce. For the majority of employees pay rose steadily during the Blair decade and, for those at the upper end, often substantially so. Most escaped the rawer edges of the flexible labour market. But it was precisely the failure to arrest pronounced inequalities in the labour market that might have surprised observers in 1997.

Physical and mental health. This once-neglected area is now attracting the attention of researchers, unions and Government agencies. Whatever the successes of flexible labour markets in generating new jobs, lowering costs and suppressing inflation its impact on the quality of working life, it appears, is distinctly less impressive. Research conducted by the Rowntree Foundation found that the growth of insecurity and loss of control at work caused by the drive to increase efficiency were strongly associated with a decline of physical and mental well-being (Rowntree, 1999). Of particular concern has been what seems to be an emergent pattern of a rising incidence of mental illness. According to the Health and Safety Executive 'work-related stress accounts for over a third of all new incidences of ill health' with a total of 12.8 million working days lost to stress, depression and anxiety in 2004/5 (Health and Safety Executive, 2007). A number of characteristics of the employment experience, all associated with the flexible labour market, appear to be correlated with deteriorating mental health. These include job insecurity, insecurity of income streams, long hours, work intensification, low control at work, strict performance management (imposition of targets, performance-related pay and so forth) and an authoritarian style of management (Beresford, 2005: 476). In what follows, some of the evidence is briefly reviewed.

'Over-work in our society' according to the ESRC Work-Life Balance programme 'is seen as a primary cause of growing ill health, both physical and mental ... Stress has become an increasingly intractable problem in the modern workplace' (Taylor, R, 2001b: 9. For international findings, see Gospel, 2003). Forty-five per cent of men and 32 per cent of women in the United Kingdom worked more hours than they were contracted for. The percentage of people working more than 48 hours a week has increased from 10 per cent in 1998 to 26 per cent in 2003 and (from 1992) the proportion of women working over 60 hours has more than doubled from 6 per cent to 13 per cent. A quarter of those who work long hours do so reluctantly (Bunting, 2004: 7, 9–10). The Blair Government's negotiated opt-out from EU Regulations appears to have had an effect because, according to a TUC report, a larger proportion of the workforce – one in six – work over 48 hours a week than they did when the EU 48-hour rule was brought in (Toynbee, 2003: 218). Research by Rubery and her colleagues disclose a relentless trend in both public and private sectors towards longer and less predictable work schedules, encroaching on time available for family commitments and leisure activities (Rubery, Ward, Grimshaw and Beynon, 2005).

The ability of British employers to bear down on costs and respond to fluctuating market conditions through tighter control over work schedules may have strengthened their competitive position and boosted profits but has not brought unalloyed benefits to those they employ. 'Study after study is showing a sharp increase in hours worked, causing rising stress and a matching sharp decrease in work satisfaction' (Toynbee, 2003: 218). Work intensification and long working hours were cited by 68 per cent of respondents in a wide-ranging study as major causes of high levels of stress, which, in turn (according to research) renders sufferers more vulnerable to cancer and heart disease (cited in Bunting, 2004: 187–8, 195. See also data compiled by the British Social Attitudes Survey, Crompton and Lyonette, 2007). According to a 2004 TUC survey of almost 5,000 health and safety staff 'anxiety over heavy workloads, long hours and the threat of redundancy is fuelling an epidemic of stress, with 58 per cent of union health and safety representatives citing it as the major cause of complaints' (*The Observer*, 31 October 2004). Equally, research findings reviewed by Fryer showed that 'job insecurity is associated with experienced powerlessness, impaired mental health (depression and reported psychosomatic symptoms), reduced job satisfaction, reduced organisatisational commitment, and reduced trust in management, resistance to change and poorer industrial relations' (Fryer, 1999: 8).

Whatever its claimed efficiency effect, evidence suggests that the reassertion of managerial prerogatives – another major aspect of flexible labour markets – has had clear negative effects on employee well-being. Low control over and low status at work, Professor of Epidemiology and Public Health Sir Michael Marmot found, not only contributed to a greater propensity to fall victim to heart disease but also to a greater risk of developing psychiatric disorders such as depression (Marmot, 2004: 130–1). In 1999 the Royal College of Psychiatrists reported that pressures of work – including boring repetitive tasks, uncertainty about the future and domineering management – were helping to tip a third of all employees every year into depression or other mental health problems (*The Guardian*, 10 September 1999). A major ESRC research programme concluded that 'today's world of work is much less satisfying to employees than the one they were experiencing ten years ago' (Taylor, R, 2002: 9). A Government minister put the matter in a nutshell: 'the long hours culture is alive and kicking ... We are all working too long hours and it is making us ill' (Margaret Hodge in the *Guardian*, 21 November 2000).

Although there was a rising incidence in official pronouncements of references to the importance of the 'work-life balance' and although a number of remedial steps were taken (e.g. improved parental leave) the falling quality of life so strongly associated with a 'lightly regulated' labour market was not a matter that preoccupied the Government. Indeed Blair and Brown urged a 'lighter touch' in the inspection of businesses to prevent breaches of existing health and safety laws and actually reduced the budget of their main enforcer, the Health and Safety Executive (Taylor, R, 2005a: 192, 189). But perhaps most significant, as an indicator of its priorities, has been its own initiatives in areas over which it holds direct responsibility.

Jobs with the highest stress levels are all in the public sector: local government employees, teachers and nurses (*The Guardian*, 6 January 2003). Research conducted by Andrew Oswald and Jonathan Gardner of Warwick University uncovered a major increase in depression, strain and sleep loss among public employees especially in health and education (cited in the *Guardian*, 22 March 2001). Indeed there is evidence of a direct linkage between the Government 's efforts to engineer a more 'entrepreneurial' and competitive culture in the public sector and ill health. Professor Green's research indicated that the much greater insistence on meeting targets, job intensification and incessant re-organisation is leading to a level of pressure before which growing numbers are beginning to buckle (cited in the *Guardian*, 30 October 2004). Government economic advisor Lord Layard identified performance-related pay – a key plank in the effort to foster a more 'enterprising spirit' among public employees – as likely to cause more stress, demoralisation, loss of self-respect and a general deterioration of mental health (Layard, 2006: 31). The Audit Commission identified six main factors that underpinned the decision by public sector employees to quit their jobs: virtually all were connected with the quality of the work experience. They were: 'the sense of being overwhelmed by bureaucracy, paperwork and targets; insufficient resources, leading to unmanageable workloads; a lack of autonomy; feeling undervalued by Government, managers and the public; pay that is not "felt fair" and a change agenda that feels imposed and irrelevant' (Audit Commission, 2002: para 49).

Conclusion: New Labour, employment relations and patterns of representation

What does this brief survey of the Blair Government's policies in the sphere of industrial relations tell us about New Labour's representational role? The Employment Relations Act and the ending of its predecessors' stalling on EU directives marked a major shift from the Conservative approach. On some matters, such as the institution of a minimum wage, the strengthening of employee rights at work, the adoption of the EU's Social Chapter, the phasing out of the two-tier workforce (to name but a few measures) Government actions, to varying degrees, indicated a willingness to accommodate trade union demands. The individual and collective rights of the workforce have been extended and the Government has set an important precedent by establishing by statute a minimum wage. Furthermore, its measures extending employee representation rights (e.g. over grievances, redundancies, transfer of undertaking and through union recognition), afforded a little more job security and improved procedures for consultation (Undy, 1999: 332). On all these issues New Labour exhibited a receptivity to the trade unions' representations that contrasted starkly with their experience under the Tories.

On other issues, including the retention of most of the existing legal framework governing the conduct of industrial disputes, the negotiation of opt-outs from EU directives, the insistence on preserving a lightly regulated labour market and the extension of private managerial practices to the public sector, Government measures showed scant sympathy towards union wishes. Union recognition procedures are complex and cumbersome, the laws regulating industrial action are highly restrictive and EU directives have usually been acceded to only with 'generous derogations and exceptions' (Undy, 1999: 331). Further, while the onus has been on extending employees individual rights, these largely depend for their practical application (in the private sector at least) on a strong trade union presence which is generally lacking and, as a result, for many workers they remain paper rights.

Utilising a more 'objective' concept of interest it would appear that, on the one hand, the Government's labour market strategy has had positive effects on the quantity of jobs generated in the economy. Its impact on remuneration levels is difficult to compute though the following points are worth making. In general most employees have experienced a sustained rise in living standards and there have been particular gains which can be directly attributed to Government measures for public sector workers, especially in health and education. But particular groups, notably the rapidly growing numbers employed in private service sector occupations such as catering, retail and cleaning have gained little in terms of pay and conditions. Turning to the quality of work experience the overall impact of Government labour market policy has been rather negative. The longer hours, diminished security, work intensification and stricter managerial regulation entailed by this policy is clearly associated with a decline of physical and (especially) mental well-being.

A key driver of the New Labour approach is the attempt to reconcile 'social justice' with 'economic efficiency'. 'If our labour market or our economy becomes too rigid', the Prime Minister warned, 'if it is too hard for businesses to function effectively or too expensive for them to employ, the result is merely another form of injustice' (Blair, 1998b). Regulations, the Treasury insisted, must not impose disproportionate costs on employers: they must be allowed to 'adjust total pay, including overtime and bonuses, as well as employment numbers quickly and flexibly in response to changes in market conditions' (quoted in Smith and Morton, 2006: 404). Labour markets encumbered by rigid systems of employment protection and too generous social assistance programmes wages would stultify the vibrancy of the economy. In short (from the Government's perspective) the price to be paid for creating a dynamic, inventive and entrepreneurial economy – with steady increments to the national wealth, the improvements in public services this rendered feasible, rising living standards, and employment for most – was that a substantial portion of the workforce must (at least for the time being) acquiesce in rather poorly paid and insecure jobs with sparse rights and entitlements. For some commentators, the Government had no real option. If social democratic parties 'are serious about full employment,' Peter Hall contends,

> they must be willing to pay the price – forms of labour market deregulation they would never have countenanced in previous eras, including the relaxation of restrictions on hiring and firing, measures to encourage part-time employment, and provisions for more flexible labour contracts.
>
> (Hall, P, 2002: 38)

Be that as it may, it would be unwise to over-state the degree to which the Government felt constrained to follow policies for which it had little natural enthusiasm. These external and structural factors have been coupled with an overt redefinition of the party's representational role. New Labour was, as one minister put it, 'unashamedly pro-business' because it was 'business that creates wealth and jobs and sustains our quality of life' (Hewitt, 2001b). It does not follow that it was anti-union. The Tory Government after 1979 was animated by a degree of hostility to trade unionism not seen since the inter-war years. The Blair Government ended this outsider status. The advice and comments of trade unions were sought as a matter of routine on a whole host of questions. Their representatives were invited to participate in deliberations on proposed measures which would affect the interests of their members. The Government provided large sums of money to help fund union training and educational efforts. The TUC and senior trade unionists 'now had ready access to ministers and their involvement in the Government's proliferating Task Forces afforded another opportunity to influence its thinking' (Undy, 2002: 643).

But if the trade unions were restored by the Government to the premier league of interest organisations equally it made certain that they languished at the lower end. They were seen to represent but 'one pressure group among many, with no special claim on government attention, sympathy or support' (Ludlam, Bodah and Coates, 2000: 229). Unlike its predecessors, the Blair Government did not require union co-operation in efforts to tackle key problems such as combating inflation, improving productivity or tempering industrial disturbances. In the years since the party was last in power the unions had experienced relentless decline in membership, organisation and industrial leverage. They had little to offer the Government in exchange for allowing it a status as a privileged and respected interlocutor (Undy, 2002: 642). They were more or less confined (in the words of former *Financial Times* Employment Editor, Robert Taylor) to 'a small and rather marginal role, mainly as voluntary learning organisations designed to help improve corporate performance'. The transformation of the United Kingdom as a world economic leader means ensuring 'that the needs of business and not those of trade unions or employees should become the main priority of employment relations and labour market policies' (Taylor, R, 2005a: 190, 191).

What was truly novel about New Labour was the rapprochement with business. As Tony Blair explained, 'the partnership we have tried to build with [business] over these past years is one that I am deeply committed to. It is a founding principle of New Labour and it will not change' (*The Guardian*, 6 November 2001). The new Labour Government, Blair reassured American financiers in New York in April 1998, 'attaches enormous importance to its relations with business both here and in the UK and abroad. ... We want to go out and have a proper dialogue with business and be the natural party of business' (quoted in Grant, 2000: 24).

Inevitably there were tensions between employers and the Government. Business – especially its peak association, the CBI – bemoaned any attempt by the Government to institute measures of labour regulation as more 'red tape', complained regularly about the imposition of 'stealth' taxes and felt impelled to regret virtually every concession the Government made to the unions. But much of this was muscle flexing. In truth it had 'little genuine to grumble about' (Taylor, R, 2005a: 191). New Labour viewed industry and finance as (what may be called) public interest organisations with the right to act as partners in the economic governance of the country. Interests like the unions and the anti-poverty lobby, in contrast, were awarded a secondary status as pressure groups whose demands were sectional since their interests did not objectively align and indeed were frequently at odds with the common economic welfare, as now defined. As TUC General Secretary John Monks put it, trade unions were often regarded 'as embarrassing elderly relatives at a family get-together' (*The Observer*, 20 June 1999).

'Labour's approach to the business community', a minister declared, 'has been transformed. Instead of being in conflict, the Labour Party and the business community are now increasingly effective partners' (Hewitt, 2001b). The broad correspondence between the interests of 'the wealth-creators' and those of the community at large, it was assumed, should be properly embedded in the machinery of government. Businessmen were enthusiastically recruited into ministerial positions, including Lord Sainsbury (of the retail chain, and a massive contributor to Labour party funds); Lord Simon, former group chief executive and chairman of BP; and Lord Drayson. Large numbers of prominent industrialists and financiers were invited to serve on numerous Government task forces. 'The wholesale importation of business expertise into the interstices of government at all levels is one of New Labour's most distinctive and enduring features ... This scale of business penetration was quite unprecedented in peacetime' (Smith, P, 2003: 588). There was a growing and widespread practice of recruitment and secondment of staff from major financial and industrial firms to government departments with which their firms had some tutelary relationship. This included staff from oil giants BP and Esso, British Aerospace (now Marconi), the United Kingdom's top defence contractor, accountancy and business consultancy firms, private medical insurers and from private contractors, all of whom worked in areas (e.g. taxation and the negotiation of PFI contracts) to which the Government felt they could contribute and from which they would certainly derive material advantage. New Labour's conversion to the 'harmony of interests' axiom persuaded it that a greater intermingling between government and business – a revolving door of personnel – was a positive benefit to both and it could see little of merit in the argument that conflicts of interest and the misuse of access, contacts and information for personal or corporate benefit could occur. Former ministers and political advisors flocked to well-remunerated jobs in the private sector where their skills and experience could be properly appreciated

Since society as a whole benefits from a dynamic and competitive market economy, New Labour holds, it follows that there is a pronounced congruence between the needs of investors and entrepreneurs in the market and those they employ – and, indeed, society at large. Hence the Prime Minister called for 'a real sense of shared national purpose' in which business and government would work together in 'a genuine partnership' (Blair, 2000). The party's traditional mistrust of and antipathy towards business had to be cast aside. In effect, a major modification has occurred in the role Labour performs in the political system and thereby in the pattern of interest representation. We discuss the implications of this in Chapter Nine.

7 The dynamics of New Labour

Not to extinguish our free will, I hold it to be true that Fortune is the arbiter of one-half of our actions, but that she still leaves us to direct the other half, or perhaps a little less.

(Machiavelli, *The Prince*)

The preceding chapters have sought, through a series of case studies, to delineate the programmatic trajectory of the Blair Government. This chapter will seek to unravel the general processes at work that may be said to account for it. We noted in the Introduction that two major schools of thought, globalisation and 'varieties of capitalism', have dominated scholarly discourse. The first section of this chapter briefly reviews them and then reflects upon their adequacy as explanations of New Labour. We conclude that while the structural and institutional factors they adduce did indeed constrain and delimit what was possible, they did not predetermine the course of action actually embarked on.

To explain the evolution of New Labour requires, this chapter suggests, elucidating how its key figures understood the situation in which they found themselves and defined the key challenges they confronted – in short their reasons for acting in the way they did. Here, the chapter maintains, there are three key questions: what were the lessons drawn from the party's unhappy past? How, in the New Labour view, could the legacy of electoral failure be overcome? And in what ways and to what extent was globalisation deemed to circumscribe policy discretion?

Globalisation and varieties of capitalism

Globalisation theory explains New Labour in terms of what can be called 'the logic of accommodation'. It emphasises the degree to which the freedom of manoeuvre of governments, especially those of a social democratic stripe, are constrained by the imperatives of globalisation. Globalisation designates a global political economy characterised by the internationalisation of production, free trade, massive and free-flowing capital movements and the general deregulation of economic and financial relations. 'The logic of accommodation' is encapsulated in Cerny and Evans' claim 'that the Labour government in the UK has adopted a policy agenda which in its most crucial aspects reflects the continuing transformation of the British industrial welfare state into a competition state' in which 'the imperatives of international competitiveness and consumer choice' supersede equality and social justice as the prime objectives of state policy (Cerny and Evans, 2004: 51, 60). Globalisation has substantially diminished the state's capacity to project its power inside its borders, with its choice of policies and the balance of its strategic priorities heavily constricted by the need to placate forces emanating from the international environment. It is deemed an inexorable process which has squeezed the power of the nation-state to such an extent that traditional social democracy has ceased to be a viable political project.

The varieties of capitalism approach rejects the thesis that all Western states are being impelled onto a convergent course. It draws attention to 'the role that political-economic institutions play in co-ordinating the behaviour of economic agents, the relationship among the institutions of a given country and the tight linkage between those institutions and particular patterns of economic growth' (Howell, 2004: 3). These institutions fall into two distinct types – liberal market economies and co-ordinated market economies – to which correspond two welfare state regimes, the liberal and the social democratic (Esping-Andersen, 1990). The prevailing institutional type imparts a logic deriving from functional interdependence that restricts the range of policy options available to governments. 'There are,' Soskice avers, 'strong interlocking complementarities between different parts of the institutional framework. Each system depends on the other systems to function effectively' (quoted in Pierson, 2000a: 812). Systemic logic or institutional path dependence replaces economic forces as the principal propellant of policy choice – though perhaps in an equally deterministic way. 'The self reinforcing character of institutions makes it extremely difficult to jump paths from one type of political economy to another' (Howell, 2004: 4). Applied to the study of social democratic transformation, Hall explains,

> Systematic variations in the organization of the political economy and social policy regimes ... [condition] both the direction taken by social democratic parties as they search for new policies and the likely success with which any particular type of policy can be implemented in a nation. The character of the political economy affects both the complexion of the problems it faces and the feasibility of specific solutions.
> (Hall, P, 2002: 42)

As we have seen (Introduction pp. 12–14) the United Kingdom has been firmly lodged by most varieties of capitalism as a liberal market economy/ welfare state regime. Thus the two schools of thought broadly concur in their predictions of a Labour Government's programmatic orbit: it has no real alternative but to adjust to the compulsions of globalisation in such a way as to reinforce Britain's neo-liberal character. The argument can be summed up in terms of three general propositions: that welfare state retrenchment is inevitable, that state intervention must be geared to the imperative of fostering competitiveness and that the role of the state must be re-engineered from being a producer to an enabler of services:

1. *Welfare state retrenchment.* The fiscal basis of the state is eroding because business corporations and financial institutions – indeed the monied in general – can avoid high taxes by shifting their assets to low-tax countries. Increasing reliance on inward investment coupled with the (relative) ease with which companies can relocate means that investment decisions will be highly sensitive to tax rates. High taxes repel and low taxes attract foreign investment so a Labour government would have no option but to maintain a business-friendly tax regime. As the revenue basis of a country abates so governments find it progressively harder to fund welfare spending. Globalisation thus 'exerts a downward pressure on systems of social protection and social expenditure by prioritizing the reduction of deficits and debt and the lowering of taxation as key objectives of state policy' (Mishra, 1999: 15). Goldthorpe summarises (but does not agree with) the proposition thus:

   > Intensified global competition and the centrality thus given to productivity impose strict limits on the resources that can be raised through taxation in order to fund social welfare services and, in effect rule out attempts to use the welfare state as a redistributive mechanism.
   > (Goldthorpe, 2002: 5)

2. *Structural re-organisation of state functions.* Notwithstanding the state remains a potent actor. However a structural transformation and strategic reorientation has occurred in the ordering and performance of its functions among which the maximising of economic competitiveness in a highly globalised world economy has emerged as the primary one. This is made manifest in the shift from 'welfarist' to 'workfarist' modes of organising welfare with the extension of social rights of citizens being displaced by the structural subordination of social policy to the demands of labour market flexibility and economic competitiveness. There is now deemed to be an inescapable trade-off between labour protection and incomes equality on the one hand and employment for all on the other. The maintenance of highly fluid labour markets, Hall suggests, is a functional requisite of the United Kingdom's liberal market economy, which no Labour government could ignore (Hall, P, 2002: 41). By the same token 'welfare to work' approaches which tie the right to benefit with the duty to seek work are vital to ensure that the cost of welfare is contained and the labour market adequately lubricated. The pressure to subordinate the social sphere to the needs of economic competitiveness is

of such a scale as to transform the welfare state from a collective shelter protecting people from international market pressures into 'a competition state' or 'Schumpeterian workfare state' (Cerny and Evans, 2004: 51; Jessop, 1999b, 1999c). Thus, in place of the priority given by the welfare state to promoting the population's welfare through affording protection against market forces, the principal objective of the competition state is to intensify competitiveness by extending the sway of the market.

3. *The enabling state.* By the same token the institutional logic of the liberal welfare state accelerates a shift from the 'collectivist' to the 'enabling' state in which the monopoly state provision of key public services (such as healthcare and education) is replaced by the 'mixed economy of welfare'. The exigencies of constrained public resources and higher consumer expectations impart a powerful impetus to extending the role of (allegedly) more efficient and responsive non-state actors (including profit-seeking organisations) in delivering public services, and to the wholesale adoption of techniques and practices honed in the private sector to shake-up a lethargic public sector. Hence the mixed economy of welfare is characterised by the growing centrality of private–private partnerships and market-style mechanisms including competition, performance management and consumer choice (van Kersbergen, 2003; Jessop, 1999c).

By way of comment on these three propositions – or predictions – findings from earlier chapters can be very briefly summarised:

Welfare state retrenchment

Some trends are clearly consistent with the projections sketched above. Tax levels on corporations and higher income groups remain stubbornly below the West European average in the United Kingdom, with rampant tax avoidance further reducing liabilities. The Government has clearly been reluctant to jeopardise the stream of inward investment by hiking corporate taxes (Peston, 2005: 252–7).[1] Income tax remains very distinctly less progressive than in most comparable EU countries, though electoral factors (see below) seem to be more important here. On the spending side there has been a further drift to means-testing and stricter conditionality, and benefits for those of working age have stagnated following the path of 'recommodification' anticipated by institutional theory. Most dramatic over all, the first two years of the Blair Government witnessed public spending rounds of almost unprecedented severity.

But then followed a major and sustained boost to spending, particularly in health and education but in many other areas too (e.g. urban regeneration, child poverty programmes). Education and health budgets now absorb a higher proportion of the GDP than at any time for a generation (i.e. before the full onset of globalisation) and compare favourably with most EU countries. At the same time, through a combination of stealth taxes, increase in national insurance contributions and higher revenues flowing from steady economic growth the amount of money available to the Chancellor has risen very appreciably. Predictions of welfare retrenchment have not been borne out. Combating social exclusion has been a major New Labour goal and as a result of a battery of policies the proportion of the population in poverty (defined in relative terms) has fallen significantly. Universality in health and education has been resolutely maintained and the quality of provision notably improved.

Structural re-organisation of state functions

Here the orbit of Government policy corresponds more closely than in any other to that predicted by globalisation and varieties of capitalism theories. 'Recommodification', that is the 'dismantling of those aspects of the welfare state that shelter workers from market pressures, forcing them to accept jobs on employers' terms' (Pierson, 2001: 9) has continued apace. The New Labour insistence on a flexible labour market in the interests of raising international competitiveness and absorbing surplus labour had as its corollary the survival – even expansion – of a large pool of poorly paid, weakly protected and insecure workers. Trade union recognition and collective bargaining rights remain limited, employees still lack many of the rights they routinely enjoy elsewhere in Western Europe and none of the tight restrictions governing the taking of industrial action established by the Tories have been eased.

However, even here, we should be cautious about over-generalisation. The lightly regulated labour market of the Blair Government is different from the sparsely regulated one bequeathed by the Tories. The Blair Government 'has radically departed from the neo-liberal doctrine that labour markets work best when wages are free to vary as much as possible' (Hamann and Kelly, 2003: 646). Thus, for the first time in British history, a minimum wage now provides a floor below which wages cannot fall, low wages are supplemented by tax credits and some re-regulation of the labour market has taken place. The competition state, as envisaged by Cerny, has not fully displaced the welfare state (Cerny, 2000: 177).

The enabling state

Far from shrinking, the public sector, whether defined in terms of spending levels, share of national income, proportion of the workforce or role in the social organisation of life, has grown substantially. The principle of schooling and healthcare available free at the point of consumption and provided according to need is now notably more firmly embedded than in 1997. On the other hand there has been a major reconfiguration in the structure, mode of operation and pattern of delivery of the public services. A wholesale import of methods, organisational principles and practices borrowed from the market sector has occurred with a major expansion in the role of profit-seeking firms in the provision of public goods. Much of the responsibility for delivering new capital projects for the public services has been devolved to commercial interests through the Private Finance Initiative.

However it does not follow that just because policy followed the track predicted by the structuralist and institutionalist theories reviewed above, that it was because of the factors adduced by them. Indeed, far from being hemmed in by 'institutional path dependence' the Blair Government's 'modernisation' programme deliberately challenged major centres of institutional power (the professional associations and the unions) and the parameters of established policy. The interviews conducted by this author with key policy players (ministers and Downing Street advisors) emphatically substantiate Marquand's judgement that if New Labour 'pushed marketisation and privatisation forward, at least as zealously as the Conservatives did' it was because it believed that these were the right policies to follow and not because it felt compelled to do so (Marquand, 2004: 118). In short, as with Regini's comparative investigation of EU countries, the pattern that emerges from our case studies is one in which 'the interconnection between contiguous policy areas' was 'much less than one might have expected' from globalisation and varieties of capitalism theory (Regini, 2000: 9–10).

Why is this? Whatever their differences – which are substantial – both theories operate within a (broadly speaking) positivist methodology. This posits explanation as the search for regularities in which a particular event or process – the dependent variable – is explicable in terms of a set of independent variables: 'x because of y'. In this context causality is seen as primarily a matter of first establishing correlations between quantifiable variables and then seeking to demonstrate causality by formulating and empirically testing hypotheses defining the relationship between these variables. From this perspective cause and effect are separate and independent objects and the relationship between them an external one. Economic forces, systemic properties and institutional formats are seen 'as the givens that constitute actions' (Bevir, 2005: 3).

This gives rise to a deterministic bias. This is self-evidently the case with the globalisation thesis of the 'logic of accommodation' that does not admit the possibility of deviating from the track laid down by immanent economic and technological forces. It is almost equally true of 'varieties of capitalism' though in a more indirect and functionalist way. Its advocates follow a labelling strategy which 'inspects the characteristics of an empirical case and decides which of a limited number of theoretical models (ideally two) it most closely resembles. The case is then considered to be "an example" of that model and labelled accordingly.' The logic ascribed to the model is then applied to the empirical instant by which it is alleged to be bound (Crouch, 2005: 452).

Such modes of analysis by their very nature neglect the ideas and pre-ferences of political actors and the way they construe policy problems (Clasen, 2002: 71; Bevir, 2005: 13). In reality, as Simon points out, external forces cannot directly cause action but can only do so through the media-tion of political agents: the social world is apprehended 'not as it appears "objectively" but subjectively to the actor' (Simon, 1985: 298). There is an inevitable gap between objective and subjective environments because of the pervasive effects of uncertainty. Uncertainty has been defined as 'the char-acter of situations in which agents cannot anticipate the outcome of a decision and cannot assign probabilities to the outcome' (Beckert, 1996: 804). Dequech has distinguished between three types of uncertainty: *sub-stantive, procedural* and *fundamental*. Substantive uncertainty is due to lack of information, procedural 'refers to the gap between the complexity of a situation and the agents' competence in processing information', while fun-damental uncertainty reflect the fact that events (even momentous ones such as the collapse of the Soviet Union) are frequently unpredictable (Dequech, 2001). In a world of uncertainty and indeterminacy, where information-processing and environment-scanning capabilities are con-strained and events cannot be foreseen, the human mind inevitably relies upon 'cognitive shortcuts', more or less elaborated notions or hypotheses of how the world works which guide policy-makers in how to perceive the environment, draw inferences from evidence and thereby reach decisions (Jervis, 1985: 321).

Such cognitive shortcuts or mental maps '"orient" people to situations much as maps orient travellers', forming connections 'between the objective conditions in which human agents find themselves and the choices of action in them' (Eckstein,1996: 486). Mental maps can therefore be conceived as frames of reference, which, by imparting some degree of intelligibility, help political actors find their bearings in a complicated, confusing and evanes-cent world. Most crucially, by selecting, highlighting and structuring aspects of a perceived reality so as to form a pattern of understanding, they 'pro-mote a particular problem definition, causal interpretation, moral evalua-tion, and/or treatment recommendation for the item described' (Entman, 1993: 52). In other words, while structural and institutional arrangements supply the conditions, the resources and restraints, the risks and opportu-nities that actors have to consider when selecting a policy, it is the appre-hension of realities and not the realties themselves that, in the final resort, determine what that selection will be. It is ultimately 'not in the real world but in the actors' mental image of the world that the attribution of causes and expected effects must be located' (Scharpf, 1997: 61).

From this perspective, external forces and institutional inheritances can best be seen not as the determinants of action but as shaping conditions which, as apprehended, help formulate notions of which courses of action can be deemed realistic, feasible, appropriate and desirable. How can this analysis be applied to explaining the dynamics of Labour's transformation?

Here it may be useful to rely on Weber's insights. What distinguishes social action from other phenomena is that it has meaning for the actors. Hence to account for why one course of action was taken rather than another it is necessary to reconstruct a context of meaning, that is the actor's own appreciation of their circumstances and how they impinge on the choice of favoured goals (Eckstein, 1996: 483; Ekstrom, 1992: 112; Farr, 1985: 1090). This is what this chapter, in what follows, seeks to do by reconstructing the formation and the distinctive attributes of the New Labour mindset.

Here the concept if 'policy learning' is of real value. Policy learning can be defined 'as a deliberate attempt to adjust the goals or techniques of policy in response to past experience and new information' (Hall, P, 1993: 278). Hall distinguishes between two forms of policy learning, the incremental, which 'adjusts policy without challenging the overall terms of a given policy paradigm', and the radical, involving discontinuities in policy, and amounting to a challenge to the principles of the prevailing frame of reference (or paradigmic view of the world) (Hall, P, 1993: 279). The hypothesis advanced here is that New Labour is rightly viewed as a phenomenon that is, in some ways at least, qualitatively different from Labour in the past because it has engaged in 'radical learning'.

Radical learning, it can be postulated, can occur for three (mutually compatible) reasons. The first is perceived paradigm exhaustion, arising from a sense that existing policy instruments or levers of action have become ineffectual, that serious anomalies inexplicable in terms of the established paradigm were occurring and that traditional goals had ceased to be feasible. The second reason is electoral shock, defined in terms of repeated and serious electoral defeat whose effect is to shake confidence in the electoral palatability and viability of established programmes. The third is the impact of a new configuration of power. Other things being equal, all politicians will be tempted to pursue policies with lower risks and costs attached – which correspond, in short, to the grain of power. Hence if the balance of power in society is altered in some substantial manner, with the effect of magnifying the costs and risks involved in pursuing policies derived from an established paradigm, then political actors are likely to consider shedding this paradigm in favour of one which commands more support among power wielders (Hall, P, 1993: 280). What matters in this case is less the substantive qualities of a policy than its political viability.

We argue below that all three of these processes were at work to produce New Labour's metamorphosis. The rest of the chapter will consist of the following sections. The first will investigate New Labour's perception of 'paradigm exhaustion', derived from its analysis of past Labour governmental failure. The second will examine the impact of electoral shocks, the succession of electoral debacles culminating in the trauma of 1992. The third explores the effect of shifting power configurations, New Labour's understanding of the new systemic pressures and imperatives arising from the advent of a globalised world economy and the effect this was seen to have on the feasibility of various policy options.

'Old Labour': exorcising the past

> Tony saw the Labour party, like a restaurant that poisoned its guests ... Think of that restaurant. If you had come home after what you thought was a good meal and had been violently ill for a week, what would make you return?
>
> (Peter Hyman, Downing Street aide in Hyman, 2005: 53)

The starting point for failure-induced learning is 'the prevalence of pressing policy problems for which the standard recipes from past policy experience no longer apply' (Hemerijck and Schludi, 2000). The perception of programmatic impasse or paradigm failure operates as a powerful lever of change by subverting traditional beliefs and faith in established policy repertoires, thereby creating 'political space, windows of time, and political entrepreneurs begin to search out and try new policy prescription' (Goldstein, 1993: 13). The late 1980s witnessed the emergence of a new cohort of 'political entrepreneurs', led by Blair and Brown, who steadily gained in influence in the years of the Kinnock leadership (see Shaw, 1994). The sudden death of John Smith in 1994 provided them with the opportunity to gain full control of the party, with Blair elected as leader and Brown as shadow chancellor. These 'modernisers' brought with them an 'explicit, conscious, deliberate, and – above all – aggressive assumption' of a new political identity (Moschanas, 2002: 229). Indispensable to grasping the dynamics of this process was their analysis of the impasse of 'Old Labour'.

'Old Labour' should not be understood as a descriptive reference to Labour in its earlier guise, still less as relating to a historically verifiable view of the party's past,[2] but as the centre-piece of a past that was constructed and imagined for political purposes. It was both a strategic and an operative concept. As a strategic concept it was designed to emphasise – for public consumption – the novelty of New Labour, the dazzling white of the new against the tawdry, stained 'brand X' of the old. But it was also an operative concept in that it informed and helped organise the "modernisers'' understanding of where Labour had in the past gone wrong. 'Understanding the psychological imprint on the minds of Tony and Gordon, of what they saw as their political inheritance,' Peter Hyman, a Number 10 staffer, explained, 'is crucial to understanding their actions in government' (Hyman, 2005: 53). The transition of 'Old Labour' to New Labour symbolised, publicised and registered the party's 'paradigm shift'.

For New Labour (Blair, Brown and their followers) 'Old Labour' was a spent force irretrievably bound to a stockpile of ill-conceived, irrelevant, dogma-driven and damaging policies. Attempts to propitiate union power by seeking its co-operation in moderating wage growth through various types of 'social contracts' had merely stoked-up inflationary pressures. Nationalised industries, excessive state intervention and the propping-up of 'lame-ducks' had reduced productivity growth, pushed-up costs and squandered resources into non-productive outlets. Deficit financing had undermined financial and business confidence, destablised the economy and provoked repeated financial crises. New Labour, Blair declared 'has learned from the lessons of the Seventies and Eighties that Keynesian-style expansionary measures to raise the demand for labour only generated inflationary spirals, which through a squeeze on profits and investment, destroyed jobs' (the *Daily Telegraph*, 17 September 1996). Second-guessing the market had distorted price signals and misused investment opportunities. Reckless and profligate policies had heedlessly alienated the financial markets. The resulting total lack of market credibility had imposed a huge burden of servicing alarmingly high public debt levels, caused turmoil on the currency and bond markets, and driven up interest rates to economically stifling levels – culminating in the humiliating IMF-enforced cuts in public spending. But the real denouement of the 'Old Labour' government was the 'Winter of Discontent' of 1978/9. For Blair, 'the effect of the Winter of Discontent, the piles of rubbish, the dead not buried, the economic incompetence, the high taxes, the unilateral disarmament policy, was to poison the electoral bloodstream' (Hyman, 2005: 53). From these events emerged a 'remembered folk history of the Labour governments of the 1970s as having been brought to their knees by public sector producer interests' (written communication from Perri 6) that fired a determination within the Blair Government that it, unlike its predecessors, would stand adamantly firm against the 'dictates' of public sector unions.

The New Labour image of 'Old Labour' was equally shaped by recollections of the fraught 1980s, the formative political experiences for most of its leading lights. 'Common to all modernisers,' Hyman reflected,

> were the scars caused by the battles with the Left – including Militant – in the eighties. For this generation, Labour was a party that lost elections, that had a series of unpalatable, extreme often suicidal policies and that was crucified by the newspapers.
>
> (Hyman, 2005: 52)

From the Blair-Brown standpoint, Kinnock's attempts to renew the party between 1983 and 1992 had been too tepid, too cautious, too hesitant about expunging the legacy of 'Old Labour'. For the New Labourites, Kinnock's leadership (as a one-time New Labour insider put it) 'was seen, not as the beginning of the long road to recovery, but as a botched and hopelessly incomplete separation from "Old Labour"' (written communication from Perri 6).

For New Labour the blemishes and defects of 'Old Labour' were endemic and permeated the entire party. In this view 'the left, the right and the centre within the Labour party were more or less equally implicated in its failures' and, indeed, 'the dilemmas of the party were insoluble in the terms of the left–right discourse within which party business was routinely conducted' (Cronin, 2004: 10). In short, there was little or nothing to be salvaged from the 'graveyard of failed programmes' and the obsolete modes of thinking and understanding of the world by which they were inspired (Cronin, 2004: 14). The repudiation of 'Old Labour' was 'not just a matter of policy, but of what the party has become, of what it now stands for, how it works and who, quite literally, it is' (Cronin, 2004: 2).

This repudiation was as much psychological as political or intellectual in character. 'Old Labour' was an emotionally charged image which, for Blair and supporters at least, encapsulated a sense of alienation from all the party had represented in the past. 'Tony,' Downing Street aide Peter Hyman explained,

> has an allergy to old Labour. It's not just that he finds policies such as nationalisation and high direct taxes barmy. He also hates losers, hates impotence, hates meaningless protest. He breaks out into a rash at the thought of being lumped with the failures of Labour's past.
>
> (Hyman, 2005: 11)

Above all, it was a party driven by ideology, not practical concern for the lives and aspirations of real people. According to a senior Downing Street aide,

> for Tony the Labour party was addicted to a set of views which were not about the improvement in lives of ordinary people but were about devotion to certain characteristics, means, institutions, rules which were not in themselves about the fundamental goals of a progressive party but had become reified.
>
> (interview with Mathew Taylor, 2007)

Equally, for Gordon Brown the 'failures of his party's past loomed large'. He

> had seen too many Labour Chancellors lurch from profligate post-election boom to fatal pre-election bust. Stability, rules, discipline, prudence, and transparency: the mantras were more than election slogans. They were the means by which the New Labour government would exorcise the past.
>
> (Stephens, 2001: 186)

It was not, then, the legacy of the party's past as such that permeated the New Labour mentality and so governed its behaviour in office – it was that past as re-imagined and reconstructed in a very particular way. The New Labour leadership, one one-time member of its intellectual entourage recalled, developed 'a memory of 1994 as a kind of watershed, before which all was capitulation to trade union militancy and craven capitulation to public sector middle class producer interests' (written communication, Perri 6). It was against this past that they defined themselves. 'Old Labour' so construed may have had only a tangential resemblance to reality but, and absorbed into the New Labour mindset, its effects were no less real for that.

Electoral shocks

> One woman said to me [Philip Gould] just weeks before the 1997 election, 'When I was a child there was a wardrobe in my bedroom. I was always scared that one night, out of the blackness, a monster would emerge. That is how I think of the Labour Party.' This was typical.
>
> (Gould, 1998: 21)

Exogenous shocks delivered by the electorate are widely seen as a crucial catalyst releasing unremitting pressures for policy renovation. They create windows of opportunity for a new generation of policy entrepreneurs with the courage, determination and capacity to sweep aside established patterns of thought. The unexpected and cataclysmic 1992 defeat – the fourth in a row – in particular had a devastating impact on Labour. Given that circumstances seemed exceptionally propitious (a serious downturn in the economy) the effect was to precipitate a collapse of morale, a dire loss of political and ideological self-confidence – a collective nervous breakdown – which eliminated much of the surviving opposition to the party's right-ward thrust and offered a virtual carte blanche to anyone who appeared to possess the secret of electoral success. As New Labour insider Mathew Taylor recalled, 'following the gut wrenching defeat in 1992,' Labour's modernisers 'took it as read that Labour could not be elected unless they had completely eradicated any connection to the discredited party of the winter of discontent and the 1983 manifesto' (Taylor, M, 2002). The lesson, for Brown, was that Labour was

> still seen as a party that taxes irresponsibly ... that spends money inefficiently ... that will always take the easy option ... whose economic policy may well be run by the unions. Generally a party that will hold people back rather than help people on, in other words that we are a threat to people's aspirations.
>
> (quoted in Hyman, 2005: 44)

With Tony Blair's accession to the leadership in 1994 the modernisers seized the reins of the party. Central to their drive for change was their analysis of the changing shape of the class structure and its implications for Labour's electoral future (Heath, Jowell and Curtice, 2001: 10). The working class was fragmenting and decomposing. The proportion of the population employed in manufacturing industries and manual occupations was shrinking remorselessly while middle class numbers leapt. Furthermore, internal differentiation within the working class was widening. Skilled workers in high tech sectors in the booming South East – 'Essex' or 'Mondeo man' – had thrived at the same time as the conditions of unskilled and casualised labour and the unemployed, especially in the North, Scotland and Wales – Labour's heartlands – had deteriorated (Heath, Jowell and Curtice, 2001, 10–11). The era of sharply defined social classes and class-driven political cleavages had come to an end, replaced by a society characterised by blurred class boundaries, loosening class and partisan attachments, high rates of social mobility, overlapping and pluralistic interest structures and issue-based voting. The dissolution of class structures has unwound the links binding class and party and pronounced the irrevocable decay of class-configured partisan loyalties.

This sociological analysis informed what elsewhere I called the 'new strategic paradigm' (Shaw, 1994: 59–62). This was largely a product of a group of advertising agents, pollsters, communications specialists and party officials assembled in the mid-1980s under the rubric of the Shadow Communications Agency (though the term ceased to be used after 1992).[3] In effect, they constituted what Haas has called an epistemic community, that is 'a network of professionals with recognised expertise and competence in a particular domain and an authoritative claim to policy-relevant knowledge within that domain' (quoted in Yee, 1996: 86) The more the area in which an epistemic community sustains a claim to competence is characterised by uncertainty, bewilderment and insecurity the greater the dependence of others on its advice (Radaelli, 1995: 165). This was the case with Labour's strategic community. Although notionally neutral experts, they were closely associated with, indeed an integral part of, the modernising faction. With the exception of the brief period of the Smith leadership, the quality of their insight into the roots of electoral behaviour, the validity of their methods of plumbing public opinion and the accuracy of the inferences they drew about the policy changes required to appeal to voters were never seriously questioned.

A major role in monitoring the feelings and beliefs was played by Tony Blair's senior polling and strategy adviser, Phillip Gould. According to Blair's biographer, no single strategic adviser in any party has ever had 'the continuity of influence [or] the same degree of penetration ... that Gould has had on Labour's' leadership' (Seldon, 2004: 136). He was 'New Labour's guru, explaining the outside world to his client, and his client to the outside world. Tony Blair found the perfect man to help him articulate what he believed needed to be done' (Seldon, 2004: 137). He was responsible for organising focus groups, sometimes personally acting as moderator, analysing the raw data, communicating his finding to the PM and providing an interpretative slant on their significance (interview with former cabinet member, 2006).

The key to the New Labour strategy was the courting of Middle England. It was to the voters of Middle England, a well-informed journalist close to

Tony Blair wrote, 'that all political blandishments are now tailored' (Martin Kettle, *The Guardian*, 18 March 1997). If New Labour's first crucial strategic concept was 'Old Labour', the second, of equal significance, was 'Middle England'. But what was 'Middle England'? It is a most elusive concept. At times it was defined as that segment of the electorate that identified itself as middle class. 'Over 60 per cent of people,' Gould wrote,

> now believe that they are, to one degree or another, middle class. This new middle class does not just include people in white-collar jobs: 50 per cent of people in skilled manual occupations consider themselves to be to some extent described by the term 'middle class'.
>
> (Gould, 1998: 396).[4]

At other times it was defined in terms of objective social characteristics. Thus Gould proffered the alternative definition of Middle England as 'the aspirational working class in manual occupations, and the increasingly insecure white-collar workers with middle-to-low-level incomes' (Gould, 1998: 396). Another Downing Street strategist characterised 'Middle England' as 'the affluent working class and the middle class south of Watford' (interview, Mathew Taylor, 2006). At yet other times it was defined in terms of newspaper readership – specifically the readers of the *Mail* and the *Sun* (interviews with Government advisors and MPs). On the point of those who were *not* Middle England there was more agreement: the 'heartland' working class (especially in Scotland, Wales and the North), ethnic minorities (Hyman, 2005: 54) and the more progressive elements within the public sector middle class, '*Guardian* and *Independent* readers' as they were unenthusiastically dubbed (interviews with New Labour advisors).

It was 'Middle England's' views that were 'repeatedly solicited on the issues of the day' in focus groups (Martin Kettle, *The Guardian*, 18 March 1997). This implies a more operational definition of Middle England for members of focus groups had to be recruited. Certainly prior to 1997 focus group members were drawn principally from the ranks of Conservative voters who had considered switching to Labour in 1992 then changed their mind and returned to their traditional allegiance. They flocked in large numbers to Labour in 1997 and a New Labour strategic priority was to retain their support (interview, Mathew Taylor, 2005). It was the portrait of their collective mindset that so heavily influenced party strategy both in the run-up to 1997 and subsequently.

This delineated 'Middle England' as aspirational, consumer-oriented, and individualistically minded with few of the collective sentiments and attachments that had defined Labour's constituency in the past. Its members wanted higher quality public services and they were strongly averse to shouldering more tax burdens, and to 'wasteful' spending by 'profligate' public authorities (Gould, 1998: 3–4). The principal theme in the portrait of 'Middle England' that emerged was estrangement from 'Old Labour'. It was deemed 'an old-fashioned party, remote from their concerns and aspirations, wedded to high taxation and extravagant expenditure and not competent to run the country' (Radice and Pollard, 1993: 13). 'To millions of voters Labour became a shiver of fear in the night, something unsafe, buried deep in the psyche' (Gould, 1998: 21).

For one close observer of New Labour 'the recognition in the early 1990s that Labour was not just distrusted but positively loathed by electorally absolutely key constituencies is central and formative to the development of New Labour' (written communication from Perri 6). This posed a real strategic dilemma and it would not have been surprising if strategists had concluded that the caricature of the party was so deeply lodged in the public psyche that there was no real alternative but to repudiate it in favour of a totally new 'brand'. But perhaps the most intriguing aspect of New Labour strategic thinking was the belief that this 'Middle England's' grim and sombre image was, far from being a tabloid-driven caricature, essentially accurate. Labour was, indeed, the monster from Gould's wardrobe. Voters had decisively repudiated 'Old Labour' in four successive elections – and they had been quite right to do so. 'Old Labour' (New Labour's principal strategist contended) had 'failed to understand that the old working class was becoming a new middle class: aspiring, consuming, choosing what was best for themselves and their families. They had outgrown crude collectivism and left it behind in the supermarket car park' (Gould, 1998: 4). It had become ever more 'enslaved by dogma ... had abandoned the centre ground and ... camped out on the margins' (Gould, 1998: 3–4). It had not merely stopped listening, it had 'declared political war on the values, instincts and ethics of the great majority of decent, hard-working voters' (Gould, 1998: 19).

'Old Labour', in short, was beyond redemption. Its 'stubborn refusal to modernise was unique to the British Labour Party, buried deep in its character, its ethos, implicit in its founding moments' (Gould, 1998: 23). The clutter in the attic had all to be swept away. Labour – 'New' Labour – had to start afresh. 'We would never again have penal tax rates, never again take risks with the economy, never again be weak on defence, never again pander to the unions, never again be anti-business or anti-market or anti entrepreneurship.' For Blair these beliefs were 'non-negotiable' (Hyman, 2005: 54).

Throughout the period of the Blair Government the views of 'Middle England' continued to be tirelessly scrutinised via the ubiquitous focus groups. All governments, of course, want to keep their finger on the pulse of the public. What was distinctive of New Labour was (as a former Cabinet minister put) its 'persistent and obsessive attention to the perceived electoral consequences' of any contemplated measure (interview, 2006) and the heavy reliance on a form of opinion survey research which, by its nature (extremely small numbers), could not lay claim to be representative. But establishing the precise extent to which and the way in which the opinions of Middle England (as unravelled by focus groups) shaped policy is not easy to establish. Two obvious areas were law and order and race/asylum seekers/ immigration. But in the policy areas covered in this study the most pervasive impact was on tax.

An entrenched part of the New Labour mentality was that the public (or, more specifically 'Middle England') was deeply tax-averse. According to the well-connected economic editor of the *Observer*, Bill Keegan, after the shock of the 1992 defeat Gordon Brown was 'terrorised by fear of doing anything to offend ... Middle England', who had felt threatened by John Smith's tax plans (Keegan, 2003: 11. See also Seldon, 2004: 242). Quanti-tative surveys that appeared to suggest public support for higher tax and spending were greeted with deep scepticism (interviews with Charles Clarke, 1998; Frank Dobson, 2004). A senior Downing Street advisor summed-up the New Labour view:

> The hard fact is that when offered a choice between competing parties they [electors] will vote for the one that's cutting taxes, as they did it in 1992, when tax was a big issue. ... I think when you ask people a question about whether they would pay more tax, it is interpreted by respondents in this way: would you pay more tax, or are you just a mean bastard? Though the inner voice is I'm a mean bastard, I'll keep my money, I don't think you get a very fair answer.
>
> (interview, 2002)

How correct this view was is a moot point. According to Paul Whiteley, one of the United Kingdom's leading electoral analysts, the proposition that Labour lost the 1992 election because of John Smith's proposals on tax was little more than 'an urban myth'. The evidence compiled by the British election survey indicates 'that voters swung away from Labour in 1992 because of a lack of faith in the party's ability to improve services such as health and education, rather than because of its position on taxation' (Paul Whiteley 'The great myth about tax', *The Guardian*, 27 June 2003). Myth or otherwise, key New Labour players subscribed to it. The belief that the party was highly vulnerable to the 'tax and spend' charge had major and tangible consequences – it was a key reason for the harsh squeeze on public spending in the first years of the Blair Government (Keegan, 2003: 143–4). Taxes (especially 'stealth' taxes) have risen significantly since 1999 to fund the large increases in public service budgets, but the Government's sensitiv-ity to a (tabloid-orchestrated) tax backlash is a key reason for its reluctance to raise income tax rates on wealthier groups – the upper band of 40 per cent is one of the lowest in Western Europe and below the 50 per cent band which existed for most of the Thatcher years.

'The one clinching argument with Blair,' a well-informed *Times* jour-nalist wrote, was 'to remind him of what made Labour look extreme or cost the party votes during the 1980s, whether it was being seen as favouring high taxes, being anti-business, pro-union, anti-Europe or anti-American'

(Riddell, 2005: 22). In this general sense electoral considerations were never far from the New Labour mind. But in practical terms this impact has to be seen in conjunction with the importance it assigned to winning favourable coverage from the press.

Power of the media

Meyer claims that 'a profound functional transformation of democracy' is occurring in which 'the media have acquired a decisive role in the political process, above all in shaping public opinion and decision-making' (Meyer, 2002: xii, xv). This is partly because political loyalties are now far more fragile and tentative and partly because of the all-pervasive, enveloping reach of the media. Most politicians believe that a favourable hearing in the media is the only reliable means by which they can convey their messages, manage their images and assert some control over the political agenda. The result is 'the colonization of politics by the mass media', the emergence of a 'media democracy' which 'fundamentally changes the role and mode of operation of political parties' (Meyer, 2002: 24). Party competition is now driven by 'a competitive struggle to influence and control popular perceptions of key political events and issues through the mass media' (Blumler, 1990: 103). For New Labour, 'media democracy' was an inescapable fact to which the party must accommodate.

For a generation Labour had operated in an intensely hostile press environment. It had not (contrary to myth) always been so. Between 1945 and 1970 Labour had substantial support among national newspapers, always less than the Conservatives but at 10–15 per cent (in terms of readership) it did not lag too far behind (Thomas, 2005: 55). From the mid-1970s the gap began to widen alarmingly, largely because of the switch of the *Sun* (under Rupert Murdoch) from being a pro-Labour paper to being a pugnaciously Thatcherite one, and its massive gains in circulation at the expense of the Labour-backing *Mirror*. Between 1979 and 1992 the press was more hostile – and more furiously and overwhelmingly so – to Labour than at any time since before the war (Thomas, 2005: 59, 111). The tabloid press played a crucial part in the construction of 'Old Labour' in which supine parliamentary leaders were portrayed as at the beck and call of belligerent union 'bosses' and fanatical constituency extremists led by power-mad demagogues like Tony Benn (see e.g. Hollingworth, 1986). All this culminated in the Winter of Discontent in which (in the tabloid depiction) heaps of the dead lay unburied, rats scavenged, patients were denied treatment and the country slid under the weight of uncollected garbage.[5]

As a result of relentless and venomous attacks, by the late 1980s the relationship between the Kinnock leadership and the right-wing tabloids (especially the *Sun*) had soured irretrievably. There is much debate among commentators about the scale of the press's influence in shaping voter preferences and fixing the political agenda but, for key New Labour strategists, there was no doubt and no ambiguity. 'In their view the media were supreme. What the media believed was what the country believed; and what the media believed decided elections' (McKibbin, 2007: 23). They were convinced that the ferocious and unremitting attacks on Kinnock and the Labour party by the tabloids – and above all (because of its huge readership) the *Sun*[6] – had inflicted near fatal damage on its electoral prospects. It would be difficult to exaggerate the extent to which this experience seared the collective mind of what was to be New Labour (McKibbin, 2003. Interviews conducted by the author). Its key figures were utterly convinced that a repetition of this treatment would have the most damaging effects on the party's electoral prospects. Hence, early in his leadership Blair and his two strategic advisors, Mandelson and Campbell, engaged in a determined bid to woo Rupert Murdoch (already estranged from John Major). The success of the courtship (with the *Sun* backing New Labour in three successive general elections) was, in Alastair Campbell's mind, his biggest achievement in politics (Seldon, 2004: 250, 253).[7]

The Government, the eminent *Guardian* journalist Hugo Young commented, allowed itself 'to be held hostage by inordinate fear' of press power (quoted in Thomas, 2005: 144). No major policy initiative, which might offend the tabloid pack, was launched – a former cabinet minister recalled – without the most wary and vigilant consideration (interview, 2006). 'To a lot of us in government,' one Blair aide reflected, 'the media was an uncontrollable rampaging beast. It would look for the weakest prey and then hunt it remorselessly, finding every angle to bring it down and then devour it' (Hyman, 2005: 264, 252).[8] But estimating the precise impact of this on policy is difficult. The most obvious and visible was in broadcasting where the Government reversed the party's traditional preference for public regulation and anti-monopoly legislation in favour of deregulation and liberalisation, especially where this benefited News International (Tunney, 2007: 120–7). Fear of how the fervently anti-EU *Sun* (and its stable-mates) would react if a referendum on membership of the single currency area was held undoubtedly also played heavily with Government decision-makers (BBC Radio 4 'A Very Special Relationship', 5 February 2007). In law and order policy the Government perennially played to the tabloid gallery.[9] Another consequence was the cluttering of the policy agenda and the unsettling of the public services as one new policy followed another in a breathless sequence of 'modernisation' and 'reform' designed to grab the headlines.

In terms of its objective – securing a much more favourable reception in the tabloids than Labour was normally accustomed to receive – the policy of cultivating Murdoch and other media magnates had some real success. But 'that embrace was double-edged: endorsement meant that, in return, media-baron influence on public affairs would be even greater in future' (Smith, P, 2003: 586). Perhaps most profoundly it strengthened a New Labour propensity to (in Hugo Young's words) accept the 'Conservative version of social reality' propagated by the right-wing press (quoted in

Thomas, 2005: 144). On issues such as industrial relations, social benefits and, of course, taxation, the probable effect was to fortify the Government in its conviction that what it was doing was popular as well as right: a 'tough' stance on trade unions, strikers and the irresponsible poor could always guarantee favourable media coverage. Overall, it is probably most accurate to conclude that the primary way the influence of the right-wing tabloids made themselves felt was as an ever-present menace, a fear and apprehension never far from the collective mind of New Labour. In short, fear of the tabloids nourished and sustained a reluctance to contemplate any policy innovation to which the established circles of power and privilege might take real exception.

The media contribute heavily to the fashioning of the prevailing consensus, and this has acted as another restraint upon New Labour. The terms of the ruling political discourse privilege some lines of policy more than others by delineating 'the accepted boundaries of state action', by defining the 'context in which many issues will be understood' and by lending greater representative legitimacy to some social interests rather than others (Hall, P, 1993: 290. See also Korpi, 1985: 38). The effect of almost two decades of Conservative rule and the tilting of power away from the state and the unions in conjunction with the world-wide celebration of neo-liberal ideas (often propagated by influential and prestigious international organisations such as the OECD, the IMF and the World Bank) has been to convert the free market paradigm into a pervasive orthodoxy, permeating virtually all aspects of public policy (Wilkes, 1997: 692). All the components of the belief structure which Crosland had believed to be obsolescent – individualism, the insistence on the unconditional rights of private property, the conviction that the invisible hand of the market maximised the welfare of the community (Crosland, 1964) – have been reinserted into the new ruling consensus and the Blair Government has by no means been impervious to its influence. Underpinning the resurgence of free market thinking no force has been more powerful than globalisation.

Globalisation, power constellations and the limits of Government action

'The driving force behind the ideas associated with the Third Way,' Tony Blair has explained, 'is globalisation because no country is immune from the massive change that globalisation brings' (Blair, 1998a). The most palpable political impact of globalisation lies in the way its operations have transformed the landscape of power. The core proposition advanced here is that the ruling constellation of power acts as a key variable effecting 'choice within the repertoire of possible strategies open to rational actors' (Korpi, 2001: 245). Their notions of what is feasible and attainable reflect their assessment, when considering alternative courses of action, of the relative risks and costs likely to be incurred and the prospects of success in light of a calculation of the hard realties of power (Korpi, 1989: 313; Korpi and Palme, 2003: 427; May, 1986: 113). All other things being equal, politicians will select policy options most likely to secure the support, or at least acquiescence, of those groups or institutional forces on whose approval the effective management of the economy depends (Farnham, 1990: 101). If the strategic calculus is unfavourable 'certain policy alternatives that societal actors might otherwise find attractive will not even be considered'. Power constellations, in short, impact on 'actors' perceptions of a realistic and legitimate range of debate ... and of their own capacity to shape policy in accordance with their preferences, and therefore their political strategies' (Huber and Stephens, 2001: 323).

In the 1950s Crosland argued that a decisive factor in the rise of social democracy in the post-war years was a shift in the balance of power from private capital to the state. The levers of fiscal, monetary and regulatory power and the ability to 'severely limit the autonomy of business decisions' were formidable weapons in the state's armoury (Crosland, 1964: 8). This was paralleled by a movement of industrial power from management to labour. Full employment and the growth in union density, cohesion and organisational capacity 'by transposing at once the interests, and therefore the attitudes, of the two sides, has dramatically altered the balance of power at every level of labour relations' (Crosland, 1964: 12). However from the late 1970s the currents of power flows reversed themselves. The deregulation and liberalisation of the international economic order, the increasing inter-nationalisation of capital and the massive expansion in the scale and velocity of capital flows have significantly eroded the capacity of the nation-state to command its own destiny.

Such, plainly, was the view taken by the Blair Government. The financial markets, Brown emphasised, now have

> more choice and freedom then ever before, and day to day flows of capital are greater and faster than ever before ... Today, the judgment of the markets – whether to punish or to reward government policies – is as swift as it is powerful.

The practical lesson from this was stark: to succeed a government has no option but to 'convince the markets that they have the policies in place for long-term stability' (Brown, 1997). Credibility was the 'elusive elixir of modern macroeconomics' (Balls, 1998: 120). The credibility New Labour craved was in the eyes of international investors – convincing them that it could be relied upon to resist short-term temptations to boost spending and stick to sound and judicious long-term policies (Brown, 1998a). Losing credibility meant higher interest rates and bond prices, more money spent on servicing the government's debt, less investment, less growth and fewer jobs. Confidence depended heavily on the dependability of market signals and the solidity of the vital measure of value – money. If money is sound, savings will be converted into long-term investment producing high levels of growth and employment (Brown, 1998a). 'It is upon the rock of stability that we can and must build a sustainable competitive position' (Brown, 2005).

The problem, as key New Labour policy-makers saw it, was how to reassure deeply mistrustful investors that a Labour government would not relapse into old habits. The answer was by reducing the capacity of government to steer economic policy by institutionalising constraints upon its freedom of action – what Burnham has called the strategy of 'depoliticisation' (Burnham, 2001). This took two principal forms: the transfer to the Bank of England of a crucial instrument of economic policy, the determination of interest rates; and the adoption of a binding framework of rules to govern the conduct of fiscal policy. In combination they would form a clear and transparent rules-based institutional framework for monetary and fiscal policy which could 'command market credibility' (Brown, 2001).

On 6 May 1997, within a week of Labour's victory, the new Chancellor announced his decision to give to the Monetary Policy Committee of the Bank of England (comprising the Governor, the Deputy Governors and six members) operational responsibility for setting interest rates. 'Price stability,' Brown explained in a letter to the Governor of the Bank,

> is a precondition for high and stable levels of growth and employment, which in turn will help to create the conditions for price stability on a sustainable basis. To that end, the monetary policy of the Bank of England will be to deliver price stability (as defined by the Government's inflation target of 2.5%) and without prejudice to this objective, to support the Government's economic policy, including its objectives for growth and employment.
>
> (letter from the Chancellor to the Governor, 6 May 1997)

The 2.5 per cent target was a symmetrical: if the Bank undershot as well as overshot it would be required to adjust interest rates accordingly.

The second arm of the strategy was to constrain the Government's fiscal discretion by setting firm rules and binding targets. Strict rules in the fiscal arena were designed to tie all government departments to rigorous expenditure limits. Fiscal policy was to be conducted within the following parameters: first, the so-called 'golden rule' stipulated that 'over the economic cycle the Government will borrow only to invest and that current spending will be met from taxation'; second, 'as a proportion of national income, public debt will be held at a prudent and stable level over the economic cycle'; and third, the Government would follow a 'five year deficit reduction plan' (Brown, 1998b). This would restrict government autonomy since clear, precise and transparent guidelines and targets made it easier for the financial markets to monitor the Government's performance and to take appropriate compensatory action against any shortfalls. This, in turn, would boost entrepreneurs' confidence, encourage them to invest more, produce higher levels of growth and employment and more tax outlays for the Treasury which could be used to fund better public services (Brown, 1997).

What have been the implications of this for the general thrust of Government policy? For both globalisation and variety of capitalism theorists the shift to a more orthodox monetary and fiscal policy, the heavy reliance on interest policy as the main instrument for managing the economy, and the accent on price stability and budgetary balance are all policy manifestations – driven by globalisation – of the discarding of traditional social democratic goals in favour of low taxation, labour market flexibility, welfare retrenchment and fiscal austerity (see, e.g., Cerny, 2000; Hall, P, 2002). As applied to the United Kingdom at least, both schools of thought concur that globalisation acted as 'a nonnegotiable external economic constraint, circumscribing the parameters of both political possibility and political choice' (Watson and Hay, 2003: 290).

This line of reasoning has come under critical scrutiny from Hay who points to the lack of hard evidence to substantiate globalisation theory (see Hay, 2004 and Hay, 2006 for details). He counters that the Blair Government was constrained 'as much – indeed, rather more – by the ideas it came to embrace than by the "reality" those ideas purportedly represented' (Hay, 2002a: 460). Watson and Hay suggest that 'the distinction between the "inevitable" and the "desirable" was subtly and ... strategically blurred in order to increase the potency of the message being relayed'. In short, New Labour chose to present as inevitable what in fact was contingent by deploying a 'particular political discourse of globalisation' (Watson and Hay, 2003: 290). The reason was political: 'the image of non-negotiable exogenous economic imperatives was harnessed strategically in order to displace responsibility for otherwise unpalatable social and economic reforms, arguably pursued for entirely different ends' (Watson and Hay, 2003: 291). But they agree with both globalisation and varieties of capitalism theory that – whatever the causal mechanism involved – New Labour has adopted a broadly neo-liberal agenda.

The Government objects to this line of reasoning on two grounds. First, it claims that, far from shredding the central values of social democracy by adopting policies more suited to the exigencies of a globalised world economy New Labour has preserved them. The evidence compiled in this study does not wholly support this conclusion but nor does it substantiate the proposition that it has renounced social democracy in favour of neo-liberalism. Second, the Government strongly refuted the contention that the economic programme it has adopted in response to globalisation has impelled it to forsake traditional social democratic goals. While it acknowledged that globalisation had a major constraining effect it held that it constrained *governments to act in economically rational ways*. The judgements made by the financial markets on the sustainability of economic policies where in fact, for the large part, well-informed (Arestis and Sawyer, 2002). It follows that policies designed to gain the confidence of investors would *ipso facto*, be sound policies: globalisation was, in Brown's phrase, 'made for

Britain' (Brown, 2005). Once the 'elixir of credibility' was secured, international investors would no longer inspect every initiative launched by a Labour government with a suspicious and mistrustful eye. The new binding fiscal rules, for example, reassured the markets by alleviating their anxieties that the Government might pile up excessive public debt (Stephens, 2001: 192). Equally (as Balls contended), relinquishing control over monetary policy to the Bank of England would be the means by which a Labour government could 'do the things a Labour Government should do' without fear of financial crisis. 'You should lose control in order to gain greater control' (Keegan, 2003:156).

For the Government it was precisely the credibility of its commitment to monetary and fiscal discipline that allowed it to pump new investment into the public services in 2000 and 2001 with hardly a murmur in the financial markets (Balls, 2002; Peston, 2005: 172, 190–1; Keegan, 2003: 169). Thus public expenditure rose steadily and substantially under New Labour – from 40.8 per cent of GDP in 1997 to a planned 42.3 per cent by 2008 – yet its reputation in the eyes of the City has remained intact (Peston, 2005: 152). The Blair Government 'was the first Labour government ever to have survived without either being derailed or seriously diverted by the advent of a financial crisis' (Keegan, 2003: 237). Instead of slicing back public spending – as successive Labour governments in the 1960s and 1970s had felt impelled to do to settle turbulent money markets – it had been able to persevere with a sustained expansion in government programmes enabling it to make substantial inroads into poverty and educational disadvantage, improve the range and quality of healthcare and embark on a comprehensive assault on squalor and deprivation. Though initially controversial, the transfer of conduct of monetary policy to the Bank of England appeared to have made a significant contribution to economic stability and expansion while the rules-based fiscal policy had not prevented large sums of money streaming into cash-starved public services. Indeed it is notable that Brown's management of the economy – in contrast to Government policies on health and education – attracted little criticism from within the party, indeed was regarded as one of New Labour's main accomplishments.

All this showed that, as Ed Balls, Economic Secretary to the Treasury and Brown's senior economic advisor put it, the proposition that in a globalised world economy national Governments had no option but to cut the size of the state, retrench public spending and abandon the fight against poverty was a 'myth'. The Blair Government had demonstrated 'that you can have a national minimum wage … a full employment economy and … enhanced rights at work' (Balls, 2006). Similarly, reflecting on his seven years as senior Downing Street advisor, Geoff Mulgan agreed that 'strong forces do limit government's room for manoeuvre' but then added:

> It is widely assumed that governments have lost power – upwards to a globalised market or Brussels, downwards to the people, or outwards to

the private sector and the media. This is one of the reasons why social democratic governments have reined in their ambitions, and I expected to leave government more conscious of its constraints than of its possibilities. But instead I came away convinced that the perception of powerlessness is an illusion ... the basic powers of governments have not diminished. The capacity to tax, for example, remains in rude health. Across the OECD, governments' share in GDP has risen over the past few decades; even the tax take (as opposed to the rates) on profits has gone up. Many of the world's most competitive economies are overseen by relatively big governments. ... The idea that governments have become impotent is an illusion, albeit one that can provide a useful alibi.

(Mulgan, 2005)

Conclusion

None of this is to deny that globalisation has operated as a substantial restraint on the Blair Government and in particular in the sphere of labour market and taxation policy. More generally, global economic and institutional factors undeniably set the perimeters of government action. But the evidence, as reviewed in this and earlier chapters, does not substantiate the grander claims made (by globalisation and varieties of capitalism theorists) about the degree to which governments are helpless to act. In fact in the two areas of domestic policy where New Labour policy has most inflamed opinion within the party – healthcare and education – documentary evidence as supplemented by interviews with a number of key players clearly indicates that it was the preferences of key ministers rather than any perceived external constraints that were the principal drivers of policy choice. More broadly, the decision in many spheres (including labour relations, and the organisation of healthcare and secondary education) to refine rather than to scrap many Thatcherite reforms was 'not just a reluctant concession to what was politically feasible' but a belief that many of them had been right (Cronin, 2004: 394).

In short, the Blair Government's overall programmatic thrust is not explicable exclusively or even predominantly in terms of constraint-bound adjustment to external reality nor as a form of functional adaptation to systemic needs. Rather it was, to a substantial degree, the outcome of a political process in which the ideas, values and preference of key political actors feature prominently. It is to these that we now turn.

8   For what does New Labour stand?

Introduction

New Labour's performance in government has in many ways been impressive. Levels of unemployment are lower than in most comparable countries, more jobs have been generated, average rates of economic growth have been historically better than average, there has been consistently low inflation and living standards have steadily risen. In a report produced on the eve of the 2005 election the National Institute for Economic Research commented that 'Labour's economic record has been very satisfactory. Nothing has gone badly wrong with the economy over the period since 1997' (quoted in Riddell, 2005: 71). Any earlier Labour chancellor would have been delighted with such a performance. Furthermore, the growth of inequality has been arrested, if not reversed, poverty, especially among the young and the elderly, has fallen (for most) in both absolute and relative terms, social benefits have generally become more generous, there has been a big expansion in pre-school and nursery provision and few can gainsay that the public services are not only more generously funded but in a far better shape than in 1997. Giddens finds it 'difficult to think of a single area of government intervention since 1997 which has not been related to questions of poverty and inequality' (Giddens, 2004a).

For two influential adherents, New Labour stands 'in the proud philosophical tradition of modernising social democracy' (Mandelson, 2002: x–xiii), a claim which some commentators would endorse. For Bevir it has demonstrated that it firmly lies in the social democratic tradition defined by 'the ideals of social justice, citizenship, and community' (Bevir, 2005: 63). 'Foundation hospitals, trust schools, city academies and greater financial independence for universities', some of the most contentious items in the New Labour programme were – Will Hutton, a one-time keen critic, assures us – 'all part of the Blairite programme to build a more plural society with social democratic values embodied nearer the people' (the *Observer*, 10 September 2006).

Others, while acknowledging the Blair Government's achievements, are less sure. For Roy Hattersley 'at this moment Labour stands for very little that can be identified with social democracy' (the *Observer*, 24 June 2001).

According to Peter Kilfoyle MP – who, as a tough party organiser had spearheaded the fight in Liverpool against the entryist Trotskyist group, the Militant Tendency – Labour had been 'hijacked by a small group antagonistic to the collective values which characterise the party' (*The Guardian*, 25 January 2006). 'Far from being a centre-left project,' Ruth Levitas avers, 'New Labour could more accurately be characterised as centre-right, combining a neo-liberal commitment to the market with notions of "community" replacing the role of the state in Thatcherism' (Levitas, 2005: ii). The effect of the 'New Labour project', Jon Trickett MP, chair of the centre-left Compass group of MPs writes, has been to 'effectively dissolve the Labour party as we have known it' (Trickett, 2006). Hence we have two different interpretations: the one which maintains, with Peter Hall, that the New Labour programme is the only realistic one available to a British social democratic government given prevailing economic constraints (Hall, P, 2002); and the other which contends, with Stuart Hall, that New Labour made a deliberate strategic decision to adopt a programme that was fundamentally neo-liberal in character (Hall, S, 2003).

'To explain New Labour's ideas,' Bevir has suggested, 'we have not only to locate it in the tradition from which its representatives set out, but also to grasp how they then modified this tradition in response to specific dilemmas' (Bevir, 2000: 281). Such has been the approach this book has sought to apply. Thus preceding chapters have sought to uncover 'the orientations or premises of action that support, perhaps through intervening levels of thought and feeling, a set of particular attitudes displayed in behaviour' (Beer, 1969: 403). The object has been to define the New Labour creed in terms of action-principles – applied to problem-situations – which drove actual policy choice. Now we seek to draw together the threads, to trace the political tapestry that is New Labour. The first chapter suggested that the British social democratic tradition was constituted by two dimensions, the redistributive social democratic and the ethical socialist. The discussion in what follows is framed by the two principle components of each of the dimensions – equality and collectivism in the former case, fellowship and the public service ethos in the latter – in an attempt to delineate the essential features of the New Labour morphology.

Redistributive social democracy

Equality

For Driver and Martell 'the debate about equality goes to the very heart of third way politics' (Driver and Martell, 2000: 151). Chapter Two suggested that New Labour's distributional philosophy can be defined in terms of four key principles: social inclusion, fairness for all (or 'priority'), common advantage and equal worth/equality of opportunity. Social inclusion refers to the right of all to engage fully in society; priority to the precedence to be assigned to redressing deprivation among the most vulnerable members of the community; common advantage to the limits to redistribution imposed by the imperatives of wealth creation; and equal worth/equality of opportunity to ensuring that all people have the ability to realise their own potential. This, *in toto*, constituted the New Labour distributional creed.

For the Blair Government the principal route to social inclusion, for those capable of work, was through paid employment. Paid work not only provided the income which enabled one to participate fully in society but was also the means to gain self-esteem, control over one's life and a sense of social identity. The Blair Government's strategy for achieving 'employment for all' was twofold. First, through promoting 'employability', that is the acquisition through education and training of the skills and aptitudes which could secure a niche in the labour market. Second, a re-engineering of the structure of welfare to gear it more closely to the needs of the labour market. These included 'job facilitation' measures such as the various New Deals, the provision of childcare facilities and advice on job-search, and efforts to 'make work pay' (enlargening the gap between benefits and pay) through instituting a minimum wage and providing tax credits for working families. It also entailed an emphasis on conditionality in which, in return for material and other forms of assistance from the state, the workless accepted the duty to accept such training and jobs as were available.

For the poor and socially excluded not available for work New Labour invoked the principle of priority. Priority was, in effect, a reaffirmation of Crosland's principle of social welfare which he defined as giving an 'exceptional priority over other claims on resources' to the redress of poverty (Crosland, 1964: 76–7). We suggested that 'priority', as an operative value, could be distinguished from both equality and a safety-net approach (that is the relief of absolute poverty). On the one hand equalising the distribution of income, wealth and status was not in itself an objective: what mattered was that all should have the opportunity to rise. But, on the other, poverty alleviation was defined in terms relative to the median income, an acknowledgment that meaningful social participation varied according to the standards prevailing at any one time. Hence 'the traditional social democratic goal of improving the relative position of the worst-off in relation to the average' has been, for the Blair Government 'a crucial objective' (Diamond and Giddens, 2005: 1034).

Chapter Two charted the Government's steady progress in achieving this objective with substantial reductions in poverty in particular among the very young – though it failed to hit its own targets. The Institute of Fiscal Studies concluded that 'the tax and benefit reforms introduced by the Labour government over this time have been strongly redistributive, favouring lower-income families, especially those with children and older people' (Brewer, Goodman, Shaw and Sibieta, 2006: 25). As Riddell argues, the Blair Government pursued a policy of redistribution by stealth and eventually emerged as 'a recognisably social democratic government' – though it 'only half-heartedly admits to beings so' (Riddell, 2005: 21–2, 67).

It is true that Government reforms have done little to arrest the trend to higher levels of inequality in the distribution of income and wealth. IFS researchers calculated that 'the net effect of eight years of Labour government is to leave inequality either slightly higher or slightly lower' but 'not substantially different' from its level in 1996/97' (Brewer, Goodman, Shaw and Sibieta, 2006: 24). But, for New Labour, greater equality of outcome per se was neither a feasible nor perhaps even desirable goal since distributional politics had to take account of the principle of 'common advantage'. This stipulates that inequality is acceptable to the extent that it is a condition of a more efficient and productive economy, from which all, especially those on lower incomes, will benefit. The party in the past, New Labour alleged (not wholly accurately), had failed to recognise that social justice and economic efficiency were integrally inter-related and that a dynamic economy was a precondition for the fulfilment of its social goals (Diamond and Giddens, 2005: 106). It had failed to appreciate the scale of the 'substantial personal incentives and rewards [that] are necessary in order to encourage risk-taking and entrepreneurialism' (Mandelson and Liddle, 1996: 64). It had overlooked the importance of rewarding the 'drive, initiative or creativity' of the businessman or 'entrepreneur' (Diamond and Giddens, 2005: 103). For New Labour the ample rewards assumed to be essential to spur businessmen to greater effort would, by enlarging the pie, advantage all. Hence – and in contrast to what 'Old Labour' might have thought – the swelling and abundant share of income and wealth flowing into the hands of the richest 5 per cent of society has not been deemed a problem. Indeed it was seen 'as a sign of a new entrepreneurial spirit, the rising levels of personal enrichment, the acknowledgment of leadership skills, risk-taking and business acumen that benefits all' (Lansley, 2006: xii).

Equally, however, New Labour insists, such a market-governed order is only fair to the extent that all have an equal opportunity to excel. What is important is not *how* resources are distributed but whether all people have the opportunity to better themselves by dint of effort, ability and enterprise. To the Blair Government 'the equal worth of all citizens, and their right to be treated with equal respect and consideration despite their differences' was an absolutely 'fundamental' principle (Blair, 2001c). The principle of equal worth, as understood by New Labour, postulated that 'all deserve to be given an equal chance in life to fulfil the potential with which they were born' (Brown, 1999: 40). In short, equal respect and consideration meant, in the New Labour lexicon, giving all people the opportunity to rise in the social world. This was the doctrine of meritocracy.

A meritocratic society is one where 'a hierarchy of more and less desirable, superior and inferior positions' will remain but access to these positions, that is 'the assignment of individuals to places in the social hierarchy is determined by some form of competitive process, and all members of society are eligible to compete on equal terms' (Arneson, 2002b). Thus New Labour envisaged a society in which, as Blair put it, 'nobody is left behind;

in which people can go as far as they have the talent to go; in which people can achieve true equality – equal status and equal opportunity rather than equality of outcome' (Blair, 2002a). From this perspective substantial inequalities in the distribution of rewards were justified insofar as all have the opportunity to compete for them. 'Hurdles which bar the path to personal advancement must be torn down and prizes must be awarded to those who have covered the ground most successfully. In short, life should be a flat race not a steeple chase' (Roy Hattersley, *The Guardian*, 14 September 1998).

How was a meritocracy to be built? For the Blair Government the answer was through education. A core New Labour proposition – one upon which the feasibility of its meritocratic vision rested – was that equality of educational opportunity was possible without a substantial levelling in the distribution of income and wealth. Hence it is worth considering how far this proposition was correct. To explore the issue is may be useful to draw upon Hirsch's concept of education as a 'positional good'. Hirsch distinguishes between two dimensions of education: the intrinsic (a good in itself) and the instrumental (a means to career advancement). In this latter sense, Hirsch argues, education is a positional good. Positional goods are products and services whose value is contingent on ranking, that is the utility its consumption confers on any one person is a function of that which it confers on others. Thus 'the value to me of my education depends not *only* on how much I have but also on how much the man ahead of me *in* the job line has' (Hirsch, 1977: 3. Emphasis in original).

Hirsch's insight has profound implications for New Labour-style meritocracy. The more important education is for future individual success, the more intense will be 'positional competition'. By

> positional competition is meant competition that is fundamentally for a higher place within some explicit hierarchy and therefore yields gains for some only by dint of losses for others ... The contrast is with competition that improves performance or enjoyment all round ... the positive sum game.
>
> (Hirsch, 1977: 52)

Positional competition, he suggests, is a zero sum game since, to the extent that jobs in the upper reaches in a hierarchy are socially scarce, the educational system will inevitably act as 'a general filtering device through which excessive demand has to be matched to available supply' (Hirsch, 1977: 52). Improving the overall standard of education may be economically and socially beneficial but it will not lessen the degree of positional competition, for what matters in the job market is not how much education you have but how much you have in relation to others (Barry, 2005: 177).

The problem for the New Labour meritocratic project is that the stiffer the positional competition, the stronger the incentive for those who are materially and culturally advantaged to use their access to superior resources to ensure the reproduction of that advantage to their children. The ability of the upper echelons of society to secure their offspring's future by tapping their wealth, their social connections and know-how, is well-attested. Comparative research into mobility patterns, a leading expert notes, indicates that 'the effects of class origins on educational attainment are highly resistant to change' largely because parents from the professional and business middle classes are able to exploit their economic, social and cultural resources to give their children a competitive edge (Goldthorpe, 2005). The greater the importance attached to credentials in the career market, the more the better-off will be motivated to mobilise their surplus income to advance their children's education. The corollary is – crucially – this: the greater the gap between those who have surplus income to dispense and those who do not, the greater the imbalance in educational opportunities (Hirsch, 1977: 7; Goldthorpe, 2005).[1]

In a highly competitive environment, where rewards, reputation and status for schools are integrally linked to their place in an institutinalised pecking order, schools, equally, will have the incentive to use whatever discretion they may have to recruit the 'right kind' of pupil. 'If this process proceeds unchecked,' Crouch maintains, 'inequalities of achievement between schools ... will spiral' (Crouch, 2003: 34). This may well be already happening. Thus while (as the evidence suggests) educational standards in schools in the more deprived areas – and, indeed, the overall quality of education – may be, in absolute terms, improving, the prospects of a substantial evening-out of educational disadvantage seems as elusive as ever. As a result the pronounced correlation between class background, admission to education in high-performing secondary schools (both public and private), entrance to top universities and, ultimately, access to high-status and well-paid jobs will not be significantly loosened. All this underlines the long-familiar point that (something like) an equal race in life presupposes (something like) an equal start. The lesson of comparative research into social mobility is that if we want 'to create greater equality of opportunity – we will first need to create a greater equality of condition' (Goldthorpe, 2005).

It may well be that the Blair Government recognises that anything approaching real equality of opportunity is (in the circumstances) unattainable and this may not, in reality, be an operative goal. It may be useful here to distinguish between what can be called 'thin' and 'thick meritocracy'. 'Thick meritocracy' is akin to Rawls' 'society of liberal equality' which holds that

> those who are at the same level of talent and ability, and have the same willingness to use them, should have the same prospects of success regardless of their initial place in the social system, that is, irrespective of the income class into which they are born.
>
> (Rawls, 1971: 73)

This would appear to entail a degree of redistribution which has never been seriously contemplated by the Blair Government. It seems more plausible to assume that its real aim can be described as 'thin meritocracy'. Thin meritocracy demands – as Philip Collins, director of the pro-New Labour Social Market Foundation explained – creating conditions which enable the most energetic, able and ambitious to overcome inherited social handicaps and achieve in a competitive society, thereby ensuring that society makes most efficient use of available talent (Collins, 2001).

Collectivism

The welfare state, its architects believed, should be 'built on values (need, not ability to pay) and a structure (collective rather than individual provision) that embodied an alternative way of living to that offered by free market capitalism' (Driver and Martell, 2006: 88). The two central pillars of the social democratic notion of collectivism were an emphasis on the public good as something separate from – and often transcending – private interests and the idea of positive government, that is faith in the capacity of the state, served by enlightened public servants, to effect major improvements in people's lives (see Chapter One). The copingstone of the two pillars was the concept of a distinctive public domain. While the private domain was the sphere of the market and the pursuit of private advantage, the public was defined by 'the values of citizenship, equity and service' where goods were distributed on the basis of need and 'where strangers encounter each other as equal partners in the common life of the society' (Marquand, 2004: 27). It followed that the public domain should be regulated by its own rules and norms, operate as the arena within which collective (rather than individual) choices were formulated and be protected from the compulsions of the market (Ranson and Stewart, 1994: 88).

For New Labour socio-cultural changes have rendered such collectivist notions obsolete. The collectivist mentalities which had once sustained popular support for the welfare state had largely faded. 'The 1945 settlement,' Blair explains, 'was the social equivalent of mass production, largely state-directed and managed, built on a paternalist relationship between state and individual, one of donor and recipient. Individual aspirations were often weak, and personal preferences were a low or non-existent priority' (Blair, 2002a). The mass of the population was no longer homogenous, deferential and compliant. Society had been transformed by rising prosperity, the increasing diversity of people's needs and aspirations and, above all, by the advent of a consumer culture. The key measure of systems of common welfare now was their capacity to satisfy individual claims and aspirations. In this more instrumental world 'more people may come to feel they can provide health and education or security for themselves, and thus be less inclined to support tax-based universalism' unless they could be persuaded that collective welfare could deliver more effectively and at less expense (Taylor, M, 2006: 18). People demanded choice and personalised services closely tailored to their preferences and unless the Government heeded this the public services would forfeit their legitimacy in the eyes of the population (see e.g. Office of Public Services Reform, 2002: 8; Joint Government Memorandum, 2005; Hewitt, 2006a).

In this New Labour narrative the citizen has re-emerged as the consumer (or, at least, the citizen-consumer). What has occurred is a subtle shift in Labour's understanding of the nature and purposes of human freedom. An older vocabulary which associated freedom and autonomy with the concept of self-development – 'the full and free development of every individual person' in the words of Labour's 1950 manifesto (Craig, 1970: 127) – has been marginalised by an increasing emphasis on freedom as the extension of choice in competitive markets: 'the consumer exercises personal autonomy through the freedom to choose' (Needham, 2003: 21). The self-regarding instrumental rationalism typical of people enacting the role as a consumer now (in the New Labour view) defines their broader social roles. People 'view public services through a frame of reference grounded in the experience of being treated as consumers elsewhere'. Consumer culture in effect 'constitutes the reference points' against which, in New Labour discourse, 'public services should be judged' (Clarke *et al.*, 2007: 38, 34). Its rhetoric has been 'saturated with the language of consumerism' (Marquand, 2004: 118). Hence (as has been seen in Chapters Three and Five) the relationship between the service-user and public providers is increasingly remodelled on that between the consumer and the private firm – a relationship that is 'individualised, instrumental and transactional' within an institutional setting increasingly reliant on individual choice and market mechanisms as key allocative devices (Needham, 2003: 14).

According to New Labour, choice was sweeping through society 'like a tidal wave' (Alan Milburn quoted in Which, 2005: 25). However evidence about public attitudes falls short of unequivocally substantiating this proposition. The British Social Attitudes survey did indeed find that around two-thirds of patients favoured choice over such matters as which hospital to attend and what kinds of treatment they received (Appleby and Alvarez-Rosete, 2005: 120–1). The Public Administration Select Committee in its study of choice found that people welcomed the opportunity 'to make decisions which have a direct and immediate impact on the quality of their lives' and appreciated the availability of options (Public Administration Select Committee, 2005a: 3). But its overall conclusion was that 'while public attitudes towards choice are generally positive, few people are likely to name it as their first priority for public services' (Public Administration Select Committee, 2005a: 41). A MORI survey, conducted for the National Audit Office, similarly revealed that while people favoured choice they did not see it as a key to improving standards (National Audit Office, 2004: Ev 68. See also the review of relevant literature research in Coulter, 2005 and Greener, 2004). An extensive programme of research commissioned by

Which (formerly the Consumers Association) found that 'people want more choice and more responsive public services, but they often see choice as less important than quality and access'. In neither healthcare nor education was it a top priority (Which, 2005: 4, 8. See also Clarke *et al.*, 2007). Research conducted on behalf of the Healthcare Commission, the government's health watchdog, disclosed that for most patients choice was far less important than confidence in a hospital's doctors and nurses, the availability of accurate information and hygiene (*The Guardian*, 14 May 2007).

In short, while people generally appreciated choice there was no evidence of a spontaneous groundswell of demand – 'a tidal wave' which cannot be resisted, in Milburn's metaphor. How, then, can we account for the pivotal role it occupied in New Labour's narrative? Two considerations seem relevant here. First, the Blair Government appeared convinced that, unless offered greater choice, there would be a mass defection by the more affluent sections of the middle class from the public services. Middle class flight to private health and education would, one Blairite minister declared, put at risk 'universal provision funded through general taxation' and ultimately lead to 'the break up of public service provision as we know it today' (Byers, 2003. See also Milburn, 2003b). While it was estimated that 12 per cent of the population had private health insurance this figure rose to as high as 30 per cent in marginal rich South Eastern England (Mohan, 2003). The figures for private education were 7 per cent in England but three times as much in parts of London. Equally it was this section of the middle class – disproportionately numerous in the highly populated south-east of England – whose interests and concerns where most volubly and vociferously championed by what New Labour regarded as *the* organ of 'Middle England', the *Daily Mail*. As we have seen (Chapter Seven) exhibiting sensitivity to the needs of 'Middle England' was seen as crucial to Labour's electoral prospects.

The second consideration was more ideological: a major re-orientation in Labour thinking about the relative merits of collective and individual choice. For traditional social democratic thinking there was a qualitative difference between the two. Individual consumer choice – for example, which television to buy – was typically piecemeal, short term and took little account of wider horizons or longer-term consequences. Decisions over the allocation of public goods, in contrast, typically have to take account of 'problems of conflicting rights, differences between individual and collective rights, and differences of the long and the short-term impact of the exercise of rights' (Walsh, 1995: 254). The interests of different users have to be balanced with each and with those of the community at large – not least because of the finite nature of public sector resources. The combination of a host of individual choices may well produce longer-term social effects which none may have wanted – such as school segregation along religious, social and ethnic lines. Decisions over how to deliver and apportion public goods thus frequently raised legitimate differences over values that could only be resolved by collective choice (Plant, 2003a: 578).

In contrast, while recognising that the state must retain final responsibility for defining and implementing the public interest, the Blair Government saw in the demanding consumer a major driver for more effective and higher quality public services. People were the best judges of their own interests and just as in the private sector so too in the public the hidden hand of competition – suitably regulated, controlled and monitored – would operate to align these interests to the common good. One minister explained the reasoning thus:

> Our default position should ... be to give the individual choice over what the government provides for them – over where their children go to school, what kind of medical treatment they get, what kind of support they receive if they are disabled or growing old. ... All this explains why choice and competition are such important tools for people with Labour values. They put the power in the individual's hands.
>
> (James Purnell in the *Guardian*, 23 September 2006)

Ethical socialists such as Titmuss and Tawney had seen the universal welfare state not only as a collective means for providing material security but as an institutional framework 'capable of bonding people through an increased awareness of common need and common frailty before the overwhelming contingencies of social life' (Harris, D, 1987: 74). The accent, in short, was on common needs and interests collectively sustained. In the New Labour view such solidaristic modes of thought were rooted in collectivist forms of organisation – of class, workplace experience, occupational communities - which were rapidly disappearing. The new popular spirit was one of individual self-assertion and ambition, embodied in the concept of the confident, demanding consumer. It followed that the welfare state – the provision of needs through public services – could only continue to command popular support to the extent that it demonstrated a sensitivity to increasingly powerful and pervasive individual aspirations and expectations (interview, senior Downing Street advisor, 2007). It is to the wider ramifications of this perceived shift towards a more individualistic social order that we now turn.

Ethical socialism

Fellowship

Ethical socialism sought not only a fairer division of income and wealth and an equalising of life-chances but a remodelling of social relations. It promised 'not merely equity and efficiency but a restoration of collective virtue', a reversal of the subordination of the public good, aesthetic principles, fellowship and community to the unappeasable striving for private gain, the culture of materialism, of competitive individualism and the "cash nexus" (Cronin, 2004: 55–6). In Crosland's words, it connoted 'a desire to replace competitive social relations by fellowship and social solidarity and the motive of personal profit by a more altruistic and other-regarding motive' (Crosland, 1964: 54).

It has been argued that one of the defining features of New Labour is its determination to revive this tradition (Savage and Atkinson, 2001: 11; Buckler, 2007: 46). For Mandelson and Liddle, New Labour stands for 'an ethical socialism that draws on the ideas of Tawney and Ruskin' (Mandelson and Liddle, 1996: 4). New Labour's communitarianism, one commentator maintains, 'is in part a reassertion of traditional co-operative values, and often in stronger terms than were articulated by the left in earlier decades' (Nuttall, 2006: 157). 'Blair's own definition of ethical socialism,' another adds, shared with it such notions 'as common good, rights and responsibilities, and an organic society in which individuals can flourish only by working together' (Carter, 2003: 189–90). Indeed, Bevir and O'Brien remind us, Blair 'constantly evokes a thick view of the person as integral to a vision of community that he contrasts sharply with the individualistic society sought by the New Right' (Bevir and O'Brien, 2003: 326). For Giddens community was 'fundamental to the new politics' of the Third Way (Giddens, 1998: 79).

There are undoubtedly points of contact between New Labour and ethical socialism. The foundation concept of ethical socialism is that people are, by nature, social beings who could only fully express and fulfil themselves in social relationships – not the isolated, calculating utility maximisers of neoliberal thinking. This is a view New Labour would appear to share. 'People,' Blair declared, 'are not separate economic actors competing in the marketplace of life ... We are social beings, nurtured in families and communities and human only because we develop the moral power of personal responsibility for ourselves and each other' (Blair, 1997). A society that denies this, and sees people simply as atomised beings, is a 'fragmented and divided' one, 'where people feel no sense of shared purpose', and one which is 'unlikely to produce well-adjusted and responsible citizens' (Blair, 1995, quoted in Driver and Martel, 2000: 151). Thus the Blair Government emphasised the responsibility of the state for the welfare of all citizens, defined in terms of the collective pooling against risk, through the consolidation of universal welfare (notably in the NHS and education). The need to strengthen social cohesion and ensure that all have the right to participate fully in the life of the community are constantly recurring motifs in New Labour discourse. If people are socially, economically and culturally impoverished and deprived of hope then inevitably they will slide to the margins of social life: hence the priority given to tackling social exclusion through policies addressing urban decay, crime, drug-abuse and other forms of social malaise.

Blair insisted that community, rooted firmly in solidarity, 'is the governing idea of modern social democracy' (Blair, 2002a: 9–10). However the concept of community is protean, ambiguous, notoriously difficult to unravel, and one whose meaning varies according to the broader discourse into which it is inserted. For present purposes, one can distinguish between an ethical socialist and a conservative variant. Ethical socialism, as we have seen, equated community with fellowship and defined these concepts in terms of cooperation and mutuality, altruism and public service. Fellowship could only exist within a common culture, which, in turn, could only flourish where there was 'a large measure of economic equality' (Tawney, 1952: 43). The conservative variant, in contrast, stressed duty and obligation within a hierarchical social order, the regulation of conduct by precepts derived from traditional moral codes and the role of established institutions in inculcating respect, personal responsibility and self-reliance. It was this latter notion of community, which has proved the more appealing to New Labour. 'The only way to build social order and stability', Tony Blair maintained, 'is through strong values, socially shared, and inculcated through individuals, family, government and the institutions of civil society' (Blair, quoted in Driver and Martell, 1997: 34–5).

Within the New Labour mind-set community is integrally related to responsibility. 'Without responsibility to each other,' Blair declared, 'we create a nation where community evaporates. If I take without giving, enjoy rights without accepting obligations, then I betray the trust of those who exercise responsibility in a responsible way' (Blair, 1997). For New Labour, 'rights' refer to claims made by people to a share of those national resources that are disbursed by the state. Such rights cannot be treated as entitlements – as unconditional – since to allow this (the reasoning runs) would be to give the beneficiaries the incentive to 'free load' on the community as a whole. This would, in turn, feed 'welfare dependency', reward the indigent, undermine personal responsibility and injure the social fabric.

In contrast to Labour social thinking since the 1950s[2] – which tended to shy away from personal judgmentalism – New Labour stressed that all must bear responsibility for their conduct. 'New egalitarianism ties rights to corresponding responsibilities ... benefits depend not only on a person's means but also on his or her behaviour' (Diamond and Giddens, 2005: 107). The contingency of rights on the performance of responsibilities was embodied in the concept of 'welfare contractualism': access to benefits is part of a contract between citizens and the community 'which has as its reverse side various responsibilities that the individual citizen is obliged to meet; as a condition of eligibility for welfare benefits, the state may legitimately enforce these responsibilities, which centrally include the responsibility to work' (White, 2000: 508). Thus New Labour acknowledges that the state had a moral responsibility for providing all its citizens with opportunities to improve their personal circumstances but, in return, people had the duty to act as responsible and productive members of the community. Blair summed it up thus: 'modern civic society is an ethic of mutual responsibility or duty. It is something for something. A society where we play by the rules. You only take out if you put in. That's the bargain' (Blair, 1997a).

For some commentators, this yoking of rights and responsibilities 'expresses a conception of fairness and mutuality that has deep roots in the social democratic tradition' (White, 1999: 166). Ethical socialists such as Tawney indeed agreed that all rights were 'conditional and derivative conditional on contributing to the end of society and derived from such an end' and that a besetting fault of society was that rights were too often divorced from obligations (quoted in Carter, 2003: 53–4). But the conditionality that he had in mind was not simply attached to rights to resources dispensed by the state but to those derived from all sources, including market remuneration and inheritance. For New Labour the most appropriate targets of the admonition that 'rights must be coupled with responsibilities' seemed to be social security recipients, assumed to be peculiarly 'lacking in civic virtue and deserving of the imposition of duties' (Lockwood, 1996: 539). Ethical socialists believed this admonition should apply to all. Rights (or claims) to income, whatever its sources, were, for Tawney, only acceptable to the extent that they were associated with the performance of a social function, which he defined as 'an activity which embodies and expresses the idea of social purpose' (Tawney, 1961 [1921]: 40). In short, the distribution of income and wealth should be regulated by 'a principle superior to the mechanical play of economic forces, which ought to determine the relative importance of different occupations' (Tawney, 1961 [1921]: 40). New Labour communitarianism, in stark contrast, effectively excludes the sphere of economic activity from such ethical regulation. The sense that the right to accumulate large sums of money is in any way contingent upon the performance of a social function has been largely abandoned. In effect the balancing of rights with responsibilities has been disconnected from the wider context of fairness in the social system (White, 1999: 171).

Thus while for ethical socialists fellowship (or community) is integrally related to greater equality of condition, for New Labour the two are severed. For the former fellowship can only thrive where there is equality of regard and this, in turn, presupposes the avoidance of deep and entrenched material inequalities. Equal worth – which in the New Labour lexicon simply meant the opportunity of individuals to climb the social ladder – for ethical socialists only makes sense as an *attribute of social relationships*. As such, it referred to the social distribution of esteem and respect, hence the way in which people were collectively treated and regarded by others and by society as a whole. Community and (substantive) equality are, from this perspective, mutually reinforcing and there can be no real equality of worth where people are divided from each other by huge gaps in the division of income, wealth and status. Major material inequalities, Wilkinson explained, were 'socially distancing: they are read as status differences and so as differences in people's intrinsic merits'. Thus, on the one hand, the rich 'are seen as valued, successful, and significant people' while on the other 'the poor appear as inadequate failures of little or no account'. Sharp disparities in income and wealth are, thus, 'fleshed out by cultural differences, which help support perceptions of superiority and inferiority and enable relations between us to be coloured by rank' (Wilkinson, 2005: 201).

For New Labour this was old-fashioned thinking that failed to grasp that collectivist values had crumbled, that people were fired by ambition to rise in the social scale, that the wealthy – in a celebrity-drenched culture – were less objects to be envied than role models to be emulated. In the past, driven by its determination to iron-out differences in social position, the party had lost touch with the aspirations of the mass of the people. Obsessed by a determination to advance 'absolute equality', Patricia Hewitt complained, 'Old Labour' seemed to 'punish anything that was exceptional, particularly if it was success, particularly if it was financial success' ('Analysis', 2000). The levelling urge smothered individuality, discouraged initiative and scorned fully merited largesse. Deploring those who wished to reinstitute 'penal levels of taxation' the chair of the party Hazel Blears MP stressed that in today's society,

> people want to get on and do well. They want to own their own home, and to see their children do better than they did. This is the spirit that New Labour tapped into in the 1990s. Any whiff of the politics of envy … and these families will go over to the Tories. There must be no caps on aspiration.
>
> (the *Independent*, 2 June 2007)

No phrase more starkly demonstrated the distance New Labour had travelled than 'the politics of envy'. It implied that while lifting the living standards of the poor and socially marginalised, and the extending to them of opportunities to better themselves, were wholly admirable, indeed essential, objects of public policy, the belief that a substantial compression of inequalities should be pursued *as a matter of principle*, was inspired by wrong-headed, antiquated and dogma-driven sentiments which had lost touch with the individualism of the new consumer culture.

Yet, ironically, New Labour's disowning of the party's traditional egalitarian creed occurred just as evidence began to accumulate that inequality per se, and not just impoverishment, was – as ethical socialists in particular had long proclaimed – detrimental to both physical and social well-being. After reviewing copious evidence, Professor of Social Epidemiology Richard Wilkinson, a leading expert in the field, found that ill-health tended to be less common 'in societies where income differences are smaller, even after average incomes, absolute poverty, and a number of other socioeconomic factors have been controlled for'. Although absolute material standards did have an impact, socioeconomic differences in health within developed countries, the data indicated, 'result primarily from differences in people's position in the socioeconomic hierarchy' (Wilkinson, 1997. See also Wilkinson, 2006). Similarly, research findings surveyed by Professor of Epidemiology Sir Michael Marmot clearly showed that 'the psychological experience of inequality – and not just poverty – has profound effects on body systems' and 'may be a major factor in generating the social gradient in health'. Studies have repeatedly demonstrated that 'being low in the hierarchy means a greater susceptibility to just about every disease that is going' (Marmot, 2004: 7, 23).

Furthermore, data gathered by experts indicated that, as ethical socialists had long claimed, high levels of inequality rent the social fabric by producing among those who occupied the lower rungs in the social ladder feelings of alienation, bitterness and anger. This was because the greater the inequality in income and wealth, the wider the disparities in status positions and socially sanctioned esteem patterns. These disparities, in turn (Wilkinson observed) 'have a huge impact on whether people feel valued, appreciated and needed or, on the other hand, looked down on, ignored, treated as insignificant, stigmatised and humiliated' (Wilkinson, 2005: 26). Substantial and entrenched material inequalities, in short, undermined ties of community and fellow-feeling, subverted co-operation and trust and fostered more aggressively competitive and more socially disruptive societies. 'As well-being becomes more dependent on individual material achievement and less dependent on the strength of our social relations, interaction becomes more self-serving and competitive, people trust each other less, they withdraw from social and community activities, and aggression becomes more common' (Wilkinson, 2005: 201). In such circumstances it is difficult to envisage the communitarian spirit – which the Blair Government ostensibly wished to promote – flourishing. The New Labour renunciation of equality may prove to be premature and short-sighted.

The public service ethos

As we have seen (chapter one) the original grand ethical socialist ambition to reconstitute social relationships through a wholesale transformation of capitalism was (by the 1950s) supplanted by a more modest one: to carve out strategic social enclaves in which more altruistic and co-operative modes of behaviour could flourish and thereby temper and dilute the impulses of the market and egoistic man. The key here was the construction of a powerful, autonomous public domain, charged with meeting basic human needs, with its own distinct rationality and values. The public domain should embody 'the collective life of the community: those activities and decisions which need to be, can only be undertaken by the community as a whole' (Ranson and Stewart, 1989: 24). The commitment to a distinct public domain regulated according to the precepts of what came to be known as the public service ethos thus became the cornerstone concept of ethical socialism.

The Blair Government claimed to be a staunch custodian of the ethos. The values of 'compassion, fairness, a belief in the strength of community, co-operation with others as the basis for individual progress', Milburn reassured sceptics, lay at the heart of the Government's public sector reform programme. 'It would be folly to sacrifice these values and these principles' (Milburn, 2001a). 'The ethos of the NHS,' his successor as Health Secretary, John Reid, affirmed, 'remains the glue of the service' (*The Guardian*, 1 October 2003). Critics were wholly unconvinced and this became a major point of issue with New Labour. Former senior cabinet minister Robin Cook lamented that Government reforms had 'the consistent feature of squeezing out of the NHS the public service ethos that makes it popular' (in the *Guardian*, 4 February 2005). To another former Labour minister, Angela Eagle, 'the unique benefits of the public sector ethos have been overlooked and undervalued' by a government which appears to regard 'private sector management expertise' and 'shareholder pressure for increased profits and dividends' as stronger motivating forces than 'the goodwill and commitment of the workforce' (Eagle, 2003: 34). In what follows we suggest that these critics were essentially correct – that, as Brendan Barber, TGWU general secretary put it – Government policy was informed 'by an ideological preference for the private sector that fails to recognise the importance of the distinct public sector ethos' (ePolitix.com, 23 January 2007).

Assumptions concerning human motivation, Julian Le Grand has suggested, are 'the key to both the design and the implementation of public policy'. In shaping their policies policy-makers make assumptions – conscious or otherwise – about the likely responses of both those who deliver the policies and those who are expected to benefit from them (Le Grand, 2003: 2). The public service ethos saw qualified public servants as, in the aggregate, 'primarily motivated by their professional ethic' (Le Grand, 1997: 155). Public servants 'can and do transcend individual utility maximization for the sake of the public interest; they are motivated, at least in part, and for some of the time, by a sense of service and of civic duty' (Marquand, 2004: 91). This belief 'dominated thinking' in social democratic circles 'about the motivation, character and moral importance of the public sector within the political community' (Plant, 2003a: 561). Professionalism lay at the heart of the public service ethos. 'Those in the public service have a vocation to serve the public. In doing so, they are guided by professional values which emphasise service' (Plant, 2003a: 562). Professional behaviour is behaviour regulated by a code of conduct that specifies the proper ends of the profession and commits its members to deliver services according to needs in an impartial and equitable manner. The corollary was that trained professionals should be allowed very considerable autonomy on how they discharged their functions without too much risk that the power so devolved would be abused.

There were those, especially on the left on the party, who feared such abuse of power – that professionals would stake out 'areas of professional monopoly to their own rather than the public benefit' and give preference, in the way they organised their services, to 'professional skills and ideas rather than ... to client needs' (Wilding, 1981: 4–5, 8). As Townshend wrote as early as 1961, Tawney tended to 'romanticise the professions. He appears to give too much weight to the traditions of service to the community and too little to the arrogant self advancement recognised by latter-day critics of professionalism' (Townshend, 1971). Resentment of the powerful grip the consultants had secured over the NHS was common especially among more radical elements in the Labour party. The favoured left-wing response was to exert greater political control and install more effective forms of democratic accountability. But little progress was ever made, partly because most Labour ministers (with notable exceptions such as Crossman and Castle) were reluctant to incur the political risks of challenging the citadels of professional power and hence manifested a tendency to yield to 'professional claims to expertise, independence and authority' (Wilding, 1981).

However, after the election of the Conservative Government in 1979 the assumptions underpinning the public service ethos were challenged in a far more formidable and forthright manner – and from a radically different political direction. The organising assumption of neo-liberalism (heavily influenced by theories of rational choice and 'the new public management') was that people were essentially self-seeking utility-maximisers. In the market sector, via the pressures exerted by competition and profit-maximisation, self-interest could be corralled to the public advantage. This was not the case in the public sector. Public sector workers (and the organisations that represented them) were seen as empire-builders and rent-seekers, their appetites for feathering their own nests unconstrained by the disciplines of the market. Benign views of disinterested public sector professionals ('knights') were displaced by more jaundiced ones perceiving them as 'knavish' (self-interested) (Le Grand, 2003: 39).

Labour's return to power in 1997 seemed to presage a revival of faith in the public service ethos. Blair attested that 'there is something special about public service. At its best the notion of public service embodies vital qualities – loyalty, altruism, dedication, long-term relationships with users, a sense of pride' (Blair, 2002a). However it became evident during the course of its first term that New Labour's attitude towards the public service ethos was, at best, ambivalent. Professionalism is not merely a claim to expertise and a code of behaviour but a system for appropriating and wielding power through specifying 'what counts as valuable knowledge, who knows it, and who is empowered to act in what ways as a consequence' thereby allowing it to lay claim to a very considerable degree of professional autonomy (Clarke, Gewitz and McLaughlin, 2000: 8. See also Evetts, 2003: 403). New Labour increasingly came to the conclusion that professional power was too often being suborned for purposes of producer advantage. Public employees might talk of the public service ethos, former Downing Street aide Geoff Mulgan reflected, 'but often there was not much sense of service to the public' (interview, 2006). There was a growing propensity to view public sector organisations as producer cartels whose behaviour was too often driven by narrow personal and institutional interests and which exhibited only muted regard for the public good (interviews with ministers and political advisors). In a major statement of the New Labour public sector reform programme Tony Blair drew attention to the malign consequences of

> the legacy of professional domination of service provision. The sixties and seventies were a period of unprecedented expansion in public services. Government provided the funds for services but allowed the professionals and their managers at the local level ... to define not just the way services were delivered but also the standards to which they were delivered. And this too often meant services where standards were too low, an unacceptable variability in delivery, which entrenched inequality and service users ... who were disempowered and demoralised.
>
> (Blair, 2004a)

New Labour – in contrast to the new right – never wholly accepted public choice theory and its defence of the public service ethos was never merely rhetorical. But claims by professional organisations that their members were primarily inspired by disinterested considerations were treated with growing scepticism. Ministerial experience of negotiations with shrewd and tough-minded representatives of bodies such as the BMA and the Royal Colleges helped them acquire (as one government insider recalled) 'an extremely jaundiced view of the medical profession' (interview, 2006). Public servants were (in the words of a Number 10 advisor) 'remarkably adept at convincing themselves that what's in their own interest is also in the public interest' (interview, 2006). While it was only realistic 'to recognise that public sector employees will have their own interests, their own axe to grind', one former minister recalled, there was within Downing Street 'too much of a tendency to dismiss all they say as self-interested, too great a willingness to discount the fact that they have front-line experience' (interview, 2006). Indeed, New Labour came to reformulate the very concept of the public service ethos. Public service should mean service *to the public*, not by the public. It should express itself in the sensitivity and responsiveness to consumer preferences commonly to be found among commercial enterprises rather than in any claim to be animated by a superior virtue. The public service ethos was not 'a function of ownership', one senior aide averred, but 'characteristic of an interaction' not tied to either the public or private sector (Taylor, M, 2006: 22). As a former prime ministerial advisor observed, 'the public sector has no monopoly on virtue, the private sector has no monopoly on vice. Public institutions are not only run by knights; private firms are not run only by knaves' (Le Grand, 2006a: 29).[3]

The shift in Labour's outlook can be elucidated by distinguishing between two models of organisational functioning. The first model – which can be called the professional-normative – analyses organisations as common cultures 'held together by strong social norms about motivation, work and professional ethics' in which members cooperate of their own accord to attain its goals (Rothstein, 1998: 87). The second model – which can be dubbed the managerial-instrumental – views organisations as incentive systems in which the managerial task is 'for the "principal" to create an economic structure that rewards self-interested "agents" who fulfil the goals of the organization' (Rothstein, 1998: 87). 'Agents' can only be expected to discharge their responsibilities effectively to the extent that they are 'incentivised' with rewards or sanctions applied on the basis of a rigorous monitoring of performance. Rather than assuming that public servants are 'knightly' in inclination it sees people as 'knavish' – utility maximisers – 'who are motivated to help others only if by so doing they will serve their private interests' (Le Grand, 2003: 27).

These are models and not empirical categories but do represent two ends of a pole between which policy-makers are pulled. A major theme of this study is that, under the Blair Government, Labour had moved closer to the managerial-instrumental pole. For example, in the early years of the Government, a major policy statement emphasised that the NHS was an

> organisation glued together by a bond of trust between staff and patient or, what some have called, 'principled motivation'. Our aim is to renew that for today's world, not throwing away those values to market mechanisms, but harnessing them to drive up performance.
>
> (Department of Health, 2000: 57)

But those who held such views steadily lost ground. There was, within highly influential circles, a waning confidence 'in the reliability of the public sector ethos as a motivational drive and a growing conviction that self-interest was the principal force motivating those involved in public services' (Strategy Unit, 2006: 59). In what one ex-cabinet minister called a 'very revelatory' speech (interview, 2006) Tony Blair gave vent to his vexation with 'people in the public sector' who tended to be cautious, unimaginative and reluctant to experiment at a time when 'the private sector, in its reward and motivation, has moved on apace' (Blair, 1999). From this perspective, the concept of a public service ethic seemed – to a considerable degree – to be a rather convenient rationalisation for the single-minded pursuit of 'producer interests'.

Hence the Blair Government became more and more convinced (especially in its second term) that the running of public organisations would benefit greatly from the bracing effects of competition and the entrepreneurial spirit. Crouch defines this shift towards the managerial-instrumental model as 'commercialisation', that is reforms 'premised on the assumption that the quality of public services will be improved if the existing practices and ethos of public services are replaced by those typical of commercial practice' (Crouch, 2003: 4). Summarising, 'commercialisation' took a threefold form:

1. *Pruning professional power through choice and competition.* Uncon-strained by competitive disciplines, public organisations were seen as afflicted by endemic problems of risk aversion, organisational inertia and lack of institutional drive and enterprise (Strategy Unit, 2006: 22; inter-view with Government political advisor, 2006). The key to service improvement was consumer empowerment, through 'a continuous drive to increase the scope and scale of choice available to public service users' (Blair, 2004a). Milburn put it thus: Where people can opt for a hospital where the waiting times are shorter and where money follows patient then he is empowered. The hospital losing patients then has a choice – to continue to under perform or improve: getting doctors working as they should be and therefore getting patients back (interview, 2006).

2. *Incentivisation.* Greater efficiency, better quality and more responsive service delivery were seen to 'require establishing appropriate institu-tional incentives and disciplines to evoke the required motivation and commitment' (Smith, 2000). 'Incentivisation' can be defined as the link-age of 'incentives to performance in order to foster greater entrepre-neurialism and closer attention to cost cutting and organisational efficiency' (Doig and Wilson, 1999: 28). The PM's Strategy Unit was confident that public service workers would 'respond positively to pay incentives, without this necessarily crowding out altruistic motivations' (Strategy Unit, 2006: 59). 'Incentivisation' has typically taken the form of performance-related pay, sharper differentiation of rewards at the individual level, the deployment of quantitative methods for appraising performance, the widespread use of targets to measure organisational effectiveness and exposure to consumer pressure (Doig and Wilson, 1999: 28). 'The assault on professionalism – teachers, doctors, lecturers, police,' Simon Caulkin, man-agement editor of the *Observer*, pointed out, was 'not an unfortunate by-product of policy: it is the policy. Ministers want doctors and lecturers to be motivated by money and league tables' (*The Observer*, 25 2007).[4]

3. *Professional accountability via performance management.* This can be characterised as a way of securing professional compliance with organi-sational goals through greater reliance on setting explicit standards via elaborate systems of monitoring and auditing. Hence the explosion of agencies (and the stock of rules they spawned) engaged in checking, measuring, evaluating and appraising the performance of public sector workers – a veritable nomenklatura of audit. The paraphernalia of tar-gets, league tables and performance measures has been used to create systems 'which mimic as far as possible the competition and discipline of markets' as well as providing levers by which managers can assert more control over employees (Rustin, 2000: 122). All this is underpinned by the assumption that, to significantly raise standards, public service pro-fessionals could not be allowed too much discretion but would have to be made more accountable through regulation, inspection and rigorous performance management (Blair, 2004a).

New Labour-style 'commercialisation' can be conceptualised in terms of the 'imposition of a secondary economic coding' on operations or activities that remain primarily non-commercial in their orientation. The process occurs (Jessop suggests) 'in so far as choices among formally non-commercial activities are influenced by "profit-and-loss" or at least economic "cost-benefit" calculations'. It is further reflected 'in the growing role of market proxies in non-commercial organizations' and the 'increased sensitisation of non-commercial institutions to the perceived needs of an internationally competitive economy' (Jessop, 1999a). 'Whereas the welfare system was once thought to be the embodiment of a value-system complementary to capitalism – that of care and mutual responsibility – it is being turned into a means of inculcating mentalities deemed necessary to a market economy' (Rustin, 2004a: 113–4). In essence the assumption is that public organisations would function more efficiently, produce a higher standard of service and develop more sensitivity to user needs to the extent that they emulate 'the enterprise culture' of the private sector. 'All public services,' former health minister John Denham wrote,

> have to be based on a diversity of independent providers who compete for business in a market governed by consumer choice. All across Whitehall, any policy option has now to be dressed up as 'choice', 'diversity' and 'contestability'. These are the hallmarks of the 'new model public service'.
>
> > (Denham, 2006: 20. For the similar views of other former ministers see Eagle, 2003; Whitehead, 2000)

Conclusion

Does New Labour under the Blair administration constitute 'a social democratic government, modernising public services, addressing problems of social exclusion, social injustice and elitism?' (Clarke, 2004a: 42). Or are we witnessing 'a radical revision of the very nature of social democratic politics, superseding its traditional role and political identity and essentially forming a new force in party politics'? (Schmidtke, 2002: 2).

There is no simple answer to these questions. New Labour is ideologically eclectic. It has exhibited receptivity to a range of ideas and values of diverse origins and has articulated a range of aspirations, some of which 'are clearly continuous with the Labour Party's tradition of egalitarian social democracy. Others are much less so' (White, 2001: 4). Party ideologies and governmental programmes are, Clarke points out, 'rarely "pure" expressions of larger logics'. Rather they are 'compound formations' and 'articulations of different discourses' constructed to achieve tangible goals, both electoral and programmatic – and such is the case with New Labour (Clarke, 2004a: 41). Given the irreducible elements of uncertainty and indeterminacy in political life, given, equally, that any broad political tradition will incorporate diverse beliefs with varying provenance and given, finally, that politicians have ceaselessly to wrestle with conflicting pressures, competing interests and manifold complex challenges, intellectual coherence is likely to be perceived as one of the lesser political virtues.

Some commentators, however, go further. The presumption of a single New Labour project, they suggest, is misconceived because there are in fact *two* New Labours, and the programme of the Blair Government, rather than being an expression of a single project, has in reality been formed through a series of bargains, compromises and trade-offs between two rival projects, one Blairite and the other Brownite. Thus Will Hutton discerned

> a fault-line in the Government ... between Rawlsian social democrats, led by Gordon Brown, and social liberals led by Tony Blair ... it is why the rows over foundation hospitals, specialist schools, top-up fees and the pensions regime are so ideologically charged. They go to the heart of the nature of the social settlement the Government is trying to build and why, sooner or later, there will be a breakdown between New Labour's two wings.
>
> (the *Observer*, 1 December 2002)

For Rustin the 'difference within government seems to have been buried in the party walls dividing numbers 10 and 11 Downing Street' (Rustin, 2004a: 114). An echo of this is the warning that has issued forth from some Blairites who caution about Brown's dangerously 'Old Labour' tendencies.

This is plainly a tendentious claim that ignores Brown's vital role, evident to any dispassionate observer, in the formation of New Labour. The existence of rival Blairite and Brownite tendencies which have operated throughout the life of the Labour Government and have frequently collided with each other is certainly a fact of life. Equally, there is no doubt that Brown has had the capacity, at least in some areas of policy, to pursue his own agenda. Compared to past Labour governments, which exhibited pluralist structures of power, the one formed in 1997 has been highly centralised (see Shaw, 2002; Shaw, 2004b). But this system of concentrated power has been one of dyarchy, almost of divided sovereignty. The power of the Treasury within British government has always been very considerable but – according to one very well-informed journalist – Brown's power was 'unprecedented'. Blair never had a free hand in many aspects of economic and social policy but had to take account of 'what Gordon would think' (Riddell, 2005: 16–17). The Prime Minister, former economic advisor Derek Scott bewailed, 'delegated an unprecedented amount of prime-ministerial authority to the Chancellor', effectively ceding to him 'control over economic policy' (Scott, 2004: 2, 1). Another senior Downing Street advisor distinguished between two domains of policy-making, a Prime Ministerial one in which Blair exercised predominant control (e.g. education, healthcare, law and order); and a shared domain – extending from the management of the economy to large tranches of social policy – in which policy had to be hammered out by agreement between the PM and his Chancellor (interview, 2007). The result is that, on some issues, resistance from Brown had to be overcome, for example, the extension of choice and of private sector involvement in the NHS; on others policy had to some degree to be watered-down, for example foundation trust hospitals (interview, Chris Ham, 2007); while on still others – notably higher education variable top-up fees – even diluted versions just scraped through.

Whether it is correct to conclude that Blair and Brown comprise rival 'social democratic' and 'social liberal' projects is difficult to say. It as an issue upon which even New Labour insiders cannot agree. For some, the most progressive (or regressive, according to standpoint) aspects in the New Labour programme have been mostly inspired by Gordon Brown and would not have been implemented without his support. For others, the Brownite camp has been primarily a faction of expediency rather than principle, with policy differences exploited to embarrass Blair and hasten his removal (interviews, 2006, 2007). Even the extent to which Brown is the animator of a more traditionally social democratic outlook is a matter of debate. On the one hand, his enthusiasm for combating poverty and extending opportunity, and his reservations about some of the Prime Minister's more radical neo-market initiatives are a matter of record. Further, Brown 'defined himself, with no trace of doubt or irony, as the living embodiment of the spirit of the labour movement' (Peston, 2005: 16). On the other hand, he was 'the leading architect' of the party's 'conversion to the values of enterprise, innovation, competition, flexible Labour markets, financial incentives and fiscal prudence' (Crewe, 2006: 210); the driving force behind the Private Finance Initiative (which may prove to be one of the Government's most expensive mistakes); and is a huge enthusiast for the American 'enterprise culture'. For an answer we must await the experience of the Brown premiership.

9   For whom does New Labour stand?

Introduction

At the heart of the New Labour project has been a reformulation of the party's traditional representational role and this chapter seeks to elucidate what form this has taken.

The role of interest representation has been defined as the way in which a party collates and aggregates the demands articulated by interest associations, processes them into policy proposals and translates them into acts of public policy. Few would dissent from the proposition that, under the Blair leadership, this role has been transformed; it is the nature of that transformation that is at issue. From one perspective Labour has ceased to be 'the embodiment of a narrowly working-class interest' and has been transformed into the people's party, the custodian of the interests of all sections of the community whose policies are framed to appeal to as broad a social catchment area as possible (Cronin, 2004: 401). From a second perspective, the real significance of the shift is that New Labour has shunted to one side the party's traditional role as the guardian of the interests of 'ordinary working people'. It has gone 'beyond the rapprochement and co-operation with business interests which is essential to all social democratic parties to becoming simply a business party' (Crouch, 1999: 80). The main task this chapter sets itself is to explore the way in which its key figures envisaged and enacted the representational role of New Labour and the ramifications this has had for the function the party now performs in the political system.

Labour and the pluralist frame of reference

A key factor shaping the way in which a social democratic party construes its representational role is the frame of reference it utilises to define the nature of the relationship between the two great repositories of social and economic interests, business – the owners, controllers and managers of capital – on the one hand, and the unions – the representatives of the employed – on the other. The proposition advanced here is that a party's dominant frame of reference shapes the way it conceives and attributes legitimacy to the demands of competing interests and therefore its willingness to incorporate them into public policy. Drawing upon the work of Alan Fox, a distinction is made between three such frames: the unitary, the adversarial and the pluralist (Fox, 1966, 1974).

The unitary frame of reference sees the social order as fundamentally unified and regards both capital and labour as stakeholders in a common enterprise, social partners for whom collaboration is the most rational arrangement. In the past this view, which appears to validate the existing distribution of power and resources and legitimate managerial authority, has had few adherents within the Labour party. The adversarial frame views the social order as basically fractured, with capital and labour locked in a conflictual relationship defined by a persistent opposition of class interest. According to one influential school of thought Labour's traditional representational role can best be defined in terms of this model. It was grounded in 'a strongly etched map of the social world, which began with the proposition that capitalism created social classes in conflict with one another. In this setting, the central conflict was between capital and the working class' (Rose and Ross, 1994: 449). Thus in government Labour adhered to 'a fundamental belief that working-class interests are separate, collective, and antipathetic to the interests of other social groups' and it exhibited a 'determination to protect those interests as they have come to be embodied in working-class communities and institutions' notably the trade unions (Cronin, 2006: 53). The obverse side of this was an 'attitude of suspicion' to business 'routinely combined with specific policies that business found onerous and inhospitable' (Cronin, 2004: 71, 74. See also Hall, P, 2002: 32).

While the adversarial model did indeed have its adherents on the left of the party and in the unions, we shall suggest that it never shaped the mindset of its leadership. The ruling frame of reference was emphatically pluralist. This frame concurs with the adversarial in perceiving genuine divergence of interest between those who own industrial property and those who do not, between those who occupy positions of power and prestige and can command high emoluments in the major institutional hierarchies and those who fill more subordinate roles and live on more modest incomes. But equally it held that these differences could be accommodated through institutionalised forms of social conflict regulation (Panitch, 1986: 57). As Forrester pointed out, Labour politicians were 'not concerned with fighting the class war ... but with creating the conditions for gradual, peaceful reform by winning over the middle classes and the ruling class through the moral force and economic sense of their arguments' (Forrester, 1975: 40).[1] The party was, of course, seen as the political wing of the labour movement. However, the ideological setting was not the promotion of class power but the integrationist concept of social citizenship in which public power and programmes were to be used to contain the inegalitarian social consequences of the market. 'Neither trade union leaders steeped in labourism ... nor certainly Labour's political leaders thought of society as a battlefield upon which the working class was engaged in a permanent and irrevocable struggle against domination and exploitation' (Ralph Miliband, quoted in Coates and Panitch, 2001). Rather they viewed the party's role as the protection of the institutional interests of unions against attacks from hostile sources (the Tories, the Judiciary) and the advancement of the material needs of their members. But they also believed that industrial stability could be maintained by developing procedures and institutional arrangements which facilitated the orderly and equitable resolution of disagreements.

The precise way in which Labour's leaders conceptualised the party's representational tasks varied somewhat over time. As class boundaries began to blur and the size of the middle class to swell, they became increasingly uneasy with the language of class. In government 'far from proclaiming any special concern with the interests of the working classes', the sociologist and historian Alan Fox wrote in 1978, they asserted that Labour's status as a national party required that all must make sacrifices to meet its objectives – including such 'non-class' ones as defence of the pound, reassuring markets and restoring profitability. 'Class and class interests are felt to be embarrassing concepts left over from a less sophisti- cated era and rarely mentioned' (Fox, 1978: 6). Indeed much of the effort of Labour governments in the 1960s and 1970s was expended in designing an institutional fabric that could entrench a system of quasi-corporatist co-ordination and thereby cement a stable relationship between business, unions and the state.

However, aspiring to a model of corporatist-style sustainable pluralist accommodation was not the same as achieving it. Time and again Labour governments found themselves seeking – not very effectively – to contain inflationary wage settlements through various forms of incomes policy while pursuing a macro-economic strategy designed both to accelerate growth rates and preserve the status of sterling as an international currency. The compromises that Labour governments in the 1960s and 1970s struck were fragile, transient and normally took the form of short-term and sometimes counter-productive trade-offs, and they signally failed to construct the cor- poratist arrangements which alone could institutionalise compromise between capital and labour. Industrial relations were characterised by tur- bulence and strife that contrasted with the more orderly management of conflict in the social democracies of northern Europe. All this of course culminated in the emblematic 'Winter of Discontent' of 1978/9.

New Labour and the unitary frame of reference

The disappointing record of successive Labour Governments had a pro- found effect on the outlook of the New Labour leadership. The corporatist formula, it believed, had shown itself to be unworkable in Britain. The TUC (and, indeed, the employers' peak association, the Confederation of British Industry) lacked the power to ensure that tripartite bargains between government, business and the unions would be honoured while the system of wage bargaining was becoming ever more fragmented and decentralised. In addition, the reshaping of the global economy coupled with the emergence of a new, knowledge-based, service-oriented domestic economic structure rendered the corporatist approach obsolete even in countries where it had previously functioned effectively. The politics of corporatist pluralism, in short, were unsustainable.

Past failures and crises and current challenges conjoined with the arrival into positions of control in the Labour party of a cohort of politicians which was more weakly socialised into the culture of a 'labour movement' than earlier generations, contributing to a reconfiguration in the way in which the relationship between capital and labour, employers and employees, was regarded. The notion that the party and the unions were bound together in a 'shared historical project' (Minkin, 1991: 4–5) was emphatically abandoned. Indeed it was viewed as a device which had been used to legitimate the preferential treatment accorded to the unions in successive Labour governments – to the detriment both of the national interest and ultimately (and disastrously) of the party itself. What was in traditional discourse seen as a natural partnership between the 'two wings of the movement' was now perceived as the improper exercise of influence – 'favours, not fairness'. It was the dead weight of this heritage that the leadership of the party after 1994 was determined to shed.

At the root of New Labour thinking was the conviction that, in the interests of economic efficiency, the inhibitions which in the past had always muted the party's approval of the market economy had to be shredded. The Blair Government, from its inception, demonstrated 'a new-found appreciation for the profitability of business' (Hall, P, 2002: 32), a willingness to be attentive and obliging towards business needs, to render the state's 'exactions ... more limited and its demands less intrusive' (Cronin, 2004: 435). In effect it adopted (a modified version of) the unitary frame of reference. Put in its simplest terms, since the welfare of society as a whole was contingent upon a flourishing private sector, there could be no real opposition between the private interests of business and the public good. Conflicts between management and labour were seen to arise from a malfunctioning of the system, or as a result of short-sighted, self-interested behaviour. From the perspective of this 'unitary philosophy ... there are no longer held to be any significant social conflicts left to resolve, class divisions being now held to have disappeared, or to be residues of the past' (Rustin, 2004b: 113). Different claims inevitably have to be juggled and reconciled but the assumption that if one 'side' benefits then the other suffers was to fundamentally misunderstand the nature of the employment relationship and the realities of a modern economy. Thus, as we have seen (Chapter Six), a lightly regulated labour market was deemed, by maximising competitive efficiency, to be in the interest of all. 'Everyone benefits,' Blair insisted, 'employees and business alike' (*The Guardian*, 9 September 2003).

'What pattern of behaviour do we expect,' Fox enquires, 'from the members of a successful and healthily functioning team? We expect them to strive jointly towards a common objective, each pulling his weight to the best of his ability' (Fox, 1966). Within the 'team' both employers and employees have rights and duties. Indeed, the team analogy implies that

> if the members have an obligation of loyalty towards the leader, the obligation is certainly reciprocated, for it is the duty of the leader to act in such ways as to inspire the loyalty he demands. Morale and success are closely connected and rest heavily upon personal relationships.
>
> (Fox, 1966: 3)[2]

Teamwork in New Labour parlance is 'partnership'. The Blair Government's legislative programme was designed, Blair explained, 'to replace the notion of conflict between employers and employees with the promotion of partnership' (foreword, Department of Trade and Industry, 1998). The aim was to foster a collaborative spirit which 'sought to stress the common interests that bound companies and their employers together and not their differences' (Taylor, R, 2001a: 253). As Blair told delegates to the Labour party conference prior to taking office: 'forget the past. No more bosses versus workers. You are on the same side. The same team' (Blair, 1997).[3]

New Labour has, however, incorporated into its frame of reference important pluralist elements. Unlike the Conservatives, it regards trade unions as legitimate interlocutors on behalf of their members and, far from excluding them from the policy process (their fate during the Tory years), has both engaged them fully in consultation over matters of common interest (though not with the same rights of access as business) and fostered a union–business dialogue. Collective representation of individuals at work can be, the Government accepts, 'the best method of ensuring that employees are treated fairly', and concedes that 'individual contracts of employment are *not always* agreements between equal partners' (note the important qualification. My emphasis. Department of Trade and Industry, 1998).

This unitary-pluralist hybrid is given expression in the distinctively New Labour accent on the mutuality of obligations on the part of both employers and employees, management and trade unions, to be enforced if necessary by statute. Employers must treat their workforce justly and respect the 'very minimum infrastructure of decency and fairness around people in the workplace' (Blair, foreword to Department of Trade and Industry, 1998). As noted above (Chapter Six) an impressive series of measures have been passed to enhance the collective and individual rights of employees, including the right to union recognition, to be accompanied by union representatives in grievance and discipline cases, the minimum wage, controls over working time, rights for working parents to request flexible working, protection for workers transferred to the private sector and so forth. The overall aim was to ensure 'that employer obligation to their employees be underpinned by the provision of minimum labour standards and collective representation at the workplace' (Gennard, 2002: 588–9). As the head of the TUC declared, 'Since 1997 vitally important rights and protections for workers have been won after two decades when deregulation was almost a state religion' (Barber, 2003). Equally, however, the Government has enjoined upon the unions and their members their responsibility to promote harmony and co-operation in the workplace. In return for being granted new rights employees must 'help achieve important business objectives' and 'accept their responsibilities to co-operate with employers. There will be no return to the days of industrial conflict' (Department of Trade and Industry, 1998).

Labour's traditional pluralism regarded trade unions as the indispensable sentinels of employee interests. Combination and organisation enabled workers to rectify a structural imbalance of power, restrain employer advantages over setting terms for the wage-effort bargain and afford protection against the arbitrary exercise of managerial power. Labour saw trade unionism as an essential democratic countervailing influence against the unilateral power of employers. Relations between organisational heads and their workforces were best regulated by collective bargaining. *In Place of Strife*, the controversial White Paper issued by Barbara Castle when Employment Secretary, defined collective bargaining as

> essentially a process by which employees take part in the decisions that affect their working lives. If it is carried on by efficient management and representatives of well-organised unions, negotiating over a wide range of subjects, it represents the best method so far devised of advancing industrial democracy in the interests of both employees and employers. It offers the community the best opportunity for securing well-ordered progress towards higher levels of performance and the introduction of new methods of work.
>
> (Department of Employment, 1969: para. 19)

The Blair Government, in contrast, sees collective negotiation as only one of several alternative methods of securing the well-being of employees. 'It does not accord to unions and the collective bargaining process the sole, or even the primary, responsibility for articulating workers' interests and seeing that they are met' (Cronin, 2006: 63). Thus the Government noted that employers and employees often choose representational methods that do not involve trade unions but nonetheless 'achieve good employment relations' (Department of Trade and Industry, 1998). 'For sure', Brendan Barber, TUC General Secretary observed, New Labour ministers

> recognise our right to exist, and a citizen's right to join. They can see that individuals may benefit from belonging to a union. They recognise that the legal pendulum swung too far away from workers during the

Thatcher/Major years. But this is not the same as recognising that unions, and the collective bargaining and right to effective representation that we pursue, are in general a force for good.

(Barber, 2003)

As Cronin observes, this shift in policy amounts to 'a major break with the collectivist traditions of the trade unions, of the Labour Party, and of the classic British system of industrial relations' (Cronin, 2006: 63).

Thus, rather than the rights of unions to organise, secure recognition and bargain with employers being inherent in a democratic society, they are conditional ones, which have to be earned. Unions' success depends not only on convincing employees of their value but on convincing employers too. As the *Fairness at Work* White Paper put it, *where* 'trade unions are able to demonstrate value to employers', *where* they can show 'how much help they can bring to the success of an enterprise for employers' *then* they are more likely to gain – and by implication to merit – recognition (Department of Trade and Industry, 1998). The role of the union, from the New Labour perspective, is a significant but ultimately rather modest one: to protect 'their members against arbitrary and unfair treatment', to help them acquire appropriate skills and to work 'with business to promote business performance' (Byers, 1999).

The notion that the employment relationship is an inherently unequal one, that managerial authority that is not checked by union organisation constitutes a threat – especially when the demand for their labour is weak – to employees' employment security, conditions or income levels, is not one given much credence by New Labour. Once an infrastructure of basic rights and minimum standards is established and a wage floor provided by the minimum wage, then it is not so far-fetched as Labour once assumed to envisage the contract of employment as one of voluntary and free exchange between individuals and firms in which all parties benefit. Thus, 'the primary task of industrial relations institutions is not to correct an imbalance of power in the workplace, but to create a context in which the productivity and creativity of workers is properly harnessed for the good of the firm' (Howell, 2004: 14).

To the pluralist the legitimacy of managerial rule 'in the eyes of subordinates is not automatic but must be actively pursued and maintained' (Fox, 1974: 263). As Kay points out, 'for a century, the legitimacy of corporate and managerial authority was a central political question' as the labour movement challenged 'the basis on which private entrepreneurs exercised seemingly arbitrary authority' (Kay, 2004: 76). Such a concern has little resonance with New Labour. As long as managerial authority is not exercised in too overtly autocratic a manner, it is unproblematic. Thus the Government does not favour any substantial reform to the structure of authority or the decision-making process within the firm – and, indeed, has striven to block modest EU-inspired measures to make mandatory more extensive employee consultative rights. As Smith and Morton point out, once the notion of structured power inequalities inherent in the employment relationship is abandoned then the case for collective organisation and the assertion of a strong collective voice is much less compelling (Smith and Morton, 2006: 403).

New Labour's adhesion to the unitary frame reflected a degree of enthusiasm for big business never before found in the party. As *The Financial Times* reported early in his premiership, one of Blair's 'most striking traits' was 'reverence for big companies. His empathy with professional managers... is infinitely greater than any fraternal bond with trade unionists' (*The Financial Times*, 4 February 1998, quoted in Grant, 2000: 14). Equally Brown was insistent that 'we must never return to a situation here in Britain where, unlike in America and most of Europe, one party is seen as pro-business and the other anti-business' (the *Daily Telegraph*, 11 November 1996). As we have seen (Chapters Two, Four and Six) he was, in policy terms, as good as his word.

This shift from a pluralist frame of reference to a more hybrid unitary-pluralist one should be seen in the context of a new power setting. The power of organised labour in the United Kingdom (as in many other countries) has, over the last quarter-century, slumped, with a drastic fall in membership and union density, a result of the combination of the legacy of high unemployment, the shrinkage of manufacturing employment and a much tougher institutional framework. Globalisation has recalibrated the balance of power in favour of capital and at the expense of the state and organised labour. The outcome has been a decisive shift in the distribution of power resources with 'a major weakening of political forces pursuing labour interests, seeking redistributive taxation, or egalitarian access to identified basic needs through public provision based on citizenship rights rather than market power' (Crouch, Eder and Tambini, 2001: 10). The countervailing forces which developed in the post-war era – the trade unions, a state willing and able to check and regulate the power of capital and an ideology (the Keynes-Beveridge consensus) which legitimated this – have been attenuated and economic liberalism has been restored as the collective reference point setting the parameters of political debate, inculcating accepted notions of the appropriate responsibilities of the state and the market and stipulating the terms on which policy is judged.

This is the significance of New Labour's 'big tent approach'. It reflected the Blair Government's acute sensitivity to the realities of power, its determination to minimise political risks by sedulously avoiding giving serious offence to those – in the City, the corporate sector and the media – who had in the past abundantly demonstrated their capacity to derail Labour administrations. The big tent can be most accurately characterised as the politics of business accommodation. In 2002 Anthony King described the 1997–2001 Blair administration as 'the first-ever Labour government to be openly, even ostentatiously pro-business' [and] ... ministers were instructed to be, and were, continuously sensitive to business interests' (King, 2002: 9). This has remained a leitmotiv of the New Labour approach. 'We should be proud,' an eagerly Blairite minister pronounced, 'that, after years of ideological opposition to the means of wealth creation in this country, New Labour has a relationship with business' (Tessa Jowell, interview in the *New Statesman*, 25 September 2006). As a senior Number 10 aide reflected, 'part of the magic of New Labour was that Tony was able to bring such people – big business, the rich – over to the party's side. He was very, very nervous about losing these people, fearful of alienating new friends' (interview, 2007).[4] This nervousness inevitably imposed political constraints. As another key Downing Street advisor wrote, the 'big tent approach made it hard to take on the most powerful interests – the London media, the super-rich, big business and the City – that often stood in the way of progressive reform' (Mulgan, 2005).

It does not follow that the Blair Government has neglected the cause of the socially excluded. Indeed as we have seen consistently throughout this book, it has taken seriously its responsibility for alleviating abject poverty and health inequality, for tackling educational underperformance and for extending opportunities for advancement to those in the past routinely denied them. Furthermore, the core of the Labour constituency remains a mix of working class and public sector voters and their needs and preferences must to some degree be propitiated. Indeed the central proposition of the unitary frame of interest was that policies designed to foster corporate competitiveness, far from being in opposition to, were a condition of the success of the struggle against poverty and social exclusion.

This recasting of the party's role can be conceptualised in terms of a shift from being a 'programmatic' to being an 'adjustive' party (see Introduction p. 6). The latter conceived its function as balancing and accommodating interests within the framework of the established distributional order. The former sought 'to change basic institutions and social arrangements' in favour of the disadvantaged (Jupp, 1968: 30). As such, it operated as a vehicle for the pursuit of 'contentious politics', a form of political activity defined by the sustained effort of previously marginalised and disadvantaged groups to shake off the shackles of subordination and, through organised action, break into the political realm and challenge established structures of power and privilege (McAdam, Tarrow and Tilly, 1995). From the perspective of New Labour's unitary frame of reference contentious politics, whatever virtue they may once have had, had been rendered thoroughly outmoded by social and economic changes. Questions about the social distribution of resources and power were now seen as distractions from the real issue of enhancing economic competitiveness and running a market economy more productively.

For some commentators all this represents a long-delayed but essential process of modernisation – a belated recognition that Labour must end its 'deep ambivalence' about business and the market economy and free itself from the manacles of trade union power (Cronin, 2004: 72). Every social democratic party has to strike a balance between the politics of accommodation and contention, between retaining 'the dynamism and enterprise of capitalism while preventing firms and their executives from exercising power to a degree incompatible with democracy' (Crouch, 2004: 105). But for some critics that balance, under New Labour, has been lost. Moschanas, for instance, maintains that 'defence of the interests of the subaltern classes' has ceased to be a *raison d'être*. 'Perhaps for the first time since the beginning of the twentieth century, popular strata are *deprived of a political representation that is at once uncontested and more or less effective*' (Moschanas, 2002: 299. Emphasis in the original).

This judgement seems a little premature. Labour remains a coalition to which affiliated trade unions are institutionally bound and which remain (not least because of the 'cash for coronets' scandal)[5] major sources of finance and other organisational resources. Equally it is as yet far too early to determine the impact of Brown's accession to the party leadership and the premiership. To the extent that, under its new leadership, Labour remains committed to 'the big tent' – the politics of accommodation and adjustment – it may well be that (as Crouch suggests) Britain will drift towards a system (as in the United States) where 'politics is really shaped in interaction between elected governments and elites that overwhelmingly represent business interests' (Crouch, 2002: 4).[6] But it may be that Labour finds the 'big tent' too unwieldy, that the strain of sustaining an alliance spanning so may diverse interests may begin to tell and it may have to reformulate its relationship to the key interests in society.

Whatever the truth, there is no doubt that the representative dynamics of the British party system (or, more accurately, the party system at Westminster) have changed. Indeed this was a principal objective of the New Labour 'project' which Blair clearly enunciated even before becoming premier. 'People don't even question for a moment that the Democrats are a pro-business party. They should not be asking that question about New Labour. New Labour is pro-business, pro-enterprise and we believe that there is nothing inconsistent between that and a just and decent society' (*The Financial Times*, 16 January 1997, quoted in Grant, 2000: 14–15). Party politics, in short, should be contained within the format of the established structure of power, wealth and privilege – as in the United States. That objective has been, to an impressive degree, realised. As Adair Turner, former head of the CBI, commented, 'we are now much closer to the American model of Democrats and Republicans, pro-business parties, than the continental socialist v capitalist model' (*New Statesman*, 5 November 1999).

10 Conclusion: losing Labour's soul?

How far are we are prepared to allow every nook and cranny of our society to be governed by the values of the market? How far are we prepared to allow the view that every relationship is essentially transactional, only valid and efficient if it suits our self-interest? And how far are we prepared to allow that the values that govern social relationships – trust, empathy, mutual regard, altruism, conscience – are economically inefficient and thus second rate?
Will Hutton, 'Death of Community Spirit', the *Observer*, 16 November 2003)

For what is a man profited, if he shall gain the whole world, and lose his own soul?
(Matthew xvi. 26)

'At every point in our history,' Gordon Brown declared, 'Labour needs not just a programme but a soul' (Brown, 2003a). Has the party, under the aegis of 'New Labour', lost that soul? Chapter One suggested that a party's soul can be seen as its essential animating force, its 'characteristic spirit as manifested in attitudes and aspirations' (*Shorter Oxford Dictionary*). The character of Labour's soul, it was further suggested, was encapsulated in Gaitskell's reformulated Clause 4. He had the party stand for

social justice, for a society in which the claims of those in hardship or distress come first; where the wealth produced by all is fairly shared among all; where differences in rewards depend not upon birth or inheritance but on the effort, skill and creative energy contributed to the common good; and where equal opportunities exist for all to live a full and varied life.

Equally, it was a party that repudiated 'the pursuit of material wealth by and for itself as empty and barren'. It deplored 'the selfish, acquisitive doctrines of capitalism' with their belief that 'our relations with one another should be based ... on ruthless self-regarding rivalry'. Instead it strove 'to create instead a socialist community based on fellowship, co-operation and service in which all can share fully in our cultural heritage' (Labour Party, 1959: 12–13; Brivati, 1997, 340–1).

Does this spirit continue to inspire New Labour? As will be evident from the case studies compiled in this account, there is no easy answer to this question. Social democracy has always been a synthesis, often an uneasy and unstable one. As Moschanas has pointed out, it was 'historically constructed at the intersection of two dynamics, that of the market and that of democracy' (Moschanas, 2002: 292). What emerged was the mixed economy welfare state: less a fixed type than a shifting equilibrium of forces and pressures – labour and capital, producer and consumer, state and market. The equilibrium between these forces was always fluid and delicate in the United Kingdom but was finally disrupted after the 1970s, partly because of intensifying contradictions within the Keynesian welfare order as a whole, partly because of a failure of the British version to embed itself either structurally or normatively, partly because of globalisation and partly because of the impact of the Thatcherite assault. For New Labour the old equilibrium was beyond repair or recovery but the new Thatcherite one was equally unacceptable. A new synthesis had to be forged which could meet a range of imperatives: it could form the basis of a winning electoral coalition, it would pose no serious challenge to the new pattern of power and privilege which had crystallised by the 1990s, it was economically viable and it made possible an attack on poverty and disadvantage.

The New Labour synthesis that emerged is a hybrid, a yoking together of two 'thematics', one 'more or less classically social-democratic', pursuing the traditional values of equality, social welfare and full employment, the other neo-liberal, 'extolling market logic, monetary stability, labour market flexibility, lower taxation, privatisation, and deregulation' (Moschanas, 2002: 159–60). Social democratic and neo-liberal elements variously combine in ways that can produce a variety of stances according to electoral needs, political competition, the hunger for good publicity, the interplay of inner-party power and – not least – chance and circumstance. To explore the nature and properties of this synthesis it may be useful to return, as twin ideological and programmatic reference points, to our two dimensions of the British social democratic tradition: redistributive social democracy and ethical socialism.

New Labour and redistributive social democracy

What we have called redistributive social democracy can be summarised in terms of a series of propositions: that there existed social needs and public purposes that could only be served by deliberate collective action and that a foremost objective of the state should be to promote them; that the good of the public could never be equated with the preferences of individuals as registered in market choices; that large and unjustified disparities in the apportionment of resources and life-chances were an inevitable consequence of the free market system – hence that positive state action to produce fairer allocations was both necessary and desirable; and that this action should take the form of public provision of high-quality goods and services to be financed in large part by a progressive system of taxation.

Summing up his exhaustive account of 'the new social democracy' Moschanas concludes that New Labour lies 'outside the social-democratic tradition, and breaks sharply with it' (Moschanas, 2002: 328). This is not a conclusion that this study can sustain. Our survey of policies implemented by the Blair Government indicates that, far from repudiating key propositions of redistributive social democracy, New Labour has reaffirmed many of them. This is above all manifested in the centrality to its programme of the concepts of social inclusion and widening opportunities. Hence such measures as the relentless drive to reduce child poverty; the provision of extra support for the disadvantaged through programmes such as Sure Start, the National Childcare Strategy, the various employment New Deals, multiple efforts to boost educational attainment and skills in order to improve life chances for all – not to mention the various other initiatives, such as Employment Zones, urban improvement schemes and community action programmes in policy areas not explored in this study (Social Exclusion Unit, 2004: 29–30).

As we have seen, New Labour has poured substantial additional monies into healthcare and education, has through a range of inventive tax, benefit and childcare strategies, lifted by appreciable amounts the living conditions of many of the poorest in the land, has introduced (and regularly upgraded) a minimum wage, has either initiated or (if EU-sponsored) enacted legislation which procured significant improvements in the working conditions and entitlements of millions of employees, has protected the rights of workers transferred to the private sector, has even at times levied taxes and charges which have been borne most heavily by those with the broadest shoulders: has, in short, undeniably pursued the politics of redistribution even if, sometimes, 'by stealth'.

Even several of New Labour's more controversial departures from inherited policies and long-established modes of thought can still be construed as responses, within the social democratic tradition, to difficult problems that have for long dogged the party. Thus it has sought to resolve entrenched weaknesses – unaccountable bureaucratic and professional power, inefficiencies, lack of responsiveness to user needs – of public service delivery that past Labour governments have been reluctant to confront. Its accent on economic competitiveness has been used to relegitimate large-scale investment in goods under-provided by the market but functional to higher productivity, such as education and training.

It is true that taxes on higher income groups remain light, corporation taxation is significantly lower than in most other EU countries and even these rates inflate the Government's take since tax avoidance is so rampant. Equally, the Government's adamant insistence on maintaining a flexible labour market has exposed many workers to low pay, insecurity, poor working conditions and the arbitrary exactions of managerial power. But – New Labour could riposte – in an open and highly integrated world economy painful policy choices had to be made if economic competitiveness was not to be jeopardised. This imposes strict limits on the capacity of any government to re-apportion resources through fiscal or other measures – yet the Blair administration has nevertheless filled the coffers of the cash-starved public services. The logic of the liberal market economy – the Blair Government could by the same token contend – enforces a trade-off, unpalatable as it may be, between full employment on the one hand and high levels of labour protection on the other. In opting for a lightly regulated labour market it has a record in generating jobs considerably more impressive than most comparable EU countries (outside Scandinavia). And it can claim that the combination of the minimum wage and the subsidising of low paid jobs by tax credits has relieved the worst cases of poverty in work. It would willingly concede that it has taken steps to dismantle the traditional social democratic collectivist state. But the enabling state by which it has been replaced con-tinues, as a matter of principle, to guarantee access to core public goods (health, education etc.) according to need and free at the point of use. The New Labour programme is, in short, 'one answer at least to the question of how best to empower individuals in a society scarred by inherited inequalities and self-sustaining cycles of deprivation' (Patmore and Coates, 2005: 138).

It is all this that allows Giddens to conclude that while New Labour has accommodated itself to a greater degree than the party previously regarded as acceptable to a market economy it nonetheless 'is a distinctively left of centre project – it is about the modernisation of social democracy' (Gid-dens, 2003: 2). It is a new synthesis that Buckler and Dolowitz term 'social-liberal in that it embraces fundamental liberal individualist assumptions but also retains a commitment to redistributive social justice' (Buckler and Dolowitz, 2000a: 102). Above all its steadfast allegiance to 'the principle of redistribution' has been made manifest by its determination to extend equality of opportunity and thereby ensure that 'those with similar abilities and skills' were given 'similar life chances regardless of social background' (Buckler and Dolowitz, 2000b: 308–9, 2000a: 102).

Our review of the New Labour record indicates that these claims overstate the mark. We have suggested that Labour's stance on resource-distribution was actuated by four normative principles: widening opportunity (or 'thin meritocracy'), social inclusion, priority and common advantage. While the outcome has been a substantial movement of resources to the least well endowed, it falls well short of any significant advance towards equality of opportunity. Indeed, we pointed out that comparative research showed that most progress towards achieving this end has been made by those countries with the least unequal distribution of income and wealth. As a leading expert in income distribution commented, 'inequality of outcome today is the cause of inequality of opportunity in the next generation' (Tony Atkin-son, quoted in Lansley, 2006: 203). Hence this account's conclusion, on the basis of extant evidence, that there is unlikely to be a substantive inroad into the intergeneration transmission of advantage.

Nor, equally, should the significance of the Blair Government's relin-quishing of equality of outcome as an object of political endeavour be overlooked. The New Labour concept of social justice does not visualise any major alterations to the distributional order. Thus it has 'eradicated the conception of class from its lexicon' (Freeden, 1999a: 49). Entrenched inequalities, New Labour acknowledges, persist, but these derive from the denial of life-advancement opportunities due to particular configurations of circumstances rather than from sources embedded within the social structure itself. The scale, basis and intensity of class-based differences and the most appropriate means of compressing them have long been debated within the Labour Party but with the common presumption that such differences exist, are inequitable and should be narrowed. For New Labour the whole notion of class-structured inequality – the conception of the social order as composed of structurally differentiated social positions to which correspond markedly disparate life-chances – is obsolescent. 'The assumption seems to be that social risks and class inequalities that emanate from the market can be overridden if we target policy so that all compete on an equal footing' (Esping-Andersen, 2002: 4–5). Indeed major equalities in income and wealth must realistically be conceded as functional to the success of the economic system since this is the price to be paid for high levels of productive investment and for eliciting the commitment of those upon whose energy, ingenuity and entrepreneurial drive national prosperity depends.

Equal opportunity, Gaitskell commented, 'is sometimes taken to mean a highly competitive and materialistic affair in which all start on the same line and proceed through racing against each other to amass as much well as possible. This is not what I mean' (Diamond, 2004: 98). But it is what New Labour means. Disparities in reward may be reasonable, Labour traditionally held, but these must not only be due and proportionate but justifiable in terms of some moral code. When, in his introduction to the 1997 manifesto, Blair dismissed such a view as 'the politics of envy' he was signalling a 'key turning point in Labour's central philosophy' (Lansley, 2006: 25). New Labour (according to Mandelson's oft-quoted formulation) has no objection to people becoming 'filthy rich'. Widening opportunities within highly stratified structure of rewards ('thin meritocracy') as the ultimate egalitarian goal would have received at best a muted approval from Labour in the past. Crosland had pointed out that since ability was to a substantial degree a product of either social background or inherited genetic endowment 'no one deserves either so generous an award or so severe a penalty for a quality implanted from the outside and for which he can claim only a limited responsibility' (quoted in Kogan, 2006: 74). But this was not a view that impressed New Labour. In truth, the abandonment of the goal of greater equality of outcome amounted to 'a revision of ends and not means' (Plant, 2004: 117).

New Labour and ethical socialism

The New Labour relationship with redistributive social democracy is a complex and ambivalent one, but with ethical socialism it is clear-cut for it is here its rupture with the past is at its sharpest and most abrupt. Ethical socialism recoiled from a society with sharp and conspicuous social and status demarcation lines, one which celebrated the virtues of the unabashed and ruthless pursuit of self-advancement and the heaping-up of vast fortunes. The narrow pursuit of meritocracy (Michael Young predicted in his 1958 satire) would drive a deeper fracture between members of the privileged elite reassured in their knowledge 'that success is a just reward for their own capacity, for their own efforts, and for their own undeniable achievement' and those who fail and can contemplate the fact that the failure is thoroughly deserved (Young, 1958: 106). It would thereby severely strain the social fabric.[1] Ethical socialism instead urged a pattern of social relations rooted in social solidarity, co-operation and a commitment to the common good. Such views are alien to the spirit of New Labour.

Nowhere is this more plainly demonstrated than in its market-oriented programme of public sector modernisation. For those who wondered, former Number 10 advisor Peter Hyman declared, where 'the [New Labour] "project" is heading, the renewal of public services provides the answer' (Hyman, 2005: 170). 'Renewal' meant ensuring the survival of well-funded collective institutions as the main suppliers of key public goods and services, on the basis of need rather than ability to pay. It most assuredly did *not* mean that New Labour was continuing the Conservative assault on the public services: privatising and outsourcing as much as possible with the long-term objective of reducing the role played by the state. Such a view not only ignores the large sums pumped by the Blair Government into the public sector but equally the fact that – as Geoff Mulgan pointed out – the price mechanism was *not* being used to determine the flow of resources and that services were *not* being broken down into commodities to be sold on the market and that they remained free at the point of use (interview, 2006).

But there was a second meaning attached to 'renewal': the application to the public services of rules, norms and incentive structures borrowed wholesale from world of private commerce. This prescribed, in Stuart Hall's summary, that the public sector:

1 Must open the door to private investment or blur the public/private distinction;
2 It must meet market criteria of efficiency and value-for-money;
3 It must put managerial authority in command;
4 It must reform working practices in a less collective, more individualised direction;
5 It must stimulate competition and divide workers by introducing incentive pay schemes and undermining collective bargaining.

(Hall, S, 2003: 22)

'I believe in the public service ethos,' Tony Blair insisted in 2001, 'that is why I am trying to reform and deliver better public services, not privatise them' (*The Guardian*, 11 September 2001). However, as Ed Balls (then Gordon Brown's chief economic advisor) warned, 'if you go down [the] marketising route, you run grave risks with [the] ethic of public service' (the *Guardian*, 4 November 2002). Designing institutions on the assumption that people are self-interested is likely to be self-fulfilling as the norms, rules and conventions which restrain such behaviour are relaxed or abandoned (Plant, 2003a: 576; Vines, 1999: 77). 'If you assume bad motives and devise rules on the assumption that people have bad motives, then do not expect them to behave from good motives ... the bad motives will drive out the good' (Plant, 2001).

In the short term such effects are unlikely to be obtrusive. However, major social changes tend to be incremental and their real import usually only becomes apparent after the passage of years as they slowly gather momentum – by which time they may have acquired the character of unstoppable forces. So it is important to reflect upon the longer-term impact of the New Labour project of public sector 'modernisation'. Here it may be useful to draw upon Hirsch's analysis of 'the commercialisation effect'. He defines this as the 'effect on the characteristics of a product or activity of supplying it exclusively or predominantly on commercial terms rather than on some other basis – such as informal exchange, mutual obligation, altruism or love, or feelings of service or obligation' (Hirsch, 1977: 87). The greater the expectation that the behaviour of organisational members will be driven by self-interest regulated only by contractual obligations, the lower the stock of other norms such as mutual obligation and trust. 'By influencing social norms and expectations in this way, commercialisation or its equivalent embodies its own dynamic' (Hirsch, 1977: 88).

Initially the impact of commercially oriented behaviour may well be mitigated by the survival of older cultural norms and expectations and the reluctance of people socialised into older normative patterns to follow the new commercial cues. Thus 'the erosion of conventions about mutual obligations could extend a certain distance within society without setting off dynamic effects'. But at a certain point at which the costs and risks incurred by such behaviour mounts then a narrow instrumental mentality will take hold (Hirsch, 1977: 89). People will learn 'to speak the vocabulary of economic calculation' to regard themselves as 'entrepreneurial' subjects seeking to further 'economic efficiency' and generate organisational income (Newman, 2001a: 102). The weakening of social norms which uphold public goods is then 'likely to become self-aggravating. Once such conventions can no longer be counted on as the typical basis of behaviour ... then the change in behavioural norms will feed on itself" (Hirsch, 1977: 89).

The increasing permeation of an institution by market relations and patterns of behaviour will, in other words, *in time* tend 'to drive out previous patterns of co-operation' and create 'clearer differences of interest and incentives to pursue interests' (Walsh, 1995: 198. See also Skidelsky, 2001; Parekh, 2001). The moral basis of public services will be slowly dismembered.

Disapproval of purely instrumental or calculative behaviour will abate and the accent on personal incentives with their appeal to self-interest will erode altruism, trust and a sense of vocation as people are encouraged to give priority to their own narrow interests (Vines, 1999: 60, 68, 7). Hence will the final knell of ethical socialism – in its very heartland – be sounded. 'The history of social democracy,' Robin Cook wrote shortly before his death,

> can be expressed as the struggle to set limits to the market and to define those areas where priorities should be set by social policy rather than commercial forces. Yet this government is dismantling the barriers that its predecessors had erected to keep those commercial forces off the public-service turf.
>
> (Robin Cook, *The Guardian*, 17 June 2005)

Conclusion

So, then, has Labour under the Blair Government lost its soul? If we return to Gaitskell's formulation, the evidence reviewed in this study indicates that it retains a firm commitment to social justice, that is 'a society in which the claims of those in hardship or distress come first' and, no less, to the promotion of opportunities for all. Real progress has been made in alleviating poverty among the most vulnerable in society. The Government has evinced a steadfast determination to revive public service that, under the Conservatives, had been left to languish. What one of Blair's biographers, Philip Stephens, calls the 'fashionable reflection' that the Blair Government did little more than 'soften the edges of Thatcherism' is 'belied by unprecedented investment in health and education, by discretionary increases in taxes and by a determined effort to reduce poverty' (*The Financial Times*, 11 May 2007). To this extent Labour's soul remains intact.

However the party no longer sees 'the pursuit of material wealth by and for itself as empty and barren': interest in striving 'to create instead a socialist community based on fellowship, co-operation and service' has been quite thoroughly dissipated. Though Blair declared that New Labour 'believes in a "fraternal" community, where our relationship with each other is not just instrumental or efficient' (Blair, 2002b: 9–10) the conclusion reached in this account is that such a belief has in fact been banished to the outer edges of the party's ruling creed. 'When it comes to fraternity,' as Hennessy points out, New Labour 'is pretty well tone deaf' (Hennessy, 2004). The increasing acceptance in many quarters of society of the propriety of the single-minded and zealous pursuit of wealth has evoked from New Labour a firm and unstinting approval. When asked whether it was possible for anyone to earn too much money, Blair riposted: 'Not really, no. Why does that matter?' (the *Guardian*, 23 November 2005). The values of competition, individual self-assertion and 'entrepreneurialism', and not 'fellowship, co-operation and service' are those that New Labour extols. Over half a century after he had drafted Labour's 1945 manifesto, the eminent ethical socialist Michael Young observed that, for the Blair Government, private enterprise was regarded

> as all-round superior to public services with their own more altruistic ethic ... The superiority of private enterprise is now dinned into the public service by the practice of calling upon it to save the day when the public authorities are said to have "failed" ... Private enterprise has become the icon. The premium it places on competition, on profit-motivated judgements, and on acquisitiveness, has been given a seal of approval.
>
> (Young, 2000)

To this extent Labour has lost its soul.

Notes

Introduction

1 There is a notable omission which meets all four conditions: the highly controversial introduction of variable top-up fees. I very reluctantly excluded this primarily because I felt a proper treatment would have entailed a general discussion of higher education policy, an additional case study which limitations of space and time did not allow me to pursue. For the same reason I did not cover another major policy decision, the rejection by the Government of the Sutherland Commission's recommendation that free personal care for the elderly infirm be introduced – a recommendation that was, in contrast, accepted by the new Scottish Executive.

2 It is worth noting that Crouch has raised some serious questions about the empirical validity of this classification. See Crouch, 2005.

3 By explanation I mean here giving a plausible account of why something occurred in a situation in which there was at least one other possibility (Therborn, 1991: 178).

1 The British social democratic tradition

1 These three terms are used as synonyms.

2 Another step to widen educational opportunities – though only taken (for budgetary reasons) after some hesitation – was the raising of the school leaving age from 15 to 16.

3 Most of the industries nationalised in the 1960s and 1970s (such as the docks and British Leyland) were scarcely if at all profitable and the prime objects were to conserve jobs and exports.

4 'People' the Chancellor Denis Healey exclaimed in Cabinet in 1975, 'will be shocked, not pleased, when they saw how much we were spending on social services. They already felt too much of our national resources were going on the public services'. When the doughty left-winger Barbara Castle demanded that Healey 'name them' he riposted: 'schools for one, and other forms of education' (Castle, 1990: 463).

5 There were specific reasons for this outcome, including the energy and ability of the two key left-leaning social policy ministers, Crossman and Castle, and their close relationship with Prime Minister Harold Wilson; and the support (in 1976) of the most powerful of trade union leaders, Jack Jones, for the universalist Child Benefits measure.

6 Donne expressed the same sentiment more poetically: 'No man is an Island, entire of itself; every man is a piece of the Continent, a part of the main; if a clod be washed away by the sea, Europe is the less, as well as if a promontory were, as well as if a manor of thy friends or of thine own were' (John Donne, *Meditation XVII*)

7 Thus Tawney believed that 'professional solidarity' and responsibility, with the large degree of autonomy and discretion this allowed, could help avoid 'the elaboration of cumbrous regulations' (Tawney, 1961 [1921]: 149).

8 All of whom had, at one time, ministerial responsibility for health.

9 The attempted revision was defeated for internal political reasons.

2 New Labour and social justice

1 In Scotland the Sutherland report was implemented in full.

2 For example, the elderly infirm suffering from mental disease (such as dementia) who own capital assets of over £21,000 (as of 2007) are not eligible for any significant degree of support to pay for their personal needs while those with less than £12,000 receive substantial aid.

3 He urged instead a better system of data exchange about suspected tax evaders.

4 Detailed investigation by the reporter Nick Davies found 'multinationals were not being fined like other taxpayers when they were caught out being fraudulent or negligent.' In effect their tax submissions were not subject to the same scrutiny as ordinary tax-payers although the sums involved were immeasurably larger (the *Guardian*, 17 October 2002).

5 A Gini coefficient value of 0 corresponds to the absence of inequality, a value of 1 corresponds to absolute inequality (Brewer *et al.*, 2006: 22–3).

3 Equality of opportunity: the case of secondary education

1 This chapter will concentrate on education in England. The educational system in Scotland has always been substantially different and, after 1999, education became a devolved issue so that Westminster education legislation applied only to England.

2 To achive this goal the Government sponsored a range of measures such as Excellence in Cities, Beacon Schools, Leadership Incentives Grants and most recently (in 2005) the launch of Education Improvement Partnerships (Dyson, Kerr and Ainscow, 2006: 56).

3 This proved highly controversial but, for reasons of space, it is not discussed in this book.

4 There has been some disagreement over whether the Academies were recruiting fewer pupils who were entitled to free school meals, the most common measure of social deprivation. See National Audit Office, 2007: 23; Wilby, 2007.

5 The salaried refers to the professional, semi-professional and managerial middle class as distinct from a broader 'middle class' classification which incorporates routine clerical workers.

6 What matters is less 'specialism' per se than its type: specialising in languages, for example, was more conducive to recruiting a more middle class intake than, say, sport (Taylor *et al.*, 2005: 63). Despite the importance of this issue, the Government has not gathered statistics upon the impact of aptitude selection (interview, Fiona Miller, 2007).

7 This included policies such as Education Action Zones and neighbourhood and urban regeneration initiatives not covered in this account.

4 Is what matters what works?: the case of the Private Finance Initiative

1 The term is used a little more broadly in the following chapter.

2 There was an additional problem caused by the introduction of payment by results (money following patient choice) in the NHS designed to ensure that

funds flowed into hospitals favoured by health consumers (see Chapter Five). PFI-funded hospitals would be locked into paying off annual charges on long-term contracts even if the capacity they financed considerably exceeded demand for their services (Ham, 2006).

3 An article published in the accounting journal *Public Money and Management* contended that such a conclusion was based on flimsy evidence and fundamental analytical flaws. Pollock, Price and Player, 2007.

4 However a BBC Panorama investigation into the running of one private prison uncovered an extremely poor level of performance – in an institution which had already received two damning reports by HM's Chief Inspector of Prisons. Panorama, 2007.

5 The Blair Government has not only been responsible for the recruitment of an unprecedented number of people from the private sector to Whitehall and has encouraged the secondment of personnel from leading firms to key positions in the government machine but has sought to relax the rules regulating the flow of former ministers and civil servants into lucrative jobs in the private sector (see e.g. the *Guardian*, 16 August 2004).

5 Modernisation in action: the case of NHS reform

1 The focus in this chapter is on healthcare in England since, under devolution, the direction of policy in Scotland and, to a lesser extent, Wales, has been significantly different.

2 According to one Downing Street advisor who had many discussions with rebel MPs another major concern was that, under Foundation Trust arrangements, MPs would no longer be able to lobby the Secretary of State to articulate constituency complaints about their local hospitals (interview, 2007).

3 I owe this point to Simon Stevens, written communication, March 2007.

4 Milburn felt confident that the impulses generated by the measure would be unstoppable and the concessions would in due course be reversed (interview with Alan Milburn, 2006).

5 PbR's objectives included:

1. achieving a better matching between what purchasers want and what hospitals provide;
2. improving cost-effectiveness and value for money;
3. facilitating the flow of funds to new providers;
4. making the allocation of funds more transparent;
5. enabling patient choice;
6. increasing activity in areas with high waiting times in order to meet waiting time targets (Appleby and Jobanputra, 2004: 197).

6 The Government also reasoned that short-term contracts would discourage long-term investment in new facilities since commercial operators required the prospect of a long term profit stream before committing substantial funds (Milburn in *The Guardian*, 25 May 2002).

7 In fact the rules of the first wave of ISTCs precluded the ISTCs actually buying in the time and expertise of NHS specialists. Rather only specialists from outside the NHS, mostly from overseas, would be allowed to work in the ISTCs, in what was to be called 'additionality' rules.

8 As the Health Secretary commented, it was striking 'how NHS waiting lists miraculously shrink when consultants are faced with the prospect of an independent treatment centre down the road or patients being sent to empty beds in a private hospital' (Hewitt, 2005a).

9 Ricketts acknowledged that 'we have seen a big increase in cataract activity and a fall in waiting times from before the ISTC' (Health Select Committee, 2006b: question 52).

10 Given the importance of the issue, the Committee added, it was 'surprised that the Department has made no attempt systematically to assess and quantify the effect of competition from ISTCs on the NHS' (Health Select Committee, 2006: 25).

11 There were also general concerns about ISTC treatment, including the quality of specialist care offered, the loss of continuity in medical provision, the lack of long-term patient care and the qualifications and specialist expertise of doctors working in the treatment centres (BMA, 2005: 9–10).

12 The difficulties of making cost comparisons between ISTCs and NHS hospitals should be noted. Such comparisons could be misleading since the latter's marginal costs of producing an extra operation was often well in excess of the average cost used to compare with ISTCs (my thanks to Simon Stevens for pointing this out).

13 Whether ISTCs were providing the same standard of treatment as NHS producers has been a matter of dispute. BMA researchers expressed concern about the quality of care provided by ISTCs, noting that after-care treatment was hampered by poor communication with independent treatment centres and that a significant number of patients developed complications following treatment in treatment centres and required readmission to NHS hospitals (which had to bear the cost) (BMA, 2005: 9–10. See also reports in the *Guardian*, 10 March 2006).

14 A BMA study of clinical directors found that more than two-thirds of respondents reported that ISTCs had had a negative overall impact on services provided by their NHS trust (Health Select Committee, 2006a: 18, 35).

15 The Committee could not calculate 'how great the dangers might be' since while the Department of Health had conducted an analysis of the possible effects of the ISTC programme on NHS facilities 'it has refused to disclose the analysis to us' (Health Select Committee, 2006a: 36).

16 A survey published in the *Health Service Journal* found that 86 per cent of chief executives in the NHS felt 'battered and bruised' by constant re-organisation (*Health Service Journal*, 1 March 2007). In a survey of mental health trust chief executives, one gave vent to a general sense of anger and exasperation: 'There is so much that has been rushed through without looking at the consequences. If something doesn't work we don't just tweak it, we throw it in the air and start all over again' (*Health Service Journal*, 15 March 2007).

17 'The only contribution the private sector is going to make,' Frank Dobson acidly commented, 'is sending a man with a bag marked swag and taking it away again' (interview, 2004).

18 Under existing arrangements private sector involvement in elective surgery had been capped at 15 per cent. This was largely for political reasons. As Health minister John Hutton told the Public Administration Committee it was a way of repudiating the claim 'that the whole NHS is going to be privatised' (Public Administration Select Committee, 2005b: Ev 156–7).

6 New Labour's representational role: the case of employment relations

1 This was because rising inflation would automatically lead to higher interest rates which would depress demand for labour.

2 According to one piece of research 62 per cent of new starters in outsourced NHS jobs were paid less, 44 per cent had more unsocial hours, 58 per cent had worse sick pay, 73 per cent had less holiday, 51 per cent had worse pensions, 44 per cent has less job security. Added to this have been endemic insecurity of pay and employment and paltry provision for pensions, sickness and holidays (Toynbee, 2003: 79, 57–9).

3 For example the Employment Relations Act of 2004 requires unions, when balloting members for industrial action, to provide employers with highly specific information about those who might participate (Smith and Morton, 2006: 408).
4 Although the new recognition procedures probably helped arrest the pace of union decline they have not reversed it as 'employers have learned to mitigate, control or oppose its limited provisions' (Smith and Morton, 2006: 406, 408. See also Glyn and Wood, 2001: 62; Undy, 1999: 331).

7 The dynamics of New Labour

1 However, it has been argued that the historical reliance of welfare states on corporate taxation has been over-stated since, according to estimates, it represent only 10–15 per cent of total revenue collections in the OECD with more revenue deriving from sources less subject to significant international pressures, such as VAT, excise and national insurance contributions and income tax (Hines, 2006: 33).
2 For the author's own take on Labour's past, see Shaw, 1994 and Shaw, 1996.
3 Leading figures included Peter Mandelson, Philip Gould, Chris Powell and Patricia Hewitt. For a fuller account, see Shaw, 1994.
4 Such, at least, was the New Labour view, though the data upon which it was based were unclear. The British Social Attitudes Survey for 2006 found that while there had been 'an increase in the proportion of people identifying themselves as middle class, and a decline in those saying they are working class', reflecting real changes in the balance of manual and non-manual jobs, 'a working-class identity is still much more common than a middle-class identity: 37% of people now identify themselves as middle class, compared with 57% identifying as working class' (British Social Attitudes press release, 24 January 2007).
5 Derek Jameson, then editor of the *Daily Express*, recalled, 'we pulled every dirty trick in the book; we made it look like it was general, universal and eternal when it was in reality scattered, here and there, and no great problem' (Thomas, 2005: 80–1).
6 The *Sun* was not only read by a very substantial portion of the electorate but contained a disproportionately high number of (mainly working class and lower middle class) floating voters (Miller, 1991: 191–2).
7 Campbell also tried hard to win the *Mail* over (Seldon, 2004: 253).
8 'We, at Number 10,' the aide added, ' believed that unless we had daily control over the news agenda, unless we fought for every headline, rebutted every lie or inaccuracy, we would sink under the media onslaught' (Hyman, 2005: 261).
9 A leaked memorandum in 2000 revealed Blair demanding policy initiatives that demonstrated 'toughness and standing up for Britain'. His proposals included: highlighting 'tough measures' on crime such as compulsory tests for drugs before bail, more burglars jailed under 'three strikes and you're out', and firm action on street crime, 'especially in London' for example by locking up street muggers. 'Something tough, with immediate bite, which sends a message through the system' (Tony Blair's memo reproduced in the *Guardian*, 17 July 2000).

8 For what does New Labour stand?

1 One interesting example of this is the increasing pervasiveness of tutoring. This has long been rampant in secondary education particularly in the struggle to gain entry to over-subscribed high-performing schools. According to research conducted by King's College London, in London *primaries* 'private tutoring has grown exponentially: it has become almost the norm among the middle classes, and it is increasing the social-class differences in educational attainment' (Jenni Russell, the *Guardian*, 8 April 2002).

2 But with some striking resemblance to the early Fabians.
3 In a memorandum to the Select Committee on Public Administration, the New Labour think tank, the New Local Government Network found 'very little evidence' for the proposition that motivation in the public sector is in any way 'more pure' or that profit-seeking 'muddies' motivation (Stoker and Williams, 2001: paras 12, 13, 15).
4 After summarising much research on the topic Government advisor Lord Layard concluded that the Government's reliance on rewarding individual performance rather than 'stressing the importance of the job and of professional norms and professional competence' has been seriously misguided. 'It is not surprising that reform of the public services is proving so difficult when the wrong levers are being pulled and the workers so often demoralised' (Layard, 2005a: 160).

9 For whom does New Labour stand?

1 As early as 1926 the major policy document *Labour and the Nation* affirmed that the party 'speaks not as the agent of this class or that, but as the political organ created to express the needs and voice the aspirations of all those who share in labour which is the lot of mankind' (quoted in Panitch, 1986: 67).
2 The unitary frame of reference often uses the analogy of the professional football team, 'for here, combined with the team structure and its associated loyalties, one finds a substantial measure of managerial prerogative at the top ... Team spirit and undivided management authority co-exist to the benefit of all' (Fox, 1966: 3). Compare this with the pluralist view, as articulated by the former TUC General Secretary George Woodcock: 'unions and management exist – not as part of the same team but as two separate groups with different aims working in the same sphere' (Taylor, R, 2000a: 141).
3 In fact a survey conducted as part of an ESRC research programme uncovered a 'significant deterioration' in personal commitment among employees to the companies in which they worked. Despite the rhetoric of partnership at work and the importance of enhancing human capital the survey found little evidence that they were translated into practical measures (Taylor, R, 2002: 11).
4 The aide added that placating the powerful 'doesn't always pay off because if you continually pander to a constituency it thinks it can get away with murder' (interview, 2007).
5 This refers to the investigation of allegations that, in return for generous donations and 'loans' to the party, wealthy individuals were honoured by peerages and knighthoods.
6 Under such a system, Crouch predicts, the parameters of policy debate will narrow, effectively excluding the 'agenda of strong egalitarian policies for the redistribution of power and wealth, or for the restraint of powerful interests' (Crouch, 2002: 2).

Conclusion: losing Labour's soul?

1 Mulling over the policies of the Blair Government shortly before his death, Michael Young concluded thus: 'It is hard indeed in a society that makes so much of merit to be judged as having none. No underclass has ever been left as morally naked as that' (Young, 2001).

Bibliography

Abel-Smith, B, (1984) 'Social Welfare' in Pimlott, B (ed.) *Fabian Essays in Socialist Thought*, HEB.

Ainscow, M and Dyson, M, (2006) *Equity in Education: Mapping the Territory Centre for Equity in Education*, Manchester University Press.

Allen, G, (2001) 'The Private Finance Initiative' *House of Commons Library Economic Policy and Statistics Section Research Paper*, 01/117, December.

Allsop, J and Baggott, B, (2004) 'The NHS in England: from modernisation to marketisation?' in Ellison, N (ed.) *Social Policy Review 16*, Policy Press.

'Analysis', (1995) BBC Radio Four 'Pay Your Money, Take Your Choice?', 9 November.

—— (2000) BBC Radio Four 'Equally Different', 16 March.

—— (2001) BBC Radio Four, 'Going Private', 16 August.

Anderson, A and Camiller, P, (1994) *Mapping the Western European Left*, Verso.

Andrews, David M, (1994) 'Capital Mobility and State Autonomy: Toward a Structural Theory of International Monetary Relations' *International Studies Quarterly*, 38 (2).

Appleby, J and Alvarez-Rosete, A, (2005) 'Public Responses to NHS Reforms' in Park, A, Curtice, J, Thomson, K, Jarvis, L and Bromley, C (eds) *British Social Attitudes: the 22nd report*, Sage.

Appleby, J and Jobanputra, R, (2004) 'Payment by Results: The NHS financial revolution', *New Economy*, 11 (4).

Appleby, J, Harrison, A and Devlin, N, (2003) *What is the Real Cost of More Patient Choice?*, King's Fund.

Arestis, P and Sawyer, M (2001) 'The Economic Analysis Underlying the "Third Way"', *New Political Economy*, 6 (2).

—— (2002) '"New Consensus," New Keynesianism, and the Economics of the "Third Way"', *Levy Economics Institute Working Paper*, No. 364. www.levy.org/pubs/wp/364.pdf.

Arneson, R J, (1997) 'Egalitarianism and the Undeserving Poor', *Journal of Political Philosophy*, 5 (3).

—— (1999) 'Human Flourishing versus Desire Satisfaction', *Social Philosophy and Policy*, 16 (1).

—— (2002a) 'Egalitarianism' in *Stanford Encyclopaedia of Philosophy*. http://plato.stanford.edu/archives/fall2002/entries/egalitarianism/.

—— (2002b) 'Equality of Opportunity' in *Stanford Encyclopaedia of Philosophy*. http://plato.stanford.edu/archives/win2002/entries/equal-opportunity/.

Artis, M and Cobham, D, (1991) 'Summary and Appraisal' in Artis, M and Cobham, D (eds) *Labour's Economic Policies 1974–79*, Manchester University Press.

Atun, R A and McKee, M (2005) *Is the Private Finance Initiative Dead?*, Editorial BMJ 331 (7), October.

Audit Commission, (2002) *Recruitment and Retention: A public service workforce for the 21st century*, Audit Commission.

—— (2003) *PFI in Schools*, Audit Commission.

—— (2004) *Choice in Public Services*, Audit Commission.

—— (2005a) *Higher Standards, Better Schools for All: More choice for parents and pupils*, Audit Commission.

—— (2005b) *'Early Lessons from Payment by Results,'* Audit Commission.

Babb, P, (2005) *A Summary of Focus on Social Inequalities*, Office for National Statistics.

Baker, J, (1987) *Arguing for Equality*, Verso.

Ball, S J, (2003) 'The teacher's soul and the terrors of performativity', *Journal of Educational Policy*, 18 (2).

—— (2004) 'Education For Sale! The Commodification of Everything?' King's Annual Education Lecture, Institute of Education, University of London. www.asu.edu/educ/epsl/CERU/articles/CERU-0410-253-OWI.pdf.

Balls, E, (1997) 'Open Macroeconomics in an Open Economy', *Centre for Economic Performance Occasional Papers*, No. 13.

—— (1998) 'Open Macroeconomics in an Open Economy', *Scottish Journal of Political Economy*, 45 (2).

—— (2002) *'Devolution and Localism in Public Policy – a view from the Treasury,'* Speech by the Chief Economic Adviser, to the CIPFA annual conference in Brighton, H M Treasury.

—— (2006) *Britain's Next Decade*, Speech to the Fabian Society, November. www.fabian-society.org.uk/documents/document_latest.asp?id = 149&catid = 52.

Barber, B, (2003) *New deal or no deal*, Unions 21 10th anniversary conference, March. www.tuc.org.uk/the_tuc/tuc-6360-f0.cfm.

Barker, R M, Pearce, M S and Irving, M, (2004) 'Star wars, NIIS style', *British Medical Journal*, 329.

Barry, B, (2005) *Why Social Justice Matters*, Polity Press.

Bartlett, W and Le Grand, J, (1993) 'The Theory of Quasi-Markets' in Bartlett, W and Le Grand, J, *Quasi-Markets in Social Policy*, Macmillan.

Becker, F and Cuperus, R, (2004) 'The Party Paradox: Political Parties Between Irrelevance and Omnipotence' FE Foundation *Europäische Politik*, June.

Beckert, J, (1996) 'What is sociological about economic sociology? Uncertainty and the embeddedness of economic action', *Theory and Society*, 25 (6).

Beckett, F and Hencke, D, (2004) *The Blairs and their Court*, Aurum.

Beech, M, (2006) *The Political Philosophy of New Labour*, I.B. Tauris.

Beer, S, (1969) *Modern British Politics*, Faber.

Benn, T, (1989) *Against The Tide: Dairies 1973–76*, Hutchinson.

Beresford, P, (2005) 'Redistributing profit and loss: the new economics of the market and social welfare', *Critical Social Policy*, 25 (4).

Bevan, Aneuran, (1978) [1952] *In Place of Fear*, Quartet.

Bevir, M, (2000) 'New Labour: a Study in Ideology', *British Journal of Politics and International Relations*, 2 (3).

—— (2003) 'From Idealism to Communitarianism: The Inheritance and Legacy of John Macmurray', *History of Modern Political Thought*, 24 (2).

—— (2005) *New Labour: A critique*, Routledge.

Bevir, Mark and O'Brien, David, (2001) 'New Labour and the Public Sector in Britain', *Public Administration Review*, 16 (5).

Black, L, (2003) *The Political Culture of the Left in Affluent Britain, 1951–64*, Palgrave Macmillan.

Blackstone, T, (1980) 'Education' in Bosanquet, N and Townsend, P (eds) *Labour and Equality: A Fabian study of Labour in power 1974–79*, Fabian Society.

Blair, Tony, (1995) *Let us Face the Future*, Fabian Society.

——(1997) Speech on *Faith in the City Ten Years On*, at Southwark Cathedral, January.

—— (1997a) *Speech in Southwark,*.

—— (1997b) *Speech in Lambeth*, December.

—— (1998a) *The Third Way: New Politics for a New Century*, Fabian Society.

—— (1998b) *Speech to the French National Assembly*, March.

—— (1999) *Speech to the British Venture Capitalist Association*, July.

—— (2000) *Speech at the CBI Annual Dinner*, May.

—— (2001a) *Speech on Public Service Reform*, July.

—— (2001b) *Speech to 2001 Labour Party Annual Conference,*.

—— (2001c) *Speech to the Christian Socialist Movement*, March.

—— (2001d) *Speech to the CBI Conference*, November.

—— (2002a) *The Courage of our Convictions: Why Reform of the Public Services is the Route to Social Justice*, Fabian Society.

—— (2002b) 'New Labour and Community', *Renewal*, 10 (2).

—— (2002c) *Speech 'A Britain in which nobody is left behind'*, September.

—— (2003a) *Speech at South Camden Community College*, January.

—— (2003b) *Speech to the Progressive Governance Conference*, July.

—— (2003c) *Lecture to the Fabian Society.*

—— (2004a) *Speech at the*, Guardian's *public services summit*, January.

—— (2004b) *Prime Minister's speech on 'Choice, excellence and equality'*, June.

—— (2004c) *Prime Minister's speech to the Fabian Society*, July.

—— (2005) *Speech on Education*, October.

—— (2006) *Speech to New Health Network*, April.

Blair, Tony and Schroeder, Gerhard, (1999) *The Third Way/Die Neue Mitte*, Labour Party.

Blomqvist, P, (2004) 'The Choice Revolution: Privatization of Swedish Welfare Services in the 1990s', *Social Policy and Administration*, 38 (2).

Blumler, J, (1990) 'Elections, the Media and the Modern Publicity Process' in Ferguson, M (ed.) *Public Communication: The New Imperatives*, Sage.

Bosanquet, N, (1980) 'Labour and Public Expenditure: an overall view' in Bosanquet, N and Townsend, P, *Labour and Equality: A Fabian Study of Labour in Power 1974–79*, Heinemann.

Bower, T, (2004) *Gordon Brown*, HarperCollins.

Bowles, S and Gintis, H, (1998/99) 'Is Equality Passé? Homo reciprocans and the future of egalitarian politics', *Boston Review*, December 1998/January 1999.

Boyle, S and Harrison, A, (2000) *Investing in Health Buildings: Public-Private Partnerships*, King's Fund.

Brettingham, M, (2005) 'Local control over foundation trusts is "rhetoric"', *British Medical Journal*, 330, 18 June.

Brewer, M, Clark, T and Wakefield, M (2002) *Social Security Under New Labour: What did the Third Way mean for welfare reform?*, Institute for Fiscal Studies. www.ifs.org.uk/conferences/socsec/clark. pdf.

Brewer, M, Goodman, A, Muriel, M and Sibieta, L, (2007) *Poverty and Inequality in Britain: 2007*, Institute for Fiscal Studies.

Brewer, M, Goodman, A, Shaw, J and Shephard, A, (2005) *Poverty and Inequality in Britain: 2005*, Institute for Fiscal Studies.

Brewer, M, Goodman, A, Shaw, J and Sibieta, L, (2006) *Poverty and Inequality in Britain: 2006*, Institute for Fiscal Studies.

Briggs, A, (2001) *Michael Young*, Palgrave.

British Medical Association (BMA), Health Policy and Economic Research Unit, (2005) *Impact of Treatment Centres on the Local Health Economy in England*, BMA.

—— (2006) *Evidence submitted to the Health Select Committee hearing on ISTCs*, BMA.

British Orthopaedic Association, (2006) *Evidence submitted to the Health Select Committee hearing on ISTCs*.

Brivati, B, (1997) *Hugh Gaitskell*, Richard Cohen Books.

Broadbent, J and Laughlin, R, (2005) 'The Role of PFI in the UK Government's Modernisation Agenda, *'Financial Accountability & Management 21 (1)*.

Brown, Gordon, (1997) *Mansion House speech*, May.

—— (1998a) *The World Economy and the Role for Global Policy Makers*, Speech to the Federation of Bankers Association, Tokyo, September.

—— (1998b) *Speech to Labour Party Conference*, September.

—— (1999) 'Equality – then and now' in Leonard, D (ed.) *Crosland and New Labour*, Macmillan/Fabian Society.

—— (2001) *Speech to the Annual Conference of the European Bank for Reconstruction and Development*, April.

—— (2002a) *Building World Class Public Services*, Speech given at the Unison conference, February.

—— (2002b) *On Economic Stability and Strong Public Services*, Speech given to the Social Market Foundation, March.

—— (2003) *A Modern Agenda for Prosperity and Social Reform*, Speech to the Social Market Foundation, February.

—— (2003a) *Speech to Labour Party Conference*, September.

—— (2004) *Speech to Conference of Compass*, October.

—— (2005) *Speech to the Institute of Directors*, November.

Brown, W, (2000) 'Putting partnership into practice in Britain', *British Journal of Industrial Relations*, 38 (2).

Brown, W, Deakin, S, Hudson, M and Pratten, C (2001) 'The Limits of Statutory Trade Union Recognition', *Industrial Relations Journal*, 32 (3).

Buchanan, A E, (1985) *Ethics, Efficiency and the Market*, Clarendon.

Buckler, S, (2007) 'Theory, Ideology, Rhetoric', *British Journal of Politics and International Relations*, 9 (1).

Buckler, S and Dolowitz, D (2000a) 'New Labour's Ideology: A Reply to Michael Freeden', *Political Quarterly*, 71 (1).

—— (2000b) 'Theorizing the Third Way: New Labour and social justice', *Journal of Political Ideologies*, 5 (3).

—— (2004) 'Can Fair be Efficient?', *New Political Economy*, 9 (1).

Bunting, M, (2004) *Willing Slaves*, Harper-Collins.

Burnham, P, (2001) 'New Labour and the politics of depoliticisation', *British Journal of Politics and International Relations*, 3 (2).

Byers, S, (1999) *Speech to the London Business School*, October.

—— (2003) *Speech to Social Market Foundation*, May.

Cairncross, A, (1985) *Years of Recovery: British Economic Policy 1945–51*, Methuen.

Callaghan, J, (2000) *The Retreat of Social Democracy*, Manchester University Press.

Calman, K, Hunter, D J and May, A, (2005) *Lost in Translation: A commentary on Labour's health policy four years into the NHS Plan*. www.dur.ac.uk/public.health/news/losttrans/

Carter, M, (2003) *T H Green and the Development of Ethical Socialism*, Imprint Academic.

Castle, B, (1990) *The Castle Dairies 1964–1976*, Macmillan.

Centre for Public Services, (2001) *Private Finance Initiative and Public Private Partnerships: What future for public services?* www.centre.public.org.uk

Cerny, P, (1995) 'Globalisation and the Changing Logic of Collective action', *International Organisation*, 49 (4).

—— (2000) 'Globalization and the Disarticulation of Political Power: Towards a New Middle Ages?' in Goverde, H, Cerny, P, Haugaard, M and Lentner, H, *Power in Contemporary Politics*, Sage.

Cerny, P G and Evans, M, (2004) 'Globalisation and Public Policy under New Labour', *Policy Studies*, 25 (1).

Chadwick, A and Heffernan, R, (2003) *The New Labour Reader*, Polity Press.

Chitty, C, (2004) *Education Policy in Britain*, Palgrave.

Clark, T, (2001) *The Limits of Social Democracy? Tax and Spend under Labour, 1974–79*, Institute for Fiscal Studies.

Clarke, J, (2004a) *Changing Welfare, Changing States*, Sage.

—— (2004b) 'Dissolving the Public Realm? The Logics and Limits of neo-liberalism', *Journal of Social Policy*, 33 (1).

—— (2004c) 'Consumerism and the remaking of state-citizen relationships', Paper prepared for ESPAnet conference, Oxford, September.

—— (2004d) 'A Consuming Public?' Lecture in ESRC/AHRB Cultures of Consumption series, Royal Society, April 22.

—— (2004e) 'Creating CitizenConsumers: the trajectory of an identity', Paper prepared for CASCA annual conference, London, Ontario, May.

—— (2005) 'The People's Choice? New Labour and public service reform', *Renewal*, 13 (4).

Clarke, J, Gewitz, S and McLaughlin, E, (2000) 'Reinventing the Welfare State' in Clarke, J, Gewitz, S and McLaughlin, E, *New Managerialism, New Welfare*, Open University Press.

Clarke, J, Smith, N and Vidler, E, (2005) 'Consumerism and the reform of public services: inequalities and instabilities' in Powell, M, Bauld, L and Clarke, K (eds) *Social Policy Review 17*, Policy Press.

Clarke, J, Newman, J, Smith, N, Vidler, E and Westmarland, L, (2007) *Creating Citizen-Consumers*, Sage.

Clasen, J, (2002) 'Modern Social Democracy and European Welfare State Reform', *Social Policy and Society*, 1 (1).

—— (2003) 'From Unemployment to Worklessness: the transformation of British unemployment policy' in Clasen, J, Ferrera, M and Rhodes, M (eds) *Welfare States and the Challenge of Unemployment*, Routledge.

—— (2005) *Reforming European Welfare States*, Oxford University Press.

Clegg, D, (2005) 'A Rootless Third Way' in Powell, M, Bauld, L and Clarke, K (eds), *Social Policy Review 17*, Policy Press.

Coates, D, (2001) 'Capitalist Models and Social Democracy: the case of New Labour', *British Journal of Politics and International Relations*, 3 (3).

—— (2005) *Prolonged Labour*, Palgrave.

Coates, D and Panitch, L, (2001) *'The Miliband School of Labour Scholarship: an Internal Retrospective'*, Past Paper presented to the Labour Movements Group of the Political Studies Association, University of Salford, July.

Cohen, G, (1994) 'Back to Socialist Basics', *New Left Review*, 207.

Collins, P, (2001) 'A Story of Justice' *Prospect*, May.

Coote, A, (1999) 'The Helmsman and the Cattle Prod', *Political Quarterly*, 70 (S1).

Coulson, A, (1998) 'Trust and Contract in Public Sector Management', in Coulson, A (ed.) *Trust and Contracts*, Policy Press.

Coulter, A, (2005) 'What do patients and the public want from primary care?', *British Medical Journal*, 331, 19 November.

Craig, F W S, (1970) *British General Election Manifestos*, Political Reference Publications.

—— (1990) *British General Election Manifestos*, Parliamentary Research Services.

Craig, D with Brooks, R, (2006) *Plundering the Public Sector*, Constable.

Crewe, I, (2006) 'New Labour's Hegemony: Erosion or Extension?' in Bartle, J and King, A *Britain at the Polls 2005*, CQ Press.

Cribb, A and Ball, S, (2005) 'Towards an Ethical Audit of the Privatisation of Education', *British Journal of Educational Studies*, 53 (2).

Crick, B, (1984) 'Equality' in Pimlott, B (ed.) *Fabian Essays in Socialist Thought*, HEB.

—— (1987) *Socialism*, Open University Press.

Crinson, I, (2005) 'The Direction of Health Policy in New Labour's Third Term' *Critical Social Policy*, 25 (4).

Crompton, R and Lyonette, C, (2007) 'Are we all working too hard? Women, men, and changing attitudes to employment' in *British Social Attitudes: the 23rd Report – Perspectives on a changing society*, Sage Press Release. www.natcen.ac.uk/natcen/pages/news_and_media_docs/BSA_%20press_release_jan07.pdf.

Cronin, J E, (2004) *New Labour's Pasts: The Labour Party and its Discontents*, Pearson, Longman.

—— (2006) 'New Labour's Escape from Class Politics', *The Journal of The Historical Society*, 6 (1).

Crosland, Tony, (1964) *The Future of Socialism*, Jonathan Cape.

—— (1974) *Socialism Now*, Jonathan Cape.

Crossman, R H S, (1960) *Socialism and the New Despotism*, Fabian Society.

—— (1976) *Diaries of a Cabinet Minister, Vol. 3*, Hamish Hamilton and Jonathan Cape.

Crouch, C, (1997) 'The Terms of the Neo-Liberal Consensus', *Political Quarterly*, 68 (4).

—— (1999) 'The Parabola of Working-Class Politics', *Political Quarterly*, 70 (1).

—— (2001) 'A Third Way in Industrial Relations?' in White, S (ed.) *New Labour: The Progressive Future?*, Macmillan.

—— (2002) *Coping With Post-Democracy*, Fabian Society.

—— (2003) *Commercialisation or Citizenship?*, Fabian Society.

—— (2004) *Post-Democracy*, Polity Press.

—— (2005) 'Models of capitalism', *New Political Economy*, 10 (4).

Crouch, C, Eder, K and Tambini, D, (2001) *Citizenship, Markets and the State*, Oxford University Press.

Cruddas, J MP, (2002) 'Return of the Working Class', *Tribune*, 14 March.

Cutler, T and Waine, B, (2000) 'Managerialism Reformed? New Labour and Public Sector Management', *Social Policy and Administration*, 34 (3).

Daguerre, A, (2004) 'Importing Workfare: Policy Transfer of Social and Labour Market Policies from the USA to Britain under New Labour', *Social Policy and Administration*, 38 (1).

Dalton, R J and Wattenberg, M, (2002) *Parties without Partisans: Political Change in Advanced Industrial Democracies*, Oxford University Press.

Dalyell, T, (1989) *Dick Crossman*, Weidenfeld and Nicolson.

Darling, A, (1999) *Speech by the Secretary of State for Social Security*, February.

Dash, P, (2004) 'New providers in UK health care', *British Medical Journal*, 328, 7 February.

Dawson, D, (2001) 'The Private Finance Initiative: A public finance illusion?', *Health Economics*, 10 (6).

De Botton, A, (2004) *Status Anxiety*, Hamish Hamilton.

Deacon, A, (1998) 'The Green paper on Welfare Reform: A case of Enlightened Self-Interest?', *Political Quarterly*, 69 (3).

—— (2003) 'Levelling the playing field, activating the players: New Labour and the cycle of disadvantage', *Policy and Politics*, 31 (2).

Deacon, A and Mann, K, (1999) 'Agency, Modernity and Social Policy', *Journal of Social Policy*, 28 (3).

Deakin, N and Walsh, K, (1996) 'The Enabling State: The role of markets and contracts', *Public Administration*, 4 (1).

Delorenzi, S and Reed, J, (2006) 'Returning through the Back Door: social class and social mobility', *Renewal*, 14 (1).

Denham, J, (2006) 'How Not to Make Policy', *Chartist*, 219, March/April.

Denham, J, Eagle, A, Morris, E, Raynsford, N and Whitehead, A, (2005) *Shaping the Education Bill Reaching for Consensus*, Compass. www.compassonline.org.uk/campaigns/educationdebate/.

Dennis, N and Halsey, A H, (1988) *English Ethical Socialism*, Clarendon.

Department of Education and Skills, (2005) White Paper *Higher Standards, Better Schools For All More choice for parents and pupils*, The Stationery Office, October.

—— (2006) *Summary of The Education and Inspections Act 2006*. www.dfes.gov.uk/publications/educationandinspectionsact/

Department of Employment, (1969) *In Place of Strife*, HMSO.

Department of Health, (1999) *PFI Questions and Answers*, The Stationery Office, December.

—— (2000) *The NHS Plan: A Plan for Investment, a Plan for Reform*, The Stationery Office.

—— (2001) *For the Benefit of Patients: A Concordat with the Private and Voluntary Health Care Provider Sector*, The Stationery Office.

—— (2003) *Building on the Best Choice, Responsiveness and Equity in the NHS*, The Stationery Office.

—— (2004) *The NHS Improvement Plan: Putting People at the Heart of Public Services*, The Stationery Office.

—— (2006) *Written Evidence submitted to Health Select Committee hearings on ISTCs*, The Stationery Office.

Department of Social Security, (1998) *New Ambitions for Our Country*, Green Paper on Welfare Reform, The Stationery Office.

Department of Trade and Industry, (1998) *Fairness at Work*, White Paper, The Stationery Office.

Dequech, D, (2001) 'Bounded Rationality, Institutions, and Uncertainty', *Journal of Economic Issues*, 35, December.

Diamond, P, (2004) *New Labour's Old Root: Revisionist Thinkers in Labour's History 1931–1997*, Imprint Academic.

Diamond, P and Giddens, A, (2005) 'The New Egalitarianism: economic inequality in the UK' in Diamond, P and Giddens, A (eds) *The New Egalitarianism*, Polity Press.

Dixon, J, (2003a) 'Framing the debate' in Dixon, J, Le Grand, J and Smith, P, *Can Market Forces be Used for Good?*, King's Fund.

—— (2003b) 'Foundation trusts: Where next?', *British Medical Journal*, 326, 1 June.

—— (2004) 'Payment by results – new financial flows in the NHS' *British Medical Journal*, 328, 24 April.

Dobrowolsky, A and Jenson, J (2005) 'Social investment perspectives and practices: a decade in British politics' in Powell, M, Bauld, L and Clarke, K (eds) *Social Policy Review 17*, Policy Press.

Dobson, F, (2003) *Foundation Trusts and the new health service market: what future for the NHS?*, Speech to Catalyst fringe meeting at TUC Congress, 9 September.

Doig, A and Wilson, J, (1999) 'Ethics, Integrity, Compliance and Accountability in Contemporary UK Government–Business Relations', *Australian Journal of Public Administration*, 58 (4).

Driver, S and Martell, L, (1997) 'Labour's new Communitarians' *Critical Social Policy*, 17 (3).

—— (2000) 'Left, Right and the Third way', *Policy and Politics*, 28 (2).

(2002) *Blair's Britain*, Polity Press.

—— (2006) *New Labour*, Polity Press.

Dunleavy, P and Hood, C, (1994) 'From Old Public Administration to New Public Management', *Public Money and Management*, 14 (3).

Durkheim, E, (1982) [1895] *The Rules of the Sociological Method*, Free Press.

Dworkin, R, (1984) 'Liberalism' in Sandel, M (ed.) *Liberalism and its Critics*, New York University Press.

Dwyer, P and Heron, E, (1999) 'Doing the Right Thing', *Social Policy and Administration*, 33 (1).

Dyson, A, Kerr, K and Ainscow, M, (2006) 'A "pivotal moment"? Education policy in England, 2005' in Bauld, L, Clarke, K and Maltby, T (eds) *Social Policy Review 18*, Policy Press.

Eagle, Angela MP, (2003) *A deeper democracy: Challenging market fundamentalism*, Catalyst.

Ebbinghaus, B, (2005) *Can Path Dependence Explain Institutional Change?*, MPIfG Discussion Paper 05/2.

Ebbinghaus, B and Manow, P (eds), (2001) *Studying Varieties of Welfare Capitalism*, Routledge.

Eckstein, H, (1996) 'Culture as a Foundation Concept for the Social Sciences', *Journal of Theoretical Politics*, 8 (4).

Education and Skills Select Committee, (2005) *Secondary Education*, The Stationery Office.

Edwards, N, (2005) 'Using Markets to Reform Health Care' *British Medical Journal*, 331, 17 December.

Edwards, T and Tomlinson, S, (2002) *Selection isn't working: Diversity, standards and inequality in secondary education*, Catalyst Working Paper, Catalyst.

Ehrke, M, (2000) 'Revisionism Revisited: The Third Way and European Social Democracy', *Concepts and Transformation*, 5 (1).

Ekstrom, M, (1992) 'Causal Explanation of Social Action Acts', *Sociologica*, 35 (2).

Ellison, N, (1994) *Egalitarian Thought and Labour Politics*, Routledge.

Entman, R M, (1993) 'Framing: Towards Clarification of a Fractured Paradigm', *Journal of Communication*, 43 (4).

Esping-Andersen, G, (1990) *The Three Worlds of Welfare Capitalism*, Polity Press.

—— (1999) *Social Foundations of Post-industrial Economies*, Oxford University Press.

—— (2002) 'Towards the Good Society, Once Again?' in Esping-Andersen, G (ed.) *Why We Need a New Welfare State*, Oxford University Press.

Etzioni, A, (2001) 'The Third Way is a Triumph', *New Statesman*, 25 June.

European Foundation for the Improvement of Living and Working Conditions, (2002) *Quality of work and employment in Europe Issues and challenges,*. www.eurofound. eu.int.

Evetts, J, (2003) 'The Sociological Analysis of Professionalism', *International Sociology*, 18 (2).

Exworthy, M, Powell, M and Mohan, J, (1999) 'The NHS: Quasi-market, Quasi-hierarchy and Quasi-network?', *Public Money and Management*, October–December.

Fabian Society, (2006) *Narrowing the Gap: The Fabian Commission on Life Chances and Child Poverty*, Fabian Society.

Farnham, B, (1990) 'Political Cognition and Decision-Making', *Political Psychology*, 11 (1).

Farr, J, (1985) 'Situational Analysis', *Journal of Politics*, 47.

Ferge, Z, (1997) 'The Changed Welfare Paradigm: The Individualisation of the Social', *Social Policy and Administration*, 31 (1).

Field, J E and Peck, E, (2004) 'Concordat or Contract Factors facilitating or impeding the development of public/private partnerships in healthcare in England', *Public Management Review*, 6 (2).

'File on Four', BBC Radio Four, (2004a) 'Primary Care Trusts', 1 June.

'File on Four', BBC Radio Four, (2004b) 'The Private Finance Initiative', 6 July.

'File on Four', BBC Radio Four, (2006) 'Private Corporations in the NHS', 17 October.

Fitzpatrick, T, (2003) *After the New Social Democracy*, Manchester University Press.

Flinders, Matthew, (2005) 'The Politics of Public–Private Partnerships', *British Journal of Politics & International Relations*, 7 (2).

Forrester, T, (1975) *The Labour party and the Working Class*, Heinemann.

Fox, A, (1966) *Industrial Relations and Industrial Sociology*, Research Papers 3, Royal Commission on Trade Unions and Employment Associations, HMSO.

—— (1974) *Beyond Contract: Work, Power and Trust Relations*, Faber and Faber.

—— (1978) *Shop Floor Power Today*, Fabian Research Series 338.

Francis, M, (1997) *Ideas and Policies under Labour 1945–51*, Manchester University Press.

Freeden, M, (1996) *Ideologies and Political Theory*, Oxford University Press.

—— (1999a) 'The Ideology of New Labour', *Political Quarterly*, 70 (1).

—— (1999b) 'True Blood or False Genealogy: New Labour and Social Democratic Thought', *Political Quarterly*, 70 (S1).

Fryer, D, (1999) *'Insecurity, the restructuring of unemployment and mental health'*, Paper presented to Conference on Social Security and the Restructuring of Unemployment, Graz, Austria.

Gaffney, D, and Pollock, A M, (1999) *Downsizing for the 21st Century: A report to UNISON Northern Region on the North Durham Acute Hospitals PFI scheme*, 2nd Edition, Unison.

Gaffney, D, Pollock, AM, Price, D and Shaoul, J, (1999a) 'NHS capital expenditure and the private finance initiative', *British Medical Journal*, 319, 3 July.

—— (1999b) 'PFI in the NHS: is there an economic case?', *British Medical Journal*, 319, 10 July.

—— (1999c) 'Planning the new NHS: downsizing for the 21st century', *British Medical Journal*, 319, 17 July.

—— (1999d) 'The politics of the private finance initiative and the new NHS', *British Medical Journal*, 319, 24 July.

Gaitskell, H, (1956) *Socialism and Nationalisation*, Fabian Society.

Gamble, A and Wright, T (eds), (1999a) *The New Social Democracy*, Blackwell.

Gamble, A and Wright, T, (1999b) 'Introduction: the New Social Democracy', *Political Quarterly*, 70 (S1).

Garrett, G, (1998) *Partisan Politics in the World Economy*, Cambridge University Press.

Garrett, G and Lange, P (1991) 'Political Responses To Interdependence: What's "left" for the left?', *International Organisation*, 45 (4).

Garrett, G and Mitchell, D, (1999) *'Globalization and the Welfare State'*. www.yale.edu/leitner/pdf/1999–04.pdf.

Gennard, J, (2002) ' Employee relations public policy developments, 1997–2001 A break with the past?' *Employee Relations*, 24 (6).

George, A, (1967) *The Operational Code: A Neglected Approach to the Study of Political leaders and Decision-Making*, Rand.

Gewirtz, S, Dickson, M and Power, S, (2004) 'Unravelling a "spun" policy: a case study of the constitutive role of "spin" in the education policy process', *Journal of Education Policy*, 19 (3).

Giddens, A, (1998) *The Third Way: The Renewal of Social Democracy*, Polity Press.

—— (1999a) 'Third Way must reduce inequality of outcome', *New Statesman*, 12 February.

—— (1999b) 'Why the old left is wrong on equality', *New Statesman*, 25 October.

—— (2000) *The Third Way and its Critics*, Polity Press.

—— (2002) *Where Now for New Labour?*, Polity Press.

—— (2003) 'Neoprogressivism: A New Agenda for Social Democracy' in Giddens, A (ed.) *The Progressive Manifesto*, Polity Press.

—— (2004a) 'We can and should take action if the earnings of the rich set them apart from society', *New Statesman*, 24 September.

—— (2004b) 'Egalitarianism: old and new' Miliband lecture, London School of Economics, 7 October.

Glatter, R, (2004) 'Choice and Diversity of Schooling Provision: Issues and Evidence', Written Evidence to *Public Administration Select Committee Choice, Voice and Public Services,*.

Glennerster, H, (2001) 'Social Policy' in Seldon, A (ed.) *The Blair Effect*, Little, Brown and Co..

—— (2005) 'The Health and Welfare Legacy' in Seldon, A and Kavanagh, D (eds) *The Blair Effect 2001–2005*, Cambridge University Press.

—— (2007) *British Social Policy*, 3rd Edition, Blackwell.

Glyn, A (1998) 'The Assessment: Economic Policy and Social Democracy', *Oxford Review of Economic Policy*, 14 (1).

Glyn, A and Wood, S, (2001a) 'New Labour's Economic Policy: How Social-Democratic is the Blair Government?' in Glyn, A (ed.) *Social Democracy in Neo-Liberal Times*, Oxford University Press.

—— (2001b) 'Economic policy under New Labour: how social democratic is the Blair government?' *Political Quarterly*, 72 (1).

Goldstein, J, (1993) *Ideas, Interests and American Trade Policy*, Cornell University Press.

Goldthorpe, J H, (2002) 'Globalisation and Social Class', *West European Politics*, 25 (3).

—— (2005) 'Perpetuum mobile?', *Prospect*, 116, November.

Goodman, A, Johnson, P and Webb, S, (1997) *Inequality in the UK*, Oxford University Press.

Gospel, H, (2003) *Quality of working life: A review on changes in work organization, conditions of employment and work-life arrangements*, International Labour Organisation.

Gough, I, (1994) 'Economic institutions and the satisfaction of human needs', *Journal of Economic Issues*, 28 (1).

Gould, P, (1998) *The Unfinished Revolution*, HarperCollins.

Gould Mattinson Associates (GMA), (1992) *Monitor for Fabian Society Election and Post Election Polling*, Fabian Society.

Grant, W, (2000) *Globalisation, Big Business and the Blair Government*, Centre for the Study of Globalisation and Regionalisation Working Paper No. 58/00, University of Warwick.

Gray, A, (1997) 'Editorial: Private Finance Initiative', *Public Money and Management*, July–September.

Greenaway, J, Salter, B and Hart, S, (2004) 'The Evolution of a "Meta-Policy": The Case of the Private Finance Initiative and the Health Sector', *British Journal of Politics and International Relations*, 6 (4).

Greener, I, (2003) 'Who's Choosing What? The Evolution of the use of "choice" in the NHS and its importance for New Labour' in Bochel, C, Ellison, N and Powell, M (eds) *Social Policy Review 15*, Policy Press.

—— (2004) '*Marketing Health: waste of public money or driver if change?*,' Paper presented to the Annual Conference of the Political Studies Association.

Greenleaf, W H, (1983a) *The British Political Tradition. Vol. I: The Rise of Collectivism*, Routledge.

—— (1983b) *The British Political Tradition. Vol. II: The Ideological Heritage*, Routledge.

Green-Pedersen, C, van Kersbergen, K and Hemerijck, A, (2000) 'Neo-Liberalism, the "Third Way" or What? European Social Democracy and the Welfare State at the Beginning of the New Millennium' Paper for the Twelfth International Conference of Europeanists, Chicago.

Grieve-Smith, J, (2006) 'Unequal Britain', *Chartist*, 219, March/April.

Hall, P A, (1993) 'Policy Paradigms, Social Learning and the State: The case of economic-policy making in Britain', *Comparative Politics*, 25 (3).

—— (1998) *Organized Market Economies and Unemployment in Europe: Is it Finally Time to Accept Liberal Orthodoxy?*, Paper prepared for the 11th International Conference of Europeanists, Baltimore.

—— (2002) 'The Comparative Political Economy of the Third Way' in Schmidke, O (ed.) *The Third Way: Transformation of Social Democracy*, Ashgate.

Hall, P A and Taylor, R, (1998) *Political Science and the Three New Institutionalisms*, MPIFG 96/6. www.mpi-fg-koeln.mpg.de/pu/mpifg_dp/dp96–6.pdf.

Hall, S, (1998) 'The Great Moving Nowhere Show', *Marxism Today*, Special Edition.

—— (2003) 'New Labour's Double Shuffle' *Soundings*, 24, Autumn.

Ham, C (2004) *Health Policy in Britain*, 5th Edition, Palgrave.

—— (2006) 'Unsteady as she goes', *Guardian*, 27 April.

Hamann, K and Kelly, J, (2003) 'The Domestic Sources of Differences in Labour Market Policies', *British Journal of Industrial Relations*, 41 (4).

Hampshire-Monk, I, (1996) 'The Individualist Premise and Political Community' in King, P (ed.) *Socialism and the Common Good*, Frank Cass.

Harker, L, (2006) 'Tackling Poverty in the UK. Have we reached the limits?', *Public Policy Research*, 13, March–May.

Harris, A and Ranson, S, (2005) 'The Contradictions of Education Policy: disadvantage and achievement', *British Educational Research Journal*, 31 (5).

Harris, D (1987) *Justifying State Welfare*, Blackwell.

Harris, J, (2005) *So Now Who Do We Vote for?*, Faber and Faber.

Harrison, S and Smith, C, (2004) 'Trust and moral motivation: redundant resources in health and social care?', *Policy and Politics*, 31 (4).

Harvey, J, (1998) 'Heuristic Judgment Theory', *Journal of Economic Issues*, 32 (1).

Hattersley, Roy (Lord), (2005) Memorandum to Public Administration Select Committee *Choice, Voice and Public Services Volume III Oral and written evidence*, The Stationery Office.

Hay, C, (1999) *The Political Economy of New Labour: Labouring under false pretences?*, Manchester University Press.

—— (2001) *What Place for Ideas in the Structure–Agency Debate? Globalisation as a 'Process Without a Subject'*, First Press: Writing in the Critical Social Sciences. www.theglobalsite.ac.uk/press/.

—— (2002a) 'Globalisation, "EU-isation" and the space for social democratic alternatives: pessimism of the intellect: a reply to Coates', *British Journal of Politics and International Relations*, 4 (3).

—— (2002b) 'Common Trajectories, Variable Paces, Divergent Outcomes?' Paper presented at the Biannual Conference of Europeanists, Chicago, March.

—— (2004) 'Re-stating Politics, Repoliticising the State', *Political Quarterly*, 75 (S1).

—— (2005) 'The Political Economy of New Labour: A Preliminary Assessment', Conference on *Cool Britannia: Britain After Eight Years of Labour Government*, Université de Montréal, 4–6 May.

—— (2006) ',What's Globalization Got to do with it? Economic Interdependence and the Future of the European Welfare State', *Government and Opposition*, 41 (1).

Hazareesingh, S, (1994) *Political Traditions in Modern France*, Oxford University Press.

Heald, D, (2003) 'Value for money tests and accounting treatment in PFI schemes', *Accounting, Auditing & Accountability Journal*, 16 (3).

Heald, D and Geaughan, N, (1997) 'Accounting for the Private Finance Initiative', *Public Money and Management*, 17 (3).

Healey, D, (1989) *The Time of My Life*, Michael Joseph.

Health and Safety Executive, (2007) 'Why tackle work-related stress?'. www.hse.gov.uk/stress/why.htm.

Health Select Committee, (1999) *Future NHS Staffing Requirements*, The Stationery Office.

—— (2002) *The Role of the Private Sector in the NHS*, The Stationery Office.

—— (2003) *Foundation Trusts*, The Stationery Office.

—— (2006a) *Independent Sector Treatment Centres*, The Stationery Office.

—— (2006b) *Uncorrected transcript oral evidence. Independent Sector Treatment Centres*, The Stationery Office.

Heath, A, Jowell, R and Curtice, J, (2001) *The Rise of New Labour*, Oxford University Press.

Heffernan, R, (2000) *New Labour and Thatcherism: Political Change in Britain*, Macmillan.

Helleiner, E, (1994) *States and the Reemergence of Global Finance: from Bretton Woods to the 1990's*, Cornell University Press.

Hemerijck, A and Schludi, M, (2000) 'Sequences of Policy Failures and Effective Policy Responses' in Scharpf, F W and Schmidt, V (eds) *Welfare and Work in the Open Economy – From Vulnerability to Competitiveness*, Oxford University Press.

Hemertijick, A and van Kersbergen, K, (1998) 'Negotiated Change: Institutional and Policy Learning in Tightly Coupled Welfare States', *European Consortium for Political Research Joint Sessions*, Warwick University.

Hennessy, P, (2004) 'Michael Young and the Labour Party'. www.chu.cam.ac.uk/archives/about/Young_Hennessy.shtml.

—— (2005) 'Michael Young and the Labour Party' *Contemporary British History*, 19 (3).

Hewitt, P MP, (2001a) 'The Principled Society: Reforming Public Services', *Renewal*, 9 (2/3).

—— (2001b) 'Business And Society – Roles and Responsibilities' Speech at the *Guardian*, and the *Observer*, Conference, London, July.

—— (2005a) *Speech to Fabian Society*, 20 July.

—— (2005b) *LSE Annual Health and Social Care Lecture*, December.

—— (2006a) *Speech to Braunstone Health Centre*, Leicester, March.

—— (2006b) *Speech to Institute of Public Policy Research*, 19 September.

Hills, J, (1998) *Thatcherism, New Labour and the Welfare State*, Centre for Analysis of Social Exclusion, London School of Economics.

Hines, J R, (2006) 'Will Social Welfare Expenditures Survive Tax Competition?', *Oxford Review of Economic Policy*, 22 (3).

Hinton, J, (1983) *Labour and Socialism*, University of Massachusetts Press.

Hindess, B, (1991) 'Taking Socialism Seriously', *Economy and Society*, 20 (1).

Hinnfors, J, (2006) *Reinterpreting Social democracy*, Manchester University Press.

Hirsch, D with Millar, J, (2004) 'Labour's welfare reform: Progress to date', Joseph Rowntree Foundation Ref 44 2004. www.jrf.org.uk/knowledge/findings/foundations/n44.asp.

Hirsch, F, (1977) *The Social Limits to Growth*, Routledge and Kegan Paul.

Hirst, Paul, (1999) 'The Strange Death of New Labour England?', *Renewal*, 7 (4).

HM Treasury, (1997) *Employment Opportunity for All – A New Approach*, The Stationery Office.

—— (1998) *Modernising Public Services for Britain*, The Stationery Office.

—— (1999a) *Economic Briefing, Issue 9, the Private Finance Initiative*.

—— (1999b) *Tackling poverty and extending opportunity: The modernisation of Britain's tax and benefit system*, The Stationery Office.

—— (2000) *Public Private Partnerships: The Government's Approach*, The Stationery Office.

—— (2001) *Public Private Partnerships*, The Stationery Office.

—— (2002) *Budget 2002: Report*, The Stationery Office.

Hoggett, P (1996) 'New Modes of Control in the Public Service', *Public Administration*, 74 (1).

Hollingworth, M, (1986) *The Press and Political Dissent*, Pluto Press.

Hood, C C, (1991) 'A Public Management for all Seasons', *Public Administration*, 69 (1).

House of Commons Library, (2003) *Research Paper 03/07 The Private Finance Initiative*, House of Commons Library.

Howell, C, (1998) '*From New Labour to No Labour? The Blair Government in Britain*', Paper presented to the Conference of the American Political Science Association, Boston.

—— (2001) 'The End of the Relationship between Social Democratic Parties and Trade Unions?', *Studies in Political Economy*, 65, Summer.

—— (2004) 'Is There a Third Way for Industrial Relations?', *British Journal of Industrial Relations*, 42 (1).

Huber, E and Stephens, J D, (2000) 'Welfare State and Production Regimes in the Era of Retrenchment' in Paul Pierson (ed.) *The New Politics of the Welfare State*, Oxford University Press.

—— (2001) *Development and Crisis of the Welfare State*, University of Chicago Press.

—— (2002) 'Globalisation, Competitiveness, and the Social Democratic Model' *Social Policy and Society*, 1 (1).

Hunter, D J, (2002) 'A tale of two tribes: the tension between managerial and professional values' in New, B and Neuberger, J (eds) *Hidden Assets*, King's Fund.

—— (2003) 'Foundation Hospitals: Back to the Future', *Public Money and Management*, October.

—— (2005) 'The National Health Service 1980–2005' *Public Money and Management*, 25 (4).

Hutton, John MP, (2005) *Speech to the Social Market Foundation*, August.

Hutton, Will (1995) *The State We're In*, Jonathan Cape.

Hyman, P, (2005) *One out of Ten*, Vintage.

Ignatieff, M, (1984) *Needs of Strangers*, Picador.

Ingle, S J, (2000) *The British Party System*, Pinter.

International Labour Organisation (ILO), (1995) 'Combating unemployment and exclusion: Issues and policy', International Labour Organisation.

Jackson, B and Segal, S, (2004) *Why Inequality Matters*, Catalyst Working Paper, Catalyst.

Jackson, P M, (1991) 'Public Expenditure' in Artis, M and Cobham, D (eds) *Labour's Economic Policies 1974–79*, Manchester University Press.

Jayasuriya, K, (2000) 'Capability, Freedom and the New Social Democracy', *Political Quarterly*, 71 (3).

Jervis, R, (1985) 'Cognition and Political behaviour' in Lau, R R and Sears, D O, *Political Cognition*, Lawrence Erlbaum.

Jessop, B, (1994) 'The Transition to Post-Fordism and the Schumpeterian Welfare State' in Burrows, R and Loader, B (eds) *Towards a post-Fordist welfare state?*, Routledge.

228   *Bibliography*

—— (1999a) 'The Social Embeddedness of the Economy and its Implications for Economic Governance'. www.comp.lancaster.ac.uk/sociology/soc016rj.html.

—— (1999b) 'The Changing Governance of Welfare: Recent Trends in its Primary Functions, Scale and Modes of Coordination', *Social Policy and Administration*, 33 (4).

—— (1999c) 'Narrating the future of the national economy and the national state' in Steinmetz, G *et al.*, (eds) *State/Culture: State Formation after the Cultural Turn*, Cornell University Press.

Johnson, P, (2004) 'Education Policy in England', *Oxford Review of Economic Policy*, 20 (2).

Joint Government Memorandum, (2005) presented to the House of Commons Public Administration Select Committee.

Jordan, Bill, (1998) *The New Politics of Welfare*, Sage.

J½rgensen, T B and Bozeman, B, (2002) 'Public Values Lost? Comparing cases on contracting out from Denmark and the United States', *Public Management Review*, 4 (1).

Jupp, J, (1968) *Political Parties*, Routledge and Kegan Paul.

Kay, J, (2003) 'The Embedded Market' in Giddens, A (ed.) *Progressive Manifesto*, Polity Press.

—— (2004) 'The State and the Market', *Political Quarterly*, 75 (S1).

Keat, R, (2000) 'Market Boundaries and Human Goods' in Haldane, J (ed.) *Philosophy and Public Affairs*, Cambridge University Press.

Keegan, W, (2003) *The Prudence of Mr Gordon Brown*, Wiley.

Kelly, Gavin and Le Grand, Julian, (2000) 'Should Labour go private?', *New Statesman*, 11 August.

Kelly, S P, (2005) 'Recurring Policy Errors: blind spots over cataracts', *Lancet*, 12 November.

—— (2006) 'Cataract care is mobile', *British Journal of Ophthalmology*, 90.

King, A, (1998) *New Labour Triumphs: Britain at the Polls 1997*, Chatham House.

—— (2002) 'Tony Blair's First Term' in King, A (ed.) *Britain at the Polls, 2001*, Chatham House.

King's Fund, (2002) *The Future of the NHS: A framework for debate*, King's Fund.

—— (2005a) *An Independent Audit of the NHS under Labour 1997–2005*, King's Fund.

—— (2005b) *Memorandum to House of Commons Public Administration Select Committee Choice*, Voice and Public Services London: Stationery Office Volume III Oral and written evidence.

Kitschelt, H (1994) *The Transformation of European Social Democracy*, Cambridge University Press.

Kitson, M, Martin, R, Wilkinson, F, (2000) 'Labour Markets, Social Justice and Economic Efficiency', *Cambridge Journal of Economics*, 24: 631–41.

Klein, R (2001) *The New Politics of the NHS*, Longman.

—— (2003) Editorial 'Governance for NHS foundation trusts', *British Medical Journal*, 326, 25 January.

—— (2005) 'Transforming the NHS: the story in 2004' in Powell, M, Bauld, L and Clark, K (eds) *Social Policy Review 17*, Policy Press..

—— (2006) 'The Troubled Transformation of Britain's National Health Service', *The New England Journal of Medicine*, 355 (4), July.

Kmietowicz, Z, (2001) 'News roundup', *British Medical Journal*, 27 October.

Kogan, M, (2006) 'Anthony Crosland: intellectual and politician', *Oxford Review of Education*, 32 (1).

Korpi, W, (1985) 'Power Resources Approach vs Action and Conflict: On Causal and Intentional Explanation in the Study of Power', *Sociological Theory*, 3 (1).

—— (1989) 'Power, Politics and State Autonomy in the Development of Social Citizenship', *American Sociological Review*, 54 (3).

—— (2001) 'Contentious Institutions: An Augmented Rational-Action Analysis of the Origins and Path Dependency of Welfare State Institutions in the Western Countries', *Rationality and Society*, 13 (2).

Korpi, W and Palme, J, (2003) 'New Politics and Class Politics in the Context of Austerity and Globalisation', *American Political Science Review*, 97 (3).

Krieger, J, (1999) *British Politics in the Global Age: Can Social democracy Survive?*, Polity Press.

Labour Party, (1959) *Annual Conference Report, 1959*, Labour Party.

—— (1960) *Annual Conference Report, 1960*, Labour Party.

—— (1964) *Let's Go with Labour for the New Britain*, Election Manifesto.

—— (1974) *Britain Will Win with Labour*, Election Manifesto.

—— (1989) *Meet the Challenge, Make the Change*, Labour Party.

—— (1996) 'Renewing the NHS: Labour's agenda for a Healthier Britain', *International Journal of Health Services*, 26 (2).

—— (1997) *Britain will be Better with New Labour*, Election Manifesto.

—— (2001) *Investing in Strong Communities*, Election Manifesto.

Lane, R, (2005) 'The NHS is being dismantled', *Guardian*, 21 April.

Lane, R E, (1986) 'Market Justice, Political Justice', *American Political Science Review*, 80 (2).

Lang, S, Wainwright, C and Sehdev, K, (2005) *A Review of Patient Choice in the NHS*, Cranfield University Healthcare Management Research Group.

Lansley, S, (2006) *Rich Britain: The Rise and Rise of the New Super-Wealthy*, Politico's Publishing.

Lawton, D, (2005) *Education and Labour Party Ideologies*, Routledge.

Layard, R (Lord), (2003a) 'Income and happiness: rethinking economic policy' *Lionel Robbins Memorial Lectures*, LSE, March.

—— (2003b) 'Towards a happier society', *New Statesman*, 24 February.

—— (2005a) *Happiness*, Allen Lane.

—— (2005b) Interview with Nick Pearce, *Public Policy Research*, 12 (3).

—— (2006) 'Happiness and public policy: a challenge to the profession' *Economic Journal*, 116 (510).

Le Grand, J, (1997) 'Knights, Knaves or Pawns? Human Behaviour and Social Policy', *Journal of Social Policy*, 26 (2).

—— (1998a) 'Ownership and Social Policy', *Political Quarterly*, 69 (4).

—— (1998b) *UK-policy: The appropriate role of the state*. uk policy@netnexus.org.

—— (2001) *The Provision of Health Care: Is the Public Sector Ethically Superior to the Private Sector?*, LSE Health and Social Care Discussion Paper No. 1.

—— (2003) *Motivation, Agency and Public Policy*, Oxford University Press.

—— (2006a) The Blair Legacy? Choice and Competition in Public Services Public Lecture LSE, 21 February.

—— (2006b) 'Equality and choice in public services', *Social Research*, June.

Lecky, W E H, (1910) [1865] *The Rise and Influence of Rationalism in Europe*, Longmans, Green and Co..

Levitas, R, (2005) *The Inclusive Society?: Social Exclusion and New Labour*, Palgrave Macmillan.

Lewis, J, (2004) 'Modern Challenges to the Welfare State' in Lewis, J and Surender, R (eds) *Welfare State Change: Towards a Third Way?*, Oxford University Press.

Lewis, R, (2003) 'Cutting edge' *Guardian*, 29 January.

Lewis, R and Dixon, J, (2005a) *NHS market futures: Exploring the impact of health service market reforms*, King's Fund.

——(2005b) *The Future of Primary Care: Meeting the challenges of the new NHS market*, King's Fund.

Lewis, R and Gillam, S, (2003) 'Back to the Market: Yet More Reform of the NHS', *International Journal of Health Services*, 33 (1).

Leys, C, (2001) *Market-driven Politics. Neoliberal Democracy and the Public Interest*, Verso.

Lieberman, E S, (2001) 'Causal Inference in Historical Institutional Analysis', *Comparative Political Studies*, 34 (9).

Lieberman, R C, (2002) 'Ideas, Institutions, and Political Order: Explaining Political Change', *American Political Science Review*, 96 (4).

Lindblom, C, (1978) *Politics and Markets*, Basic Books.

—— (2002) *The Market System*, Yale University Press.

Lipsey, D (Lord), (2005) 'Too much choice', *Prospect*, 117, December.

Lister, R, (2004) 'The Third Way's social investment state', in Lewis, J and Surender, R (eds) *Welfare State Change: Towards a Third Way?*, Oxford University Press.

Lloyd, C, (1986) *Explanation in Social History*, Oxford University Press.

Lockwood, D, (1996) 'Civic Integration and Class Formation', *British Journal of Sociology*, 47 (3).

Lonsdale, C, (2005) 'Risk Transfer and the UK Private Finance Initiative: a theoretical analysis', *Policy and Politics*, 33 (2).

Lowe, R, (2004) 'Education policy' in Seldon, A and Hickson, K (eds) *New Labour, Old Labour: The Wilson and Callaghan Governments, 1974–79*, Routledge.

Ludlam, S, (2004) 'New Labour and the Union Link' in Ludlam, S and Smith, M (eds) *Governing as New Labour*, Palgrave Macmillan.

Ludlam, S and Taylor, A, (2003) 'The Political Representation of the Labour Interest in Britain', *British Journal of Industrial Relations*, 41 (4).

Ludlam, S, Bodah, M and Coates, D, (2002) 'Trajectories of Solidarity: Changing Union-party Linkages in The UK and The USA', *British Journal of Politics and International Relations*, 4 (2).

Lukes, S, (1972) *Emile Durkheim: his life and work*, Penguin.

—— (1977) 'Socialism and Equality' in Hampshire, S and Kolakowski, L (eds) *The Socialist Idea*, Quartet.

—— (2005) *Power: A Radical View*, 2nd Edition, Macmillan.

McAdam, D, Tarrow, S and Tilly, C, (1995) *To Map Contentious Politics*, Center for Studies of Social Change, University of Michigan.

—— (2001) *Dynamics of Contention*, Cambridge University Press.

McCarthy, W E (Lord), (1998) 'Freedom, Democracy and the Role of the Trade Unions in Modern Industrial Society', *Labour Party papers*, PD: 1395, March.

McDermott, R, (2001) 'The Psychological Ideas of Amos Tversky', *Journal of Theoretical Politics*, 13 (1).

McKay, S (2001) 'Between Flexibility and Regulation: Rights, Equality and Protection at Work', *British Journal of Industrial Relations*, 39 (2).

McKibbin, R, (2002) 'Nothing More Divisive', *London Review of Books*, 24 (23).

—— (2003) 'Tell a friend how to put the politics back into Labour', *London Review of Books*, 25 (13).

—— (2006) 'Sleazy, Humiliated, Despised', *London Review of Books*, 28 (17).

—— (2007) 'Defeatism, Defeatism, Defeatism', *London Review of Books*, 29 (6).

McMurray, R, (2007) 'Our Reforms, Our Partnerships, Same Problems: The Chronic Case of the English NHS', *Public Money and Management*, February.

Machin, S and Stevens, M, (2004) 'The Assessment: education', *Oxford Review of Economic Policy*, 20 (2).

Mahoney, J, (2000) 'Path Dependence in Historical Sociology', *Theory and Society*, 29 (4).

Mair, Peter, (2000) 'Partyless democracy – Solving the paradox of New Labour?', *New Left Review*, 2 (2).

Maltby, P and Gosling, T, (2003) *Ending the two-tier Workforce*, Institute for Public Policy Research, August.

Mandelson, P, (2002) *The Blair Revolution Revisited*, Politico's Publishing.

Mandelson, P and Liddle, R, (1996) *The Blair Revolution*, Faber and Faber.

Manheim, K, (1960) [1936] *Ideology and Utopia*, Routledge and Kegan Paul.

March, J G A, (1994) *Primer on Decision-Making: how decisions happen*, Free Press.

Marmot, M, (2004) *Status Syndrome*, Bloomsbury.

Marquand, D, (1988) *The Unprincipled Society*, Fontana.

—— (1991) *The Progressive Dilemma*, Heinemann.

—— (1998) 'One year on' *Prospect*, May.

—— (2000) 'The fall of civic culture', *New Statesman*, 30 November.

—— (2004) *Decline of the Public*, Polity Press.

Marshall, T H, (1950) *Citizenship and Social Class and other essays*, Cambridge University Press.

Mason, P, (2007) 'New Dawn for Workers', *New Statesman*, 17 April.

May, P J, (1986) 'Politics and Policy Analysis', *Political Science Quarterly*, 101 (1).

Maynard, A, and Street, A, (2006) 'Seven years of feast, seven years of famine: boom to bust in the NHS?', *British Medical Journal*, 332, 15 April.

Mayston, D J, (1999) 'The Private Finance Initiative in the National Health Service: An Unhealthy Development in New Public Management?', *Financial Accountability and Management*, 15 (3 and 4).

—— (2002) *Private Finance and Opportunities Foregone in Health Care Capital*, Memorandum to the House of Commons Select Committee on Health, The Stationery Office.

Meredith, S, (2005) 'Labour Party Revisionism and Public Expenditure: Divisions of Social Democratic Political Economy in the 1970s', *Labour History Review*, 70 (3).

Merkel, W, (2001) 'The Third Ways of Social Democracy', in Giddens, A (ed.) *The Global Third Way Debate*, Polity Press.

Meyer, T, (1999) 'The Third Way at the Crossroads', *International Politics and Society*, 3.

—— (2002) *Media Democracy*, Polity Press.

Michie, J and Sheehan, M, (2003) 'Labour market deregulation, "flexibility" and "innovation"', *Cambridge Journal Of Economics*, 27 (1).

Michie, J and Wilkinson, D, (1994) 'The Growth of Unemployment in the 1980s' in Michie, J and Grieve-Smith, J, *Unemployment in Europe*, Academic Press.

Milburn, A, (1999a) 'More Private Finance Initiative Deals Expected', HM Treasury News Release 103/99, June.

—— (1999b) *Speech at launch of the IPPR Commission into Public Private Partnerships*, HM Treasury News Release 152/99, September.

——— (2001a) 'Interview with Alan Milburn', *New Statesman*, 23 July.

——— (2001b) *Speech to the NHS Confederation Conference*, July.

——— (2002a) *Speech to Annual Social Services Conference*, Cardiff, October.

——— (2002b) *Speech on Foundation Hospitals*, May.

——— (2002c) *Speech to NHS Confederation annual conference*, May.

——— (2003a) *Speech to the Social Market Foundation*, 30 April.

——— (2003b) *Speech to NHS executives*, February.

——— (2003c) *Speech to Labour's local government, women's and youth conference*, SECC, Glasgow, February.

——— (2006) 'Preface' to Milburn, A *et al.* (eds) *Private Investment for Public Success*, Policy Network.

Miliband, D, (2005) 'Life Chances: the positive agenda Fabian lecture', Institute of Education, March.

Miliband, E, (2006) *Why ideology matters*, Speech to Fabian Society Northern Conference 'The next future of socialism', 16 September. www.fabian-society.org.uk/documents/ViewADocument.asp?ID = 142&CatID = 52.

Miller, D, (1989) 'In What sense Must Socialism be Communitarian?', *Social Philosophy and Policy*, 6 (2).

——— (1991) 'The Relevance of Socialism', *Economy and Society*, 20 (4).

——— (2001) 'Distributing Responsibilities', *Journal of Political Philosophy*, 9 (4).

——— (2003) 'What's Left of the Welfare State?', *Social Philosophy and Policy*, 20 (1).

Miller, W L, (1991) *Media and Voters*, Clarendon Press.

Minkin, L, (1978) *The Labour Party Conference*, Allen Lane.

——— (1991) *The Contentious Alliance*, Edinburgh University Press.

Mishra, R, (1999) *Globalisation and the Welfare State*, Edward Elgar.

Mohan, J, (2003) *Reconciling Equity and Choice? Foundation Hospitals and the future of the NHS*, Catalyst.

Morgan, K O, (1984) *Labour in Power, 1945–1951*, Clarendon Press.

——— (1997) *Callaghan: A Life*, Oxford University Press.

Morrell, K, (2006) 'Governance, Ethics and the NHS', *Public Money and Management*, January.

Moschanas, G, (2002) *In the Name of Social Democracy*, Verso.

Mulgan, G, (2005) 'Lessons of power', *Prospect*, 110, May.

Myles, J and Quadagno, J, (2002) 'Political Theories of the Welfare State', *Social Service Review*, 76 (1).

National Audit Office, (1999) *The PFI Contract for the new Dartford & Gravesham Hospital*, The Stationery Office.

——— (2001) *Managing the Relationship to Secure a Successful Partnership in PFI Projects*, The Stationery Office.

——— (2004) Memorandum to The Public Administration Select Committee hearing on *Choice, Voice and Public Services*, The Stationery Office.

——— (2005) *The Refinancing of the Norfolk and Norwich PFI Hospital*, The Stationery Office.

——— (2007) *The Academies Programme*, The Stationery Office.

Needham, C, (2003) *Citizen-consumers: New Labour's Marketplace Democracy*, Catalyst Working Paper, Catalyst.

Newman, J, (2000) 'Beyond the NPM: Modernising Public Service' in Clarke, J, Gewitz, S and McLaughlin, E (eds) *New Mangerialism, New Welfare*, Sage.

——— (2001a) *Modernising Governance*, Sage.

—— (2001b) 'What Counts is What Works: Constructing Evaluations of Market Mechanisms', *Public Administration*, 79 (1).

Norman, R, (1999) 'Equality, Priority and Social Justice', *Ratio*, 12 (2).

Nuttall, J, (2003) 'The Labour Party and the Improvement of Minds', *Historical Journal*, 46 (1).

—— (2006) *Psychological socialism: The Labour Party and qualities of mind and character, 1931 to the present*, Manchester University Press.

Offe, C, (1996) *Democracy Against the Welfare State*, Polity Press.

Office of Public Services Reform, (2002) *Reforming our Public Services*, The Stationery Office.

Olsen, G, (1991) 'Labour Mobilisation and the Strength of Capital: The Rise and Fall of Economic Democracy in Sweden', *Studies in Political Economy*, 34.

O'Neill, O, (2002) *Reith Lectures: A Question of Trust*, BBC. www.bbc.co.uk/radio4/reith2002/.

Palmer, G, MacInnes, T and Kenway, P, (2006) *Monitoring poverty and social exclusion 2006*, Rowntree Foundation. www.jrf.org.uk/knowledge/findings/socialpolicy/1979.asp.

Palmer, K, (2005) *How Should we Deal with Hospital Failure? Facing the challenges of the new NHS market*, King's Fund.

—— (2006) *NHS Reform: How to get back on track*, King's Fund.

Panitch, L, (1986) 'Ideology and Integration: The Case of the British Labour Party' in Panitch, L (ed.) *Working Class Politics in Crisis*, Verso.

'Panorama', (2006a) 'Tony Blair's Long Goodbye', BBC One, 12 March.

—— (2006b) 'The NHS Blame Game', BBC One, 26 March.

—— (2007) 'Life Behind Bars', BBC One, 16 April.

Parekh, B, (2001) Lords Hansard text for 24 October.

Paterson, L, (2003) 'The Three Educational Ideologies of the British Labour Party, 1997–2001', *Oxford Review of Education*, 29 (2).

Patmore, G and Coates, D, (2005) 'Labour Parties and the State in Australia and the UK', *Labour History*, May.

Pauly, L, (1995) 'Capital mobility, state autonomy, and political legitimacy', *Journal of International Affairs*, 48 (2).

Paxton, W and Dixon, M, (2004) *An Audit of Injustice in the UK*, Institute for Public Policy Research.

Perkins, A, (2003) *Red Queen: the authorised biography of Barbara Castle*, Macmillan.

Peston, R, (2005) *Brown's Britain*, Short Books.

Piachaud, D, (2005) 'Social Policy and Politics', *Political Quarterly*, 76 (3).

Pierson, C, (2001) 'Globalization and the End of Social Democracy', *Australian Journal of Politics and History*, 47 (4).

—— 2001a Pierson, C, 2001a *Hard Choices*, Polity

Pierson, P, (2000a) 'Three Worlds of Welfare State Research', *Comparative Political Studies*, 33 (6–7).

—— (2000b) 'The Limits of Design: Explaining Institutional Origins and Change', *Governance*, 13 (4).

—— (2001) 'Coping with Permanent Austerity: Welfare State Restructuring in Affluent Democracies' in Pierson, P (ed.) *The New Politics of the Welfare State*, Oxford University Press.

Pimlott, B, (1992) *Fabian Essays in Socialist Thought*, Heinemann.

Piven, F F, (1991) 'The Decline of Labour Parties: An Overview' in Piven, F F (ed.) *Labour Parties in Post-Industrial Societies*, Polity Press.

Plant, R (Lord), (1989) 'Citizenship, Liberty and Markets: Ideological Renewal in the Labour Party', Paper presented to the Annual Conference of the Political Studies Association.
—— (1991) *Modern Political Thought*, Blackwell.
—— (2001) Evidence to Public Administration Select Committee hearings on *The Public Service Ethos*, The Stationery Office.
—— (2003a) 'A Public Service Ethic and Political Accountability', *Parliamentary Affairs*, 56 (2).
—— (2003b) 'Citizenship and Social Security', *Fiscal Studies*, 24 (2).
—— (2004) 'Ends, Means and Political Identity', in Plant, R, Beech, M and Hickson, K (eds) *The Struggle for Labour's Soul*, Routledge.
Plant, R, Beech, M and Hickson, K (eds), (2004) *The Struggle for Labour's Soul*, Routledge.
Pollock, A, (2004) *NHS plc*, Verso.
Pollock, A and Price, D, (2003) *In Place of Bevan?*, Catalyst.
Pollock, A, Price, D and Dunnigan, M, (2000) *Deficits Before Patients: A Report on the Worcester Royal Infirmary PFI and Worcestershire Hospital Reconfiguration*, School of Public Policy, University College London.
Pollock, A, Price, D and Gaffney, D, (1999) *The Only Game in Town? A Report on the Cumberland Infirmary Carlisle*, UNISON Northern Region.
Pollock, A, Price, D and Player, S, (2007) 'An Examination of the UK Treasury's Evidence Base for Cost and Time Overrun Data in UK Value-for-Money Policy and Appraisal', *Public Money and Management*, April.
Pollock, A, Shaoul, J, Rowland, D and Player, S, (2001) *Practical Policies for the Redistribution of Wealth, Power and Opportunity: A response to the IPPR Commission on Public Private Partnerships*, Catalyst.
Ponting, C, (1989) *Breach of Promise: Labour in power 1964–1970*, Penguin.
Porter, R, (2000) *Enlightenment*, Penguin.
Powell, M (ed.), (1999) *New Labour, New Welfare State? The 'third way' in British social policy*, Policy Press.
—— (2000) 'Something old, something new, something borrowed, something blue: the jackdaw politics of New Labour', *Renewal*, 8 (4).
—— (2001) 'Third Ways in Europe: concepts, policies, causes and roots', *European Consortium of Political Research Joint Sessions*, Grenoble.
—— (2002) *Evaluating New Labour's Welfare Reforms*, Policy Press.
—— (2003) 'Quasi-markets in British Health Policy: A Longue Durée Perspective', *Social Policy and Administration*, 37 (7).
Powell, M and Barrientos, A, (2004) 'Welfare regimes and the welfare mix', *European Journal of Political Research*, 43 (1).
Powell, M, Bauld, L and Clarke, K (eds), (2005) *Social Policy Review 17*, Policy Press.
Pring, R, (2005) 'Labour Government Policy 14–19', *Oxford Review of Education*, 31 (1).
Public Accounts Select Committee, (1999) *Getting Better Value for Money from the Private Finance Initiative*, The Stationery Office.
—— (2000) *The PFI Contract for the new Dartford and Gravesham Hospital*, The Stationery Office.
—— (2003) *Delivering Better Value for Money from the Private Finance Initiative*, The Stationery Office.
—— (2007) *Update on PFI Debt Refinancing and the PFI Equity Market*, The Stationery Office.

Public Administration Select Committee, (2002) *The Public Service Ethos*, The Stationery Office.

—— (2005a) *Choice, Voice and Public Services*, The Stationery Office.

—— (2005b) *Minutes of Evidence to enquiry on Choice, Voice and Public Services*, The Stationery Office.

Putnam, R, (1973) *Beliefs of Politicians*, Yale University Press.

—— (1993) 'The Prosperous Community: Social Capital and Public Life', *The American Prospect*, 13, Spring.

Radaelli, C M, (1995) 'The Role of Knowledge in the Policy Process', *Journal of European Public Policy*, 2 (2).

Radice, G and Pollard, S, (1993) *More Southern Comfort*, Fabian Society.

Ranson, S and Stewart, J, (1989) 'Citizenship and Government: The Challenge for Management in the Public Domain', *Political Studies*, 37 (1).

—— (1994) *Management for the Public Domain: Enabling the Learning Society*, Macmillan.

Rawls, J, (1971) *A Theory of Justice*, Oxford University Press.

Reeve, S, (2006) 'Introduction to Public Private Partnerships' in Milburn, A *et al*,. (eds) *Private Investment for Public Success*, Policy Network.

Reeves, R, (2004) 'Without ideology', *New Statesman*, 24 September.

Regini, M, (2000) 'Between Deregulation and Social Pacts: the Response of European Economies to Globalisation', *Politics and Society*, 28 (1).

Reid, J, (2005) *Limits of the Market, Constraints of the State*, Speech to Social Market Foundation.

Reisman, D, (1997) *Crosland's Future: Opportunity and Outcome*, Macmillan.

Rhodes, M, (2000) ',Desperately Seeking a Solution: Social Democracy, Thatcherism and the "Third Way" in British Welfare', *West European Politics*, 23 (2).

—— (2001) 'The Political Economy of Social Pacts' in Pierson, P (ed.) *The New Politics of the Welfare State*, Oxford University Press.

—— (2002) 'Welfare States and Europe', in Heywood, P, Jones, E and Rhodes, M (eds) *Developments in West European Politics 2*, Palgrave.

Riddell, P, (2005) *The Unfulfilled Prime Minister*, Politico's Publishing.

Rieger, R and Liebfried, S, (1998) 'Welfare State Limits to Globalization', *Politics and Society*, 26 (3).

Riesman, D, (1997) *Crosland's Future*, Macmillan.

Robinson, Geoffrey, Paymaster-General (1998) *Speech at the Private Finance Initiative Conference*, 27 April.

Robinson, J, (1962) *Economic Philosophy*, Penguin.

Robinson, P and Stanley, K, (2005) 'A progressive consensus in the making?', in Powell, M, Bauld, L and Clarke, K (eds) *Social Policy Review 17*, Policy Press.

Robinson, R and Bevan, G, (2002) *Economic Ideas and Political Constraints: 15 years of health policy reform in the UK*, LSE Health and Social Care.

Robinson, R and Dixon, A, (2002) *Completing the Course: Health to 2010*, Fabian Society.

Roche, D, (2004) 'Choice: rhetoric and reality. Introducing patient choice in the NHS' *New Economy*, 11 (4).

Rodger, J L, (2003) 'Social Solidarity, Welfare and Post-Emotionalism', *Journal of Social Policy*, 32 (3).

Rose, B and Ross, G, (1994) 'Socialism's past, New Social Democracy, and Socialism's Futures', *Social Science History*, 18 (3).

Rose, N, (1999) *Powers of Freedom*, Cambridge University Press.

Rothstein, B, (1998) *Just Institutions Matter*, Cambridge University Press.

Rowntree Foundation, Research Findings, (1999) 'Job insecurity and work intensification'. www.jrf.org.uk/knowledge/findings/socialpolicy/849.asp.

—— (2005) *Monitoring poverty and social exclusion in the UK 2005*, Rowntree Foundation.

Royal College of Anaesthetists, (2006) 'Evidence submitted to the Health Select Committee hearing on ISTCs', The Stationery Office.

Royal College of Nursing, (2004) Memorandum to the Public Administration Select Committee hearing on *Choice, Voice and Public Services*, The Stationery Office.

Royal College of Ophthalmologists, (2006) 'Evidence submitted to the Health Select Committee hearing on ISTCs', The Stationery Office.

Royal College of Surgeons of England, (2006) 'Evidence submitted to the Health Select Committee hearing on ISTCs', The Stationery Office.

Ruane, S, (2006) 'Independent Sector Treatment Centres', *Health Matters*, Autumn.

Rubery, J, Ward, K, Grimshaw, D and Beynon, H, (2005) 'Working Time, Industrial Relations and the Employment Relationship', *Time and Society*, 14 (1).

Russell, J, (2007) 'This Charming Vision of inclusion isn't Working', *Guardian*, 11 January.

Rustin, M, (2000) 'The New Labour Ethic and the Spirit of Capitalism', *Soundings*, 14, Spring.

—— (2004a) 'Rethinking Audit and Inspection', *Soundings*, 26, Spring.

—— (2004b) 'Is there a Future for Social Democracy?', *Soundings*, 28, Winter.

Rutherford, J and Shah, H, (2006) *The Good Society: Compass Programme for Renewal*, Compass.

Sanderson, I, (2003) 'Is it "what works" that matters? Evaluation and evidence-based policy-making', *Research Papers in Education*, 18(4).

Sartori, G, (1976) *Parties and Party Systems: A Framework for Analysis*, Cambridge University Press.

Sassoon, D, (2000) 'Socialism in the twentieth century: an historical reflection', *Journal of Political Ideologies*, 5 (1).

Savage, S P and Atkinson, R (eds), (2001) *Public Policy under Blair*, Palgrave.

Saville, J, (1973) 'The Ideology of Labourism', in Benewick, R, Berki, R N and Parekh, B (eds) *Knowledge and Belief in Politics – The Problem of Ideology*, Allen and Unwin.

Sawyer, M, (2003) 'The Private Finance Initiative: A Critical Assessment', in Coffey, D (ed.) *Industrial and Labour Market Policy and Performance*, Routledge.

Scharpf, F W (1991) *Crisis and Choice in European Social Democracy*, Cornell University Press.

—— (1997) *Games Real Actors Play: Actor-Centered Institutionalism in Policy Research*, Westview.

—— (2000) *Globalization and the Welfare State Constraints, Challenges and Vulnerabilities*, Conference on Social Security, Helsinki, September.

Schmidt, V (1995) 'The New World Order Inc.; The Rise of Business and the Decline of the Nation State', *Daedalus*, 124 (2).

Schmidtke, O (2002) 'The Dilemmas of Social democratic regimes in the Age of Globalisation' in Schmidtke, O (ed.) *The Third Way: Transformation of Social Democracy*, Ashgate.

Schwartz, B (2004) *Paradox of Choice*, Harper.

Scott, D, (2004) *Off Whitehall*, I B Tauris.

Sefton, T, (2005) 'Give and Take: attitudes to redistribution' in Park, A *et al.*, (eds) *British Social Attitudes: 22nd Report*, Sage.

Seldon, A, (2001) *The Blair Effect*, Little, Brown and Co..

—— (2004) *Blair*, Simon and Schuster.

Seldon, A and Kavanagh, D, (2005) *The Blair Effect 2001–2005*, Cambridge University Press.

Self, P, (1993) *Government by the Market? The Politics of Public Choice*, Macmillan.

Shaoul, J, (1999) 'The Private Finance Initiative: Looking Glass World of PFI', *Public Finance*, 29 January–4 February.

—— (2003) 'A financial analysis of the National Air Traffic Services PPP', *Public Money and Management*, 23 (3).

Shaw, E, (1988) *Discipline and Discord in the Labour Party*, Manchester University Press.

—— (1994) *The Labour Party Since 1979: Crisis and Transformation*, Routledge.

—— (1996) *The Labour Party Since 1945*, Blackwell.

—— (2002) 'New Labour – New Democratic centralism?', *West European Politics*, 25 (3).

—— (2004a) 'What Matters is What Works: The Third Way and the Case of the Private Finance Initiative', in Leggett, W, Hale, S and Martell, L (eds) *The Third Way and Beyond: Criticisms, Futures and Alternatives*, Manchester University Press.

—— (2004b) 'The Control Freaks' in Ludlam, S and Smith, M J (eds) *Governing as New Labour*, Palgrave Macmillan.

Sikka, P, (2003) 'Socialism in reverse', *Guardian*, 15 April.

—— (2005) 'Accountants: a threat to democracy', *Guardian*, 5 September.

—— (2007) 'New Labour – the Tax Dodgers' Friend', *Tribune*, 9 March.

Simon, H A, (1985) 'Human Nature and Politics: The Dialogue of Psychology with Political Science', *American Political Science Review*, 79 (2).

—— (1995) 'Rationality in Political Behaviour', *Political Psychology*, 16 (1).

Simons, A, (2003) 'Evaluating the PFI: the National Audit Office Perspective', in Milburn, A *et al,*. (eds) *Private Investment for Public Success*, Policy Network.

Skidelsky, R (Lord), 2001 Lords Hansard text for 24 October.

Smith, A, (2000) *Chief Secretary to the Treasury. Speech to the IPPR Seminar on Public Private Partnerships*, April.

—— (2001) *Speech to the Office of Government*, Commerce Partnership UK Conference, October.

Smith, P, (2003) 'The case against the internal market', in Dixon, J, Le Grand, J and Smith, P (eds) *Can Market Forces be Used for Good? Benefits of Competition*, King's Fund.

Smith, P and Morton, G, (2001) 'New Labour's Reform of Britain's Employment Law', *British Journal of Industrial Relations*, 39 (1).

—— 2006 'Nine Years of New Labour: Neoliberalism and Workers' Rights', *British Journal of Industrial Relations*, 44 (3).

Smith, T (Lord), (2003) 'Something Old, Something New, Something Borrowed, Something Blue: Themes of Tony Blair and his Government', *Parliamentary Affairs*, 56 (4).

Smithers, A, (2001a) 'Labour creating secondary maze', *Guardian*, 24 May.

—— (2001b) 'Education Policy' in Seldon, A (ed.) *The Blair Effect*, Little Brown.

—— (2005) 'The Health and Welfare Legacy' in Seldon, A and Kavanagh, D (eds) *The Blair Effect 2001–2005*, Cambridge University Press.

Social Exclusion Unit, (2004) *Breaking the Cycle: Taking stock of progress and priorities for the Future*, Office of the Deputy Prime Minister.

Stanfield, J R, (1986) *The Economic Thought of Karl Polanyi*, St. Martin's Press.

Stedward, G, (2003) 'Education as industrial policy: New Labour's marriage of the social and the economic' *Policy and Politics*, 31 (1).

Stephens, P, (2001) 'Treasury under Labour' in Seldon, A (ed.) *The Blair Effect*, Little Brown.

Stevens, S, (2003) 'Equity and Choice: Can the NHS Offer Both?' in Oliver, A (ed.) *Equity, Health and Healthcare*, The Nuffield Trust.

—— (2005) 'The NHS works' *Prospect*, 107, February.

Stewart, M, (1972) 'The Distribution of Income' in Beckerman, W (ed.) *The Labour Government's Economic Record*, Duckworth.

Stoker, G and Williams, J, (2001) *New Local Government Network Memorandum to Public Administration*, Select Committee hearing on Public Sector Ethos, The Stationery Office.

(Prime Minister's) Strategy Unit, (2006) *The UK Government's Approach to Public Service Reform*, The Stationery Office.

Straw, Jack, (1998) *Speech to the Nexus Conference on Mapping out the Third Way*, July.

Sussex, Jon, (2001) *The Economics of the Private Finance Initiative in the NHS: A Summary*, Office of Health Economic. www.ohe.org/private_finance_initiative.htm.

Sutherland, H, Sefton, T and Piachaud, D, (2003) *Poverty in Britain: the impact of government policy since 1997*, Rowntree Foundation.

Sutherland, S (Lord), (1999) *Royal Commission on Long Term Care. With Respect to Old Age*, The Stationery Office.

Swank, D, (2001) 'Political Institutions and Welfare State Restructuring' in Pierson, P (ed.) *The New Political Economy of the Welfare State*, Oxford University Press.

Tallis, R, (2004) *Hippocratic Oaths*, Atlantic Books.

Tawney, R H, 1961 [1921] *The Acquisitive Society*, Fontana.

—— (1964a) [1931] *Equality*, Allen & Unwin.

—— (1964b) *The Radical Tradition*, Allen & Unwin.

—— (1964c) [1949] 'Social Democracy in Britain', in Tawney, 1964b.

—— (1964d) [1952] 'British Socialism Today', in Tawney, 1964b.

Taylor, C, Fitz, J and Gorard, S, (2005) 'Diversity, specialisation and equity in education', *Oxford Review of Education*, 31 (1).

Taylor, M, (2002) 'Modernisation' as Labour's Meta-Narrative', PERC Annual Lecture, 16 May.

—— (2006) 'A major new study shows that social background determines pupils' success', *Guardian*, 28 February.

Taylor, R, (1993) *The Trade Union Question in British Politics*, Blackwell.

—— (2000a) *The TUC*, Palgrave.

—— (2000b) 'Economic Reform and New Industrial Relations'. www.europaprogrammet. no/sider/4_publikasjoner/4_bokerhefter/hefter/98_5/taylor.html.

—— (2001a) 'Employment Relations Policy' in Seldon, A (ed.) *The Blair Effect*, Little, Brown and Co..

—— (2001b) *The Future of Work-Life Balance*, An ESRC Future of Work Programme Seminar Series, ESRC.

—— (2002) 'Britain's World of Work – Myths and Realities', An ESRC Future of Work Programme Seminar Series, ESRC.

—— (2005a) 'Third ways old and new', *Political Quarterly*, 75 (4).

—— (2005b) 'Mr Blair's Business Model – capital and labour in flexible markets' in Seldon, A and Kavanagh, D (eds) *The Blair Effect 2001–2005*, Cambridge University Press.

Taylor-Gooby, P, (1993) 'Citizenship, Dependency and the Welfare Mix – Problems of inclusion and exclusion' *International Journal of Health Services*, 23 (3).

—— (1999) 'Markets and Motives' *Journal of Social Policy*, 28 (1).

Taylor-Gooby, P, Larsen, T and Kananen, J, (2004) 'Market Means and Welfare Ends: The UK Welfare State Experiment' *Journal of Social Policy*, 33 (4).

Temple, M, (2000) 'New Labour's Third Way: pragmatism and governance' *British Journal of Politics and International Relations*, 2 (3).

Therborn, G, (1991) 'Cultural Belonging, Structural Location and Human Action: Explanation in Sociology' *Acta Sociologica*, 34: 177–91.

Thomas, J, (2005) *Popular Newspapers, the Labour Party and British Politics*, Routledge.

Thompson, P, (2002) 'The Politics of Community', *Renewal*, 10 (2).

Timmins, N, (2005a) 'Use of private health care in the NHS', *British Medical Journal*, 331, 12 November.

—— (2005b) 'Challenges of private provision in the NHS', *British Medical Journal*, 331, 19 November.

Titmuss, R, (1971) *The Gift Relationship*, Allen & Unwin.

—— 2000 [1968] 'Universalism V Selection' in Pierson, C and Castles, F (eds) *The Welfare State: A Reader*, Polity.

Tomlinson, J, (2002) 'Labour and "the Market" in historical perspective: the limits of Tawney's ethical socialism', *Contemporary British History*, 16 (4).

Tomlinson, S, (2003a) 'New Labour and Education', *Children and Society*, 17: 195–204.

—— (2003b) 'Comprehensive Success and Bog-Standard Government' Third Caroline Benn Memorial Lecture. www.socialisteducation.org.uk/CB3.htm.

—— (2005) *Education in a Post-Welfare Society*, Open University Press.

Towers, B, (1999) 'The most lightly regulated Labour market', *Industrial Relations Journal*, 30 (2).

Townshend, P, (1961) Preface to Tawney, R H, *The Acquisitive Society*, Allen & Unwin.

Toynbee, P, (2003) *Hard Work*, Bloomsbury.

Toynbee, P and Walker, D, (2005) *Better or Worse? Has Labour Delivered?*, Bloomsbury.

TUC (Trades Union Congress), (1966) *Trade Unionism*, Evidence to Royal Commission on Trade Unions and Employment Associations, TUC.

—— (2003a) Press Release on employment rights, May.

—— (2003b) Press Release on Foundation Hospitals, 2 May. www.tuc.org.uk/publicsector/tuc-6618-f0.cfm.

TGWU (Transport & General Workers' Union), (2002) *Enron NHS? Foundation Hospitals and the backdoor privatisation of the National Health Service*, TGWU.

Treasury Select Committee, (2000) *The Private Finance Initiative*, The Stationery Office.

Trickett, J, (2006) 'Saving the Labour Party from Blair', *Red Pepper*, 141, May.

Tunney, S, (2007) *Labour and the Press, 1972–2005*, Sussex Academic.

Undy, R, (1999) 'New Labour's "Industrial Relations Settlement": The Third Way?', *British Journal of Industrial Relations*, 37 (2).

—— (2002) 'New Labour and New Unionism, 1997–2001: but is it the same old story?', *Employee Relations*, 24 (6).

van Kersbergen, K, (2003) 'The Politics and Political Economy of Social Democracy', *Acta Politica*, 38: 255–73.

Vigor, A, (2005) 'An Anglo-Social Approach to Work' *Public Policy Research*, 12 (3).

Vincent-Jones, P, (2000) 'Contractual Governance', *Oxford Journal of Socio-legal Studies*, 20 (3).

Vines, D, (1999) 'Integrity and the Economy' in Montefiore, A and Vines, D, *Integrity*, Routledge.

Waddington, J, (2003) 'Heightening Tension in Relations between Trade Unions and the Labour Government in 2002', *British Journal of Industrial Relations*, 41 (2).

Walford, G, (2005) 'Introduction: Education and the Labour Government', *Oxford Review of Education*, 31 (1).

Walsh, K, (1995) *Public Services and Market Mechanisms: Competition, Contracting and the New Public Management*, Macmillan.

Walshe, K, (2003) 'Foundation Hospitals: a new direction for NHS reform', *Journal of the Royal Society of Medicine*, 96.

Walshe, K *et al.*, (2004) 'Primary care trusts', Editorial, *British Medical Journal*, 329, 16 October.

Walters, W, (1997) 'The Active Society', *Policy and Politics*, 25 (3).

Walzer, M, (1983) *Spheres of Justice: A Defense of Pluralism and Equality*, Routledge.

Watson, M, (2003) 'The Politics of Inflation Management', *Political Quarterly*, 74 (3).

Watson, M and Hay, C, (2003) 'The Discourse of Globalisation and the Logic of no Alternative' *Policy and Politics*, 31 (1).

Weiss, L, (2005) 'The State-augmenting Effects of Globalisation' *Political Economy*, 10 (3).

West, A, (2006) 'School Choice, Equity and Social Justice: The Case for More Control', *British Journal of Educational Studies*, 54 (1).

Wickham-Jones, M, (1997) 'Anticipating Social Democracy, Accommodating Anticipations: The Appeasement of Capital in the Modernisation of the Labour Party', *Politics and Society*, 25 (2).

—— (2002) 'British Labour, European Social Democracy and the Reformist Trajectory: a reply to Coates', *British Journal of Politics and International Relations*, 4 (3).

Which (formerly Consumer's Association), (2005) *Which Choice?*, www.which.co.uk/files/application/pdf/0503choice_rep-445–55216.pdf.

White, S, (1999) 'Rights and Responsibilities: A Social Democratic Perspective', *Political Quarterly*, 70 (S1).

—— (2000) 'Social Rights and the Social Contract – Political Theory and the New Welfare Politics', *British Journal of Political Science*, 30 (2).

—— (2000/2001) 'Ethics and Equality', *Boston Review*, December/January.

—— (2001) *New Labour: The Progressive Future*, Palgrave.

Whitehead, A, (2000) 'Cleaning up the dogma doings: Labour and the market', *Renewal*, 8 (4).

Whitfield, D, (2001) *Public Service or Corporate Welfare*, Pluto.

Wilby, P, (2006a) 'Education: The State We're In', *New Statesman*, 6 March.

—— (2006b) 'A Delay on the Road to Meritocracy', *Political Quarterly*, 77 (S1).

—— (2007) 'What you call a school is academic', *New Statesman*, 5 March.

Wildavsky, A, (1987) 'Choosing Preferences by Constructing Institutions: A Cultural Theory of Preference Formation', *American Political Science Review*, 81 (1).

Wilding, P, (1981) *Socialism and Professionalism*, Fabian Tract 473, Fabian Society.

Wilkes, S, (1997) 'Conservative Government and the Economy', *Political Studies*, 45 (4).

Wilkinson, R, (1997) 'Socioeconomic determinants of health: Health inequalities: relative or absolute material standards?', *British Medical Journal*, 314, 22 February.

—— (2005) *The Impact of Inequality: How to Make Sick Societies Healthier*, Routledge.

—— (2006) 'The Impact of Inequality' *Social Research*, 73 (2).

Williamson, O, (1985) *The Economic Institutions of Capitalism*, Free Press.

Wood, C M, (2007) 'Surgery for cataract', *British Medical Journal*, 20 January.

Wragg, Ted, (2004) 'Uneasy money', *Guardian*, 2 March.

Wright, Tony, 1979 *G D H Cole and Socialist Democracy*, Oxford University Press.

—— (1984) 'Tawney Revisited: Equality, Welfare and Socialism' in Pimlott, B (ed.) *Fabian Essays in Socialist Thought*, Heinemann.

—— (1987) *R H Tawney*, Manchester University Press.

Yanai, N, (1999) 'Why do Political Parties Survive? An Analytical Discussion' *Party Politics*, 5 (1).

Yeates, N, (1999) 'Social Politics and Policy in an Era of Globalization: Critical Reflections', *Social Policy and Administration*, 33 (4).

Yee, A, (1996) 'The Causal Effects of Ideas on Policies' *International Organization*, 50 (1).

—— (1997) 'Thick Rationality', *Journal of Politics*, 59 (4).

Young, M (Lord), 1958 *The Rise of the Meritocracy*, Penguin.

—— (2000) *Equality and Public Service Speech*, to British Association for the Advancement of Science, Fabian Society.

—— (2001) 'Down with meritocracy', *Guardian*, 29 June.

Index